D1118659

THE GUINNESS BOOK OF
TRACK & FIELD
ATHLETICS
FACTS & FEATS

THE **GUINNESS** BOOK OF
TRACK & FIELD
ATHLETICS
FACTS & FEATS

Peter Matthews

Guinness Superlatives Limited
2 Cecil Court, London Road, Enfield, Middlesex

Frontispiece
Jesse Owens, hurdling in 1935. The 220y hurdles was the last event he tackled at Ann Arbor on 25 May that year, when he set a record six world records in one day.   (*Ohio State University*)

All colour photographs have been supplied by All Sport with the exception of p. 100 Gulf Photo/Harold Israel and additionally the author and publishers are grateful to James MacKay for supplying the stamps on p. 275.

Editor: Josie A. Holtom
Designer: Roger Daniels
First published in 1982
© Peter Matthews and Guinness Superlatives Ltd 1982

All rights reserved. No part of this publication may be reproduced, stored in a retrieval system, or transmitted in any form or by any means, electronic, mechanical, photocopying, recording or otherwise, without prior permission in writing of the publishers.

Typeset in Times and Univers, and printed and bound in Great Britain by Fakenham Press Limited, Fakenham, Norfolk.

British Library Cataloguing in Publication Data

Matthews, Peter
The Guinness book of athletics facts and feats

1. Track-athletics-History
I. Title
796. 4'2   GV 1060.2
ISBN 0-85112-238-8

'Guinness' is a registered trade mark of Guinness Superlatives Ltd

ACKNOWLEDGEMENTS

I am extremely grateful to many historians and statisticians for help in compiling this book. I owe especial thanks for many useful comments to John Brant, Stan Greenberg, Andrew Huxtable, Richard Hymans, Peter Lovesey, Andy Milroy and Dave Terry and to many other members of the National Union of Track Statisticians, including Roger Gynn, John Keddie, Duncan McKechnie, Bob Sparks, Chris Thorne, Clive Williams and Colin Young. My thanks also go to Janis Kerr and John Goulstone.

   Valuable help in compiling sections came from: Paul Jenes (Australia), Erich Kamper (Austria), André de Hooghe (Belgium), Cecil Smith (Canada), Winfried Kramer (FRG), Ian Buchanan (Hong Kong), Gabriel Szabo (Hungary), Ole Peter Sandvig (Norway), Daniel Grinberg (Poland), Arrie Joubert, Harry Beinart and Gert Le Roux (South Africa), José Corominas (Spain), Rooney Magnusson (Sweden), Fulvio Regli (Switzerland), Peter Cava (USA), Philip Kennedy (Zimbabwe), Egon Rasmussen (Women's walks).

   While all the above made valued contributions the responsibility for the selection and compilation of items is mine alone and any errors are entirely at my behest!

   I am grateful to all those who have supplied me with photographs, including the Sports Information Departments of several Universities in the USA.

   Above all I am indebted to the following superb magazines: *Athletics Weekly* (GB), *Leichtathletik* (FRG), *Track and Field News* and *Track Newsletter* (USA). I have, over the years, also consulted many other magazines, newspapers and books and the published works of the members of the National Union of Track Statisticians and the Association of Track and Field Statisticians.   PETER MATTHEWS

Contents

Introduction

'Athletics' is derived from the Greek word 'Athlos' meaning fight, competition or combat. The thousands of claims received annually by the editors of the *Guinness Book of Records* bear striking testimony to mankind's desire to be the best at something, and sometimes it seems that anything will do. Athletics provides, more than almost any other activity, the opportunity for people to measure themselves in competitive situations.

Success at athletics calls for preparation, technique, skill and both analytical and competitive abilities. The top class athlete needs to have prepared carefully so that speed, stamina and power are all highly tuned. Technique needs to be worked out and perfected over hours of training. Tactical sense needs to be developed so that the athlete can judge the right moment to make a move in a race. Analytical ability is needed to correct technique where necessary, and above all the athlete needs the ability to rise to the occasion, to produce his or her best when it matters most.

This book features those who have had the greatest successes. Those who have broken through the psychological barriers such as the 7 foot high jump, the 10 second 100 metres and the 4 minute mile. It details those who have won the most titles, and what greater test of a sportsman can there be than to reach the top and do it again and again, despite the increasing pressures of being the man or women to beat. Thus, athletes like Al Oerter, Irena Szewinska and Viktor Saneyev feature prominently in this text.

This book is not a history but it lists the milestones in the development of the sport and the great events are detailed in the various chapters.

Track and field athletes test themselves against their opponents and against the unyielding instruments of recording – the stop-watch and the tape-measure. This book is thus full of statistics, who achieved what and when, and how often. I have not attempted to illustrate the drama behind the races, the build-up to the successful vault, the colossal determination needed to endure, sustain and win, yet behind all these facts lie just such stories.

Not everybody can aspire to match the needs of the great champions. The sport is indeed much wider than that. The tremendous growth in marathon running exemplifies the most important aspect of the sport, the ability to succeed against, and yet with one's self. No success can be complete without the will to do so, and the will is best sustained not just by desires for material benefits but for the sheer pleasure of achievement.

Running on the first London marathon on a damp March Sunday morning, I felt the desire to laugh, to embrace the world of these determined people thrusting along the roads and pavements and those crowds willing us along and sharing with us the happy madness of the venture. Mostly I trained alone, often just a morning ritual, but often quiet private times to put some perspective to problems, while following the trails through the woods or along suburban streets or even chugging up some endless hill – and feeling good and in harmony with the world.

Even after euphoria began to pale, after hundreds of discarded green and white plastic cups had been crunched under foot at the feeding stations, somehow you had to keep going. The thighs rebelled, I walked, before the mind and the crowds stirred some semblance of running, and I just made it. I am in this book. I have noted that there were '6255 finishers inside 5 hours'. I finished 3841st. There's a lot behind the figures.

PETER MATTHEWS
9/2/82

Abbreviations

In order to save space the track and field events have been abbreviated on many occasions, as follows:

m	metres	yR	yards relay
m/s	metres per second	mR	metres relay
mph	miles per hour	HJ	high jump
km	kilometres	PV	pole vault
y	yards	LJ	long jump
M	miles	SP	shot (put)
Mar	marathon	DT	discus (throw)
Dec	decathlon	HT	hammer (throw)
Pen	pentathlon	JT	javelin (throw)
h	hurdles	S/C	steeplechase
yh	yards hurdles	CC	cross country
mh	metres hurdles	(W)	Women
R	relay	(i)	indoor
		W	wind assisted

ORGANISATIONS

AAA	Amateur Athletic Association (GB)
AAU	Amateur Athletic Union (USA)
IAAF	International Amateur Athletic Federation
IOC	International Olympic Committee
TAC	The Athletics Congress of the AAU (USA)
WAAA	Women's Amateur Athletic Association (GB)
FSFI	Fédération Sportive Féminine Internationale
BAAB	British Amateur Athletic Board
IAC	International Athletes Club
NCAA	National Collegiate Athletic Association
ITA	International Track Association
ICAAAA	Intercollegiate Association of Amateur Athletes of America
NAIA	National Association of Intercollegiate Athletics
AAC	Amateur Athletic Club
RWA	Road Walking Association

COUNTRIES

Alg	Algeria	Fra	France	Ind	India	Rom	Romania
Arg	Argentina	GB	Great Britain and Northern Ireland	Ire	Ireland	SA	South Africa
Aus	Australia			Isr	Israel	Sco	Scotland
Aut	Austria			Ita	Italy	Spa	Spain
Bel	Belgium	GDR	German Democratic Republic (East)	Jam	Jamaica	Swe	Sweden
Bra	Brazil			Jap	Japan	Swi	Switzerland
Bul	Bulgaria			Ken	Kenya	Tai	Taiwan
Can	Canada	Ger	Germany (pre 1945) and German Federal Republic (West)	Lux	Luxembourg	Tan	Tanzania
Chn	China			Mex	Mexico	Tha	Thailand
Chi	Chile			Mor	Morocco	Tri	Trinidad and Tobago
Cub	Cuba			Nig	Nigeria		
Cze	Czechoslovakia	Gha	Ghana	Nor	Norway	Tun	Tunisia
Den	Denmark	Gre	Greece	NZ	New Zealand	Uga	Uganda
Egy	Egypt	Hol	Holland/ Netherlands	Pan	Panama	USA	United States
Eng	England			Phi	Philippines	Ven	Venezuela
Eth	Ethiopia	Hun	Hungary	Pol	Poland	Wal	Wales
Fin	Finland	Ice	Iceland	Por	Portugal	Yug	Yugoslavia

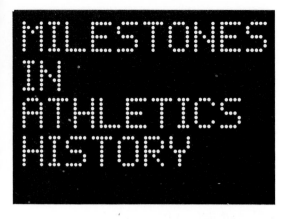

MILESTONES IN ATHLETICS HISTORY

BC

3800 Earliest evidence of organised running in Egypt at Memphis. Ritual races around the walls of the town may even have pre-dated 4100BC. Races were held between two pillars c800m apart and were normally of four lengths.

3300 Form of high jumping practised, with children jumping over linked arms of other children.

2650 Earliest representation of a runner, a stone relief in the pyramid temple at Saqqara, of King Djoser of Egypt running a race.

c1600 Evidence of running in Crete.

c1250 Vase in Cyprus depicts athletic sports.

c800 Homer's funeral games.

776 First known Olympic champion – Coroibos (see p. 82).

c500 Tailtean Games originated in Ireland.

490 Battle of Marathon and subsequent run to Athens by Pheidippides (see p. 41).

c324 First indoor athletics – in a large marquee erected in India by two generals of Alexander the Great.

c50 First known association of professional athletes in Greece was formed.

AD

3rd Century High jumping tests for military in Ireland.

393 Olympic Games abolished by decree of the Roman Emperor Theodosius.

5th Century Athletic tests celebrated in Germanic literature (Brunhilde).

7th Century St Cuthbert noted for running and leaping.

1035–1040 Harold I, King of England, known as 'Harefoot', due to his speed.

1180 William FitzSteven describes sporting events at Smithfield (Smooth Field), London.

c1275 Poem 'Havelock the Dane' includes the earliest reference to putting the weight in England.

13th/14th Century Earliest Highland Games in Scotland.

1530 International match held between England and Scotland. (See p. 195.)

1584 First evidence of running footmen.

1589 Sir Robert Carey walked from London to Berwick (c340 miles/550km) for a bet.

c1604 Robert Dover starts Cotswold 'Olympic Games'. These rural sports held annually except during Civil War (1642–60) until 1852.

1630 Regular running matches in Hyde Park, London.

1664 Running matches at Newmarket regularised.

1680 First athletics 'calendar' produced at Newmarket, giving results of leading races.

1750s Artillery Ground, London is the first enclosed ground to be used for foot races, at which an entrance fee is charged.

1766 Site of ancient Olympic Games rediscovered at Olympia by Richard Chandler.

1773 Foster Powell ran from London to York and back, 402 miles in 5 days 18 hours. Twenty years later, at the age of 59, he did it in 5 days 15¼ hours.

1793 JTF Guts Muths published *Gymnastik für die Jügend*, hints on athletics techniques, from the founder of German gymnastics.

1809 Captain Barclay's 1000 miles in 1000 hours (see p. 266).

1813 William Thom's *Pedestrianism* published – an account of the performances of celebrated pedestrians.

1820s Athletics at Shrewsbury School.

1834 Donald Walker's *Manly Exercises* published.

1837 Crick Run first held at Rugby School; originally c12½ miles, later c11 miles/18km.
Inter-class athletics first held at Eton College.
First track to be laid specifically for athletics; at Lord's Cricket Ground, London. This was a 5ft wide gravel path all round the ground, already well established as a venue for foot running matches. Earlier paths had been set

aside for races, but these can hardly qualify as tracks in the modern sense.

1839 First athletics meeting in North America, at Caer Howell grounds near Toronto.

1842 Olympic Club of Montreal formed.

1845 First amateur hurdles race, at Eton.

1849 Royal Military Academy, Sandhurst stages its first athletics meeting.

1850 Exeter College, Oxford, athletics club formed; the oldest surviving one.
Dr Penny Brookes inaugurates the Much Wenlock Olympic Games, to encourage outdoor recreation, and based on Greek ideals. Included were five athletics events (high jump, long jump and three races).

1854 Professional jumper John Howard jumps 9.01m/29ft 7in using weights.

1857 First sports meetings held at Cambridge University and at Trinity College, Dublin.

1860 First Oxford University Sports held.

1862 Chronograph patented by Adolphe Nicole (Swi).

1863 Founding of Mincing Lane AC (London AC from 1866).
First amateur indoor meeting at Ashburnam Hall (see p. 260).
Olympic festival at Mount Vernon Parade Ground, Liverpool, the most popular of a series of such festivals in the 1860s; a crowd of 12000 to 15000 attended.

1864 First Oxford v Cambridge athletics match held at Oxford.
First Civil Service Sports held.
First artificial steeplechase course (as opposed to cross-country) at RMA Woolwich.

1866 First national championships – English, organised by the Amateur Athletic Club at Beaufort House, Welham Green, London.
National Olympian Society held its first Games at Crystal Palace, London.

1868 First indoor meeting in the USA organised by New York AC (see p. 136).

1874 Madison Square Garden, New York, first used for athletics.
First US university competition at Saratoga.
Edward Weston becomes the first man to walk 500 miles in 6 days, at Newark, New Jersey, USA.

1875 ICAAAA formed in the USA.

1876 Starting gun first used; previously races started with a drum, or 'Go' or a white handkerchief.
First American championships held in New York.
London AC (actually an England team) visits Ireland.
First English cross-country championship.

1879 Northern Counties AAA formed by nine clubs in Southport.

1880 AAA founded in Oxford, first championships held.

1886 Straight-leg hurdle style pioneered by Arthur Croome of Oxford.

1887 *Athletics and Football* by Montague Shearman published.

1888 AAU formed and first championships held in the USA.

1891 Astley Cooper suggests an Empire athletic gathering.

1893 Batons first used in relay races.

1894 International conference held at the Sorbonne, Paris, organised by Baron Pierre de Coubertin; re-establishment of Olympic Games agreed.

1895 First women's meeting at Vassar College, New York. New York AC beat London AC in New York.

1896 Olympic Games revived in Athens (opened on 6 April); athletics from ten nations compete.

1898 First international cross-country race, between England and France (see p. 121).

1900 Olympic Games in Paris; athletics track a 500m grass oval on the grounds of the Racing Club de France in the Bois de Boulogne.

1903 First international cross-country championship (see p. 121).

1904 Olympic Games held in conjunction with the World Exhibition in St Louis, USA; little more than a US inter-club meeting; three laps to a mile track.

1906 Intercollegiate AA formed in the USA (changed name to NCAA 1910).
Intercalated Olympic Games in Athens.

1908 Olympic Games held at the White City, London; a new three laps to a mile track used; 22 nations competing.

1911 Inter-Empire Championships held at the Crystal Palace, London. London AC meet Stockholm and undertake Swedish tour.

1912 Olympic Games held in Stockholm;

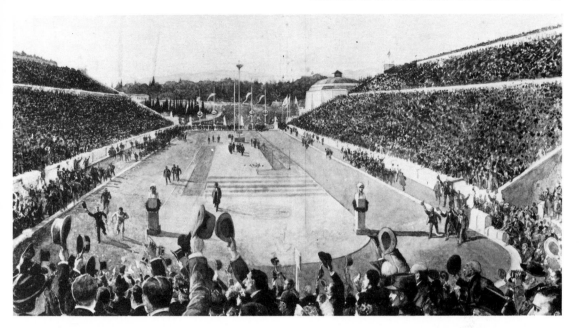

1896 marathon winner Spiridon Louis is greeted by George I, King of Greece.   *(BBC Hulton)*

383m track; lanes first marked by chalk.
International Amateur Athletic Federation (IAAF) formed on 17 July, 17 countries represented.

1913 Inaugural IAAF meeting, in Berlin; 34 countries on first membership list. Far Eastern Games held in Manila.

1914 First technical rules for international competitions and first list of world records presented at third IAAF Congress.

1917 France forms first governing body for women's athletics.

1919 South American Championships held in Montevideo, Uruguay.
In Britain, first Inter-Varsity Athletic Sports at Manchester University and Inter-Varsity Athletic Board formed (changed to Universities Athletic Union in 1930).

1920 Olympic Games at Antwerp, a 400m track; for the first time Olympic Oath and Olympic Flag introduced.

1921 First women's international match (see p. 196).
Fédération Sportive Féminine Internationale (FSFI) formed.

1922 Women's Amateur Athletic Association (WAAA) founded.

1923 First WAAA championships.

1924 Olympic Games at Colombes Stadium, Paris; 500m track. IAAF proposed reduction of Olympic programme by taking out seven events – four removed but triple jump, steeplechase and decathlon are reprieved. IAAF membership now 39, women's committee formed.

1925 English Schools Athletic Association founded.

1926 Central American and Caribbean championships held in Mexico City. Exchange zones instituted for relay events.

1927 Starting blocks invented by George Bresnahan in USA (see p. 250).

1928 Olympic Games at Amsterdam; women's events included for the first time; slow-motion apparatus used for judging close finishes.
First Spartakiade in USSR.

1930 British Empire Games held in Hamilton, Canada.

1931 First women's international cross-country race at Douai, France. First AAA Junior championships.

1932 Olympic Games in Los Angeles; newly developed photo-timer used; motion film taken of the races and made available to the Jury of Appeal; first Olympic village for the male competitors; entries limited to three

per country.
British Amateur Athletic Board (BAAB) formed.

1933 WAAA championships go metric.

1934 First European championships for men at Turin, Italy.

1935 First AAA indoor championships, at Wembley, London.

1936 Olympic Games in Berlin; first official Olympic film; introduction of torch relay (conceived by Carl Diem); first televised Games, in fact the first high definition sports' outside broadcast – live coverage was watched by 150000 viewers in 28 halls in and around Berlin.

1938 First full-scale international contested by USA (see p. 138).

1940 First televised athletics in USA – ICAAAA indoor championships in Madison Square Garden, New York, by television station W2XBS.

1947 Geoff Dyson appointed national coach by AAA.

1948 Olympic Games at Wembley, London; starting blocks allowed for first time in Olympic competition.

1950 Association of Track and Field Statisticians founded in Brussels.

1951 First Pan-American Games, at Buenos Aires, Mediterranean Games at Alexandria and Asian Games in New Delhi.
4-spike shoe invented by Adidas.
First major floodlit meeting in London at White City.

1952 Olympic Games in Helsinki.
Road Runners Club (RRC) founded.

1953 British Universities Sports Federation formed.

1956 Olympic Games in Melbourne.

1958 'Built-up shoes' banned for high jumping. National Union of Track Statisticians (NUTS) formed.

1959 International Athletics Club (IAC) founded.

1960 Olympic Games in Rome; electronic results boards used for field events for first time.

1961 Inaugural IAAF walking team competition (later the Lugano Trophy) (see p. 114).
US Track and Field Federation formed (first championships 1963).

1963 British Milers Club formed.

1964 Olympic Games in Tokyo; first official use of automatic timing.

First European Junior Games (official championships from 1970).

1965 First African Games in Brazzaville, The Congo.
First European Cup.

1966 First European Indoor Games (official championships from 1970). IAAF expels 117 athletes, mostly from Cambodia and North Korea, for competing at GANEFO (Games of the Newly Emergent Forces) Games at Phnom-Penh, Cambodia.

1968 Olympic Games in Mexico City; first Olympics on an all-weather 'Tartan' track.
Byers Committee reports on the state of athletics in Britain.
BAAB Junior Commission set up.

1969 National (later British) Athletics League introduced.
AAA championships go metric.
Discus and hammer sectors reduced from 60° to 45°.
Pole allowed to pass under PV bar.
Neck no longer considered part of torso.

1972 Olympic Games in Munich; introduction of measurement of long throws by focusing on a prismatic reflector set at the point of impact, and calculating the distance by trigonometry using a computer; first dope testing at Olympics, record 1599 competitors from 122 nations.

1973 IAAF take over jurisdiction of International Cross-Country Championships. The ITA professional series starts (see p. 267).

1974 Young Athletes League introduced in Britain.

1975 IAAF introduced automatic suspensions for athletes found to have used anabolic steroids. US team toured China.

1976 Olympic Games in Montreal. ITA folds.

1977 First World Cup competition. Automatic timing recognised for world records.

1980 Olympic Games in Moscow. First world championships outside Olympics (see p. 115).
First TAC Grand Prix road races, with prize money paid to athletes' clubs.

1982 IAAF membership of 168 nations, the greatest number for any sport.

WORLD RECORDS

official records at events no longer recognised by the IAAF and nine more that were not ratified. As two of these were better than records subsequently set by him and ratified, his grand total of world records comes to 29.

Nurmi was born on 13 Jun 1897 in Turku, Finland, later to become one of the great venues for running. He began running at the age of nine and during his long career set more records and won more honours than any other man in the history of the sport. He might have added even more if his career had not been cut short in 1932 when he was banned by the IAAF from international events for alleged violations of his expense accounts during the 1929 season. There is a statue of him outside the Olympic

The first official list of world records was submitted by the IAAF at their fifth congress in Geneva in 1921, although a committee had produced such a list at the second congress in Berlin in 1913. Since that date the IAAF have regularly recognised records, following thorough investigation into the authenticity of performances submitted. Unfortunately some record-breaking achievements have never been submitted, while others have failed to be confirmed due to minor irregularities.

The list of events at which records are ratified is now much shorter than formerly. The first lists that were prepared gave the men's records for 53 running/hurdles events, 30 walking events, three standing jumps and the 56lb weight as well as the usual eight field events. The 1976 IAAF Congress in Montreal decided to recognise only metric distances on the track, with the exception of the 1 mile. Also since 1976 records for distances up to and including 400m were only for performances timed on fully-automatic electrical devices.

The first official list of women's world records was issued by the FSFI in 1927. All five current field events were included but the list of running events looks strange to modern eyes, with the 10 × 100m relay, the 83m hurdles, and the concentration on sprints, although 800m and 1000m were also recognised events.

The greatest number of world records set at events on the current IAAF list is 14 by Iolanda Balas (Rom) at women's high jump (see p. 75) and 14 by Paavo Nurmi (Fin) at distances ranging from 1500m to 20000m.

Paavo Nurmi
To Nurmi's total should be added eight more

Paavo Nurmi set one of his 29 world records in Britain. Here he wins the 6 miles in 29:36.4 at Stamford Bridge in 1930. *(UPI)*

stadium in Helsinki, Finland, where due tribute was paid to him as he carried the Olympic torch around the track at the opening ceremony of the 1952 Games.

Possessed of what seemed at the time to be uncanny pace judgement, perfected from timed runs, Nurmi was never defeated at a distance greater than 5000m. He won a record 12 Olympic medals (nine individual and three team) including a record nine gold medals (six individual and three team). See page 83 for full details.

Summary of Nurmi's best times and world records:

Event	Best time min sec year	No. of world records
1500m	3:52.4 – 1926	2
1 mile	4:10.4 – 1923	1
2000m	5:24.6 – 1927	2
3000m	8:20.4 – 1926	4
2 mile	8:59.5 – 1931	1
3 mile	14:02.0 – 1924	3
5000m	14:28.2 – 1924	2
4 mile	19:15.4 – 1924	2
5 mile	24:06.2 – 1924	2
6 mile	29:07.1 – 1924	2
10000m	30:06.1 – 1924	2
15000m	46:49.5 – 1928	1
10 mile	50:15.0 – 1928	1
1 hour	19210m – 1928	1
20000m	1:04:38.4 – 1930	1
4 × 1500m R	16:11.4 – 1926	2

His first world record: 22 Jun 1921 Stockholm – 10000m in 30:40.2 (and 6 miles in 29:41.2).

At the end of 1928 he held all twelve world records from 1 mile to 1 hour.

His last world record: 24 Jul 1931 Helsinki – 2 miles in 8:59.5.

In addition Nurmi had tremendous success at indoor running in the USA. In his first race indoors at Madison Square Garden, New York on 6 Jan 1925 over 1 mile he beat the world indoor record holder Joie Ray (USA) and improved the record by a second to 4:13.6. An hour and a half later the same evening he beat arch-rival Ville Ritola (Fin) to set another world indoor best (as records are not officially recognised indoors) at 5000m in 14:44.6. During a sensational tour before returning to Finland in May, Nurmi ran 55 races including 45 indoors, winning all except two, a 5000m to Ritola and an 800m to Allan Hellfrich (USA) the latter it was reported 'out of politeness'.

He set about 30 world and US indoor records, and had bests at 2000m (5:22.4), 3000m (8:18.6) and 2 miles (8:58.2) which were all superior to the outdoor world records. He also improved the 1 mile indoor best to 4:12.0. He made indoor track into big business and gate receipts from the tour were reported to total almost one million dollars.

In 1922 Nurmi set world records on three successive weekends: 27 Aug 3000m in 8:28.6 at Turku, Finland; 4 Sep 2000m in 5:26.3 at Tampere, Finland; 12 Sep 5000m in 14:35.3 at Stockholm. In 1923 he set world records on successive days; 23 Aug 1500m/1M in 3:53.0/4:10.4 in one race; 24 Aug 3 miles in 14:11.2 at Stockholm. In 1924 he capped the lot, first at Helsinki on 19 Jun with 1500m in 3:52.6 and just an hour later 5000m in 14:28.2, both world records, and three weeks later with his triumphs at the Olympic Games. Nurmi also won 20 Finnish titles between 1920 and 1933 at distances from 800m to 10000m and cross-country.

The most world records set by an athlete in a day is six by Jesse Owens (USA), competing for Ohio State University in the Western Athletic Conference (Big Ten) Championships at Ann Arbor, Michigan, USA on 25 May 1935.

Owens equalled or bettered six world records within an hour. His programme was as follows:
3.15pm – 100y in 9.4sec, equalling the record and winning by 5y.
3.25pm – LJ 8.13m/26ft 8¼in. On this, his one jump of the competition in a pit which had been specially dug for the meeting in front of the stands, Owens hit the board perfectly. Second was Willis Ward 7.66m/25ft 1½in.
3.45pm – 220y in 20.3 (also a record for 200m) with Andy Dooley second, 20.7. The old record was 20.6 by Roland Locke in 1926.

Long jump rivals Jesse Owens (right) and Luz Long (left) at Berlin in 1936 transcend the political overtones behind the Games. *(BBC Hulton)*

4.00pm – 220yh in 22.6 (also a record for 200mh) with Phil Doherty second 23.2. The old record of 23.0 had first been set by Charles Brookins (USA) in 1924. This is also the only occasion on which an athlete has set a track and a field world record on the same day.

Amazingly Owens had a sore back, injured while rolling downstairs, which meant that he had had to be helped into coach Larry Snyder's car to take him to the track. The pain apparently left him at 3.15pm and returned after his epic deeds!

Although this was Owens' greatest day he won ten quadruple individual victories (100y/220y/220yh/LJ) in 1935–6 and four additional triples, including, of course, one at the 1936 Olympic Games.

His first record was for the indoor long jump when winning the 1934 AAU title at 7.70m/25ft 3¼in.

His last competition was at the White City Stadium, London on 15 Aug 1936 at the post-Olympic British Empire v USA match, when he competed for the winning US sprint relay team.

The longest time that a world record has remained unbeaten is 61 years 129 days for the 20 mile walk in 2:47:52 by Thomas Griffith (GB) on 30 Dec 1870 in London. This was finally surpassed by Arthur Plumb's (GB) 2:43:38 on 7 May 1932.

The longest duration for a running record is 35 years 39 days for 15 miles in 1:20:04.6 by Fred Appleby (GB) on 21 Jul 1902.

The longest duration for a woman's record is 26 years 156 days by Stanislawa Walasiewicz (Pol) for 60m in 7.3sec on 24 Sep 1933 in Lemburg. This was equalled but not beaten until Betty Cuthbert (Aus) ran 7.2 on 27 Feb 1960. Walasiewicz also held the 200m record for 16 years 345 days with her 23.6 in Warsaw on 15 Aug 1935, the longest lasting of any woman's event on the current records schedule.

However Nellie Halstead's (GB) 440y in 56.8 in London on 9 Jul 1932 was not bettered for 400m for 18 years 72 days, but the 400m was not at the time on the IAAF record schedule.

The longest duration for any standard Olympic event is 25 years 79 days for the 8.13m/26ft 8¼in long jump by Jesse Owens (USA) at Ann Arbor on 25 May 1935.

Charles Paddock (USA) ran 110y in 10.2sec at Pasadena on 18 Jun 1921. This was recognised by the AAU for 110y, but not for 100m, despite the fact that 110y is 0.58m *over* 100m, as the AAU rules at the time allowed records only for the distance at which the race was run. There were some doubts about the timing, but the time was not put forward to the IAAF for ratification. It was unbeaten at 100m for 29 years 111 days until Lloyd La Beach ran the distance in 10.1 at Guyaquil, Ecuador on 7 Oct 1950, but was not submitted to the IAAF.

World records – Miscellany

World indoor and outdoor records were once set at the same meeting. It happened at the 1970 NCAA Championships at Des Moines, Iowa, when Ralph Mann (USA) ran 440y hurdles in 48.8 and Jan Johnson (USA) pole vaulted 5.36m/17ft 7in indoors. The vault was moved indoors due to a torrential downpour having made conditions impossible outdoors. Johnson's previous best was 5.04m/16ft 6½in so his successive clearances of 17ft, 17ft 4in and 17ft 7in represented a startling breakthrough.

The greatest percentage improvement in a men's world best (pre IAAF records) was 10.83% by Erik Lemming's (Swe) 49.32m javelin in 1899. The greatest improvement in an IAAF men's record is 6.59% by Bob Beamon's (USA) 8.90m long jump in 1968.

The greatest single performance improvement in a women's world best is 6.43% by Nina Dumbadze's (USSR) discus throw of 57.04m in 1952, all the more remarkable as Dumbadze had also improved the record by 5.45% with 53.25m in 1948 (actually a record 10.23% on the IAAF record, but Dumbadze had four unratified records between 1939 and 1946).

The oldest world record breaker was John Flanagan (USA), who recorded a hammer best of 56.18m/184ft 4in at New Haven, Conn., USA on 24 Jul 1909 at 41 years 196 days. The oldest under IAAF jurisdiction is Gerhard Weidner (Ger) at 41 years 71 days on 25 May 1974 when he set a world 20 mile walk record.

The oldest female world record breaker is Dana Zátopkova (Cze), who was 35 years 255 days when she threw the javelin 55.73m/182ft 10in on 1 Jun 1958.

The youngest world record breaker was Carolina Gisolf (Hol) aged 15 years 5 days when she high jumped 1.61m/5ft 3¾in at Maastricht on 18 Jul 1928.

A copy of the birth certificate of the youngest ever world record breaker. Tom Ray set 8 successive pole vault bests up to 3.57m/11ft 8⅛in in 1888.

The youngest man to break a world record was Thomas Ray (GB) who was 17 years 198 days when he set his first pole vault best of 3.42m/11ft 2¾in on 19 Sep 1879. The youngest this century was John Thomas (USA) with 2.16m/7ft 1¼in to win the indoor AAU title in 1959 at 17 years 355 days. Although this was the greatest height ever jumped it could not be ratified by the IAAF as it was made indoors.

The greatest number of world records (on current or recent IAAF schedules) set in one year is ten by Gunder Hägg (Swe) in 1942 of which seven were for current events; and ten by Ron Clarke (Aus) in 1965, of which six were for current IAAF events.

Hägg's full list is given under the mile summary. Clarke's ten, out of 17 he set in all were for: 3 mile (2), 5000m (3), 6 mile (1), 10000m (1), 10 mile (1), 1 hour (1), 20000m (1). Sandor Iharos (Hun) set eight at six events from 1500m to 5000m and 4 × 1500m R in 1955. In the following year he set a new world 10000m record of 28:42.8 to achieve what must be the greatest ever percentage improvement in a world record holder's personal best, for his only previous 10000m time was 33:04.4 in 1952.

The most world records set by an individual at one event in one year is seven by Parry O'Brien (USA) at shot in 1956 and by John Pennel (USA) at pole vault in 1963, however of these marks only four and two respectively were ratified by the IAAF. The greatest number of IAAF records in a year is five, by Iolanda Balas (Rom) for women's high jump in 1958, while Gisela Mauermayer (Ger) also set five official marks plus one unratified at women's discus in 1935, before the IAAF took over verification of women's records.

Least experienced world record holders:
Jim Thorpe (USA) set a world record in his first ever decathlon competition (although he had contested an all-around event in 1911) when he won the 1912 Olympic title, although this never made the IAAF lists as Thorpe was disqualified for professionalism. Kip Keino's (Ken) 3000m record of 7:39.5 at Hälsingborg, Sweden came in his first attempt at the distance. Glenn Morris (USA) set world records in 1936 in the second and third decathlons of his three-decathlon career. Sandor Iharos (Hun) ran a world record in his second 10000m race.

Abebe Bikila (Eth) and Jim Peters (GB) both set marathon world bests at their third races at the distance.

In 1956 Glenn Davis (USA) ran a world record for 400m hurdles at his seventh attempt at the event and Bobby Morrow (USA) ran a 10.2sec world record in his second 100m, but that hardly counts as he had, of course, raced often at 100y. Fanny Blankers-Koen (Hol) ran a world record 80m hurdles in 11.3sec in 1943. Her only previous hurdles race was a 12.3 in 1940.

The longest wait for ratification is for the 9.4 100y of Daniel Joubert (SA) set in 1931 but not ratified until 1947.

The longest time span over which world records have been set by an individual is 13 years 318 days (1895–1909) in the pre-IAAF era by John Flanagan (USA) with the hammer, followed by 13 years 103 days (1899–1922) by Erik Lemming (Swe) at javelin. Nina Dumbadze (USSR) set women's discus records over a 13 years 30 day span (1939–52) but her early records were not ratified as the USSR was not then a member of the IAAF. The longest time span for IAAF records is 11 years 20 days (1965–76) for Irena Szewinska (Pol).

Athletes to have set IAAF world records at three Olympic individual events:
Men: Paavo Nurmi (Fin) 1500m, 5000m, 10000m; Jesse Owens (USA) 100m, 200m, LJ; Sandor Iharos (Hun) 1500m, 5000m, 10000m; Henry Rono (Ken) 5000m, 10000m, 3000m S/C.

Glenn Morris throws the javelin 54.52m in the ninth event of his world record and Olympic gold medal winning decathlon at Berlin in 1936.
(BBC Hulton)

Women: Gisela Mauermayer (Ger) SP, DT, Pen; Chi Cheng (Tai) 100m, 200m, 100mh; Irena Szewinska (Pol) 100m, 200m, 400m.

Way out in the lead, however, is the incomparable Fanny Blankers-Koen (Hol) who set world records at five Olympic events: 100m, 80mh, HJ and Pen, as well as at 100y, 220y 4 × 110y R and 4 × 200m R for an unparalleled spread of events.

The smallest crowd to watch a world record was possibly 48 at John Muir College, Pasadena on 11 Jul 1953 to see Fortune Gordien (USA) throw the discus 58.10m/190ft 7in.

The city where the most records have been set is Los Angeles, but the stadium with the most is Stockholm (see stadia).

The greatest era for world record breaking was the 1960s. Official world records for Olympic events by decades:
Men: 1920s – 65; 1930s – 96; 1940s – 32; 1950s – 121; 1960s – 156; 1970s – 96.
Women: 1930s – 12; 1940s – 16; 1950s – 76; 1960s – 95; 1970s – 118.
The IAAF only started to recognise women's marks in the late 1930s.

Men's World Records

100 YARDS
Although removed from the IAAF world record list in 1976, the 100 yards has been a classic event, with the bait of 'even time' a target for all aspiring sprinters.
One must regard timekeeping in the 19th century with care, and there were several claims for astounding sprint times.

The first man to better 10.0sec in a major race was John Owen (USA) with 9.8 in the AAU championships on Anastolan Island, Washington DC on 11 Oct 1890. Thomas Malone (Ire) was reputed to have run a 9.8 at Limerick on 15 Jun 1882, but this must be regarded a doubtful timing. At that time there had been at least 80 times of 10.0 recorded, from the first by John Watkins (GB) on 14 Mar 1860.

The most IAAF world records is six times of 9.6sec by Charles Paddock (USA), four in 1921 and one each in 1924 and 1926. The final one was actually 9.5, but the IAAF at the time recognised records in fifths of a second, so it was rounded up. Paddock, Olympic 100m champion

Charlie Paddock, who won two gold and two silver Olympic medals, leaps for the tape. He was the second of 16 Olympic champions to have studied at the University of Southern California.
(University of Southern California)

in 1920, was a popular and controversial character, whose 'trademark' was to take a flying leap for the tape. His second 9.6 came at Redlands, Cal. on 23 Apr 1921, when he set four more world records in two races. First he ran 100m in 10.4 (passing 100y in 9.6) and in the second broke tapes at 200m (21.2), 300y (30.2) and 300m (33.2). He died, a Captain in the Marine Corps, in 1943 and had a ship named after him.

Jesse Owens, (USA) who ran 100y in 9.4sec six times, of which two were accepted as world records, ran the distance in 9.9 in 1936 in baseball uniform. This was bettered by Dave Sime's 9.8. Sime (USA) turned down professional baseball offers to concentrate on sprinting and set three world records at 9.3 in 1956–57.

The first official 9.0sec was run by Ivory Crockett (USA) at Knoxville on 11 May 1974, although John Carlos (USA) had run a wind assisted 9.0 at San José, Cal. on 3 May 1969, a week before equalling the record at 9.1, a time first run by Bob Hayes (USA) in 1963. 9.0 was also run by Houston McTear (USA) in 1975.

The fastest ever 100y on automatic timing is 9.18 (wind assisted) by Reggie Jones (USA) at Austin, Texas on 7 Jun 1974, and the best under record conditions is 9.21 by Charlie Greene (USA) at Provo, Utah on 16 Jun 1967, both when winning NCAA titles. Greene habitually wore dark glasses while running, even indoors – he called them his re-entry shields.

The fastest 100y run backwards is 13.1 by Paul Wilson (NZ) at Tokyo on 22 Sep 1979 during a 14.4 for 100m.

The fastest three-legged 100y is 11.0 by Harry Hillman (USA) and Lawson Robertson (USA) at New York on 24 Apr 1909. Both won medals at the 1904 Olympics. Robertson was the head US coach at four Olympic Games from 1924 to 1936.

100 METRES
The first sub 11sec time was run by Luther Cary (USA), recorded as 10¾sec at Paris 4 Jul 1891.

The first sub 10sec 100m was run by Bob Hayes (USA) or Jim Hines (USA), depending on the definition of record conditions. Bob Hayes ran a wind assisted (5m/s) 9.9 at Walnut, Cal. on 27 Apr 1963. On 15 Oct 1964 in the Olympic semi-final at Tokyo he ran the first automatically timed sub-10 with 9.91, but again the wind at 5.3m/s was far too strong for a record. Hayes went on to win the final in 10.06, the best ever automatic timing, with the wind at just under 1m/s. (This was ratified at 10.0 as equalling the world hand-timed record.)

The first 9.9sec under record conditions was run by Jim Hines in a semi-final of the AAU championships at Sacramento, Cal. on 20 Jun 1968. Behind him Ronnie Ray Smith (USA) was also given 9.9, as was Charlie Greene (USA), winner of the second semi-final. Automatic timings were respectively 10.03, 10.14 and 10.10. Hines had earlier won his heat in a windy 9.8.

Hines ran the first auto-timed sub-10sec when he won the 1968 Olympic title at Mexico City in 9.95. This time, still the world record, was ratified as the inaugural automatically timed mark. A faster 9.87 by William Snoddy (USA) was aided by a strong wind of 11.2m/s at Dallas on 1 Apr 1978.

The most officially ratified 100m records is four at 9.9 by Steve Williams (USA) 1974–6.

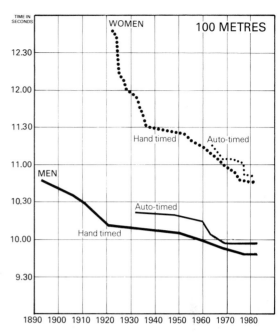

Jim Hines, double Olympic gold medallist in 1968, whose 9.95 for 100 metres lasted as a world record into the 1980s.   (E. D. Lacey)

The fastest ever hand-timed 100m is 9.8, first run by Hines in 1968 with wind assistance and then by Valeriy Borzov (USSR) in the 1972 Olympic final. On the latter occasion automatic timing (10.07) was used officially, so this mark was not ratified, and that distinction fell to Steve Williams with 9.8 at Eugene, USA on 20 Jun 1975 (but only 10.19 auto!). Since then Harvey Glance (USA) has run 9.8 in 1977 and 1981.

The first 10.0sec time was run by Armin Hary (Ger) at Zurich twice on 21 Jun 1960. For the first race (10.16 auto) the starter later admitted to Hary's flying start, but the second (10.25 auto) was allowed as a world record.

The fastest ever with automatic timing at sea-level under record conditions is 10.00 by Carl Lewis (USA) with a nil wind at Dallas on 16 May 1981. Lewis, following in the footsteps of Jesse Owens also won the 200m (20.73) and LJ (8.25m) at this meeting.

Owens himself ran the first world record 10.2sec at the 1936 NCAA in Chicago. This remained the record for 20 years until Willie Williams (USA) ran the first world record 10.1 in the Berlin Olympic stadium, where Owens won his four gold medals in 1936. Owens and Williams shared the same birthday (12 September).

200 METRES

In the original IAAF list of records there was no distinction drawn over the type of course on which world 200m or 220y records could be set. Thus most records were set on straightaways in the USA, the lack of a turn enabling times to be about 0.3–0.4sec faster. The IAAF introduced separate lists for marks round a turn in 1958 and later dropped marks on a straight track as the practice of running these died out in the USA in 1967.

The greatest number of 200m world records (turn) by one man is five by Ray Norton (USA), three of which (two of his four 20.6 marks and his 20.5) were ratified by the IAAF. All these were set in 1959 and 1960.

The first time of 20.0 around a turn was run at 220y by Tommie Smith (USA) at Sacramento on 11 Jun 1966 to take 0.2sec off Henry Carr's (USA) record. Smith improved to 19.8 on 16 Oct 1968 at Mexico City in the Olympic final, which was automatically recorded as 19.83 and was later adopted by the IAAF as the first automatically timed record. A 'faster' 19.7 (but 19.92 auto) had been run by John Carlos (USA) to win the US Olympic Trials at Echo Summit, South Lake Tahoe on 12 Sep 1968, but this mark was not ratified as Carlos wore the outlawed 'brush' spikes made by *Puma*, containing 68 mini-spikes as against the official maximum of six spikes up front and two at the heel.

Tommie Smith's 19.83 remained as the world record for nearly 11 years until Pietro Mennea (Ita) also ran at the 2240m/7347ft altitude of Mexico City and won the 1979 World Student Games title with 19.72. Mennea has also run the fastest at sea level, 19.96 at Barletta, Italy on 17 Aug 1980.

The biggest ever improvement at 200m (turn) came on 16 Jan 1932 at Sydney Cricket Ground when James Carlton (Aus) won the Australian 220y title in 20.6. This was 0.6sec faster than the previous best (220y times being about 0.1sec more than the equivalent for 200m). The referee, more shaken by the time than by the strength of the wind according to reports, ruled that it was wind assisted. Carlton was unable to prove his ability against the world's best as he retired to a monastic life before the Olympic Games later that year.

The fastest time ever clocked over 220y on a straight course was 19.5sec by Tommie Smith at San José, Cal. on 7 May 1966. This was also the first 'legal' sub 20sec clocking, while Carlos's 19.7/19.92 was the first sub-20 time around a turn.

The biggest improvement at the former classic distance of 220y straight was 0.5sec by Tommie Smith (USA), who did 19.5 at San José, Cal. on 7 May 1966 to better the old record of 20.0 by Dave Sime (USA) in 1956 and Frank Budd (USA) in 1962. Smith ran the 400m very infrequently but won all eight races at 400m or 440y 1966–68, including world records 44.5m/44.8y at San José on 20 May 1967.

The first sub 20sec time was Ralph Metcalfe's (USA) 19.8 wind assisted mark on a straight course at Toronto on 3 Sep 1932. He ran a best ever 220y straight of 20.3 in 1933.

The stylish Henry Carr, NCAA 220y champion for Arizona State University in 1963, and world record holder and Olympic champion at 200m and 4 × 400m relay. *(Arizona State)*

Lee Evans climaxed his 1968 season with world records and Olympic titles for 400m (43.86) and 4 × 400m relay. *(San Jose State University)*

400 METRES – 440 YARDS

From 1976 the IAAF no longer recognised records at 440 yards, but in the 19th century and in the early part of this century most of the best times were recorded at this slightly longer distance (402.34m). A generally accepted conversion factor is 0.3sec.

The greatest improvement in the IAAF record came on 26 Mar 1932 when Ben Eastman (USA) ran 440y in 46.4sec on his home track at Palo Alto for Stanford University. Eastman had been co-record holder for 440y at 47.4 and the 400m record stood at 47.0. Eastman ran another fast 440y, 46.5 on 21 May, but he was beaten at the ICAAAA championships by Bill Carr (USA) of Pennsylvania University 46.99 to 47.19. Carr started with a 440y best of 48.4 in June, ran 47.7 in his heat before this startling breakthrough and went on to beat Eastman again in the Olympic final in Los Angeles on 5 August. There Carr broke Eastman's world record with 46.2 to Eastman's 46.4. Carr's brief and sensational career ended when he sustained a pelvic fracture in a car crash in March 1933.

The only man to have set IAAF records on three separate occasions is Herb McKenley (Jam), with 46.3 (1947) and 46.0 (1948) for 440y and 400m records of 46.0 and 45.9 in 1948.

Barrier breakers – (* = 440 yard times)
50sec: The professional Harold Reed (GB) is credited with 48.5* in London on 25 Jun 1849. The first amateur – Robert Philpot (GB) 49.6* Cambridge 7 Mar 1871.
49sec: professional – 48¼sec* Richard Buttery (GB) Gateshead 4 Oct 1873; amateur – 48.6* Laurence Myers (USA) Birmingham 16 Jul 1881 on a slightly downhill course.
48sec: Maxie Long (USA) 47.8* New York 29 Sep 1900. Five days later Long, the reigning Olympic champion, ran 440y in 47.0sec. This, however, could not be accepted as a record as it was achieved on a straight track at the Guttenburg race-track in New Jersey. Wendell Baker (USA) had run 440y in 47¾sec on a straight track at Boston on 1 Jul 1886. For the last 100y of the race he wore only one shoe.
47sec: Ben Eastman (USA) 46.4* Stanford 26 Mar 1932.
46sec: Herb McKenley (Jam) 45.9 Milwaukee 2 Jul 1948. McKenley also ran 440y on a board-walk straightaway with a following breeze in 45.0 on 23 Aug 1947 at Long Branch, NJ.
45sec: Otis Davis (USA) 44.9 Rome 6 Sep 1960. Both Davis and Carl Kaufmann (Ger)

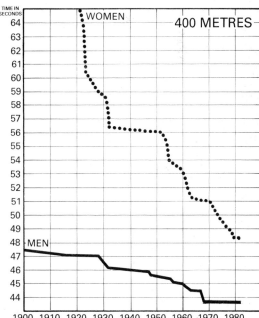

shared the world record at 44.9, but on automatic timing Davis won with 45.07 to 45.08.
44sec: Lee Evans (USA) 43.86 Mexico City 18 Oct 1968. Evans had been second, in 45.3, to his San José State team mate Tommie Smith in the latter's 1967 world 440y record of 44.8, and improved to 44.95 to win the 1967 Pan-American title. In 1968 Evans swept all before him, losing just two minor races at 400m to Ron Freeman (USA). Evans won the NCAA and AAU titles and then the US Olympic trials at Echo Summit, South Lake Tahoe, Cal. in a world best of 44.06 from Larry James, 44.19. Evans, however, wore the illegal 'brush' spikes so James was credited with the record, breaking the two-week old 44.4 by Vince Matthews (USA). In the Olympic Games Evans won in 43.86 from James 43.97 and Freeman 44.41. Three days later the great US 4 × 400m squad won that event in a world record 2:56.16 – times for each leg were: Vince Matthews 45.0, Ron Freeman 43.2 (the fastest ever relay leg), Larry James 43.8 and Lee Evans 44.1.

Both Mexico City (2240m) and Echo Summit (2249m) are at high altitude. **The fastest ever low altitude times** are 44.1 (hand timed) by Wayne Collett (USA) at Eugene, Oregon in 1972 and 44.26 by Albert Juantorena (Cub) in winning the 1976 Olympic title.

In 1868 Edward Colbeck (GB) ran a world best of 50.4sec for 440y to win the AAC title, yet he had run into and broken the leg of a sheep on the way round.

800 METRES
There have been fewer world records at 800m than at any of the other classic men's running events, just 18 from Ted Meredith's (USA) Olympic victory in 1912 in 1:51.9 to Sebastian Coe's (GB) 1:42.33 at the Bislett Games in Oslo on 5 Jul 1979 and 1:41.73 in Florence on 10 Jun 1981. The only other double world 800m record setter is Alberto Juantorena (Cub), Coe's predecessor, who won the 1976 Olympic title in 1:43.50 and then the 1977 World Student Games title in Sofia in 1:43.44.

The greatest improvement and the longest lasting record was set by the great German runner Rudolf Harbig, who was killed on the Eastern front on 5 Mar 1944. He won a bronze medal at 4 × 400m R in the 1936 Olympic Games and won a clear victory in the 1938 European championships in 1:50.6 for a German record. He improved to 1:49.4 in 1939 before he faced his great rival Mario Lanzi (Ita) on the 500m track at Milan on 15 July in the Germany v Italy match. Lanzi had earlier set an Italian record of 1:49.5 so the two appeared evenly matched. Lanzi went off fast, passing 200m in 24.6 and 400m in 52.5. He still led at 600m in 1:19.8 but had no answer as Harbig drove past in the final 100m to finish in 1:46.6 to Lanzi's 1:49.0. The previous world record had been set by Sydney Wooderson (GB) with 1:48.4 in 1938. Harbig beat Lanzi again, 1:48.7 to 1:49.2 two weeks later and again in 1:47.8 to 1:49.3 in 1940, but Lanzi beat him 1:54.2 to 1:54.7 on 29 Sep 1940 which ended a run of 48 successive victories at 800m for Harbig, starting on 23 Aug 1936, following his fifth place to Glenn Cunningham's (USA) world record 1:49.7 three days earlier. At all events Harbig beat Lanzi 8–4. Harbig's coach, the renowned Woldemar Gerschler, a pioneer of interval training, considered that but for the war Harbig would have run even faster in 1940 and 1941 when he set a world 1000m record of 2:21.5. Harbig's record remained unbroken until Roger Moens (Bel) ran 1:45.7 on 3 Aug 1955.

Before official IAAF records were introduced the American Laurence 'Lon' Myers set seven world records at 880y, from 1:56.2 in 1880 to 1:55.4 in 1885 at which time he had run the ten fastest times ever. Myers was desperately thin weighing just 52kg/8st 2lb at 1.73m/5ft 8in tall but was one of the greatest competitors of all time, setting US records for each event from 100y to 1 mile, and world records at all events from 100y (10.0 in 1880) to 880y. He was undefeated at 440y (best time 48.6) and 880y.

Barrier breakers:
2:00 Harold Reed (GB) 1:58 for 880y as a professional in 1854.
1:55 Francis Cross (GB) 1:54.4 (880y) 9 Mar 1888 Oxford.
1:50 Thomas Hampson (GB) 1:49.7 2 Aug 1932 Los Angeles.
1:45 Peter Snell (NZ) 1:44.3 3 Feb 1962 Christchurch.
Snell, who had run an 880y relay leg in 1:44.8 for the British Commonwealth v USA at the White City on 14 Sep 1960, went through 400m in 50.7sec and 600m in 1:16.4, much the fastest pace of any world record to that date. Indeed the next five world records were all run with a slower first lap, although Rick Wohlhuter (USA) in his 1:44.1 half-mile in 1974 passed 400m in 50.7 and 600m in 1:16.2. However Sebastian Coe moved the event into faster terri-

tory; in his first record he was timed at 50.6 at 400m and 1:15.4 at 600m and went even faster – 49.64 and 1:15.0 at Florence.

1000 METRES
Although this distance is raced comparatively infrequently, there have been some classic records, not least Sebastian Coe's two world records at Oslo – 2:13.40 in 1980 and 2:12.18 in 1981. He succeeded Rick Wohlhuter (USA), whose 2:13.9 also at Oslo on 30 Jul 1974 had been the greatest improvement ever, 2.1sec over Danie Malan's (SA) year-old mark.

The most records is three by Audun Boysen (Nor) 2:20.4, 2:19.5 and 2:19.0 in 1953, 1954 and 1955 respectively. All these were ratified by the IAAF. Dan Waern (Swe) also set three records in 1958–59, but only the first and last 2:18.1 and 2:17.8 were official, and Henri Deloge (Fra) made three improvements before the first IAAF list in 1900–2. Deloge's best was 2:35.8.

¾ MILE (non official event)
The first man to run this distance in under 3min was Sydney Wooderson (GB) with 2:59.5 at Fallowfield Stadium, Manchester on 6 Jun 1939. Naturally this caused speculation as to the possibility of adding another quarter mile at the same speed to obtain the 'four-minute-mile'. Wooderson, a deceptively frail looking runner (1.67m/5ft 6in tall and weighing about 56kg, just under 9 stone), shares with Peter Snell and Sebastian Coe the distinction of holding world records for both 800m and 1 mile (4:06.4 in 1937). He was Britain's greatest athlete in the immediate pre-war years when he won five successive AAA 1 mile titles 1935–9. He kept running with limited competition during the war when he was a corporal in the Pioneer Corps, and returned to great triumphs afterwards, winning the 1946 European 5000m title and the 1948 National cross-country championship. Yet in 1944 he had spent four months in hospital with severe rheumatism. In his first race less than six months after leaving hospital he bettered 4:25. His fastest ever mile came on 9 Sep 1945 in Göteborg when he ran 4:04.2 behind Arne Andersson's 4:03.8. This was his fourth British mile record, and his 1500m time of 3:48.4 was his fifth at that distance. On 6 Aug at the White City a capacity crowd was thrilled by a tremendous mile in which Andersson beat Wooderson 4:08.8 to 4:09.2. This was Wooderson's first defeat in a major race in Britain since 1935.

Sydney Wooderson wins his first major title and beats Jack Lovelock (NZ) in the 1935 AAA 1 mile in 4:17.4.

1500 METRES

The first sub 4min 1500m was run on 30 May 1908 by Harold Wilson (GB) who won the Olympic silver medal behind Mel Sheppard (USA) later in the year. Wilson's time was bettered three times by Abel Kiviat (USA) who followed him as Olympic silver medallist (behind Arnold Jackson) in 1912. Kiviat's best of 3:55.8 in 1912 was the first IAAF 1500m record.

Only one man has emulated Kiviat in setting three records – Gunder Hägg (Swe). Hägg's first record was 3:47.6 in 1941 in taking a fifth of a second off Jack Lovelock's (NZ) winning time at the 1936 Olympics. Hägg improved to 3:45.8 in 1942, then lost the record to arch-rival Arne Andersson (Swe), 3:45.0 in 1943, before regaining it at 3:43.0 in 1944, a time which was unbeaten for ten years.

Other barrier breakers:
3:50 – Jules Ladoumègue (Fra) 3:49.2 Paris 5 Oct 1930.
3:40 – Stanislav Jungwirth (Cze) 3:38.1 Stará Boleslav (Cze) 12 Jul 1957.

The previous day three runners broke the old record in one race at Turku, Finland. Olavi Salsola and Olavi Salonen shared the new record at 3:40.2 and a third Finn Olavi Vuorisalo, clocked 3:40.3 compared with the record of 3:40.6 to Istvan Rózasvolgyi (Hun). Way back in this race in 3:54.8 was Matti Nurmi, son of the great Paavo.

The biggest improvement in the IAAF record is 2.5sec by Jim Ryun (USA) on 8 Jul 1967 at Los Angeles for the USA v British Commonwealth. Fifteen days after he had set a world mile record of 3:51.1, Ryun ran 3:33.1 after tailing Kip Keino (Ken) around the second and third laps finishing with a devastating burst of speed to leave Keino way back in 3:37.2. Herb Elliott's 1960 Olympic time of 3:35.6 was shattered. Ryun put in the most devastating finish ever seen in the USA v West Germany match at Dusseldorf on 17 Aug 1967. He passed Bodo Tummler (Ger) with 300m to go and covered that distance in 36.4. Undefeated at 1500m or 1 mile in 47 races from 1965 until his Olympic silver medal in 1968, Ryun bestrode the middle distances, but a hamstring injury and glandular fever severely affected his chances in 1968 and he proved no match for Keino. Four years later he fell in the heats of the Olympic 1500m. Ryun's record stood for six and a half years before two men beat it in the 1974 Commonwealth Games – Filbert Bayi (Tan) 3:32.16 and

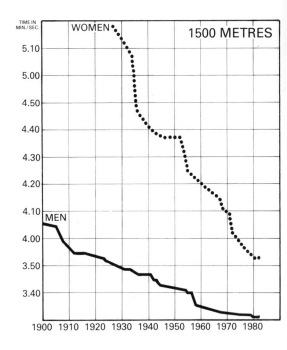

John Walker (NZ) 3:32.52, with Ben Jipcho (Ken) just outside at 3:33.16. Since then the record has been in British hands, first Sebastian Coe 3:32.03 in Zurich on 15 Aug 1979, and then Steve Ovett first ran 3:32.09 at Oslo on 15 Jul 1980 to tie the record when rounded up under the rules then in force and 3:31.36 at Koblenz on 27 Aug 1980.

1 MILE

The first IAAF mile record was 4:14.4 by John Paul Jones (USA) at Cambridge, Mass. on 31 May 1913. That was the amateur best but Walter George (GB) had run 4:12¾ as a professional.

George v Cummings
George had three times set amateur world bests, finally with 4:18.4 in 1884 while William Cummings (GB) had run 4:16.2 as a professional in 1881. George, world amateur record holder at 1, 2, 3, 6 and 10 miles as well as for one hour, turned 'pro' and the stage was set for a clash with Cummings, a Scot from Glasgow. This came at Lillie Bridge on 31 Aug 1885 with more than 30000 spectators, many of whom had fought their way into the stadium after officials had closed the gates two hours before the race. George had to climb over the wall by a ladder into his dressing room such was the melée. Cummings was the favourite with the book-

Walter George (world record of 51:20.0 in 1884) and William Cummings contest 10 miles at Lillie Bridge for £100 a side in 1885. *(BBC Hulton)*

makers, but George demolished his opponent with a sensational pace: 440y in 58.2sec and 880y in 2:02.0. Cummings was level at 1000y and George went through ¾ mile in 3:07.5. In heavy rain Cummings had to let go and George jogged through to finish in 4:20.2. He said afterwards that he could have run 4:12 and proved that to be no idle boast in the re-match the next year.

The pace in the second challenge between these great milers, again at Lillie Bridge, on 23 Aug 1886 was remarkably similar to their first race. George led through the first three laps in 58¼, 63½ and 66sec. This time Cummings was not spent, and burst into the lead with 350y to go. George was not beaten, but gained steadily and stretched through to the tape to win in the tremendous time of 4:12¾ as Cummings collapsed. George's time was not beaten by an amateur until Norman Taber (USA) ran 4:12.6 in 1915, and George had run even faster, 4:10.2 in a time-trial at Surbiton in 1885. This time was not bettered until 1931.

The first sub 4:20 mile had been run on 19 Aug 1865 in a race for 'The Champion Miler of England' by professionals William 'Crowcatcher' Lang and Welshman William Richards,

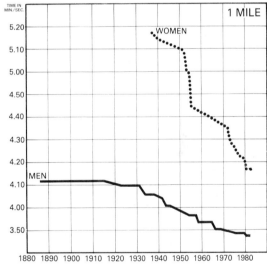

who dead-heated at Manchester in 4:17¼. George ran the first such time by an amateur, 4:19.4 at Lillie Bridge on 3 Jun 1882.

The first sub 4:10 mile was run by Jules Ladoumègue (Fra), 4:09.2 at Stade Jean Bouin in Paris on 4 Oct 1931, taking 1.2sec off Paavo Nurmi's (Fin) eight year old record.

The most IAAF mile records by any athlete is

World records set at all distances by Hägg and Andersson:

10 Aug 1941	Stockholm	1500m	Hägg 3:47.5 (2. Andersson 3:48.6)
1 Jul 1942	Göteborg	1 mile	Hägg 4:06.1 (2. Andersson 4:06.4)
3 Jul 1942	Stockholm	2 mile	Hägg 8:47.8 (2. Andersson 8:51.4)
10 Jul 1942	Stockholm	1 mile	Andersson 4:06.2
17 Jul 1942	Stockholm	1500m	Hägg 3:45.8 (2. Andersson 3:49.2)
21 Jul 1942	Malmö	2000m	Hägg 5:16.4 (2. Andersson 5:16.8)
23 Aug 1942	Östersund	2000m	Hägg 5:11.8 (2. Andersson 5:30.6)
28 Aug 1942	Stockholm	3000m	Hägg 8:01.2
4 Sep 1942	Stockholm	1 mile	Hägg 4:04.6
11 Sep 1942	Stockholm	3 mile	Hägg 13:35.4
20 Sep 1942	Göteborg	3 mile } 5000m }	Hägg 13:32.4 / 13:58.6
1 Jul 1943	Göteborg	1 mile	Andersson 4:02.6
17 Aug 1943	Göteborg	1500m	Andersson 3:45.0
25 Jun 1944	Östersund	2 mile	Hägg 8:46.4
7 Jul 1944	Göteborg	1500m	Hägg 3:43.0 (2. Andersson 3:44.0)
18 Jul 1944	Malmö	1 mile	Andersson 4:01.6 (2. Hägg 4:02.0)
4 Aug 1944	Stockholm	2 mile	Hägg 8:42.8 (2. Andersson 8:59.4)
17 Jul 1945	Malmö	1 mile	Hägg 4:01.3 (2. Andersson 4:02.2)
29 Jul 1945	Norrköping	4 × 1500m R	Hägg ran on 15:38.8 record by his club.

three by Sebastian Coe (see p. 33) and by both Gunder Hägg and Arne Andersson. These Swedish rivals took the record from Sydney Wooderson's 4:06.4 in 1937 to the brink of the four-minute mile, with Hägg's 4:01.3 in 1945. Both were suspended from amateur competition by the Swedish federation in 1946.

Under the rules then in force times were rounded up in fifths, so Hägg's time on 1 Jul 1942 was ratified at 4:06.2, and thus equalled nine days later by Andersson. In 1942 Hägg started the season on 1 July after a ten-month suspension for excessive travel expenses. Thereafter he ran and won 32 races to 11 October, and set ten world records at seven distances in 82 days, Andersson was runner-up in five of them, and three times in three weeks bettered the old world record only to lose to Hägg. From 1945 to 1948 Hägg uniquely held all seven world records from 1500m to 5000m.

In all Hägg beat Andersson 15–8 at all distances and 11–5 at 1500m or 1 mile. Hägg's 4:01.3 was unapproached until the bid for the four-minute mile started to build up in 1952. In that year John Landy (Aus) ran 4:02.1. In 1953 both Landy and Roger Bannister (GB) ran 4:02.0 and Wes Santee (USA) 4:02.4. Landy pressed hard in Australia in the early months of 1954, and in virtually solo efforts ran successively 4:02.4, and two 4:02.6s.

The most famous of all athletics barriers, the four-minute mile, went to Roger Bannister (GB) at Oxford on 6 May 1954. Bannister's long and careful preparations were vastly rewarded by his time of 3:59.4. Gusty winds before the race nearly decided him against the effort, but Bannister and his team-mates Chris

Brasher and Chris Chataway, running for the AAA against Oxford University ran the perfect race. Bannister tracked Brasher through 440y in 57.4sec and 880y in 1:58.0 before Chataway took over, to reach the three-quarter mark in 3:00.5, and with 230y to go Bannister went ahead to maintain his form before staggering over the tape to take his place in history. Chataway was second in 4:07.2 and Brasher fourth, untimed and almost lost in the swarm of well-wishers who thronged the track.

Wes Santee followed Bannister's achievements with miles in 4:01.3, 4:00.6 and 4:00.7 but the second four-minute miler was John Landy. With Chris Chataway again second (in 4:04.4), Landy smashed Bannister's record with 3:57.9 in ideal conditions at Turku in Finland on 21 June.

The confrontation between Landy and Bannister was naturally eagerly awaited and the race, when it came was no disappointment. Billed as the 'Miracle Mile' Bannister won an epic race at the Empire Games in Vancouver on 7 August, 3:58.8 to Landy's 3.59.6. Bannister closed his career, to concentrate on completing his medical studies, with the European 1500m title in Berne on 29 August. He had raced sparingly in his career and from his third place in the London v Göteborg meeting on 6 Aug 1949 ran, and won, just 15 races at 1 mile. He was knighted in 1975, following his Chairmanship of the Sports Council.

Four-minute mile progression
Numbers of runners breaking four minutes in one race:
three: 28 May 1955 White City, London. Won by Laszlo Tabori (Hun) 3:59.0.

Roger Bannister ran and won three mile races in 1954. Between his two world records he won the AAA title in 4:07.6.

(BBC Hulton)

four: 19 Jul 1957 White City, London. Won by Derek Ibbotson (GB) 3:57.2 (world record)
five: 6 Aug 1958 Dublin. Won by Herb Elliott (Aus) 3:54.5 (beat Ibbotson's world record, the biggest ever 1 mile record improvement and first sub 3:55 mile).
six: 7 Jun 1963 Compton. Cal. Won by Peter Snell (NZ) 3:55.0 (Snell had improved the world record to 3:54.4 at Wanganui on 27 Jan 1962, and later to 3:54.1 at Auckland on 17 Nov 1964).
eight: 5 Jun 1964 Compton. Won by Dyrol Burleson (USA) 3:57.4.
Jim Ryun (USA) of Wichita East High School, Kansas was just 17 years 37 days when he ran 3:59.0 for 8th in this race. This is still the youngest ever for a sub-4. After Michel Jazy (Fra) had put the record at 3:53.6 in 1965, Ryun ran two sensational world records in California, first 3:51.3 on 17 Jul 1966 at Berkeley and then 3:51.1 on 23 Jun 1967 at Bakersfield in the AAU meet. That remained the record for nearly eight years before Filbert Bayi (Tan) ran 3:51.0 in Kingston, Jamaica on 17 May 1975.

The most men breaking four minutes in one race is 13 at Berlin on 8 Aug 1980, when the winner was Thomas Wessinghage (Ger) in 3:55.04. On the same day John Walker (NZ) led 11 others under four minutes at Crystal Palace, London.

The first teenager to run sub-4 was Herb Elliott on 25 Jan 1958, when he was the 18th man to achieve the feat. By the end of 1958 Elliott was world record holder, had run five of the ten best times ever (to 3:58.0) and ten four-minute miles. By the end of his top-class career in 1960 Elliott had run 17 four-minute miles as the next highest was seven by Dan Waern (Swe).

By the tenth anniversary of Bannister's breakthrough there had been 138 four-minute miles (127 outdoor, 11 indoor) by 43 men from 15 countries.

The 500th four-minute mile came in 1972, at which time most had been run by Jim Ryun 27 and Kip Keino 23.

Tony Waldrop (USA) ran nine four-minute miles in successive finals in 1974. The first seven were run indoors from 19 January to 9 March, including a world indoor best of 3:55.0 at San Diego, Cal. on 17 February. Then outdoors he ran a personal best 3:53.2 at the Penn Relays (in the first Benjamin Franklin Mile since 1954) on 27 Apr and 3:59.8 on 14 May before his sequence

Herb Elliott finished his career with a double victory for Cambridge University v Oxford in 1961. Here he wins the 880y in 1:49.9.
(Sport & General)

of races, all of which he had won, was broken at the California Relays on 25 May when he was fourth in 4:05.0. Including his final mile in 1973 (3:57.3 on 9 Jun), the North Carolina student had run ten successive four-minute miles.

At the 1956 Olympic Games all ten four-minute milers to that date were present, five running in the 1500m final and the other five watching. Roger Bannister presented his nine successors with a black silk tie with a monogram of a silver '4' and two gold 'M's encircled in a gold laurel wreath.

The first sub 3:50 mile was run by John Walker (NZ) on 12 Aug 1975 at Göteborg with 3:49.4. Nearly four years later Sebastian Coe broke the record with 3:48.95 at Oslo on 17 Jul 1979 passing 1500m in a European record 3:32.8, an amazing breakthrough as his previous bests were 1500m – 3:42.67 and 1M – 3:57.67. Steve Ovett became the third sub 3:50 miler with 3:49.57 at Crystal Palace, London on 31 Aug 1979, and broke Coe's world record with a hand-timed 3:48.8 at Oslo on 1 Jul 1980.

440y lap times for those sub 3:50 races:

Walker	55.8 1:55.1 2:53.0 3:49.4
Coe	57.8 1:55.3 2:53.4 3:48.95
Ovett	56.3 1:55.0 2:52.8 3:49.57
Ovett	55.7 1:53.8 2:51.1 3:48.8

In 1981 Walker became the first man to run 50 four-minute miles, and by March 1982 had run 69 such races.

STEVE OVETT AND SEBASTIAN COE

Not since the era of Hägg and Andersson has the world of middle distance running been so dominated by a pair of runners from one nation. Unlike the great Swedish duo who conducted their rivalry during the war when there was very little international athletics, however, Coe and Ovett have been challenged hard by men from all over the world in a plethora of major meetings, yet they have almost invariably come out on top. Coe with his wondrously smooth, flowing action, able to sustain his 400m sprinting speed but also able to kick hard and then kick even harder with such a change of pace as to leave world class rivals floundering. And Ovett, the more powerful man, who has made his trademark a devastating burst but is also a consummate tactician and well capable of winning off any pace. Unlike the Swedes again, the racing careers of Coe and Ovett have traversed the European circuit but they have met only in

Steve Ovett (aged 18) wins his first AAA title in 1974 at 800m. From left: Ovett, Andy Carter (2nd), Byron Dyce (3rd), Peter Browne (6th), Mark Winzenried (4th), Colin Campbell (5th).
(G. Herringshaw)

the major championships while the athletics public keep waiting with ever heightening anticipation for their confrontation.

Coe v Ovett – their only meetings 1972–81
25 Mar 1972 English Schools cross-country (intermediates) at Hillingdon: 2) Ovett 21:42 ... 10) Coe 22:05 (1st Kirk Dumpleton 21:19). Ovett aged 16 and Coe 15.
31 Aug 1978 European Championships at Prague 800m: 2) Ovett 1:44.09 3) Coe 1:44.76 (1st Olaf Beyer (GDR) 1:43.84)
26 Jul 1980 Olympic Games at Moscow: 800m: 1) Ovett 1:45.40 2) Coe 1:45.85
1 Aug 1980 Olympic Games at Moscow: 1500m: 1) Coe 3:38.40.... 3) Ovett 3:38.99 (2nd Jürgen Straub (GDR) 3:38.80).

Steve Ovett was born in Brighton on 9 Oct 1955. He started his career as principally a 400m runner and has gradually moved up in distance on the track, although he has throughout his career also raced cross-country. A member of Brighton and Hove AC for most of his career, Steve changed his allegiance to Brighton Phoenix in 1981.

Sebastian Coe was born in Chiswick, London on 29 Sep 1956, and has lived for much of his life in Sheffield, where he joined the local club, Hallamshire Harriers. He gained a degree in economics from Loughborough University in 1980. Coe started his championships career at cross-country and 3000m and, contrary to Ovett, has so far tended to move down in distance.

STEVE OVETT

National and International championships

(CC = cross-country)

1970	CC	37th English Schools Juniors
	400m	1st 51.8 English Schools Juniors
1971	400m	3rd 50.4 English Schools Inters.
	400m	1st 49.8 AAA Youths
1972	CC	2nd 21:42 English Schools Inters.
	800m	1st 1:55.0 English Schools Inters.
	400m	1st 49.1 AAA Youths
1973	CC	2nd 26:35 English Schools Seniors
	800m	6th 1:47.34 AAA
	800m	1st 1:47.53 European Juniors
1974	800m	1st 1:46.84 AAA
	800m	2nd 1:45.76 European
1975	1500m	5th 3:45.9 AAA Indoor
	CC	1st 32:06 English Juniors
	800m	1st 1:46.09 AAA
1976	800m	5th 1:45.44 Olympic Games
	1500m	6th 3:40.34 Olympic Games semi-final
	800m	1st 1:47.33 AAA

1977	CC	13th 45:11 English (National)
	1500m	1st 3:37.5 UK
1978	CC	4th 42:24 English (National)
	800m	2nd 1:44.09 European
	1500m	1st 3:35.59 European
1979	CC	6th 47:41 English (National)
	1500m	1st 3:39.08 AAA
1980	800m	1st 1:45.40 Olympic Games
	1500m	3rd 3:38.99 Olympic Games
	1 mile	1st 4:04.40 AAA
1981	1500m	1st 3:42.80 UK

Other international appearances for Great Britain or England:

1973	800m	3rd 1:49.6 GB 'A' v France
	800m	1st 3:54.9 GB Jnr v Sweden
1974	800m	1st 1:46.8 GB v Poland and Canada
	800m	1st 1:48.82 GB v Czechoslovakia
1975	800m	3rd 1:47.6 GB v GDR
	1500m	2nd 3:43.3 GB v GDR (Guest)
	800m	1st 1:46.73 European Cup semi
	800m	1st 1:46.55 European Cup final
1976	800m	1st 1:46.70 GB v Poland and Canada
1977	1500m	1st 3:39.8 GB track international, Paris
	1500m	1st 3:39.13 European Cup semi
	1500m	1st 3:44.94 European Cup final
	1500m	1st 3:34.45 World Cup
1978	1500m	1st 3:53.83 GB v GDR
1979	1500m	1st 3:41.68 GB v W. Germany
	800m	1st 1:49.54 Eng v Poland and Switzerland
1980	800m	1st 1:49.17 Eng v Wales, Hungary and Holland
1981	3000m	1st 7:54.11 Eng v Belgium, Ethiopia and USA
	1 Mile	1st 3:57.92 Eng v Ethiopia, Italy and Scotland
	1500m	1st 3:46.47 European Cup semi
	800m	1st 1:47.96 Eng v Hungary, Norway and Scotland
	800m	1st 1:47.0 Eng v Norway
	800m	1st 1:46.40 Eng v Poland, Switzerland and Yugoslavia
	1500m	1st 3:34.95 World Cup

How his personal bests have improved:

400 metres

13 Jun	1970	51.6	Brighton
9 Jul	1971	50.4	Crystal Palace
10 Jul	1971	50.4	Crystal Palace
7 Aug	1971	49.8	Wolverhampton
23 Jul	1972	49.1	Kirkby
	1972	48.9	In Germany

Ovett won 45 successive races at 1500m or 1 mile after 13 May 1977 when he was narrowly beaten by Steve Scott in Kingston, Jamaica (3:39.8 each) to 1 Aug 1980 when he was third at the Olympic Games.

At 1 mile he was unbeaten (24 races) from his eighth place at the Coke meeting on 29 Aug 1975 until 9 Sep 1981, when near the end of a long and hard season he was surprised to run 3:50.23 in Rieti only to be well beaten by Sydney Maree, the black South African turned US citizen, who ran 3:48.83. At 800m only Olaf Beyer and James Robinson have beaten Ovett since 1976 and his last loss to a British athlete at this distance was on 29 Sep 1973 when he was third at the English Commonwealth Games trials to Colin Campbell and Tony Settle. Apart from Coe's Olympic 1500m victory, Ovett's last track defeat by a British athlete was by Dave

20 Aug	1972	48.4	Crystal Palace (UK Youth record)
27 May	1973	48.0	Warley
15 Jun	1974	47.5	Crystal Palace

800 metres

Jun	1970	2:00.0	Brighton
1 May	1971	1:56.8	Brighton
22 Aug	1971	1:55.3	Crystal Palace (UK age 15 best)
10 Jun	1972	1:53.3	Brighton (UK age 16 best)
17 Jun	1972	1:52.5	Brighton (UK age 16 best)
23 Jun	1973	1:48.4	Crystal Palace (UK age 17 best)
13 Jul	1973	1:47.44	Crystal Palace (UK age 17 best)
13 Jul	1973	1:47.34	Crystal Palace (UK age 17 best)
30 Jun	1974	1:46.8	Warsaw
4 Sep	1974	1:45.76	Rome (European Junior record)
25 Jul	1976	1:45.44	Montreal
27 Jul	1978	1:45.38	Turku
31 Aug	1978	1:44.09	Prague (UK record)

1000 metres

19 Mar	1972	2:34.5	Crystal Palace
29 Mar	1972	2:29.2	Crystal Palace
17 Aug	1973	2:20.0	Crystal Palace (UK Junior best)
16 Aug	1976	2:19.16	Nice
6 Sep	1979	2:15.91	Koblenz (UK record)

1500 metres

16 Dec	1970	4:10.7	Crystal Palace
10 Jun	1972	4:09.7	Brighton
10 Sep	1972	4:01.5	Newham
19 May	1973	3:53.4	Brighton
17 Jun	1973	3:51.6	Crystal Palace
25 Jul	1973	3:44.8	Motspur Park (UK Junior record)
22 Jun	1975	3:43.3	Dresden
30 Jun	1975	3:39.5	Stockholm
29 Jul	1976	3:37.89	Montreal

12 Jun	1977	3:37.5	Cwmbran
3 Sep	1977	3:34.45	Dusseldorf (UK record)
4 Sep	1979	3:32.11	Brussels
15 Jul	1980	3:32.09	Oslo (equals World record)
27 Aug	1980	3:31.36	Koblenz (World record)

1 mile

25 Jul	1973	4:00.0	Motspur Park (UK Junior record)
17 Jul	1974	3:59.4	Haringey (UK Junior record)
30 Jun	1975	3:57.00	Stockholm
28 May	1977	3:56.2	Belfast
26 Jun	1977	3:54.69	Crystal Palace (UK record)
20 Sep	1978	3:52.8	Oslo (UK record)
31 Aug	1979	3:49.57	Crystal Palace
1 Jul	1980	3:48.8	Oslo (World record)
26 Aug	1981	3:48.40	Koblenz (World record)

2000 metres

24 Sep	1977	5:04.7	Hannover
3 Jun	1978	4:57.82	Crystal Palace (UK record)

3000 metres

30 Apr	1977	8:18.8	Brighton
18 May	1977	7:53.39	Crystal Palace
23 Sep	1977	7:41.3	Wattenscheid

2 miles

15 Sep	1978	8:13.51	Crystal Palace (World best)

5000 metres

7 Jul	1977	13:53.4	Middleton
30 Jul	1977	13:25.0	Gateshead

Ovett's other best times include 22.3 for 200m, 35.3 for 300m, 1:16.0 for 600m and 1:05:38 for the half marathon which he won on 20 Aug 1977 at Dartford, in which he only competed as he had missed his plane to Edinburgh where he was scheduled to take part in a 1000m at the Highland Games.

Racing record from 1973.

First figure is the number of wins and the second the number of races at each distance.

Year	400m	800m	1000m	1500m	1 mile	3000m	Other
1973	1/3	5/10	1/1	4/4	0/2		1/1 at 600m
1974	2/2	8/11	0/1	1/1	1/2		
1975	2/2	8/10		3/6	1/3		
1976	3/5	12/16	1/2	2/4			1/1 at 600m
1977		3/3		9/10	4/4	3/4	1/2 at 5000m, 0/1 at 2000m
1978	1/1	4/5		8/8	5/5	2/3	2/2 at 2000m, 1/1 at 2 miles
1979		2/3	2/2	9/9	4/4		1/1 at 600m, 1/1 at 2000m
1980		6/6		8/8	6/6	2/2	1/1 at 600m, 1/2 at 5000m
1981		4/4	2/2	8/9	6/7	1/1	1/1 at 2 miles

Moorcroft in the heats of the 1976 Olympic 1500m.

Ovett's only other loss at 1500m was at the hands of Tom Byers in Oslo on 26 Jun 1981. Byers was the 'hare', but as the pack, including Ovett, disdained following him through his pace of 57.52 for 400m and 1:54.83 he found himself some 50m clear. This grew to 70m as Byers passed the bell and despite the uneconomic tac-

tics he somehow found the strength to hang on and pull round the last lap in 61.5sec. Ovett led the chase, but even a 52.3 lap was unavailing: 3:39.01 to Byers and 3:39.53 for Ovett. Byers' services as a pace-setter were much in demand later and the former teenage prodigy (3:37.5 in 1974) had the satisfaction during the year of reducing his seven-year-old personal best 1500m to 3:36.35 and the 1 mile to 3:55.73.

SEBASTIAN COE

National and International championships
(CC = cross country)

1971	CC	24th 14:35 English Schools Juniors
	1500m	– – English Schools Juniors
		(did not qualify in heat)
1972	CC	10th 22:05 English Schools Inters.
	3000m	13th 9:07.0 English Schools Inters.
1973	800m	4th 2:02.6 AAA Indoors
	3000m	1st 8:40.2 English Schools Inters.
	1500m	1st 3:55.0 AAA Youth
1974 – missed season due to stress fractures of the		
		tibia in both legs
1975	1500m	1st 3:54.4 AAA Indoors Juniors
	1500m	1st 3:47.1 AAA Juniors
	1500m	3rd 3:45.2 European Juniors
1976	1500m	5th 3:51.0 AAA Indoor
	1500m	4th 3:42.67 AAA
1977	800m	1st 1:49.1 AAA Indoor
	800m	1st 1:46.54 European Indoor
	800m	2nd 1:46.83 AAA
1978	800m	1st 1:47.14 UK
	800m	3rd 1:44.76 European
1979	3000m	1st 7:59.8 AAA Indoor
	400m	2nd 46.87 AAA
1980	400m	8th 47.10 UK
	800m	2nd 1:45.85 Olympic Games
	1500m	1st 3:38.40 Olympic Games
1981	3000m	1st 7:55.2 AAA Indoor
	800m	1st 1:45.41 AAA

Other international appearances for Great Britain or England

1975	1500m	1st 3:50.8 GB Juniors v Fra, Spa
1977	800m	1st 1:47.6 GB v Ger Indoor
	800m	1st 1:47.5 GB v Fra Indoor
	800m	4th1:47.61 European Cup final
	800m	1st 1:47.78 GB v Ger
	1 mile	1st 3:57.67 GB v Ger
1979	800m	1st 1:46.63 European Cup semi
	800m	1st 1:47.28 European Cup final
		(and 45.5 leg on 4 × 400mR)
1981	800m	1st 1:46.0 GB v GDR
		(World Indoor record)
	800m	1st 1:44.06 Eng v Bel, Eth, USA
		(and 45.7 leg)
	4 × 400mR	46.6 leg Eng v Eth, Ita, Sco
	800m	1st 1:47.57 European Cup semi
	800m	1st 1:47.47 GB v USSR
	800m	1st 1:47.05 European Cup final
	800m	1st 1:46.16 World Cup final

How his personal bests have improved
400 metres

| 9 Sep | 1973 | 51.8 | | Sheffield |

Coe has raced amazingly rarely at 1 mile, and his three races from 1979 to 1981 were all world records! His last mile defeat was to Rod Dixon at Gateshead on 14 Sep 1976.

At 1500m apart from a heat in the 1980 Olympic Games Coe is undefeated since his fourth place in the AAA Championships on 14 Aug 1976, when the three ahead of him were Rod Dixon, David Moorcroft and Frank Clement.

At 800m Coe's only three losses from 1978 to 1981 were in the 1978 European, 1980 Olympics and, in his last loss in a track race of more than 200m, to Don Paige (USA) at Viareggio on 14 Aug 1980.

The only blemish, if so it can be called, on Coe's 1981 record was a fourth place at 200m in 22.6 at Loughborough on 13 May. Sebastian Coe has been a regular supporter of his county and area championships. At county level he has

24 Aug	1977	49.1	Rotherham
26 Apr	1978	48.0	Crystal Palace
10 May	1978	47.7	Isleworth
19 May	1979	47.6	Cleckheaton
13 Jul	1979	46.95	Crystal Palace
14 Jul	1979	46.87	Crystal Palace

800 metres

	1971	2:08.4	
3 Jun	1972	1:59.9	Hendon
1 May	1973	1:56.6	Stretford
13 May	1973	1:56.0	Crystal Palace
8 Jun	1975	1:53.8	Cleckheaton
12 May	1976	1:53.0	Loughborough
17 Jun	1976	1:50.7	Loughborough
8 Aug	1976	1:47.7	Stretford
19 Feb	1977	1:47.6	Dortmund (UK Indoor best)
26 Feb	1977	1:47.5	Cosford (UK Indoor best)
13 Mar	1977	1:46.54	San Sebastian (UK Indoor best)
16 Aug	1977	1:46.31	Brussels
9 Sep	1977	1:44.95	Crystal Palace (UK record)
18 Aug	1978	1:44.25	Brussels (UK record)
15 Sep	1978	1:43.97	Crystal Palace (UK record)
5 Jul	1979	1:42.33	Oslo (World record)
10 Jun	1981	1:41.73	Florence (World record)

1000 metres

1 Aug	1976	2:30.8	Nottingham
15 Aug	1979	2:20.8	Zurich (In 1500m)
1 Jul	1980	2:13.40	Oslo (World record)
11 Jul	1981	2:12.18	Oslo (World record)

1500 metres

	1970	4:31.8	
12 Jun	1971	4:23.6	Sheffield
25 Jul	1971	4:18.0	Sheffield
17 Jun	1972	4:07.4	Kirkby
	1972	4:05.9	
16 Jun	1973	3:59.5	Sheffield
4 Aug	1973	3:55.0	Wolverhampton
22 Mar	1975	3:54.4	Cosford (Indoors)
13 Apr	1975	3:49.7	Cleckheaton
27 Jul	1975	3:47.1	Kirkby
23 Aug	1975	3:45.2	Athens
16 May	1976	3:43.3	Cleckheaton
25 May	1976	3:43.3	Athens
11 Jun	1976	3:43.2	Crystal Palace
14 Aug	1976	3:42.67	Crystal Palace
17 Jul	1979	3:32.8	Oslo (European record)
15 Aug	1979	3:32.03	Zurich (World record)
7 Jul	1981	3:31.95	Stockholm

1 mile

14 Apr	1976	4:07.6	Crystal Palace
1 May	1976	4:05.7	Stretford
31 May	1976	4:02.43	Crystal Palace
22 Aug	1976	4:01.7	Gateshead
30 Aug	1976	3:58.35	Crystal Palace
29 Aug	1977	3:57.67	Crystal Palace
17 Jul	1979	3:48.95	Oslo (World record)
19 Aug	1981	3:48.53	Zurich (World record)
28 Aug	1981	3:47.33	Brussels (World record)

3000 metres

2 Jul	1972	8:49.0	Leeds
23 May	1973	8:43.7	Sheffield
7 Jul	1973	8:40.2	Bebington
18 Aug	1973	8:34.6	Stretford
28 Jun	1975	8:14.8	Blackburn
27 Jan	1979	7:59.8	Cosford (Indoors)
23 Apr	1980	7:57.4	Crystal Palace
24 Jan	1981	7:55.2	Cosford (Indoors)

5000 metres

11 May	1980	14:06.2	Cudworth

Coe's other best times include 36.2 for 300m, 1:15.0 for 600m.

Racing record from 1973

First figure is the number of wins and the second the number of races at each distance.

Year	400m	800m	1000m	1500m	1 mile	3000m	Other
1973	0/1	4/7		6/7		3/4	(not all heats included)
1974	No races						
1975		1/1		8/11		1/1	0/1 at 300m
1976		4/4	1/1	3/8	4/8		1/1 at 600m
1977	1/1	11/16			1/1		
1978	2/2	10/11			1/1		
1979	3/5	11/11		1/1	1/1	1/1	1/1 at 600m
1980	0/2	10/12	1/1	4/5		1/1	1/1 at 5000m
1981	4/4	13/13	2/2	1/1	2/2	1/1	0/1 at 200m

won a Yorkshire title each year since 1975: 400m in 1979; 800m in 1978, 1979, 1981; 1500m in 1975, 1976, 1982; and 5000m in 1980.

In 1979 Coe became the first man, since Otto Peltzer (Ger) in 1926, to set world records at both 800m and 1500m.

The age of the sub 3:50 mile

At the end of 1980 the 3:50 barrier had been broken four times. The following year, as Coe and Ovett chased world records on the European circuit, the all-time lists were drastically revised. In July, Ovett four times ran within a second of the world record, twice at 1500m and twice at a mile, and Coe was but six tenths off the 1500m record. It was amazing running, but in staged races, all too easily dubbed 'failures' by the press. In ten days in August however the mile record fell three times, and by the end of 1981, a further 11 sub 3:50s had been run.

Steve Cram from Jarrow and Hepburn AC, the youngest man to run a mile in under 3:50 at the age of 20 in 1981.   *(J. Burles)*

The sub 3:50 races in 1981
11 Jul – Oslo (Dream Mile) 1) Ovett 3:49.25 2) Jose-Luis Gonzalez (Spa) 3:49.67 3) Steve Scott (USA) 3:49.68 4) John Walker (NZ) 3:50.26 5) Todd Harbour (USA) 3:50:34 6) Steve Cram (GB) 3:50.38 7) Thomas Wessinghage (Ger) 3:50.91 8) John Robson (GB) 3:52.44. These were the best times ever for positions two to eight, as the first seven took their places among the best 12 milers of all time.
14 Jul – Lausanne 1) Ovett 3:49.66 2) Gonzalez 3:50.87. Eight more men ran sub 3:55.
19 Aug – Zurich 1) Coe 3:48.53 (world record) 2) Mike Boit (Ken) 3:49.74 3) Cram 3:49.95 4) Walker 3:50.12 5) Wessinghage 3:50.95; and four more inside 3:55.

26 Aug – Koblenz 1) Ovett 3:48.40 (world record) 2) Craig Masback (USA) 3:54.14.
28 Aug – Brussels (Golden Mile) 1) Coe 3:47.33 (world record) 2) Boit 3:49.45 3) Scott 3:51.48 4) Sydney Maree (USA) 3:51.81; and five more inside 3:55.
9 Sep – Rieti 1) Maree 3:48.83 2) Ovett 3:50.23
16 Sep – Aichach 1) Maree 3:49.93 2) Boit 3:50.51.
Although the 1500m record did not fall in 1981 that too was challenged hard.

The sub 3:33 races
7 Jul Stockholm 1) Sebastian Coe 3:31.95 2) Scott 3:34.17 3) Gonzalez 3:34.41 4) Boit 3:34.68.
8 Jul Milan 1) Steve Ovett 3:31.95 2) Walker 3:35.60
29 Jul Budapest 1) Steve Ovett 3:31.57 2) Omer Khalifa (Sud) 3:34.96
26 Aug Koblenz 1) Steve Scott 3:31.96 2) Wessinghage 3:33.49; 3) Boit 3:33.92.
12 Sep Hamburg 1) Sydney Maree 3:32.30 2) Boit 3:33.67

440y lap times for the three 1981 world record miles

Coe	56.2	1:53.6	2:51.68	3:48.53
	(1500m–3:33.27)			
Ovett	56.6	1:54.5	2:51.5	3:48.40
Coe	55.23	1:53.22	2:51.90	3:47.33
	(1500m–3:32.93)			

Much the fastest first half pace was set by James Robinson in Stockholm on 7 July, when he went out in the absurd time of 52.43 for 400m and 1:49.18 for 800m. Given that pace it was truly amazing that Coe hung on to go through 1200m in 2:48.32 with a final 43.63 for the last 300m, compared to Ovett's 40.66 in his world record time of 3:31.36.

When asked about his racing tactics after setting his world indoor 800m best in 1981, Coe said 'If anyone comes up alongside you, you just go a bit quicker'.

In an interview with Mel Watman, editor of 'Athletics Weekly', in 1979 Steve Ovett said '... anything like going for a world record seems senseless to me'. He later changed his mind it seems.

2000 METRES
Although an infrequently run distance there have been some notable records, including the current one of 4:51.45 by John Walker (NZ) at Oslo on 30 Jun 1976. At that year's Bislett Games he took 4.8 sec off Michel Jazy's 9½ year old record by running successive 400m laps in

60.1, 58.5, 57.7, 57.9 (and passing 1 mile in 3:55.5) and 57.2. Walker's 4.8 sec improvement on the previous record equalled that by Gaston Reiff (Bel) when he ran 5:07.0 at Brussels on 29 Sep 1948, and by Istvan Rózsavölgyi (Hun) when he broke that record with 5:02.2 at Budapest on 2 Oct 1955.

First sub 5:30 – Paavo Nurmi (Fin) 5:26.4 Tampere 4 Sep 1922
First sub 5:00 – Harald Norpoth (Ger) 4:57.8 Hagen 10 Sep 1966.

3000 METRES
Although not on the Olympic programme, the 3000m is a much-contested event and one at which many great performances have been achieved. The record has been held by many of the great names in distance running.

Paavo Nurmi with three official and one unrecognised performances holds the most world records, taking it from 8:28.6, the first sub 8:30 mark, at Turku on 27 Aug 1922 to 8:20.4 at Stockholm on 13 Jul 1926.

The greatest improvement in the IAAF record is 7.8 sec by Gunder Hägg when he ran 8:01.2 at Stockholm on 28 Aug 1942, the fourth successive and at the time seventh out of eleven world 3000m records to be set at that venue.

The first ever 3000m record ratified by the IAAF was run at Stockholm – 8:36.8 by Hannes Kolehmainen (Fin) on 12 Jul 1912; that was a 9.8 sec improvement on the previous best time ever.

The ten second 'barriers' Since Hägg's 8:01.2, have fallen as follows:
8:00 – Gaston Reiff (Bel) 7:58.8 Gävle, Swe 12 Aug 1949
7:50 – Michel Jazy (Fra) 7:49.2 Saint Maur 27 Jun 1962
7:40 – Kipchoge Keino (Ken) 7:39.6 Hälsingborg, Swe 27 Aug 1965.
The current record is 7:32.1 by Henry Rono (Ken) at Oslo, on 27 Jun 1978.

5000 METRES
The first IAAF 5000m record was Hannes Kolehmainen's (Fin) 14:36.6 in winning the 1912 Olympic title. This, the first sub 15min time, was 24.6sec inside the previous best, the greatest margin of improvement but he only beat Jean Bouin (Fra) by 0.1sec.

The most taken off an official record is 11.3sec

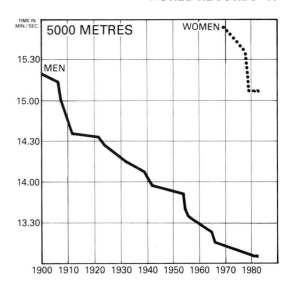

by Lauri Lehtinen (Fin) with his 14:16.9 in 1932. Since then, however, several large slices have been taken off the record in one go: Taisto Mäki (Fin) broke Lehtinen's mark with 14:08.8 in 1939 and then Gunder Hägg removed another 10.6sec with his 13:58.2 in 1942. In 1955 Sandor Iharos (Hun) (13:50.8 and 13:40.6) and Vladimir Kuts (USSR) (13:46.8) between them took 10.6sec off Kuts' 13:51.2 of the previous year and Ron Clarke (Aus) made two major improvements while sharing with Kuts the most records, four, at the distance.

Kuts set his first 5000m record at 13:56.6 in winning the 1954 European title. He then lost the record to Chris Chataway (GB) in their epic contest in the London v Moscow match on 13 Oct 1954, when Chataway ran 13:51.6 to Kuts' 13:51.7 after a duel which will never be forgotten by the 40000 crowd at London's White City Stadium or by the millions who watched on TV. The match was the first visit by a Soviet team to Britain. Ten days later Kuts ran 13:51.2, then 13:46.8 in 1955. In 1956 Gordon Pirie (GB) took the record with 13:36.8 against Kuts' (13:39.6), who was also inside the old record. However the following year Kuts had the final say in his last major race: 13:35.0 on 13 Oct in Rome.

Kuts' record stood for over seven years, until Ron Clarke ran 13:34.8 on 16 Jan 1965. A fortnight later Clarke ran 13:33.6 and on 4 Jun 1965 bettered that by 7.8 sec at Compton, Cal. with 13:25.8. The 1965 season saw a tremendous breakthrough in distance running and in all

Kuts' 13:35.0 was bettered 20 times during the year by six athletes with Kip Keino (Ken) ending with the record at 13:24.2. Keino and Clarke each had four sub 13:30 marks that year and Michel Jazy (Fra) two, and Clarke an even greater mark with 12:52.4 for three miles (worth about 13:20 for 5000m). On 5 Jul 1966 Clarke achieved 13:16.6 at Stockholm, a record which stood for over six years.

After Lasse Viren (Fin), Emiel Puttemans (Bel) and Dick Quax (NZ) had set records, a new name appeared on the books, that of **Henry Rono** of Kenya. Like Kip Keino, a member of the Nandi tribe from the Rift Valley, Rono took up the sport at the age of 19 in 1972. He first appeared in the world rankings in 1976 and, but for the African boycott would undoubtedly have made an impression at the 1976 Olympic Games, for in Montreal in pre-Games meetings he was in fine form. The following year he enrol-

The floodlit classic 5000m at the White City on 13 Oct 1954 when Chris Chataway (London) beat Vladimir Kuts (Moscow) in 13:51.6. *(BBC Hulton)*

led at Washington State University under coach John Chaplin, and at the end of the year made a sensational breakthrough at 10000m when he was second to Brendan Foster (27:36.62 on his debut) at the Coke meeting, taking over a minute off his best with 27:37.08. In 1978 he was undisputed athlete of the year, setting world records at four events, the first man to hold them all, his list reading: 8 Apr 5000m 13:08.4 Berkeley, Cal; 13 May 3000m S/C 8:05.4 Seattle; 11 Jun 1000m 27:22.5 Vienna; 27 Jun 3000m 7:32.1 Oslo. All took big chunks off the previous records. From a 1 mile loss on 25 March, Rono won 28 successive races until he was placed third at 3000m on 5 September. He went on to win double gold at the Commonwealth Games and was undefeated in 1978 at 5000m or 10000m. He continued to run well in 1979 and early 1980, but did not approach these records. Then he was troubled by malaria and by 1981 was running so poorly and concentrating on his studies that, with season's bests of only 9:00.87 for 3000m S/C and 14:03.2 for 5000m, he announced his retirement in May.

That retirement proved to be short lived. He came to Europe and ran 13:57.3 followed by 15:40.85 for last at Turku, and then 14:15.4, all in Finland in early July. After two weeks in Kenya, he was ready and swept back to the top with a European tour. From a 8:44.72 3000m S/C in London on 31 July, he just got better and better. In Koblenz on 26 Aug he won the 5000m in 13:12.15, the second fastest time ever and two days later won over 10000m in Brussels (27:40.78). The climax came with three races at 5000m in five days. On 9 Sep in Rieti he ran 13:12.47 yet was outkicked by Hans-Jörg Kunze (GDR) (European record 13:10.40) and Valeriy Abramov (USSR) (13:11.99). On 11 Sep he won at the Coke meeting in London in 13:12.34, a UK All-Comers record, and on 13 Sep broke his own world record with 13:06.20 at Knarvik, Norway. The athletics world was

Henry Rono runs for Washington State University in 1978 when he set world records at four events. For WSU he won five NCAA titles.
(Washington State University)

delighted that this wonderfully uninhibited front-runner was back on top.

10000 METRES

The first IAAF record was 30:58.8 by Jean Bouin (Fra) at Paris on 16 Nov 1911. This took 3.6 off the time clocked by Alfred Shrubb (GB) in his multi-world record 1 hour run at Glasgow on 5 Nov 1904.

The most records set have been five, by Emil Zatopek (Cze) from his 29:28.2 at Ostrava on 11 Jun 1949 to his 28:54.2 at Brussels on 1 Jun 1954. Zatopek won all these five races by huge margins.

The greatest improvement in the record is the 34.6sec that Ron Clarke (Aus) took off his own record when he ran 27:39.4 (27:39.89 auto) at Oslo on 14 Jul 1965. His previous record four weeks earlier at Turku of 28:14.0 was not put forward for ratification, so he subtracted 36.2 from his IAAF record of 28:15.6 at Melbourne on 18 Dec 1963. Like Zatopek in his record successes, Clarke had no challenge as runner-up Jim Hogan (GB) finished a lap and a half behind in 29:19.6. Clarke covered the first 5000m in an unprecedented 13:45.0, which would have been a world record at that distance as recently as eleven years earlier.

Dave Bedford (GB) emulated Clarke's devastating pace. He led at halfway in the 1972

Olympic Games race in 13:44.0, but finished sixth as Lasse Viren improved the record to 27:38.35. However on 13 Jul 1973 Bedford ran the first half even faster – 13:39.4 in the AAA Championships at Crystal Palace, London and held on to smash the record with 27:30.80. The record now stands to Henry Rono (Ken) at 27:22.5 in Vienna on 11 Jun 1978. Rono added a 13:33.5 second half to his 5000m time of 13:49.0.

The first sub 30 minute 10000m was run at Helsinki on 17 Sep 1939 by Taisto Mäki (Fin). His time of 29:52.6 beat his own 30:02.0 set the previous year.

DISTANCE EVENTS DROPPED BY IAAF FROM RECORD SCHEDULES IN 1976
2 miles
The best ever: 8:13.2 indoors Emiel Puttemans (Bel) 18 Feb 1973, West Berlin; 8:13.51 Steve Ovett (GB) 15 Sep 1978 Crystal Palace, London
The most records is three by Gunder Hägg (see list p26)
The greatest improvement is 7.2sec by Edvin Wide (Swe) 9:01.4 in 1926, when he beat Alf Shrubb's (GB) 22-year-old record.
The first sub 9min was run by Paavo Nurmi (Fin) 8:58.2 indoors on 14 Feb 1925 in New York and 8:59.5 outdoors on 24 Jul 1931 in Helsinki.

3 miles
The final IAAF record was 12:47.8 Emiel Puttemans (Bel) in his 13.13.0 5000m record on 20 Sep 1972 in Brussels.
The most records is four by Vladimir Kuts (3 IAAF) and by Ron Clarke – 13:07.6, 13:00.4, 12:52.4 (the first sub-13 min time, at the 1965 AAA championships 10 Jul 1965), 12:50.4.
The greatest improvement is 11.4sec by Lauri Lehtinen (Fin) 13:50.6 (the first sub 14min time outdoors) 19 Jun 1932 Helsinki. The first sub 14min time was run indoors by Ville Ritola (Fin) at 13:56.2 in New York on 24 Feb 1925.
The first sub 15min was 14:46.0 by James Gibb (GB) 3 Mar 1877 Cambridge.

6 miles
The final IAAF record was 26:47.0 by Ron Clarke in his 27:39.4 record 10000m on 14 Jul 1965 in Brussels. Dave Bedford ran an unofficial 26:38.6 during his 10000m world record in 1973.
The most records is two by Viljo Heino (Fin) and Emil Zatopek, although Walter George

made three improvements in pre-IAAF days.
The greatest improvement was 34.1sec by Paavo Nurmi (Fin) 29:07.1 31 Aug 1924 at Kuopio during his 30:06.2 record at 10000m.
The first sub 30min time was Jack White 29:50.0 and William Lang (both GB) 29:50.2 at Hackney, London on 11 May 1863. This was during a professional match over 10 miles. The pace was

Oxford & Cambridge in the USA 1920. From left: Alfred Shrubb (trainer), W. R. Milligan (see p. 245), Bevil Rudd (SA – 1920 Olympic 400m champion), Evelyn Montague (6th 1924 Olympic steeplechase), 'Henry' Stallard (3rd 1924 Olympic 1500m), Col. Arnold Strode-Jackson (1912 Olympic 1500m champion).

such that Lang retired after 7 miles, and White, the 'Gateshead Clipper', jogged the rest of the way to finish in 52:14. The first amateur to break 30 min was Alfred Shrubb (GB) 29:59.4 at Glasgow on 5 Nov 1904 during the hour race in which he set seven world records (each mile from six to ten as well as 10000m and 1 hour – 18742m/11 mile 1137y). Earlier in the year he had set records at 2, 3, 4 and 5 miles.

MEN'S WORLD BEST PERFORMANCES AT OTHER DISTANCES (i) = indoors
50 yards *hand timed:* 5.0(i) Kirk Clayton (USA) 1970; Herb Washington (USA) four times 1972–3; Mel Pender (USA) twice 1972; Manfred Ommer (Ger) 1975. *auto:* 5.22(i) Stanley Floyd (USA) 1982.
50 metres *hand timed:* 5.4(i) Billy Gaines (USA) 1968 and Manfred Kokot (GDR) 1971. *auto:* 5.61(i) Manfred Kokot 1973 and James Sanford (USA) 1981.
60 yards *hand timed:* 5.8(i) Herb Washington (USA) 1972. *auto:* 6.04(i) Bob Hayes (USA) 1964, and Stanley Floyd (USA) twice in 1981.

Hayes was hand timed in 5.9 in the 1964 AAU, the first sub-6 sec time.

60 metres *hand timed:* 6.3(i) Andrei Prokofiev (USSR) 1982 *auto:* 6.54. Houston McTear (USA) 1978.

300 yards 29.16(i) Dwayne Evans (USA) 1981. The first 30.0 time was credited to the great professional runner Harry Hutchens (GB) in 1885.

300 metres *hand timed:* 32.1 Jim Kemp (USA) 1971, which beat the 32.4 which Herb McKenley (Jam) had run in 1948 and 1950 *auto:* 32.23 Pietro Mennea (Ita) 1979.

500 yards 53.9(i) Larry James (USA) as a professional 1973.

500 metres 1:00.6 Josef Trousil (Cze) 1965, Horst-Rüdiger Schlöske (Ger) 1973 and Herman Köhler (Ger) 1973.

600 yards 1:07.6(i) Martin McGrady (USA) 1970 during a spectacular indoor season when he won all his ten 600y races; he set three world bests and beat Lee Evans four times.

600 metres 1:14.3 Lee Evans (USA) at the high altitude of Echo Summit, South Lake Tahoe, Cal. The best at low altitude is 1:14.9 by Martin McGrady at Melbourne in 1970.

1000 yards 2:04.7(i) Don Paige (USA) 1982.

50 yards hurdles *hand timed:* 5.8(i) Willie Davenport (USA) 1969, Marcus Walker (USA) 1970, Rod Milburn (USA) 1973, Danny Smith (Bah) 1973 and 1975, Thomas Hill (USA) 1973 *auto:* 5.92(i) Renaldo Nehemiah (USA) 1982.

50 metres hurdles *hand timed:* 6.2(i) Günter Nickel (Ger) 1976 *auto:* 6.36(i) Renaldo Nehemiah (USA) 1979.

60 yards hurdles *hand timed:* 6.7(i) Rod Milburn (USA) as a professional in 1974 and 1975 *auto:* 6.82(i) Renaldo Nehemiah (USA) 1982.

The first sub 7 sec time was 6.9 by Hayes Jones (USA) in 1962 after he had six times in three seasons equalled Milt Campbell's (USA) 7.0 record. In 1964 Jones ran the first time of 6.8. He was also the first man to better 6 sec at 50y hurdles.

A unique world record dead heat on automatic timing came on 19 Jan 1979 when Renaldo Nehemiah and Greg Foster (USA) ran 6.95.

60 metres hurdles: *hand timed:* 7.3(i) Thomas Hill (USA) 1974 *auto:* 7.54(i) Andrei Prokofiev (USSR) 1979 and Yuri Chervanyev (USSR) 1980.

300 metres hurdles: 34.6 David Hemery (GB) 1972.

2000 metres steeplechase: 5:21.2 Eshetu Tura (Eth) 1976.

The first sub-13sec 110m hurdler, Renaldo Nehemiah, who set 11 world indoor sprint hurdles records in 1978–82. *(All-Sport/Steve Sutton)*

LONG DISTANCES (10 MILES TO 30000 METRES)

The IAAF now recognises just four events of longer than 10000m: 20km, 25km and 30km and the 1 hour. Up to 1976 records at 10 and 15 miles were also recognised, and in the early years many more events were included on the world record list.

No man has broken more than two world records at any of the above distances, but Emil Zatopek (Cze) has set the most records. He set two each at 20km, 25km, 1 hour, 15 miles and one each at 30km and 10 miles – a total of ten records in four races between 1951 and 1955. Three records came in each of his runs at Stará Boleslav, (Cze) the 10 mile, 20km and 1 hour on 29 Sep 1951 and the 15 mile, 25km and 30km on 26 Oct 1952, so that from then until 1955 he held all eight world records from 6 miles to 30km, and for three months in 1954 also held the 5000m world record. No other athlete has approached this achievement.

The greatest improvements at each event
10 mile 1:10.2 Emil Zatopek 48:12.0 Stará Boleslav 29 Sep 1951
20km 1:50.6 Paavo Nurmi (Fin) 1:04:38.4 Stockholm 13 Sep 1930
1 hour 494m Emil Zatopek 20.052m Stará Boleslav 29 Sep 1951
15 mile 2:25.4 Emil Zatopek 1:14:01.0 Čelákovice, Cze 26 Oct 1955
25km 1:37.8 Albert Ivanov (USSR) 1:17:34.0 Moscow 27 Sep 1955
30km 3:30.2 Emil Zatopek 1:35:23.8 Stará Boleslav 26 Oct 1952

Barrier breakers:
10 miles
50 min: Viljo Heino (Fin) 49:41.6 Turku, 30 Sep 1945; although Walter George (GB) was reputed to have run a time-trial in 49:29 as a professional in 1886.
20 kilometres
60 min: Emil Zatopek (Cze) 59:51.8 Stará Boleslav 29 Sep 1951
1 hour (M = mile)
12M: Viljo Heino 19339m/12M 29y Turku 30 Sep 1945
20km: Emil Zatopek 20052m/12M 810y Stará Boleslav 29 Sep 1951
13M: Jos Hermens (Hol) 20944m/13M 10y Papendal 1 May 1976
30 kilometres
1½ hours: Toshihiko Seko (Jap) 1:29:18.8 Christchurch, NZ 22 Mar 1981

Long distance events – best performances recorded
Track
15km 42:54.8 Jos Hermens (Hol) 14 Sep 1975 Papendal
10 mile 45:57.6 Jos Hermens (Hol) 14 Sep 1975 Papendal
20km 57:24.2 Jos Hermens (Hol) 1 May 1976 Papendal
1 hour 20944m Jos Hermens (Hol) 1 May 1976 Papendal
15 mile 1:11:43.1 Bill Rodgers (USA) 21 Feb 1979 Saratoga, Cal.
25km 1:13:55.8 Toshihiko Seko (Jap) 22 Mar 1981 Christchurch
30km 1:29:18.8 Toshihiko Seko (Jap) 22 Mar 1981 Christchurch
20 mile 1:39:14.4 Jack Foster (NZ) 15 Aug 1971 Hamilton
2 hours 37994m Jim Alder (GB) 17 Oct 1964 Walton
30 mile 2:42:00 Jeff Norman (GB) 7 Jun 1980 Timperley

Viljo Heino (right) set eight world records from 6 miles to 20000m, following the example of Paavo Nurmi (left). Heino ran about 65 sec faster than Nurmi over 6 miles and 10000m.   *(Keystone)*

50km 2:48:06 Jeff Norman (GB) 7 Jun 1980 Timperley
40 mile 3:49:32 Joseph Keating (GB) 28 Apr 1973 Ewell
50 mile 4:53:28 Don Ritchie (GB) 28 Oct 1978 Crystal Palace
100km 6:10:20 Don Ritchie (GB) 28 Oct 1978 Crystal Palace
150km 10:36.41 Don Ritchie (GB) 15/16 Oct 1977 Crystal Palace
100 mile 11:30:51 Don Ritchie (GB) 15/16 Oct 1977 Crystal Palace
200km 16:42:31 Mike Newton (GB) 11/12 Oct 1980 Blackburn
250km 21:49:18 Jean-Gilles Boussiquet (Fra) 2/3 May 1981 Lausanne
24 hours 272624m/169M 705y Jean-Gilles Boussiquet (Fra) 2/3 May 1981 Lausanne (681 laps of the track!)

Road
Better times than the above have been achieved on road surfaces at the following distances:
10 mile 45:13 Ian Stewart (GB) 8 May 1977 Stoke-on-Trent
30km 1:29:04 Bill Rodgers (USA) 28 Mar 1976 Albany, NY.
20 mile 1:36:28 Ron Hill (GB) 25 May 1968 Huyton
40 mile 3:46:31 Barney Klecker (USA) 5 Oct 1980 Chicago

50 mile 4:51:25 Barney Klecker (USA) 5 Oct 1980 Chicago
It should be noted that strenuous efforts are made by leading road running authorities and experts to measure road running courses accurately and indeed those records recognised by the Road Runners Club of America must be set on certified loop or out-and-back courses. Such courses must have their start and finish within 10% of the race distance and must not drop more than 10 feet per mile. Nonetheless all road times must be assessed with care, as conditions can vary considerably.

MARATHON

For the 1896 Olympic Games in Athens it was determined that a long distance race would be held to celebrate the famous run of Pheidippedes (or Philippides) from the battlefield of Marathon to Athens, a distance of about 40km, to convey news of the victory of the Greeks over the Persians. He is supposed to have died from his exertions as he delivered the tidings, but such is legend. Better substantiated is Philippides' feat of running from Athens to Sparta, a distance of about 150 miles (240km).

The Olympic marathon race was preceded by two trial races, the first on 10 Mar 1896. These races, from Marathon Bridge to Athens, were over a distance of 40km (24.85 miles).

After Spyridon Louis's epic victory at the Games there was a surge of interest in the event.

The first marathon in the USA was staged by the New York Knickerbocker Athletic Club on 20 Sep 1896, over 25 miles, and marathons were also held in Hungary and Norway in 1896.

The first national marathon championship was that of Norway in 1897.

The first marathon to be run in Britain was a pre-Olympic trial over 24M 760y on 4 Apr 1908 organised by Blackheath Harriers.

The classic marathon distance of 42195m/26 miles 385 yards has only been fixed since 1924, although this was the distance run at the 1908 Olympic Games in Britain from Windsor Castle to the White City Stadium, when the winner John Hayes (USA) ran the distance in 2:55:18.4.

World records are not officially recognised for the marathon, and as courses can vary in their severity it is not always possible to compare times too precisely.

The first sub 2½ hour time was 2:29:01.8 by Albert Michelsen (USA) at Port Chester 12 Oct 1925.

The first sub 2:20 hour time was 2:18:40.2 by Jim Peters (GB) from Windsor to Chiswick 13 Jun 1953. This was the second of four world bests set by Peters. Only two other men have set even two world bests: Abebe Bikila (Eth) at each of his Olympic victories (qv) and Derek Clayton (Aus). Clayton was the first man to average sub-five-minute miling for the marathon when he ran the first sub 2:10 time – 2:09:36.4 at Fukuoka, Japan on 3 Dec 1967, before improving to 2:08:33.6 at Antwerp on 30 May 1969. Unfortunately the course was not re-measured after the race, and doubts persist that it might have been short.

Clayton's time was finally bettered after more than twelve years at the New York marathon on

Jim Peters enters Chiswick stadium to complete his fourth world marathon best, his eighth win in ten marathons. *(Central Press)*

2 Oct 1981, when Alberto Salazar (USA) won in 2:08:13. On 6 Dec 1981 Robert de Castella (Aus) ran 2:08:18 at Fukuoka, the best ever for an 'out-and-back' course. The race in which most men broke 2:20 was the 1981 Boston marathon with 64 beating that time. The record had previously been set at the US Trials race from Buffalo to Niagara Falls on 24 May 1980 when 56 men, headed by Tony Sandoval 2:10:19, did so. On the same day 52 men, headed by Vladimir Kotov 2:10:58, ran times of sub 2:20 in the Soviet championship race in Moscow.

The greatest standards in depth have been:

	Under 2:20	2:30	2:40	2:50	3:00 hours
Boston 1981	64	297	857	1788	2840
New York 1981	49	186	420	848	1603
London 1981	17	144	406	770	1294

The oldest man known to have completed a marathon is Dimitriou Yordanidis (Gre), aged 98 when he was timed in 7 hours 33 min at Athens in 1976.

The best time for an indoor marathon (surprisingly several have been run) is 2:28:09 by Johnny Nylen (Swe) at Göteborg on 27 Jan 1979.

MAJOR MARATHON RACES
BOSTON
The first Boston marathon was run on 19 Apr 1897 from Metcalf's Mill in Ashland to the Irvington Oval over a distance of 24 miles 1232 yards (39750m). The race has been run every year since, on or about the 19th April, the day being set aside as a holiday, Patriot's Day, to honour the famed ride of Paul Revere through Boston. Fifteen runners took part in that first race, which was won by John McDermott in 2:55:10.

The first 1000-plus field was 1013 in 1968 and the record field was an official 7877 plus more than 2000 'gate-crashers' in 1979, before tighter qualifying standards brought the numbers down to 5364 in 1980 and 6845 in 1981.

The course has varied over the years, with the full marathon distance being run since 1927, with the exception of 1953–6 when the course was 1207y/1104m short. The present route of Hopkinton to the Prudential Centre in Boston has been used since 1965.

The current race organiser, John Semple, first ran in the Boston in 1929 and had a best placing of seventh in 1937. Semple, with a Scottish background and a British citizen until 1932, was involved in the incident in 1967 when one K. Switzer entered the race. It was not until two miles had been passed that it was realised that this was a woman, and Semple tried to push her out of the race, but she was protected by her boy friend and finished the race in about 4:20:02. Kathy Switzer had, however, been preceded as the first woman runner by Roberta Gibb Bungay, who ran the course in an estimated 3:21:40 in 1966, but she had run unofficially. Women were admitted officially for the first time in 1972.

Winner of the most 'Bostons' is Clarence De Mar with seven – 1911, 1922–4, 1927–8 and 1930 (when he was the oldest ever winner at 41). De Mar, who started running while at the University of Vermont, first ran a marathon at Boston in 1910, finishing second. After being placed 12th in the 1912 Olympic Games, De Mar did not run for five years due to a suspected heart murmur, but returned with 3rd at Boston in 1917, and in addition to his seven wins was in the top ten on eight more occasions. In all he ran more than 100 marathons in his career from the age of 23 to 66. Gérard Côté (Can) won four times, 1940, 1943–4 and 1948, but De Mar's feat of three successive wins was not emulated until 1980, when the man to do so was Bill Rodgers (USA).

Bill Rodgers spearheaded the great upsurge in American marathoning. In 1975 at the age of 27 he placed a surprise third in the International cross-country at Rabat, Morocco, and was quoted afterwards as saying 'I'll never run another race like that as long as I live. I think I'm going to retire right now'. He stayed in the sport with the aim of regaining the AAU 30km title he had won in 1973 and entered the Boston marathon hoping for a sub-2:20 time.

Rodgers had failed to finish the 1973 race and was 14th in 2:19:34 in 1974. In 1975, running his sixth marathon, he won in 2:09:55, the fourth sub 2:10 marathon. He did not finish in 1977 but won again in 1978 in 2:10:13 just two seconds ahead of Jeff Wells. He went on to win in 1979 (2:09:27) and 1980 (2:12:11). His shop, the Bill Rodgers Running Centre, is strategically placed at the 22-mile point.

Rodgers was third (2:10:34) in 1981, when Toshihiko Seko (Jap) won in 2:09:26 from Craig Virgin 2:10:26, and fourth in 1982 when Alberto Salazar set a course record of 2:08:51 to beat Dick Beardsley by just two seconds. The women's record was set in 1981 by Allison Roe (NZ) in 2:26:46 from Patti Catalano (USA) 2:27:51.

Bill Rodgers led the marathon boom in the USA. He has won four Boston and four New York marathons. *(M. Shearman)*

The youngest Boston winner was 18-year-old Timothy Ford (USA) in 1906.

Johnny Kelley (USA) has competed in most Bostons. He ran his 51st at the age of 74 in 4:01:18 in 1982. His first was in 1928 and he won in 1935 and 1945.

NEW YORK
The first ever marathon in New York was run on 20 Sep 1896, and from 1907 to 1917 and annually since 1935 the Yonkers marathon has been run in the city.

The New York City marathon, was however first run in 1970, with 126 runners of whom 55 finished. The race really came into its own in 1976 with its sixth running. To celebrate the United States Bicentennial the course was changed from five laps of Central Park to a route through all five boroughs of the city. In that year there were 2090 starters and 71% of them finished – seven times more than the previous year. By 1977 there was a world record marathon field of 4823 and in 1978 about 11000. By 1981 the number reached a new marathon record of 14496 starters, of whom 13360 finished the course; 9172 inside four hours.

Standards improved rapidly. The first New York City winner was Gary Muhrcke (USA) in 2:31:38. Ten years later at the age of 41 he found 2:24:58 placed him only 66th in 1980.

Bill Rodgers (USA) has won a record four times, each year from 1976 (2:10:10 his fastest at New York) to 1979, before a fifth place in 1980, when the winner, Alberto Salazar (USA) ran 2:09:41, easily the fastest ever for a debut marathon. Salazar won again in 1981, with a world best 2:08:13 in the second marathon of his life.

The women's race has been won most often by Grete Waitz (Nor), who set a world best on each occasion from 1978 to 1980 (see p 76). The women's record fell again in 1981 when Allison Roe (NZ) took 13 seconds off Waitz's best with 2:25:29.

In 1980 **Ernest Conner (USA) ran the race backwards** in 5:18:00.

FUKUOKA
The Asahi marathon was first run at Kumamoto in 1947. Since the early 1960s it has been one of

the most important races, with the venue established at Fukuoka, Japan (1951, 1955, 1957, 1959–62 and since 1964) in early December each year and known as the Fukuoka International since 1968. The race is always very fast. In 1967 Derek Clayton (Aus) set a world best of 2:09:36.4 and that course record was broken in 1981 when Robert de Castella (Aus) ran 2:08:18, just 5sec off the world best.

The most wins is four by Frank Shorter (USA) 1971–4; three by Jerome Drayton (Can) 1969, 1975–6; and three by Toshihiko Seko (Jap) 1978–80. In 1980 Seko became the second sub 2:10 man at Fukuoka with 2:09:45. Fukuoka has often set new standards for the quality of performances, with record numbers of sub 2:20 runners in any marathon: 7 in 1962; 11 in 1964; and 29 in 1975.

KOSICE
Held annually in Czechoslovakia each October, the Kosice marathon was first run in 1924. Women competitors were allowed for the first time in 1980, when the 50th Kosice was staged with 1127 runners.

The most wins is four by Jozsef Galambos (Hun) 1927–28, 1932–33; and three by Pavel Kantorek (Cze) 1958, 1962, 1964.

The fastest times are 2:13:35 Chun Son Goe (N. Kor) 1978; for men and 2:37:46 Christa Vahlensieck (Ger) 1981 for women.

ENSCHEDE
This event has been held biennially in Holland since 1947.

The most wins is two by Ron Hill (GB) 1973, 1975.

The fastest times are 2:11:50 Kirk Pfeffer (USA) 1979; for men and 2:38:21 Jane Wipf (USA) 1981 for women.

ATHENS INTERNATIONAL
This event has been held biennially in Athens since 1955 from the village of Marathon to the Panathenian Stadium in Athens.

The fastest time is 2:11:07.2 Bill Adcocks (GB) 1969.

POLY
First held in 1909 in Great Britain from Windsor to Stamford Bridge, which remained the route until 1932, when the destination was changed to the White City. The race was not held during World War I, but it continued from 1940 to 1945 although not over the traditional route. From 1938–9 and 1946–72 the course was from Windsor to Chiswick. Now, however traffic problems have meant a course around Windsor. The race is organised by the Polytechnic Harriers, who also staged the race's predecessor the 1908 Olympic marathon.

The most wins were eight by Sam Ferris 1925–9 and 1931–3. Ferris, an RAF mechanic, made his marathon debut with second place to his great rival Duncan McLeod Wright in 1924, but was never subsequently beaten in the Poly (he did not run in 1930). With his first win in 1925 Ferris won the inaugural AAA marathon championship. At the Olympic Games Ferris was fifth in 1924, eighth in 1928 and a rapidly closing second in 1932, when he finished much fresher than the winner Juan Carlos Zabala (Arg). In his career Ferris won 12 of his 19 marathons. Jim Peters follows with four successive wins, 1951 to 1954. In his first ever marathon in 1951 he set a British best of 2:29:24 and in each of the last three years set world marathon bests: 1952 – 2:20:42.2; 1953 – 2:18:40.2; 1954 – 2:17:39.4.

The fastest time is 2:12:00 Morio Shigematsu (Jan) 1965, a world best at the time.

LONDON
Although by no means London's first marathon, no race has ever captured the British public's imagination like the London marathon held on 29 Mar 1981 did. It covered a route starting in Greenwich Park and finishing on Constitution Hill. Britain's biggest mass participation race to that date, there were 6255 finishers inside 5 hours, including a record 144 under $2\frac{1}{2}$ hours, out of some 7000 starters.

Winners of the 1981 race were: Men – Dick Beardsley (USA) and Inge Simonsen (Nor) dead heat 2:11:48 Women – Joyce Smith 2:29:57, the first sub $2\frac{1}{2}$ hours performance by a British woman.

As Britain's largest race, the London marathon was overtaken later in 1981 by the 'Great North Run', a half-marathon from Newcastle to South Shields on 28 June when 10681 of the over 12000 starters officially completed the course. The winner was Mike McLeod in 1:03:22, the 'retired' Brendan Foster came in 20th and

The first London marathon. Dick Beardsley (left) and Inge Simonsen (right). *(M. Shearman)*

Don Thompson in the 1956 London to Brighton walk on his way to the second of his eight wins in the race. *(H. W. Neale)*

England soccer captain Kevin Keegan was a noteworthy 491st. Then the Pony marathon, starting and finishing in Bolton on 23 August set new records for a European marathon, with 8094 runners, of whom 6547 finished.

The second London marathon was to show that marathon-fever had well and truly crossed the Atlantic, for there were some 80000 entries.

There was a record marathon field of 16350 starters, of whom 15758 finished. The men's winner Hugh Jones ran 2:09:24, the fastest ever run in Britain and Joyce Smith improved her British record to 2:29:43 to win the women's race.

LONDON TO BRIGHTON
Walking and running on the 'Brighton Road' originated in the 19th century, the first recorded time for the distance being 8 hour 37min by John Townsend, a professional runner, in 1837. In 1897 the Polytechnic Harriers promoted a walk from the Polytechnic in Regent Street, won by E. Knott in 8 hour 56min 44sec (timed from Big Ben) to the Aquarium in Brighton. The course has varied over the years due to road works, most notably for the construction of Gatwick Airport, and the present distance is 86.1km/53½ miles.

Following the 1897 race further walking races were held and the London to Brighton became an annual event in 1919.

The greatest number of wins has been eight by Don Thompson from his first attempt in 1955 to 1962 successively.

The first man to walk the distance in less than 8 hours was Harold Whitlock with 7:53:50 in 1935. This time was unbeaten until Thompson clocked 7:45:32 in 1956, and over a longer distance improved the record again to 7:35:12 in 1957.

The first women took part in 1932; with three entries including 16-year-old Lilian Salkied (12:20).

The first amateur running race was organised by South London Harriers in 1899 and won by Frank Randell in 6:58:18. Four years later the professional Len Hurst ran the distance in 6:32:34.

Arthur Newton was the first man to run the distance in less than 6 hours, with 5:53:43 in 1924.

Just 10 miles to go for 45-year-old Wally Hayward in his 1953 London to Brighton race when he improved the record by 22½ min.   *(BBC Hulton)*

Since 1951 annual London to Brighton running races have been promoted by the Road Runners Club. The South African, Wally Hayward became the first to better 5½ hours with 5:29:40 in 1953. This time was improved to 5:26:40 by Gerald Walsh in 1957, to 5:25:26 by Jackie Mekler in 1960, and 5:21:45 by Dave Levick in 1971, all South Africans. The following year Alastair Wood smashed this record with 5:11:02, thus averaging 5.89min per mile for 52¾ miles. With about 1½ miles added to the distance Ian Thompson ran 5:15:15 in 1980 to average 5.81min per mile.

The most wins is four by Bernard Gomersall 1963–6.

In 1980 Leslie Watson (GB) won the inaugural women's race in 6:56:10. The previous year she had run unofficially to clock 6:55:11.

COMRADES MARATHON
First run on Empire Day, 24 May 1921 from Pietermaritzburg to Durban, South Africa. It is held in alternate years, up from Durban, overall some 750m/2500ft in altitude, or down from Pietermaritzburg over a distance of a little over 54½ mile/88km.

The fastest recorded times:
up: 5:37:28 Bruce Fordyce (SA) 1 Jun 1981
down: 5:29:14 Alan Robb (SA) 31 May 1978

The most wins is five by Arthur Newton 1922–5, 1927; Hardy Ballington 1933–4, 1936, 1938, 1947; Wally Hayward 1930, 1950–1, 1953–4; and Jackie Mekler 1958, 1960, 1963–4, 1968. (All SA).

LONG DISTANCE RUNNING
The longest race ever staged was the 1929 Trans-America race, 3665 mile/5898km from New York to Los Angeles. The winner was Johnny Salo (USA) in 79 days, with an elapsed time of 525 hour 57min 20sec, thus averaging 6.97 mile/11.21km per hour. However he only beat Pete Gavuzzi (GB) by 2min 47sec!

The first Trans-America race, the C. C. Pyle

Bunion Derby, had been staged the previous year over a slightly shorter course of 3422 mile/5507km. Gavuzzi had run the first 2578 miles, but the winner was Andy Payne (USA) in 84 days. There were 199 starters, of whom 145 finished. Payne won $25000 but he was only paid due to the generosity of a Californian millionaire. The race organiser, C. C. Pyle was again unable to pay prize money in 1929 and this time nobody came to the rescue. Further claims to have bettered the **Trans-America record** have been (in days: hours: min) 73:08:20 Don Shepherd (SA) in 1964 for 3200 miles; 64:21:50 Bruce Tulloh (GB) in 1969 for 2875 miles; 53 days John Ball (SA) in 1972; 53:12:15 John Lees (GB), who *walked* in 1972, the same route as Tulloh; 46:08:36 Frank Giannino Jr (USA) in 1980 for 3100 mile/4989km from San Francisco to New York.

The longest ever 'non-stop' run recorded is 352.9 mile/568km by Bertil Jarlåker (Swe) at Norrköping on 26–31 May 1980. He was moving for 95.04% of the time.

The record distance achieved in a six-day 'wobble', the walk/run matches of Victorian days, was 623¾ mile/1004km by George Littlewood (GB) in 141:57:30 at Madison Square Garden, New York on 3–8 Dec 1888.

The best in modern times is 505 mile 84y/812.8km by Mike Newton (GB) at Nottingham on 8–13 Nov 1981.

Jay Helgerson (USA) ran a certified marathon (or longer distance) every week from 28 Jan 1979 to 19 Jan 1980, 52 weeks with a total racing distance of 1418 mile/2282km.

The greatest life-time distance recorded by any runner is 195855 mile/315198km by Earle Dilks (USA) to 1977.

The greatest distance run in a year is 140005½ miles/22540km by 47-year-old Tina Stone from Irvine, Cal. in 1981.

Miscellaneous long distance running feats:
Max Telford ran 5110 mile/8224km from Anchorage, Alaska to Halifax, Nova Scotia in 106 days 18 hours 45min from 25 Jul to 9 Nov 1977, averaging 47.86mile/77.02km per day. Siegfried Bauer (NZ) ran the length of New Zealand, 1320 mile/2124km, in 18 days 5hour 1min in 1975, averaging 71.42mile/114.93km per day. He also ran the length of Germany, 726mile/1169km, in 8 days 12 hour 12min in 1978, an average of 85.4mile/137.5km per day; and from Pretoria to Cape Town, South Africa, 952mile/1533km, in 12 days 21 hour 46½min in 1975, an average of 73.95mile/119km per day.

Kelvin Bowers (GB) ran from Stoke-on Trent in England to Sydney, Australia in 522 days for 10289 mile/558km from 7 Apr 1974 to 9 Sep 1975, an average of 19.7mile/31.7km per day.

Noteworthy women's long distance feats include those achieved by Mavis Hutchison (SA) 3911mile/6294km from Los Angeles to New York in 69 days 2hour 40min in 1978 (average 56.6mile/91.2km per day) and Ann Sayer (GB), 876mile/1410km from John O'Groats to Lands End in 13 days 17hours 42min in 1980 (average 63.7mile/102.5km per day).

The greatest ever claims, however, have perhaps been those for Norwegian, Ernst Mensen, who is reputed to have run from Istanbul in Turkey to Calcutta in India and back in 59 days in 1836. That would have meant an incredible 100 miles a day. Mensen was employed as a courier by several of the European Royal Houses. He is also said to have run from Paris to Moscow, 1550 mile/2500km, in 14 days 5hour 50min in 1832, again an incredible daily average of 108.6mile/175km, swimming 13 rivers on the way. It is practically impossible to authenticate such feats.

LONG DISTANCE – WALKING
The world's longest annual walking race is the Strasbourg-Paris race. The distance of the race has varied between 504 and 552km/313–344 mile. It was held from Paris to Strasbourg from 1926–37 and 1949–51 and in the current direction 1952–9 and since 1970. The fastest time recorded is 60hour 1min 10sec, after deducting 4 hours for compulsory stops, by Robert Pietquin (Bel) in 1980. He averaged 8.45km per hour or 5.25mph. The most wins is six by Gilbert Roger (Fra) 1949, 1953–4, 1956–8. Colin Young, in 1971, is the only British walker to have completed the course, taking 73hour 38min. Charles Dujardin (Fra) completed the course a record 13 times.

The longest ever 'non-stop' walk is 349.98mile/563.23km by 'Fred' Jago (GB) at Plymouth on 13–19 Sep 1980 (152hour 40min). He was moving for 98.33% of the time.

110 METRES HURDLES
The imperial distance of 120 yards is 109.73 metres, so to convert 120y times to 110m one

need add just 0.03sec. Thus while timing was in tenths the times recorded at either distance could be regarded as comparable. Times at the slightly shorter 120y could not be recognised as world records at 110m, although naturally the reverse could happen. *In the following summary times at 120yh are indicated by* *

Holder of the most IAAF records at 110mh/120yh is Rod Milburn (USA). In a tremendous season in 1971, when he won all his 28 races, he ran the first ever 13.0* performance at Billings, Montana on 4 Jun to win the NAIA title. On that occasion the following wind (+2.2m/s) was over the permitted limit, but three weeks later he again recorded 13.0*, this time the wind was acceptable at +1.95m/s, in the semi-finals of the AAU championships at Eugene for his first world record. He went on to win the final in a wind assisted 13.1*. In 1972 he ran two more wind-aided 13.0* times and a world record 13.2 (later the first automatic timed record to be recognised, at 13.24) at 110mh in winning the Olympic title. Then in 1973 three more world records followed to bring his tally to five: two at 13.1 for 110mh and another 13.0*, again at Eugene. Milburn turned professional with the ITA in 1974 but was reinstated as an amateur in 1980 when he again competed with success at the very highest levels, although by then a new star had taken over as the world's number one ... Renaldo Nehemiah (USA).

Rod Milburn won 80 out of 82 races at 110m/120y hurdles in 1971–3. He turned pro in 1974 but returned and ran 13.1 in 1982.

(Southern University)

Nehemiah, known as 'Skeets' became the first man to break 13sec when at the age of 20 he was hand-timed at 12.8 in the Manley Games at Kingston, Jamaica on 11 May 1979. Already he had set world records with automatic timing at 13.16 on 14 April at San José, USA and 13.00 at Westwood on 6 May. On 1 Jun 1979 at Champaign, Ill., USA, he ran the first automatic timing sub-13 with 12.91 to win the NCAA title, but the wind at +3.5m/s was almost twice the permitted limit. On 19 Aug 1981 at Zurich he improved his world record to 12.93 into a 0.2m/s wind at the Weltklasse meeting.

The biggest ever improvement in the 110mh record came with the first sub 14sec performance on 27 Aug 1936 at the Bislett Stadium in Oslo. Forrest 'Spec' Towns (USA), ran 13.7 to take 0.4sec off his own world record, set the previous year both in the NCAA championships and in the Olympic semi-final in Berlin. Towns ran three more races in 14.1 that season but couldn't approach that magic 13.7 again.

The first sub 15sec time was achieved by the Canadian Earl Thomson, studying in the USA at Dartmouth College, who was a pioneer of the 'double-arm shift' technique. Thomson ran 14.8* at Columbia in May 1916 and after his brother-in-law Robert Simpson (USA) had twice run 14.6* in 1916, improved to 14.4* at Philadelphia on 29 May 1920, which was unsurpassed for 11 years. Thomson also ran the first sub-15 time at 110mh in winning the 1920 Olympic title in 14.8.

The modern high hurdles event is a far cry from that of a century or more ago. In 1860 Oxford University AC staged their first race at 120y over ten 3½ft sheep hurdles hired for £6 15s. These as in earlier races held at Eton College were solid hurdles fixed in the ground which the athletes definitely did not want to hit.

The hurdles were developed over the years, but there was a major breakthrough in 1935 when Harry Hillman (USA), 1904 Olympic gold medallist at 400m, 200m hurdles and 400m hurdles, invented a hurdle with an L-type base with weighted feet on the approach side, presenting a toppling moment of 8lb/3.6kg which was subsequently accepted as the standard.

Early hurdles races were run on grass. An example of the hidden hazards was the unfortunate injury to Clement Jackson (GB), holder of the world's best time of 16sec in 1865, which brought his active career to a premature conclu-

The hurdling technique of Forrest 'Spec' Towns, who set 3 world records, including the first sub-14sec time, and won the NCAA, AAU and Olympic titles in 1936. *(University of Georgia)*

sion. Jackson, one of the founders of the AAA and its treasurer from 1880 to 1910, described the incident: 'I spiked a hidden oyster shell when going full bat in a hurdle handicap after the seven-leagued legs of W. G. Grace'. He never again ate oysters or spoke to the great cricketer!

At the 1900 Olympic Games the hurdles used for the 400m hurdles event were telephone poles 6–8in in diameter and 30ft long with boxes of brush underneath. There was a water-jump 16ft wide just before the finish.

In 1970 American Steve Hanneman introduced a new non-hurdling technique. He ran 120y in 14.3 but ran down each hurdle by stepping on them.

200 METRES/220 YARDS HURDLES
The 220y hurdles, usually on a straight course, was a popular event on the US collegiate programme until it was superseded by the 400m hurdles in 1960. Both 200m and 220y hurdles were eventually dropped from the world record schedule in 1976.

The 'final' world records were:
200mh (turn): 22.5 Martin Lauer (Ger) 7 Jul 1959 Zurich.
22.5 (22.69 auto) Glenn Davis (USA) 20 Aug 1960 Berne.
220yh (straight): 21.9 Don Styron (USA) 2 Apr 1960 Baton Rouge, Fla.

Flat sprinters have often excelled at this event, and those who have set world records at 220y (straight) both flat and hurdles are Jesse Owens (USA) (20.3 and 22.6) and Dave Sime (USA) (20.0 and 22.2).

400 METRES HURDLES
This event was first held at the Olympic Games in 1900, though it was not held as a national championship in Britain or the USA and Sweden until 1914 nor in Germany until 1922, though French championships had been held since 1893. It is now established as 'the man-killer' event, calling for speed, stamina and great control and technique particularly in working out stride patterns between the hurdles.

Two men have set three 400mh world records, Glenn Hardin (USA) and Edwin Moses (USA). **Glenn Hardin** set his first record at 52.0 at the 1932 Olympic Games, the time actually being

51.9 but rounded up to a fifth of a second as per the practice of the time. However this was in second place, for the winning time of 51.7 by Robert Tisdall (Ire) was disallowed as a record because he knocked over a hurdle. Hardin improved in 1934, first to 51.8, winning the AAU title, and then with the biggest single improvement ever to 50.6 at Stockholm on 26 July. Hardin, nicknamed 'Slats' closed his career by winning the 1936 Olympic title.

Ed Moses has a clear claim to be the greatest runner in the history of this event and his record bears comparison with any athlete in the history of the sport. His first race (at 440yh) came in 1975 with a 52.0 heat of the Southern Intercollegiate Athletic Conference. He made a major breakthrough as a 20-year-old junior at Morehouse College in Atlanta in 1976. In his first race of the year and the second of his life at the event he ran 50.1 for second place at the Florida Relays, improving to 49.8 in April and 48.8 in May. After a fourth place at the AAU he won the US Olympic Trials in an American record 48.30 before a devastating Olympic victory in 47.63, his first world record, beating the time of 47.82 set by John Akii-Bua (Uga) at the 1972 Olympics. Since being placed second to Mike Shine (USA) on 14 Jul 1976 Moses has lost just one race at 400mh, to Harald Schmid (Ger) 49.07 to 49.29 at the ISTAF meeting in Berlin on 26 Aug 1977. He improved the world record to 47.45, winning the AAU title on 11 Jun 1977, and then achieved 47.13 on 3 Jul 1980 in Milan.

The stride pattern used by Moses has consistently been 20 strides to the first hurdle, 13 strides between each of the ten hurdles and then 16 strides to the finish. His predecessors as world record holder John Akii-Bua (Uga) and David Hemery (GB) each started at 13 strides between the hurdles but needed to change down to 14 then 15, or to 15 respectively.

Moses has dominated the event in the last few years. At the end of 1981, he had run 18 of the 20 sub 48sec marks and 31 out of 43 to 48.50.

Edwin Moses in 1979, when he won the AAA 400m hurdles in 48.58. From 1977 to 1981 he won 78 consecutive races at the event.

(G. Herringshaw)

An Analysis of Moses' complete career at 400m hurdles (including heats)

Year	Best time	No. races	No. wins	sub-48	48.00–48.49	48.50–48.99	49.00–49.49	49.50–49.99
1975	52.0(440y)	1	—	—	—	—	—	—
1976	47.64	20	16	1	2	5	3	4
1977	47.45	19	18	2	—	8	4	4
1978	47.94	14	14	1	2	7	1	1
1979	47.53	25	25	4	3	8	5	4
1980	47.13	21	21	4	2	9	3	2
1981	47.14	14	14	6	2	3	2	—

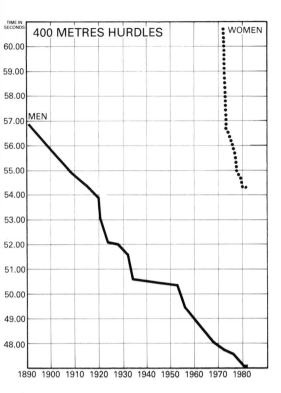

TIME IN SECONDS
400 METRES HURDLES — MEN / WOMEN

Most of these races have been in Europe over the past four years. Moses did not run in the USA in 1978, had only six races there in 1979 and only three (all at the Olympic Trials) in 1980). Moses was deeply disappointed at being forced to miss the 1980 Olympic Games but some compensation came in being voted 'Track and Field News' athlete of the year.

Barrier breakers at 400m/440y hurdles
60sec: S. Morris (GB) 59.8 (440y) 5 Jul 1886
55sec: William Meanix (USA) 54.6 (440y) Cambridge, Mass., 16 Jul 1915
50sec: Glenn Davis (USA) 49.5 Los Angeles 29 Jun 1956. This was only the ninth 400mh race of Davis' career. He had started with a 54.4 on 21 Apr 1956 and went on to place second at the NCAA and win the AAU title before 1.3sec improvement on his best to win the US Olympic trials. Davis improved further to 49.2 in 1958.

3000 METRES STEEPLECHASE
World records for the steeplechase were first recognised and rules standardised by the IAAF in 1954, and the inaugural record was 8:49.6 by Sándor Rozsnyói (Hun) in winning the Euro-

pean title that year. However several faster times had been recorded, the best at the time being 8:44.4 to Olavi Rinteenpää (Fin) in 1953.

The greatest number of world records is four by Anders Gärderud (Swe) from 8:20.08 in 1972 to 8:08.02 in winning the 1976 Olympic title in 1976. Gärderud's third record was the first ever sub 8:10 time – 8:09.70 at Stockholm on 1 Jul 1975.

The greatest improvement in the IAAF record has been 5.8sec by Ben Jipcho (Ken) when he ran 8:14.0 (8:13.91) to beat his own 8:19.8 record, the first sub 8:20 time, both races at Helsinki, on 19 Jun and 27 Jun 1973.
On 13 May 1978 Henry Rono (Ken) moved closer to the 8-min barrier with the current record of 8:05.4.

The first sub 9min performance: Erik Elmsäter (Swe) 8:59.6 Stockholm 4 Aug 1944, over 37 hurdles.

The first sub 8:30: Gaston Roelants (Bel) 8:29.6 Louvain 7 Sep 1963.

HIGH JUMP
The most world records is six by Valeriy Brumel (USSR). He succeeded John Thomas (USA) with 2.23m/7ft 3¾in at Moscow on 18 Jun 1961, improved to 2.24m and 2.25m that year, to 2.26m and 2.27m in 1962 and finally to 2.28m/7ft 5¾in at Moscow on 21 Jul 1963 in the USA v USSR match. He was born on 14 Apr 1942, curiously the same day as Ni Chih Chin (Chi), who cleared 2.29m/7ft 6¼in unofficially in 1970.

Barrier breakers:
6ft: Marshall Brooks (GB) 1.83m/6ft 0¼in at Oxford on 17 Mar 1876, after a snowstorm had delayed the start of the meeting. He improved on 7 Apr in the inter-varsity sports to 1.89m/6ft 2¼in from a grass take-off at Lillie Bridge, London before 15000 spectators, the largest crowd to watch an athletics meeting to that date.
1.95m: Michael Sweeney (USA), pioneer of the 'Eastern cut-off', known at the time as the 'Sweeney twist', 1.96m/6ft 5¼in on 29 Aug 1895.
2.00m: George Horine (USA), the first world record holder to use the 'Western roll', 2.00m/6ft 7in at Palo Alto, the Stanford University track on 18 May 1912.
2.10m: Lester Steers (USA) 2.10m/6ft 10¾in at

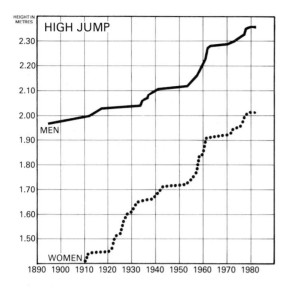

HIGH JUMP

HEIGHT IN METRES

2.30
2.20
2.10
2.00
MEN
1.90
1.80
1.70
1.60
1.50
WOMEN

1890 1900 1910 1920 1930 1940 1950 1960 1970 1980

The world's first 7ft high jump, by 19-year-old Charles Dumas of Compton Junior College at Los Angeles in 1956. He improved by over 2in to this 7ft 0⅜in, was not beaten until 1958 and went on to win the 1956 Olympic title.   *(INP)*

Seattle on 26 Apr 1941. Steers, who improved to 2.11m/6ft 11in on 17 Jun 1941, used the straddle style. Also known as the 'belly roll' the first world record with the straddle was by Dave Albritton (USA) as both he and Cornelius Johnson jumped 2.07m/6ft 9¾in at the 1936 US Olympic Trials.

7ft: Charles Dumas (USA) 2.15m/7ft 0⅝in Los Angeles 29 Jun 1956 to win the US Olympic Trials. Dumas won the 1956 Olympic title and was sixth in 1960, after which he retired. But he came back after an operation on his left knee and in his first competition for nearly four years jumped 2.14m/7ft 0¼in at Tempe, Arizona on 4 Apr 1964. A number of jumpers had been reported as having cleared 7ft unofficially, notably Walter Davis (USA), who had ended Steers' 12-year reign as record holder with 2.12m/6ft 11½in in 1953. Davis jumped 7ft in an exhibition at Port Arthur, Texas before turning professional at basketball. He had started his high jumping career in 1949 while on a basketball scholarship at college in order to get out of the gym!

2.20m: John Thomas (USA) 2.22m/7ft 3¾in Palo Alto 1 Jul 1960. Thomas had jumped 7ft

2½in, marginally less than 2.20m indoors at Chicago on 11 Mar 1960.

2.30m: Dwight Stones (USA) 2.30m/7ft 6½in Munich 11 Jul 1973. This was the first world record set with the 'flop' style, which had been pioneered by Dick Fosbury (USA), winner of the 1968 Olympic title at 2.24m/7ft 4¼in. Fosbury started using what he called a 'back float' style when he could clear only 1.78m/5ft 10in with the Western roll. He jumped 7ft for the first time on 26 Jan 1968 at Oakland, Cal. Before the Olympics his best was 2.21m/7ft 3in for third place at the US trials.

2.35m: Vladimir Yashchenko (USSR) 2.35m/7ft 8½in indoors at Milan on 12 Mar 1978. He set world records outdoors at 2.33m in 1977 and 2.34m in 1978. Unlike most of the top jumpers of the late 1970s and 1980s he used the straddle. The first outdoor 2.35m was achieved by Jacek Wszola (Pol) at Eberstadt, GFR on 25 May 1980, to be followed a day later by 18-year-old Dietmar Mögenburg (Ger). Another 'flopper' Gerd Wessig (GDR) took the record to 2.36m/7ft 8¾in at the 1980 Olympic Games.

The best combination of flop and straddle jumper is Pat Matzdorf (USA). He set a world record of 2.29m/7ft 6¼in using a bent-leg straddle technique in 1971, and after switching to the flop had a best of 2.24m/7ft 4¼in in 1975.

Synchronised high jumping record: On 4 Sep 1980 at Herne the Germans, Dietmar Mögenberg and Andre Schneider simultaneously cleared the same bar at 2.20m.

Stan Albright (USA) jumped 2.16m/7ft 1in in 1966 while at High School. After 1968, when he had a best of 7ft he dropped out of the sport. He did not jump, even in training in 1969 or 1970, but made an amazing comeback as he competed for the first time since June 1968 on 19 Mar 1971 in his home city of Cleveland, Ohio. He entered this indoor competition at 6ft 8in and went on all the way up to 7ft 1in to equal his best ever.

Early high jumpers used to jump from grass on to grass. Nowadays jumpers have plenty of foam rubber or air beds to land on, yet it was not until 1973 that the use of sawdust in pits was outlawed.

The best ever high jump by a man with one leg is 2.04m/6ft 8¼in by Arnie Boldt (Can) in the International Games for Handicapped Athletes in 1981. He had lost his leg above the knee in a

Franklin Jacobs demonstrates how high above his head is a bar set at 7ft 5¼in in 1977. He exceeded this by a further 2in in 1978 for a record differential. *(Fairleigh Dickinson University)*

farm accident at the age of three.

The greatest height jumped over an athlete's own head is 59cm/23¼in by Franklin Jacobs (USA). His 2.32m/7ft 7¼in indoors at New York on 28 Jan 1978 compares to his height of just 1.73m/5ft 8in.

Built-up shoes were used by many jumpers in 1956 and 1957, notably those of the USSR. An extra thick sole, usually of about 3cm was used on the take-off shoe. Yuriy Styepanov (USSR) set a world record of 2.16m/7ft 1in wearing such a shoe, before the IAAF restricted the maximum permissible thickness to 13mm in 1958. Styepanov's best without the artificial aid was 2.12m/6ft 11½in.

Take offs from two feet are not allowed in high jumping, but using them gymnastic experts may have been the first to clear 7ft.

In 1962 the US Tumbling champion, Gary Chamberlain, cleared 2.23m/7ft 4in with a round-off followed by a back hand-spring with a back flip over the bar placed alongside tumbling mats landing on both feet.

In April 1954 Dick Browning, AAU tumbling champion 1951–4, was reported to have somersaulted over a bar set at 2.28m/7ft 6in.

POLE VAULT

The Pole Vault record has been broken more times than any other field event from the first record ratified by the IAAF by Marcus Wright (USA) in 1912, to the present day.

Pole Vaulting originally for distance, dates back at least to the 16th century. In the 19th century heavy wooden poles, usually of ash or hickory, with iron spikes on the end were used by pioneer vaulters around Ulverston in the English Lake District. These men used a 'climbing' technique of moving their hands up the pole when it was vertical. The greatest exponent of this technique was Thomas Ray (GB) who raised the best height nine times from 3.42m/11ft 2¾in in 1879 to 3.57m/11ft 8⅜in in 1888. The 'climbing' technique was banned in 1889 in the USA but not until 1919 by the AAA.

In the early part of this century **bamboo poles**, first used in 1857, came into vogue. They were generally superseded by steel poles in the late 1940s and 1950s, as the metal poles were more consistent though not necessarily better than the best bamboo ones. Then came the transition to glass fibre poles which revolutionised the event adding about 50cm/1ft 6in to the heights cleared by the leading vaulters in a very short time span.

Up to 1936 IAAF rules specified that poles must be made of wood or bamboo. From that time any material was permitted and there were no restrictions on the length and diameter of the poles.

Early experiments with **glass fibre poles** had been conducted in the USA in the late 1940s. Herb Jenks, later with leading manufacturers AMF-Pacer tried them as did Guinn Smith, who in 1948 won the Olympic title, the last man to do so using a bamboo pole. By 1956/7 such poles began to be used in major events by such men as Giorgios Roubanis (Gre), third in the 1956 Olympics, Aubrey Dooley (USA) and Jim Brewer, the first US high school athlete to clear 15ft/4.57m. The real 'take-off' in the use of these poles and the new technique required to make best use of their properties came in 1961, when George Davies (USA) became the first man to set a world record with a fibre glass pole – 4.83m/15ft 10¼in at Boulder, Colorado on 20 May.

The greatest improvement in the IAAF record has been 12cm by Cornelius 'Dutch' Warmerdam on 6 Jun 1941 when he cleared 4.72m/15ft 5¾in at Compton, Cal. Warmerdam, born on 22 Jun 1915 at Long Beach, Cal., the third son of

Marcus Wright at the 1912 Olympic games, when he shared pole vault second place at 3.85m. A month earlier he was the first to clear 4m.

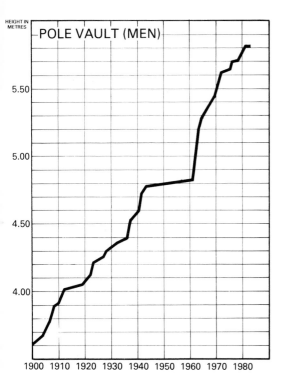

POLE VAULT (MEN)

HEIGHT IN METRES

Deacon, who amazingly had also been second to him 35 years earlier, vaulting 4.32m/14ft 2in when Warmerdam first cleared 15ft.

The world record outdoors was finally bettered by Bob Gutowski's 4.78m/15ft 8¼in on 27 Apr 1957 and Gutowski (USA) also vaulted an unratified (as his pole went under the bar, contrary to the then IAAF rules) 4.82m/15ft 9¾in on 15 Jun 1957 at Austin, Texas, still the best ever with a metal pole, to go higher than Warmerdam's indoor best.

Three men have set the greatest number of IAAF records, four by Charles Hoff (Nor) 4.12m/13ft 6¼in in 1922 to 4.25m/13ft 11¼in in 1925; John Pennel (USA) 5.13m/16ft 10¼in in 1963 to 5.44m/17ft 10¼in in 1969; Bob Seagren (USA) 5.32m/17ft 5½in in 1966 to 5.63m/18ft 5¾in in 1972. However the pace of record breaking in recent years has been so rapid that not all records have been ratified, often because they have been superseded so quickly, and Pennel has actually had the most 'world record' performances with ten.

Until 1 May 1969 successful clearances were disallowed in international competition if the vaulter's pole passed beneath the bar. This regulation cost John Pennel an Olympic medal in 1968.

The most indoor world 'bests' is 12 by Charles Hoff (Nor) all on a hugely successful American tour in 1926, from 3.99m/13ft 1in to 4.17m/13ft 8¼in. He was, however, barred by the AAU for professionalism and his records disallowed. Bob Seagren (USA) set eight successive world indoor bests from 5.19m/17ft 0¼in in 1966 to 5.33m/17ft 6in in 1969.

Barrier breakers
12ft: Norman Dole (USA) 3.69m/12ft 1¼in 23 Apr 1904 Oakland, Cal.
13ft: Robert Gardner (USA) 3.99m/13ft 1in 1 Jun 1912 Philadelphia.
4m: Marcus Wright (USA) 4.02m/13ft 2¼in 8 Jun 1912 Cambridge, Mass.
14ft: Sabin Carr (USA) 4.26m/14ft 27 May 1927 Philadelphia.
15ft: Cornelius Warmerdam (USA) 4.57m/15ft (see opposite).
16ft: John Uelses (USA) 4.88m/16ft 0¼in indoors 2 Feb 1962 New York, and 4.89m/16ft 0¾in outdoors 31 Mar 1962 Santa Barbara, Cal.
5m: Pentti Nikula (Fin) 5.10m/16ft 8¾in indoors 2 Feb 1963 Pajulahti, Fin.
17ft: John Pennel (USA) 5.20m/17ft 0¾in

an American immigrant from Holland, achieved the greatest domination of his event by any man in the history of the sport. On 13 Apr 1940 at Berkeley, Cal. he became the first man to vault over 15ft/4.57m (landing on a small pile of wood shavings) and went on to total 43 clearances at 15ft or higher in 33 competitions. Nobody else vaulted 15ft for 11 years until Robert Richards achieved 4.59m/15ft 1in indoors in New York on 27 Jan 1951. Warmerdam's eight successive improvements culminated in a world outdoor record of 4.77m/15ft 7¾in on 23 May 1942 at Modesto, Cal. and 4.79m/15ft 8½in indoors on 20 Mar 1943 at Chicago, still the best ever with a bamboo pole.

Warmerdam's 15ft competitions were as follows: two in 1940, eight in 1941, 11 in 1942, 11 in 1943 and finally exactly 15ft in winning the 1944 AAU title when his duties as a naval lieutenant held back his opportunities. After the war he was coach at Fresno State University for 33 years. In 1952 he cleared 4.37m/14ft 4in in an exhibition but did not compete again until 1975 when at the age of 60 he set a world age record at the decathlon with 4328 points at Glendale, Cal., including a 3.20m/10ft 6in pole vault. Second to him in that decathlon was Bud

24 Aug 1963 Coral Gables, Fla.
18ft: Christos Papanikolaou (Gre) 5.49m/18ft 0¼in 24 Oct 1970 Athens. Papanikolaou was the first left-handed vaulter since Wright to set a world record. The bar was set at 5.47m/17ft 11½in, but on re-measurement the true height was found to be 2cm higher.
19ft: Thierry Vigneron (Fra) 5.80m/19ft 0¼in 20 Jun 1981 Macon. Vigneron's record lasted just six days before the 21-year-old Soviet vaulter Vladimir Polyakov added a further centimetre. Then another Soviet, Konstantin Volkov jumped 5.84m/19ft 2in at Irkutsk in Siberia. However it seems likely that this performance will not be ratified as it was set in a meeting, to mark Soviet Railwaymen's Day, that did not conform with IAAF specifications.

The greatest improvements to world class standards were those of C. K. Yang (Tai) and Dan Ripley (USA). Ripley entered a competition at Saskatoon, Canada with a best of 4.97m/16ft 3½in, and cleared successively 16ft 6in, 17ft, 17ft 6in and ended with 5.38m/17ft 8in. Three weeks later he set an amateur world indoor best of 5.51m/18ft 1in. On 3 Mar 1979 he regained this world indoor best with 5.63m/18ft 5½in. C. K. Yang, as the great decathlete Yang Chuang-kwang was known in the USA, set a world indoor best of 4.96m/16ft 3¼in at Portland, Oregon on 26 Jan 1963, jumping successively 15ft, 15ft 4in, 15ft 11in and 16ft 3¼in, although his previous competition best was 4.44m/14ft 6¾in!
Steve Smith, who set a world indoor best of 5.61m/18ft 5in as a professional in 1975 two years after being the first to clear 18ft indoors, once cleared 5.26m/17ft 3in off a skateboard.

Pole Vault prodigies – first vaulters to clear their age in feet: Tobie Hatfield (USA) cleared 7ft 3in at age 7, 8ft at 8 and 9ft at 9. From age 13 upwards pioneers have been:
13: Bob Crites (USA) 3.96m/13ft 22 Jun 1968 Kokomo, Ind.
14: Bill Lange (USA) 4.28m/14ft 0½in 4 Oct 1977 Bridgewater, NJ.
15: Tim Curran (USA) 4.57m/15ft 30 Apr 1971 Encino, Cal.
16: Paul Wilson (USA) 4.87m/16ft 22 May 1964 Compton, Cal.
17: Casey Carrigan (USA) 5.18m/17ft 12 Sep 1968 South Lake Tahoe, Cal.
18: Dave Volz (USA) 5.54m/18ft 2in 13 Feb 1981 Bloomington, Ind.

The best pole vault for distance is 8.74m/28ft 8in by Jeff Chase (USA), whose 'upwards' best was 5.18m/17ft 0½in, at San José on 4 May 1963.

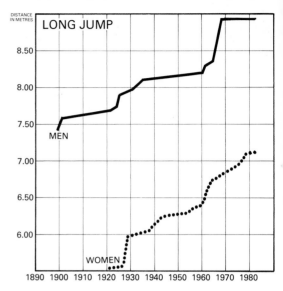

LONG JUMP
Easily the greatest improvement in the world record came when Bob Beamon (USA) added 0.55m/1ft 9¾in with his staggering performance in the 1968 Olympics at Mexico City on 18 Oct 1968. His 8.90m/29ft 2½in by-passed the first ever 28ft jump to over 29ft at a moment when everything went right for the immensely talented Beamon; the 2214.0m/7349ft altitude, the wind behind him (recorded at the maximum permitted of 2.0m/s, uncannily the same as several other readings that day), the stimulus of Olympic competition and perfect technique. This was his first jump of the competition after three other men had had no jumps and totally demoralised his main rivals. Beamon took one more jump, 8.04m/26ft 4½in before passing his remaining four jumps – his job done with a record that may well last out the century. Beamon had starred at high school in 1965, but had made his breakthrough to world class at the 1967 AAU indoor championships when he improved his best from 7.82m/25ft 8in to 8.22m/26ft 11½in. He was unbeaten in 1968 and so went into the Games as a marginal favourite over the great Ralph Boston (USA) with best performances of 8.33m/27ft 4in and 8.39m/27ft 6½in (wind assisted).
Beamon never again jumped over even 27ft. His best after 1968 was 8.20m/26ft 11in in 1969. He pulled a hamstring in 1969 and rein-

Carl Lewis long jumped over 28ft three times in 1981 and twice more in early 1982.
(University of Houston)

Bob Beamon at Mexico City in 1968 when he set the greatest of all world records – 8.90m/ 29ft 2½in. *(M. Shearman)*

jured the leg in 1970, but made a comeback in 1973, when he turned professional and had a best of 8.16m/26ft 9¼in still the third best in the world that year. A far cry from his 8.90m but when you have achieved the greatest performance in the history of the sport what else is left?

Since the IAAF first published lists with Peter O'Connor (GB/Ire) as long jump record holder at 7.61m/24ft 11¾in set at Dublin on 5 Aug 1901, there have been just 17 records ratified, and Ralph Boston (USA) has the most by one man with six, from 8.21m/26ft 11¼in in 1960 to 8.35m/27ft 5in in 1965. Boston was the closest to 28ft before Beamon came along, with a wind aided 8.49m/27ft 10¼in in the US Olympic Trials in 1964. In 1966 he was quoted as saying after he had jumped in Mexico City: 'I look for somebody to jump 28ft down there in the Olympics'. What a prediction!

The first men to exceed various targets:
24ft William Newburn (Ire) 7.33m/24ft 0½in Dublin 16 Jul 1898.
7.50m Myer Prinstein (USA) 7.50m/24ft 7¼in Philadelphia 28 Apr 1900.
25ft Edwin Gourdin (USA) 7.69m/25ft 3in Cambridge, Mass. 23 Jul 1921.
26ft Silvio Cator (Haiti) 7.93m/26ft 0¼in Paris 9 Sep 1928.
William DeHart Hubbard (USA) had jumped 7.98m/26ft 2¼in on 17 Sep 1927 at Cincinnati, but this was disallowed because the take-off board was an inch higher than the pit.
8m Jesse Owens (USA) 8.13m/26ft 8¼in Ann Arbor, Mich. 25 May 1935.
This record stood for 25 years 79 days until Boston's 8.21m. Owens jumped 26ft/7.92m or more 15 times in 1935–6, but it was 12 years before any other man exceeded that distance more than once, when Willie Steele (USA) achieved the feat. Steele, the 1948 Olympic champion, had a best of 8.07m/26ft 6in in 1947.
27ft Ralph Boston (USA) 8.24m/27ft 0½in Modesto, Cal. 27 May 1961.

The distinction of jumping **the first 28ft long jump**, staggeringly by-passed by Beamon, was realised at the 1980 Olympic Games when Lutz Dombrowski (GDR) did 8.54m/28ft 0¼in. In 1981 19-year-old Carl Lewis (USA) jumped even further and made 28ft his area of jumping. On 10 May in Los Angeles he jumped 8.63m/28ft 3¾in with the wind speed at 2.02m/s (just 0.02 above the legal limit). He emulated Jesse Owens by winning both 100m and long jump at both NCAA and TAC championships, and at the latter jumped 8.73m/28ft 7¾in, aided by a wind of 4.57m/s in the qualifying round, and a legal 8.62m/28ft 3½in in the final at Sacramento, Cal. on 20 June. In the TAC he beat Larry Myricks (USA) for the first time in nine contests. Myricks had a best of 8.52m/27ft 11½in in 1979 and eight more competitions at

8.38m/27ft 6in or better in 1980–1.

A 'flip' long jump style was evolved by Jim Wilson, former Oregon State triple jumper using partial rotation in the air. Similarly Tom Ecker, author of 'Track and Field Dynamics' suggested a somersault style of long jumping. The greatest distance reached with this method was 7.79m/25ft 6¾in by John Delamere a New Zealander at Washington State in 1974 and he later employed it as an ITA professional, but the style was banned by the IAAF at its Congress in Rome in September that year.

The best ever standing jumps (amateur)
High jump: 1.90m/6ft 2¾in Rune Almen (Swe) 1980.
Long jump: 3.65m/11ft 11¾in Johan Evandt (Nor) 1962.
   In the 19th century jumpers frequently used weights to assist their jumping, but it seems that the greatest of all these professional spring jumpers, Joe Darby (GB), did not use them when he cleared 3.70m/12ft 1½in on 28 May 1890. Darby achieved such feats as jumping 81½y/74.5m in only 17 jumps, and with weights, spring jumps of 4.50m/14ft 9in forwards and 3.94m/12ft 11in backwards, or clearing a full size Billiards table lengthwise after two jumps taking off from a raised (4in) block of wood.

TRIPLE JUMP
The first IAAF record was 15.52m/50ft 11in by Daniel Ahearn, born in Limerick and an emigrant to the USA, at Celtic Park, New York on 30 May 1911. His elder brother Tim Ahearne (Daniel dropped the final 'e') had held the previous world best of 14.92m/48ft 11¼in, with which distance he had won the 1908 Olympic title. By then the event had been standardised as the hop, step and jump; the 'hop' is taking off and landing on the same foot, the 'step' landing on the other foot and the 'jump' landing as for a long jump. Early practitioners in Ireland had used two hops and a jump. Daniel Ahearn reached 15.72m/51ft 7in with this technique in 1910.

The most triple jump world records is five by Adhemar Ferreira da Silva (Bra). On 3 Dec 1950 at Sao Paulo he equalled the 14-year-old world record of 16.00m/52ft 6in set by Naoto Tajima (Jap) in winning the 1936 Olympic title. Da Silva then improved to 16.01m in 1951 and to first 16.12m and then 16.22m/53ft 2½in at the 1952 Olympic Games. After Leonid Shcherbakov (USSR) had added a centimetre in

1953, da Silva made a decisive improvement at altitude in Mexico City to 16.56m/54ft 4in at the 1955 Pan-American Games.

The most world records in one competition is four at the 1968 Olympic Games in Mexcio City. These were preceded by another in the qualifying competition by Giuseppe Gentile (Ita). Before the Games the record was 17.03m/55ft 10½in by Jozef Schmidt (Pol) in 1960. After Gentile, Viktor Saneyev and Nelson Prudencio had finished, the record stood to Saneyev at 17.39m/57ft 0¾in (see p. 97).

The biggest improvement in the IAAF world record is 0.45m/1ft 5¾in by Joao de Oliveira (Bra) on 15 Oct 1975, again at Mexico City, when jumping the current record of 17.89m/58ft 8½in. The previous record was Saneyev's 17.44m/57ft 2¾in at sea-level at his home town of Sukhumi, Georgia on 17 Oct 1972.

Barrier breakers
15m/50ft with two hops and a jump: Daniel Shanahan (Ire) 15.57m/51ft 1in Newcastle West 8 Sep 1886; with hop, step and jump: Daniel Ahearn (USA) 15.39m/50ft 6in Boston 31 Jul 1909.
16m: Naoto Tajima (Jap) 16.00m/52ft 6in Berlin 6 Aug 1936.
17m/55ft: Jozef Schmidt (Pol) 17.03m/55ft 10½in Olsztyn 5 Aug 1960.

SHOT
Of the 43 ratified records from 1909 to date, all but seven have been set by US athletes, including all those from 1934 to 1976.

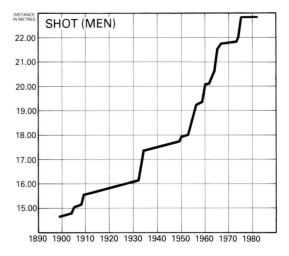

James Randel Matson set four world shot records while at Texas A&M University. He also set a US discus record at 65.16m/212ft 9in in 1967.

Parry O'Brien (USA), with ten ratified and six unratified performances, has set the most records. He succeeded Jim Fuchs (USA) with a put of 18.00m/59ft 0¾in at Fresno, Cal. on 9 May 1953, and took the record up to 19.25m/63ft 2in by 1 Nov 1956. Dallas Long (USA) equalled this before O'Brien's final record of 19.30m/63ft 4in on 1 Aug 1959 at Albuquerque. The younger generation passed him, but O'Brien continued to improve and his best put came in 1966 with 19.69m/64ft 7¼in. He did far more than break records however, for he pioneered a new style, whereby he started his throw with his right foot pointing backwards, and made a 180 degree turn before he released the shot, thus making more of the dimensions of the circle.

The biggest improvement on the IAAF record was 0.84m/2ft 9¼in by Randy Matson (USA), when his 21.52m/70ft 7¼in at College Station,

Texas on 8 May 1965 shattered Dallas Long's (USA) 20.68m/67ft 10in of the previous July. Matson, however had put 21.05m/69ft 0¾in eight days earlier, which was never submitted for ratification and thus the greatest improvement on the absolute record was 0.51m/1ft 8in by Jack Torrance (USA).

Torrance, known as the 'Elephant Baby', weighing 138kg/304lb at a height of 1.90m/6ft 2¾in, improved his own 36-day-old record to 17.40m/57ft 1in on 5 Aug 1934 at Oslo.

Matson's 21.52m was in a series of five puts of which four bettered the previous record, an unparalleled feat. His series was: 20.95m, 21.52m, 20.65m, 21.05m, 20.84m. O'Brien had come closest to matching this, for on 3 Sep 1956 he took just three trials: 18.97m/62ft 3in, 18.90m/62ft, 19.06m/62ft 6¼in, all well ahead of his previous record of 18.70m/61ft 4½in. Matson improved further to 21.78m/71ft 5½in on 22 Apr 1967, set on his final appearance for Texas A&M at College Station. By the end of 1970 he had 13 competitions with 25 puts beyond the second best performer ever to that time, Neal Steinhauer (USA) (21.01m/68ft 11¼in in 1967).

Barrier breakers
15m: Wesley Coe (USA) 15.09m/49ft 6in 5 Aug 1895 Portland, Ore.
50ft: Ralph Rose (USA) 15.39m/50ft 6in 14 Aug 1909 Seattle.
Rose set the first IAAF record of 15.45m/51ft a week later at San Francisco.
60ft: Parry O'Brien (USA) 18.42m/60ft 5¼in 8 May 1954 Los Angeles.
20m: Bill Nieder (USA) 20.06m/65ft 10in 12 Aug 1960 Walnut, Cal.
70ft: Randy Matson (USA) 21.52m/70ft 7¼in (see p. 59).

The most amazing shot performance of all-time came from a professional. Brian Oldfield (USA) had been placed sixth at the 1972 Olympics before turning professional in 1973, when he set world pro bests of 21.32m, 21.58m and 21.60m/70ft 10½in, compared to the world record of 21.82m/71ft 7in set by Al Feuerbach (USA) that year. In 1974 amateur George Woods (USA) put 22.02m/72ft 2¾in (indoors, and thus not eligible for a world record). Then in 1975 Oldfield left this far behind. First he did 21.76m and 21.87m/71ft 9in indoors at Salt Lake City on 21 February. Then he went to 22.11m/72ft 6½in indoors at Daly City on 4 April. At El Paso on 10 May he took just three throws: 21.94m/71ft 11¾in, 22.25m/73ft 0¼in and 22.86m/75ft, all ahead of the amateur world record. Even Oldfield has not approached this standard since, but he had further puts of 22.28m/73ft 1in at Edinburgh on 18 Jun 1975, and 22.45m/73ft 8in at El Paso on 22 May 1976. Reinstated as an amateur he won the 1980 TAC title with 21.82m/71ft 7in, the world's second best performance of the year, and improved to an American record 22.02m/72ft 3in on 16 May 1981. The amateur record now stands at 22.15m/72ft 8in to Udo Beyer (GDR). Oldfield used a rotational technique on his big throws. He had seen this used at the 1972 Olympic Games by Aleksandr Baryshnikov (USSR), who later set a world record of 22.00m/72ft 2¼in in 1976. Baryshnikov was the first to use this new technique with great success, but a similar method had been tried in the 1950s by some European throwers, Baryshnikov, in particular, took to the method because his height (2.00m) made it difficult for him to operate within the confines of the shot circle using the traditional methods.
    The ambidextrous shot record is held by Al Feuerbach (USA), who at Malmo on 24 Aug 1974 put 21.38m/70ft 1¼in with his right hand and 15.67m/51ft 5in with his left hand.

The world junior record was set at 20.65m/67ft 9in by Mike Carter (USA) at Boston on 5 Jul 1979, the climax of a fantastic year for the 18-year-old from Thomas Jefferson High School, Dallas, Texas. Three weeks earlier he had become the first man ever to put the 12lb/5.45kg shot over 80ft with 24.78m/81ft 3½in, the final throw of his high school career and 2.75m/9ft 0¼in better than the second best high school thrower ever. In 1979 he set seven high school records at 12lb shot and made five improvements at 16lb. A great American football prospect he was injured in his first game as an offensive lineman against Rice University, and has subsequently, to date, concentrated on throwing.

DISCUS
US throwers have set 28 of the 40 official IAAF records, and three of them have set four apiece: Fortune Gordien, Al Oerter and Mac Wilkins.

Gordien set his first record at Lisbon on 9 Jul 1949 at 56.46m/185ft 3in, improved to 56.97m that year, and after Sim Iness (USA) had thrown 57.93m/190ft in 1953, returned to the lists with 58.10m and 59.28m/194ft 6in, both at John Muir College, Pasadena. By the end of 1954 Gordien had 12 of the best 13 performances ever, with all his throws at Pasadena! He won six AAU and three NCAA titles and at successive Olympics from 1948 was placed third, fourth and second.

Al Oerter had a great duel with Rink Babka (USA) to the first 200ft throw. In 1958, Babka had a throw at Victorville, Cal. on 22 Mar which landed in a drainage ditch 201 feet from the circle. The referee computed this to be worth 60.60m/198ft 10in allowing for the drop in ground level. Then Oerter threw 61.73m/202ft 6in at Fayetteville, Arkansas on 5 Apr, but this was disallowed due to a 2½% slope (permitted limit 0.1%). The barrier remained unbroken for four years until Oerter threw 61.10m/200ft 5in at Los Angeles on 18 May 1962. Further records followed in 1963, 1964 and 1968 when he won the Olympic title with 64.78m/212ft 6in. After a seven-year absence Oerter returned, improving to 69.46m/227ft 11in at the age of 43 in 1980.

Mac Wilkins was Olympic champion in 1976, in which year he set four world records. The first was 69.18m at Walnut, Cal. 24 Apr, then, on 1 May at San Jose, Cal., he improved three times: 69.80m, 70.24m, 70.86m/232ft 6in before fin-

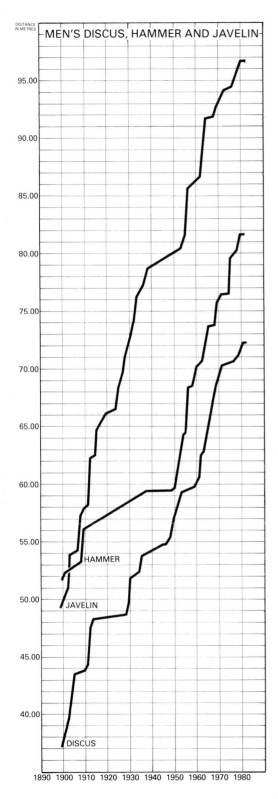

DISTANCE IN METRES

MEN'S DISCUS, HAMMER AND JAVELIN

HAMMER

JAVELIN

DISCUS

1890 1900 1910 1920 1930 1940 1950 1960 1970 1980

ishing his series with 66.98m, 68.08m and 66.58m. Wilkins' predecessor as world record holder, John Powell (USA) was second at 67.16m. Even so Wilkins professed to be unhappy with his technique, but has improved only marginally since, to 70.98m/232ft 10in in 1980. He lost the record to Wolfgang Schmidt (GDR) 71.16m/233ft 5in in 1978.

Wilkins bettered a throw of 70.38m/230ft 11in by Jay Silvester on 16 May 1971 at Lancaster, in Antelope Valley, Cal., which had not been ratified due to lack of sufficient graded officials. This had been aided by highly favourable quartering winds from the right of 40–45mph/70km/h and seven competitors threw 62.50m/205ft or more. All seven set personal bests, by an average of 3.82m/12ft 6½in! Second in this competition at 67.38m was Tim Vollmer (USA), who in June 1972 threw the 1kg women's discus 82.48m/270ft 7in at Compton, Cal. Silvester set two IAAF records, the second of which at 68.40m/224ft 5in, again with favourable strong winds, at Reno, Nevada on 18 Sep 1968 was the biggest ever discus world record improvement (1.86m/6ft 1in).

Discus world record holders have had the most massive physiques of any athletes. Tallest was John van Reenan (SA) at 2.02m/6ft 7½in and 125kg/275lb in weight, while other tall men have included Paul Jessup (USA) 1.98m (1930), Rink Babka 1.95m (1960), Ricky Bruch (Swe) 1.99m (1972) and Wolfgang Schmidt 1.98m. More massive still was Ben Plucknett (USA) who twice exceeded Schmidt's record in 1981, first with 71.20m/233ft 7in at Modesto on 16 May and then 72.34m/237ft 4in at Stockholm on 7 July. These could not, however, be ratified as world records after Plucknett had been found to have taken anabolic steroids (see p. 251). Plucknett was placed third at the 1980 US Olympic trials, ahead of Al Oerter, and weighed in at 138kg/304lb, with a height of 2.01m/6ft 7in. At Modesto he also put the shot 20.59m/67ft 6¾in for the greatest one-day SP/DT double ever and beat a great discus field, with seven men throwing over 65m/213ft 3in and Wilkins 12th at 60.92m/199ft 10in. John Powell was second at 69.98m/229ft 7in to improve from his previous best of 69.08m/226ft 8in, a world record in 1975.

Plucknett was shot twice in the stomach in January 1978 by underage youths whom he and Jim McGoldrick (1975 NCAA DT champion) had barred from a rock club at Sunnyvale, Cal. when they had been acting as 'bouncers'.

The discus was added surprisingly late to major championship programmes, the AAU in 1897 and the AAA in 1914.

Barrier breakers
40m: Martin Sheridan (USA) 40.72m/133ft 7in New York 2 Nov 1902. In all Sheridan set five world bests (pre IAAF records), culminating in 43.90m/144ft 0in in 1909.
150ft: James Duncan (USA) 47.58m/156ft 1¼in New York 27 May 1912 (First IAAF record).
50m: Eric Krenz (USA) 51.03m/167ft 5¼in Palo Alto 17 May 1930.
60m: Jay Silvester (USA) 60.56m/198ft 8in Frankfurt/Main 11 Aug 1961.
200ft: Al Oerter (USA) 61.10m/200ft 5in (see p. 60).
70m: Jay Silvester (USA) 70.38m/230ft 11in (see p. 61).

HAMMER
The origins of the modern hammer throwing event date back to throwing the sledge-hammer in England and Scotland in the 15th or 16th centuries. Henry VIII was supposedly an enthusiast. The Industrial Revolution weakened the support for rural sports in England but the hammer continued to be a major event at Highland Games in Scotland.

A 16lb round iron ball replaced the sledge head around 1865, although a stiff wooden shaft was still used. The AAA permitted a metal handle from 1896, when piano-wire handles were already in use in the USA. Originally an unlimited run-up was permitted but in 1878 a 7ft/2.13m throwing circle was introduced, although for a while this was expanded to 9ft/2.74m by the AAA. The 'round the head' style of throwing was pioneered by Donald Dinnie, a great Highland Games exponent in Scotland, who was well-nigh unbeatable between 1860 and 1890. Hammer-throwing has always been a dangerous activity, and so the hammer is now always thrown from a cage. There have been a number of tragic accidents and deaths from being hit by a hammer have been reported occasionally, the first being that of eight-year-old John Gyfford in 1566.

Hammer throwing – a costly exercise
Barry Williams, later British record holder, was fined £5 and ordered to pay £3.50 restitution after being found guilty of causing wilful damage with a 16lb hammer to a corporation football pitch at Wallasey, Cheshire in 1967.

The first IAAF record was 57.77m/189ft 6½in by Patrick Ryan (USA) in New York on 17 Aug 1913. This stood as the official record for 25 years 10 days, the second longest duration for any 'Olympic' event. Ryan's official successor was Erwin Blask (Ger) at 59.00m/193ft 7in, but a year earlier the Irishman Pat O'Callaghan had thrown 59.55m/195ft 4⅝in at the Cork County Championships. There were various irregularities which would have prevented ratification if it had been put forward, but they tended to be unhelpful – the circle was 2m/6ft 7in in diameter rather than 7ft, and the hammer was 6oz (c170g) overweight.

Ryan had set his record on his sixth throw at the Eccentric Firemen's Games, Celtic Park, Long Island. He represented the Irish-American AC and followed in the great tradition of the 'Irish Whales' as the group of men who dominated the early history of the hammer were known. The first of these great Irish-Americans was James Mitchel who took the record from 36.40m/119ft 5in in 1886 at Limerick in seven improvements to 44.21m/145ft 0¾in in New York in 1892. Mitchel won 76 national weight event titles (Irish, English, American and Canadian).

John Flanagan improved Mitchel's record to 44.46m/145ft 10½in at Clonmel, Ireland on 9 Sep 1895 and came to the USA in 1897. In all he improved the record 13 times taking it to 56.19m/184ft 4in in 1909. Flanagan won the first four Olympic titles – 1900, 1904, 1906 and 1908. He was succeeded as Olympic champion by the 1908 runner-up Matt McGrath (USA), who also improved the record to 57.10m/187ft 4in at Celtic Park in 1911. McGrath was born in Tipperary while Mitchell, Flanagan and Ryan all came from County Limerick.

The most IAAF records have been set by Mikhail Krivonosov (USSR) and Hal Connolly (USA), each with six and an additional unratified mark. Krivonosov took the record from 63.34m/207ft 9in in 1954 to 67.32m/220ft 10in in 1956 and Connolly followed, 68.54m/224ft 10in in 1956 to 71.26m/233ft 9in in 1965. They had a great battle in the 1956 Olympic Games, with Connolly's fifth round 63.18m/207ft 3in winning by just 16cm/6in.

The biggest improvement in the record was 2.48m/8ft 2in by Gyula Zsivotzky (Hun) 73.74m/241ft 11in Debrecen 4 Sep 1965.

The greatest display of world record annihilation at one event came from Karl-Hans Riehm (Ger) on 19 May 1975 at Rehlingen, when all six of his throws: 76.70m, 77.56m, 77.10m, 78.50m/257ft 6in, 77.16m, 77,28m beat the previous world record of 76.66m/251ft 6in of Aleksey Spiridonov (USSR). The 24-year-old soldier from Trier declared himself content afterwards! Riehm returned to the record lists with 80.32m/263ft 6in in 1978 and in 1980 would have given the Soviet throwers a battle at the Olympic Games but for his nation's boycott of the Games, for he had five 1980 competitions at 80m or better with a best of 80.80m/265ft 1in the day before the Olympic final.

There were also three records in one competition at Leselidze on 16 May 1980. In the third round Yuriy Syedikh (USSR) threw 80.38m/263ft 8in but was followed by Juri Tamm (USSR) 80.40m/263ft 9in. Irritated at losing the record Syedikh replied with 80.64m/264ft 7in. Eight days later another Soviet thrower, Sergey Litvinov took the record to 81.66m/267ft 11in, but Syedikh regained it when it really mattered, With the first throw of the Olympic final on 31 July, he threw 81.80m/268ft 4in and his colleagues were left to fill the other medal places: second Litvinov 80.64m, third Tamm 78.96m.

Hal Connolly breaks the world record for the first time at Boston in 1956. This unratified mark was 66.71m/218ft 10½in. *(United Press)*

Barrier breakers
150ft: John Flanagan (USA) 45.94m/150ft 8½in 31 May 1897 Bayonne, NJ.
50m: John Flanagan (USA) 50.01m/164ft 1in 22 Jul 1899 Boston.
60m: József Csermák (Hun) 60.34m/197ft 11in 24 Jul 1952 Helsinki.
200ft: Sverre Strandli (Nor) 61.25m/200ft 11in 14 Sep 1952 Oslo.
70m: Hal Connolly (USA) 70.33m/230ft 9in 12 Aug 1960 Walnut.
250ft: Walter Schmidt (Ger) 76.40m/250ft 8in 4 Sep 1971 Lahr.
80m: Boris Zaichuk (USSR) 80.14m/262ft 11in 9 Jul 1978 Moscow.

OTHER THROWING EVENTS
Best authentic performances for:
56lb weight over a bar: 5.18m/17ft Bishop Dolegiewicz (Can) 19 Aug 1980 Great Gorge, New Jersey.
35lb weight: 23.46m/76ft 11¾in Yuriy Syedikh (USSR) 10 Mar 1979 Montreal (indoors).
Scots hammer: 46.08m/151ft 2in Willie Anderson 26 Jul 1969 Lochearnhead.

JAVELIN
The most world records at the javelin and the equal most at any event is ten by Matti Järvinen of Finland. Järvinen, a member of the greatest athletics family (see p. 252), set his first record at Viipuri on 8 Aug 1930 with 71.57m/234ft 9in. Three more records followed that year, another in 1932, three in 1933, one in 1934 before culminating in 77.23m/253ft 4in in Helsinki on 18 Jun 1936. Two years later Järvinen was beaten by his compatriot Yrjö Nikkanen, when the latter took the record at 77.87m/255ft 5in and again when Nikkanen improved to 78.70m/258ft 2in. Järvinen won the Olympic title in 1932 (with five throws better than the runner-up) and European titles in 1934 and 1938. Nikkanen was second in the 1936 Olympics and in the 1938 and 1946 European Championships.

The greatest percentage improvement in a world record in the career of one man is the 40.04% by which Erik Lemming (Swe) took the world javelin record from 44.50m/146ft 0in to 62.32m/204ft 5in between 1899 to 1912. The latter was the first javelin record ratified by the IAAF. In all Lemming improved the world best at least nine times, though interspersed with these were improvements by other throwers.

The greatest single improvement in the IAAF

record is 4.70m/15ft 1in by Terje Pedersen (Nor), when he improved his own record of 87.12m/285ft 10in set at Oslo on 1 Jul 1964 to 91.72m/300ft 11in again at Oslo on 2 Sep 1964.

The most javelin world records have been set with one mighty throw in a series of much lesser throws. The only occasion when anyone has set two records in one competition was at Modesto, Cal. on 21 May 1955 when Franklin 'Bud' Held (USA) first threw 81.29m/266ft 8½in to equal the unofficial best thrown by Bill Miller (USA) the previous year, and then 81.75m/268ft 2in. Held devised a new type of aerodynamic javelin, though this was banned for the 1960 Olympics.

Barrier breakers
50m: Erik Lemming (Swe) 50.44m/165ft 6in Jönköping 1902.
60m: Mór Kóczán (Hun) 60.64m/198ft 11in Budapest 26 Oct 1911.
200ft: Juho Saaristo (Fin) 61.45m/201ft 7in Helsinki 25 May 1912.
70m: Erik Lundqvist (Swe) 71.01m/232ft 11in Stockholm 15 Aug 1928.
250ft: Matti Järvinen (Fin) 76.66m/251ft 6in Turin 7 Sep 1934.
80m: Franklin 'Bud' Held (USA) 80.41m/263ft 10in Pasadena 8 Aug 1953.
90m and 300ft: Terje Pedersen (Nor) 91.72m/300ft 11in Oslo 2 Sep 1964.

The current world record is 96.72m/317ft 4in by Ferenc Paragi (Hun) at Tata on 24 Apr 1980.

DECATHLON
The ten events of the decathlon are: 100m, long jump, shot, high jump and 400m on the first day and 100m hurdles, discus, pole vault, javelin and 1500m on the second day.

The first major decathlon with these events was staged at the 1912 Olympic Games in Stockholm and a scoring table was used based on the current Olympic records. Earlier all-round competitions were held in Ireland in the mid-19th century and the first all-round championship was that of the AAU in 1884, when the events were: 100y, SP, HJ, 880y walk, HT, PV, 120yh, 56lb weight, LJ and 1 mile, all on one day. Such an event was included in the 1904 Olympic Games. The first decathlon in Sweden was held at Malmö in 1902.

Scoring tables
The 1912 tables were modified in 1920. These

Matti Jarvinen set ten world javelin records in the 1930s. He won 15 of his 19 international appearances for Finland, including an Olympic and two European titles.

tables were replaced in 1936 by new ones devised by the Finns, until these were 'blown' by improving performances, and replaced by Swedish devised tables introduced in 1950 and modified slightly in 1952. The next set of tables was introduced in 1964 and revised in the 1970s to cater for 1/100th sec timing. As with all tables which seek to evaluate performances, the passage of time produces anomalies as different events progress at varying speeds with the introduction of new techniques, and in 1981 new tables were first accepted and then deferred by the IAAF. All the performances listed in this section have been scored with the 1964 tables, except where stated.

The greatest number of IAAF decathlon world records is three each by Paavo Yrjölä (Fin) in 1926–8, Rafer Johnson (USA) in 1955–60 and Bruce Jenner (USA) in 1975–6, but Yrjölä had an additional unratified mark in 1930.

The greatest improvement in the best mark was by Jim Thorpe (USA) at the 1912 Olympic Games. Thorpe later lost his gold medal and his performance was not ratified, see p. 105, but his total was not bettered for 15 years. On the 1964

Above: Lasse Virén (301) wins his fourth Olympic gold medal with the 1976 5000m, from Dick Quax (691), Klaus-Peter Hildenbrand (420) and Rod Dixon (689). Brendan Foster, 2nd from left, was fifth, and Ian Stewart (380) seventh.

Left: Heide Schüller is the only woman to have taken the Olympic oath, which she did in 1972, on behalf of all competitors. She was fifth at the long jump at those Games in Munich.

Above: Dietmar Mögenburg, 2.01m/6ft 7in tall, set a world record high jump in 1980 at the age of 18.

Viktor Saneyev, winner of three Olympic, four European and eight Soviet titles outdoors as well as six European indoor titles, at the triple jump.

Left: Alberto Salazar's world best for the marathon, 2:08:13, displayed on the clock as he wins at New York in 1981.

tables he scored 6756 points, compared to the previous best of 5792 by Hugo Wieslander (Swe), 6161 by Wieslander in second place and the first official IAAF record of 6270 by Aleksandr Klumberg (Estonia) in 1922. On the 1912 tables Thorpe's score was 8412.955 and Wieslander's 7724.495.

The highest ever decathlon score on the tables then in use is 9121 by Yang Chuan-kwang of Taiwan at Walnut, Cal. on 27/28 Apr 1963 on the 1952 tables. His pole vault of 4.84m/15ft 10½in was 2cm higher than the maximum height, worth 1515 points, catered for by those tables. On the 1964 tables his score is 8089. The curiosity of having different scoring tables is shown by comparing Yang's performance with the two preceding world records: Rafer Johnson (USA) (in 1960) 8683 (1952 tables) to 8063 (1964 tables), Phil Mulkey (USA) (in 1961) 8709 to 8155, Yang 9121 to 8089.

On the 1964 tables the first to exceed 7000 was Hans-Heinrich Sievert (Ger) 7003 Cologne 12/13 Aug 1933. Johnson (above) was the first to exceed 8000 at Eugene, Oregon on 8/9 Jul 1960. The first man to exceed 8500 points was Bruce Jenner (USA) with 8524 in 1975, followed by 8538 and 8617 in 1976. There were further improvements in 1980 from Daley Thompson (GB) 8622 and Guido Kratschmer (Ger) 8649.

Daley Thompson did his first four decathlons at the same venue, Cwmbran in South Wales. His first was 6685 on 28/29 Jun 1975, improving that year to 7008 and 7100 and then to 7684 to win the 1976 AAA Championships on 22/23 May 1976. Since then he has not taken part in a decathlon in Britain! Rather, all 14 from then to the end of 1981 have been overseas, including wins at the European Junior Championships and at Commonwealth and Olympic Games and a European silver medal.

The best ever first day score is 4557 (hand timed) by Joachim Kirst on 8 Aug 1968 in an unfinished decathlon at the GDR championships. Kirst also scored 4549 and 4530 in 1969. Daley Thompson (GB) has the highest first day scores with automatic timing: 4550 (with wind assistance) at Edmonton on 7 Aug 1978 and 4542 at Moscow on 25 Jul 1980.

The best ever second day score is 4320 (auto) by Bruce Jenner (USA) at Montreal on 30 Jul 1976 in the Olympic Games (8617 total), and 4341 (hand timed) in the US Olympic Trials at Eugene, Oregon on 25 Jun 1976.

Bill Toomey during his world best pentathlon at Crystal Palace in 1969. He ended that year with a world record 8417 decathlon. *(A. Huxtable)*

The first man to score over 4000 points on each day was Kurt Bendlin (Ger). His world record 8319 at Heidelberg on 13/14 May 1967 was 4214 on the first day and 4105 on the second.

A fiendish decathlon was devised by Dave Thoreson (USA), whereby all ten events had to be started within half-an-hour. Thoreson was the first to exceed 6000 points and Jürgen Hingsen (Ger) the first to exceed 7000 points, but the record is now 7243 by Jens Schulze (Ger) at Arnsberg on 7 Jul 1981.

The most decathlons completed in a career is 77 out of 79 started by Rex Harvey (USA) from 1965 to 1980. Harvey, formerly a Captain in the US Air Force, totalled 535,472 points in those completed decathlons for an average score of 6954 and a best ever of 7634 in 1979.

PENTATHLON (LJ, JT, 200m, DT, 1500m)
The best ever score is 4123 points by Bill Toomey (USA) on 16 Aug 1969 at the Crystal Palace, London. Kurt Bendlin (Ger) was the first over 4000 points with 4016 at Krefeld on 31 Jul 1965.

MEN'S RELAYS
The first relay race is thought to have been

staged at Berkeley, Cal. on 17 Nov 1883, a four-man, two mile inter-class race at the University of California. The first relay race using a baton was held in 1893 at the University of Pennsylvania and the first noteworthy performance was made that year by the University team with a 3:25.2 for 4 × 440y.

The first major relays meeting was the inaugural Pennsylvania Relay Carnival in 1895. The famous 'Penn Relays' have been held annually ever since.

The first relay race in Britain was held on 14 Sep 1895 at Stamford Bridge. Five three-man teams contested 2 miles (¼M, ¾M, 1M). the winning team being Finchley Harriers.

4 × 100m (and 4 × 110y)
Sixteen of the 26 IAAF world 4 × 100m records have been set at the Olympic Games. The imperial distance of 4 × 110y was dropped from the record lists in 1976, with the final mark 38.6sec by the University of Southern California (USC) team of Earl McCullouch, Fred Kuller, O. J. Simpson and Lennox Miller at Provo, Utah on 17 Jun 1967. This time was also a record for the slightly shorter event of 4 × 100m.

The first sub 40sec time was the 39.8 set by the US Olympic team in Berlin on 9 Aug 1936 and the record now stands at 38.03 to the credit of the US World Cup team in 1977 (see p. 116). American teams have set 15 IAAF records at 4 × 100m and 20 out of 22 at 4 × 110y.

Frank Wykoff (USA) ran on a record three world records for US Olympic teams – the first leg in 1928 (41.0), anchor leg in both 1932 (40.0) and 1936 (39.8). He also ran on the team that set an unratified 40.6 in the 1932 Olympic semi finals. Martin Lauer (Ger) also ran in the three German teams that equalled the record at 39.5 in 1958 and 1960.

4 × 200m (and 4 × 220y)
The fastest times at both 4 × 200m and 4 × 220y have not been able to be ratified due to the current IAAF rule specifying that relay records can only be set by teams comprising athletes from one nation. The 4 × 200m best is 1:20:23 by the Tobias Striders team at Tempe, Arizona on 27 May 1978.

The Tobias team, all graduates of the University of Southern California (USC) was Guy Abrahams (Pan), Mike Simmons (USA), Don Quarrie (Jam) and James Gilkes (Guy). In second place the current USC team, with all-American line-up of Joel Andrews, James Sanford, Billy Mullins and Clancy Edwards got the world record at 1:20.26. The fastest 4 × 220y time was 1:20.7, again by USC, at Fresno on 13 May 1972 by three Americans, Edesel Garrison, Leon Brown and Willie Deckard and Jamaican, Don Quarrie.

Bobby Morrow is the only man to have run on three records at this distance, once for the USA and twice for Abilene Christian College in 1956–8.

4 × 400m (and 4 × 440y)
As with the 4 × 100m, Olympic gold medal teams have dominated the record lists, with eight of the 12 4 × 400m records culminating in 2:56.16 by the USA in 1968.

The first sub 3 minute time was run by the US national team of Bob Frey, Lee Evans, Tommie Smith and Theron Lewis at Los Angeles on 24 Jul 1966.

The fastest ever 400m relay leg is 43.2sec by Ron Freeman (USA) at the 1968 Olympic Games (see p. 96), but an intrinsically faster time (by about 0.1sec) was run over 440y by Maurice Peoples (USA) on 9 Jun 1973 at the NCAA championships at Baton Rouge, Louisiana. Peoples had earlier in the day won the individual 440y title with 45.0. The 4 × 440y title was won by UCLA with 3:04.3, but behind them the Arizona State team were lying seventh after three legs before Peoples took over. He stormed through the field, running an amazing leg with very level 220y splits of 21.5 and 21.9 to be timed in 43.4 to take his team to third and barely miss second place.

4 × 800m
The world record is 7:08.1 by the USSR at Podolsk on 13 Aug 1978.

The greatest ever improvement on the record was 10.6sec by a Belgian team anchored by Roger Moens (1:46.3) that ran 7:15.8 at Brussels on 8 Aug 1956. This was also the first occasion on which a team averaged less than 1:50 per runner. This time remained a world record for ten years five days until the West German team of Manfred Kinder (1:46.9), Walter Adams (1:47.5), Dieter Bogatzki (1:47.9) and Franz-Josef Kemper (1:46.2) ran 7:08.5 at Wiesbaden. However, a few weeks earlier, on 22 Jun 1966 the British squad of Graeme Grant (1:49.5), Mike Varah (1:48.9), Chris Carter (1:48.0) and John Boulter (1:48.2) had run the longer distance of 4 × 880y in 7:14.6 but this was not put forward for ratification as the British coach John Le Masurier called out Boulter's first lap as 52sec instead of the actual over-fast 49.8 and this was considered to have assisted Boulter contrary to IAAF rules. In second place the USSR ran 7:16.0 and their time was ratified as the world record. This was the second occasion that a team finishing second has set a world record at the event, for the USA did this with 7:19.4 at the White City, London on 14 Sep 1960 when they were beaten by a Commonwealth team. The latter ran 7:18.0. Peter Snell running the last leg in 1:44.8, but this couldn't count as the team was comprised of athletes from four countries.

4 × 1500m
The world record is 14.38.8, an average of 3:39.7 per leg, by West Germany at Cologne on 17 Aug 1977 at half-time in a football match between FC Köln and Werder Bremen. The team of Thomas Wessinghage (3:38.8), Harald Hudak (3:39.1), Michael Lederer (3:43.0) and Karl Fleschen (3:36.3) ran virtually solo as the runners-up finished in 15:46.2.

Both István Rózavölgyi (Hun) and Sándor Iharos (Hun) ran in three records, the final two, culminating in 15:14.8 in 1955, for the last club team to hold the record, Budapest Honved Sport Egyesulet.

4 × 1 MILE
The 'final' record for the event before it was dropped from the IAAF recognised list was 16:02.8 by New Zealand in Auckland on 3 Feb 1972.

Mass relays
100 × 1 mile: 7 hours 53min 52.1sec. Baltimore Road Runners Club at Towson, Maryland on 17 May 1981.

The longest relay ever run was one of 9679.645km/6014.65 miles at Trondheim, Norway 21 Oct to 23 Nov 1977 by 1607 students and teachers.

WALKING
The IAAF currently ratify records made at just four men's track events.

No walker has ever set more than two official world records at any of these: 20, 30 and 50km

Maurice Peoples ran the fastest ever 440y relay leg in 1973. He also won one NCAA and two AAU individual titles.   *(Arizona State University)*

and 2 hours, but Vladimir Golubnichiy takes pride of place as he set two official and one unofficial at 20km, 1:30:02.8 in 1955, 1:27:05 and 1:26:13.2 (not put forward for ratification) in 1959.

The most records set at these four events is five by Peter Frenkel (GDR): two at 20km, two at 2 hours and one at 30km between 1970 and 1974.

The biggest margins of improvement have been:
20km 2:08.4 Janis Dalins (Latvia) 1:34:26.0 1 Jun 1933.
20 hour 918m José Marin (Spa) 28165m 8 Apr 1979.
30km 6:44.6 Hermann Schmidt (Ger) 2:30:33.6 27 Apr 1941.
50km 10:44.5 Raul Gonzalez (Mex) 3:41:39.0 25 May 1979.

Barrier breakers
20km: The first man under 1 hour 30min on the track was Leonid Spirin (USSR) with 1:28:45.2 on 13 Jun 1956 at Kiev. This performance preceded the first sub 1:30 road walk by six weeks as Josef Dolezal (Cze) clocked 1:29:59.8 on 25 Jul 1956 at Prague.
50km: The first man under 4 hours on the road was Gennadiy Agapov (USSR) with 3:55:36 on 17 Oct 1965 at Alma Ata. The first track performance was by Bernd Kannenberg (Ger) with 3:56:51.4 on 16 Nov 1975 at Nerviano, Italy.

Werner Hardmo (Swe) had perhaps the greatest domination of 'sprint' walking world records, when those were still recognised. His tally of official records was: 3000m 5, 2 mile 6, 5000m 2, 10000m 3, 7 mile 4, 1 hour 1, 10 mile 1, for 22 in all. He was the first man to walk 3000m in less than 12 minutes with 11:59.8 on 22 Aug 1944 and had a best ever of 11:51.8 at Malmö on 1 Sep 1945, a time that was not bettered officially until Paul Nihill (GB) recorded 11:51.2 on 5 Jun 1971. Nihill was also the first to better Hardmo's 5000m best of 20:26.8 in 1945. Hardmo's performances seemed well ahead of their time, but it should be noted that he was disqualified in his major international appearances, at 10000m in both the 1946 European and 1948 Olympic races.

Best recorded performances

Track

1500m	5:25.9	Erling Andersen (Nor) 26 Aug 1980 Lisleby, Nor.
1 mile	5:49.9	Erling Andersen (Nor) 26 Aug 1980 Lisleby, Nor.
3000m	10:54.6i	Carlo Mattioli (Ital) 6 Feb 1980 Milan, Ita.
5000m	18:51.2	Jozef Pribilinec (Cze) 5 May 1981 Bankska Bystrica, Cze.
10km	38:31.4i	Werner Heyer (GDR) 12 Jan 1980 Berlin, Ger.
15km	59:33.0	Daniel Bautista (Mex) 26 Mar 1980 Monterrey, Mex.
20km	1:20:06.8	Daniel Bautista (Mex) 17 Oct 1979 Montreal, Can.
30km	2:06:54	Ralf Kowalsky (GDR) 28 Mar 1982 East Berlin.
50km	3:41:38.4	Raul Gonzalez (Mex) 25 May 1979 Fana, Nor.
1 hour	15121m	Daniel Bautista (Mex) 26 Mar 1980 Monterrey, Mex.
2 hour	28338m	Ralf Kowalsky (GDR) 28 Mar 1982 East Berlin.
10 mile	1:05:07.6	Domingo Colin (Mex) 26 May 1979 Fana, Nor.
24 hour	219,500m	Derek Harrison (GB) 20/21 May 1978 Rouen, Fra.

Road

10km	39:37.0	Vladimir Yakovlyev (USSR) 4 May 1980 Softeland.
15km	58:52.0	Daniel Bautista (Mex) 29 Sep 1979 Eschborn, Ger.
20km	1:18:49.0	Daniel Bautista (Mex) 29 Sep 1979 Eschborn, Ger.
30km	2:03:06	Daniel Bautista (Mex) 27 Apr 1980 Therkassy, USSR.
20 mile	2:16:48	Willi Sawall (Aus) 15 Jun 1980 Canberra, Aus.
50km	3:37:36	Yevgeniy Ivchenko (USSR) and Boris Yakovlyev (USSR) 23 May 1980 Moscow, USSR.
100km	9:15:58	Christoph Höhne (GDR) 29 Oct 1967 Lugano, Swi.

The amazing times recorded by Ivchenko and Yakovlyev at 50km are made the more so by the curious coincidence of their arriving in the Lenin Stadium during half-time in the USSR v France soccer match to finish the race.

Daniel Bautista set three world bests on the road, including the first sub-1:20 time and two world track records at 20km.
(G. Herringshaw)

Women's World Records

100 YARDS

This event was dropped from the IAAF schedule in 1976, when the record stood at the classic figure of 10.0sec recorded by Chi Cheng (Tai) at Portland, Oregon on 13 Jun 1970. The automatic timing showed 10.10. She went on to set a world 220y record of 22.7 just 45 minutes later. Chi had three times previously equalled the old record of 10.3, which had first been run officially by Marlene Mathews Willard (Aus) in 1958, although Mathews had run a wind assisted 10.1 in 1957.

The most IAAF records set were four, by Marjorie Jackson (Aus) two at 10.8 in 1950, then 10.7 and finally 10.4 at Sydney on 8 Mar 1952. Jackson, the 'Lithgow Flash', also ran a wind assisted 10.3 in 1953.

Barrier breakers

12sec: Mary Lines (GB) 11.8 Paris 30 Oct 1921
11sec: Stanislawa Walasiewicz (Pol/USA) 10.8 Philadelphia 30 May 1930. This time and other sub 11sec times by Walasiewicz and Helen Stephens (USA) in the 1930s were not accepted by the IAAF, so the first 'official' sub-11 time was run by Fanny Blankers-Koen (Hol), 10.8 at Amsterdam on 18 May 1944. Stephens was reported to have run 100y in 10.4 at Toronto on 2 Sep 1935 in a handicap race.

100 Metres

Stanislawa Walasiewicz, or Stella Walsh as she was known in the USA, has dominated the record books for 100m. In all she broke or equalled the world record 11 times, with four of these recognised by the FSFI and two by the IAAF. The latter two were the first on the IAAF list – 11.7 at Warsaw on 26 Aug 1934 and 11.6 at Berlin on 1 Aug 1937. After Tollien Schuurman (Hol) had broken 12sec for the first time ever at Haarlem on 5 Jun 1932 with 11.9, Walasiewicz set her first records by equalling that time in each round of the 1932 Olympic Games in Los Angeles. On 24 Jun 1945 in Cleveland, Ohio she was credited with a 100m in 11.2. That time was never accepted. As she said 'At the time officials thought it was impossible for anyone to run that fast. Now the years are proving I was merely ahead of my time'.

The first 11.2sec to be ratified by the IAAF was run by Wilma Rudolph (USA) in Stuttgart on 19 Jul 1961. A year earlier, however, Rudolph had run a barely wind aided 11.0 (11.18 auto) in the Olympic final in Rome.

Helen Stephens from Missouri, Olympic 100m and sprint relay gold medallist in 1936, who was undefeated in her sprint career.

Stanislawa Walasiewicz (Stella Walsh) set more than 20 world records (five recognised by the IAAF) and won 41 AAU and 16 Polish titles.

The first sub 11sec time was run by Renate Stecher (GDR) with 10.9 at Ostrava on 7 Jun 1973 after four times equalling the record at 11.0 from 1970 to 1972. Although that was the first sub 11 sec world record, the vagaries of hand timing make comparisons with accurate automatic timings difficult. In 1972 at the Olympic final in Munich, Stecher won the 100m in 11.07, but had been hand timed in 10.8. She was recorded in exactly the same times at Dresden on 20 Jul 1973, but this time the 10.8 hand timing was official (the last hand timed world record and the 11.07 automatic was not.

After the West Germans Inge Helten (11.04) and Annegret Richter (11.01) had improved Stecher's best, Marlies Oelsner (GDR) ran the first time in sub 11sec, automatically timed, 10.88 at Dresden on 1 Jul 1977. Oelsner, now Frau Göhr, ran four more sub 11sec automatic timings in 1978–80 and the fastest ever time, 10.79 aided by an overstrong wind of 3.3m/s to win the GDR title in 1980.

200 METRES (AND 220 YARDS*)
The biggest improvements in the world 200m record came in pre-IAAF record days. Eileen Edwards (GB) made five improvements, first breaking the record, which stood at 26.8* to the credit of Mary Lines (GB) in 1922, with 26.2* at London on 28 Jun 1924. She ran the 220y in 25.8 in London on 9 Sep 1926, for the first sub 26sec time, and then made another major improvement, to 25.4, at Berlin on 12 Jun 1927. The 200m was not added to the World Games programme until 1930, but Edwards won the 250m title in 1926 with a world record 33.4. Vera Palmer (GB) came second in 34.6; as Vera Searle she was the honorary secretary of the WAAA 1927–31 and their first woman chairman 1973–81.

Edwards' 25.4 was smashed by 0.7sec in Tokyo on 19 May 1929 by the great Japanese all-rounder Kinue Hitomi. Her 24.7 was not only the first sub 25sec time, but she also registered the greatest improvement in the record. However three years later Stanislawa Walasiewicz took 0.6 off the time with 24.1 in Chicago on 18 Aug 1932, before improving further to 23.8 in 1934 and 23.6 in Warsaw on 15 Aug 1935, for the first record ratified at the event by the IAAF. This stood unbroken for 16 years 345 days. It should be noted, however, that Helen Stephens (USA) was reputed to have run the 220y on a straight track in 23.2 at Toronto on 2 Sep 1935. The timing on that occasion was said to be questionable.

The first sub 23sec time was 22.9 by Wilma Rudolph (USA) at Corpus Christi, Texas on 9 Jul 1960.

The first sub 22sec time was 21.71 by Marita Koch (GDR) at Karl Marx Stadt on 10 Jun 1979. Koch succeeded Irena Szewinska (22.21 in 1974) as world record holder with 22.06 in 1978 and whittled that down to 22.02 in 1979 before her big improvement. Koch has concentrated on the 400m in most major championships, but nonetheless at the end of 1979 had eight of the nine fastest 200m times ever recorded.

400 METRES
This event was added to the official IAAF lists in 1957. No times recorded before that year were accepted and the first times ratified, 57.0sec (for 440y) by Marlene Mathews (Aus) and Marise Chamberlain (NZ) were much slower than the best ever, 53.9 by Maria Itkina (USSR) in 1955. Itkina eventually made the record lists with the IAAF's fifth record, at 54.0, before she beat her old best for the first time with 53.6, on 6 Jul 1957.

The most world records at 400m is five by Marita Koch (GDR). Starting with 49.19sec when she won her first 400m of the year, the GDR title at Leipzig on 2 Jul 1978, she improved to 49.03 at Potsdam and to 48.94 when she won the 1978 European title at Prague. In 1979 she ran 48.89, again a record in her first 400m race of the year, on 29 July at Potsdam and a week later improved again to 48.60 at Turin in the European Cup final. Unbeaten at 400m, from her loss to Irina Szewinska (Pol), her predecessor as world record holder, in the 1977 World Cup (qv) until 1981, Koch had run the eight fastest times ever by the end of 1980. Shin Geum Dan (NK) also set five world bests, but only one, 51.9 in 1962 was accepted by the IAAF. That time was a 1.1sec improvement on two unofficial times of 53.0 that she had run. After North Korea had ceased to be a member of the IAAF, she improved again to 51.4 in 1963 and 51.2 in 1964.

Barrier Breakers:
70sec: Lidia Charushnikova (USSR) 65.0 Viatka 12 Jul 1921.
65sec: Mary Lines (GB) 64.4 (440y) London 18 Jul 1922.
60sec: Kinue Hitomi (Jap) 59.0 Miyoshino 5 Aug 1928.
55sec: Zinaida Safronova (USSR) 54.8 Leningrad 21 Jul 1955.

Nadyezhda Olizaryenko, the fifth woman to win the Olympic 800m title with a world record. She bettered her 1:54.85 set when winning the Soviet title five weeks earlier. *(G. Herringshaw)*

50sec: Irina Szewinska (Pol) 49.9 Warsaw 22 Jun 1974.
This was only the second 400m of Szewinska's career. She started with 52.0 at Warsaw on 23 Sep 1973, before this 1.1sec improvement in the world record.

800 METRES
The most world records for 800m have been set by Nina Otkalenko (née Pletnyova) (USSR) with five IAAF records and another two unofficial ones. She took the record from 2:12.0 in 1951 to 2:05.0 in Zagreb on 24 Sep 1955. Otkalenko also set world bests at 400m and 1500m and won the European 800m title in 1954, but was unable to add an Olympic title, as the event, after 1928 was not included again on the Olympic programme until 1960.

Barrier breakers
2:30 Mary Lines (GB) 2:26.6 (880y) London 30 Aug 1922.
2:25 Gladys Lane (GB) 2:24.8 (880y) London 25 Jul 1925.
2:20 Lina Radke (Ger) 2:19.6 Brieg, Berlin 1 Jul 1928. Radke won the first Olympic title with a 2:16.8 world record on 2 Aug 1928.
2:15 Zdena Koubkova (Cze) 2:12.4 London 11 Aug 1934 when winning the World Games title. However it was later decreed that Koubkova should not have been allowed to compete in women's competitions, so credit should go to runner-up Marta Wretman (Swe) 2:13.8. Gladys Lunn was third at 2:14.2.
2:10 Nina Pletnyova (USSR) 2:08.5 Kiev 15 Jun 1952

2:05 Lyudmila Shevtsova (USSR) 2:04.3 Moscow 3 Jul 1960.
2:00 Shin Geum Dan (NK) 1:59.1 Djakarta 12 Nov 1963. On the previous day she ran an Asian record 23.5 for 200m, and on the day following the 800m ran a world record 51.4 for 400m. This meeting of the Games of the New Emerging Forces (GANEFO) was not recognised by the IAAF, and neither these times nor her 1:58.0 at Pyongyang on 30 Aug 1964 was ratified. The first official sub-2:00 time was the 1:58.45 run by Hildegard Falck (Ger) at Stuttgart on 11 Jul 1971.
1:55 Tatyana Kazankina (USSR) 1:54.94 Montreal 26 Jul 1976 in the Olympic final. The current record was set in the 1980 Olympic final – 1:53.43 by Nadyezhda Olizarenko (USSR).

1500 METRES
The first official record was 4:17.3 by Anne Smith (GB), en route to her mile record on 3 Jun 1967.

The first major international championship over this distance was the 1969 European, but the first national championship dated right back to 1922 in the Soviet Union, although it was not until 1936 that another Soviet 1500m championship was staged.

The most world records is four by Lyudmila Bragina, all in 1972, first a 4:06.9 in Moscow and then her three at the Olympic Games in Munich. Her final time of 4:01.38 remained the record until Tatyana Kazankina (USSR) be-

Lyudmila Bragina at Munich in 1972 when she smashed the world 1500m record in each round. She also won eight USSR titles. *(E. D. Lacey)*

came the first woman to run the distance under four minutes, with 3:56.0 at Podolsk on 28 Jun 1976. In that race Raissa Katyukova was also under the barrier at 3:59.8 and Bragina third in 4:02.6.

Kazankina smashed her own record at the Weltklasse meeting in Zurich on 13 Aug 1980 with a stunning 3:52.47 twelve days after she had retained her Olympic title. Tracking European 800m champion Tatyana Providokhina for the first 800m, she passed 400m in 58.6, 800m in 2:04.7 and 1200m in 3:07.1. Way behind in second place, Mary Decker set an American record of 3:59.43. Kazankina's time was faster than Paavo Nurmi's 3:52.6 world record of 1924. The 56-year gap between men's and women's records is the shortest for any track or field event, although Grete Waitz's 2:25:41.8 marathon in 1980 is faster than any man ran up to 1947.

Other barrier breakers
5:00 Yevdokiya Vasilieva (USSR) 4:47.2 Moscow 30 Jul 1936
4:30 Diane Leather (GB) 4:25.0 London 21 Sep 1955.

1 MILE
Now the only imperial distance left on the IAAF schedule, the first mile record recognised was Anne Smith (GB) 4:37.0 at Chiswick, London on 3 Jun 1967.

The only woman to have set two IAAF records is Natalia Marasescu (Rom) with 4:23.8 in 1977 and 4:22.1 in 1979, but the greatest number of improvements overall is five by Diane Leather in 1953–55. She ran the first ever sub five minute mile by a woman with 4:59.6 on 29 May 1954 at Birmingham, just 23 days after Roger Bannister ran the first sub four minute mile. She reduced this to 4:45.0 in 1955.

The biggest improvement in the IAAF record and the first official sub 4:30 run was by Paola Cacchi (Ita) who with 4:29.5 at Viareggio on 8 Aug 1973 took 5.8sec off Ellen Tittel's 1971 mark.

The first sub 4:20 time was run by Mary Decker (USA) with 4:17.55 indoors on the oversized track at Houston on 16 Feb 1980. The previous month she had set an outdoor world record of 4:21.68 in Auckland. That record was improved in 1981 to 4:20.89 by Lyudmila Veselkova (USSR).

Diane Leather wins the WAAA 880y title in a world record 2:09.0. Three weeks earlier she had run the first sub-5min mile by a woman.
(H. W. Neale)

3000 METRES
This event was added to the international programme in 1974 when the first IAAF record was set at 8:52.8 by Lyudmila Bragina (USSR). After Grete Waitz (Nor) had run 8:46.6 in 1975 and 8:45.4 in 1976, Bragina returned to take an amazing 18.2sec off the record with 8:27.12 for USSR v USA at College Park, Maryland on 7 Aug 1976.

The most world records is four unofficial ones set by Paola Cacchi (née Pigni) (Ita) between 1969 and 1972.

The first national 3000m championship was that of England with the 1968 WAAA race, won in 10:06.4 by Carol Firth (later Gould).

5000 AND 10000 METRES
The IAAF added these two long distance events to the list of women's world records from 1 Jan 1982.
The best marks ever recorded at that date had been set by Loa Olafsson (Den) in 1978 when she ran the 5000m in 15:08.8 and the 10000m in 31:45.35, but as she had run against men in both races these could not be ratified as world records, so the inaugural marks were:
5000m 15:14:51 Paula Fudge (GB) 13 Sep 1981 Knarvik
10000m 32:17.19 Yelena Sipatova (USSR) 19 Sep 1981 Moscow
Ann Audain (NZ) improved the 5000m record to 15:13.22 at Auckland on 17 Mar 1982.

Other track bests
15000m 49:44.0 Silvana Cruciata (Ita) 4 May 1981 Rome
1 hour 18084m Silvana Cruciata (Ita) 4 May 1981 Rome
100 miles 15:44:27 Marcy Schwam (USA) 1/2 Nov 1980 Greenwich, Ct.
24 hours 203,457m/126M 749y Sue Medaglia (USA) 26/27 Sep 1981 Greenwich, Ct.

Best times ever recorded in road races
All road times must be assessed carefully (see note on page 41), these are the best times recorded, but are not official records.
10km 30:59.8 Grete Waitz (Nor) 1 Jun 1980 at New York in the L'Eggs Mini-Marathon. She set the previous record of 31:15.4 in the same race in 1979. On each occasion Waitz beat a top-class field, finishing over two minutes ahead of the runner-up. In 1981 she completed a hat-trick of wins, but slowed in hot and humid conditions to 32:43.
15km 48:01 Grete Waitz (Nor) Feb 1980
10 mile 53:05 Grete Waitz (Nor) 22 Sep 1979 Lynchburg, Va.
20km 1:06:52 Cathie Twomey (USA) 7 Mar 1982 Nagoya, Japan
Half-marathon 1:09:19 Grete Waitz (Nor) 4 Apr 1982 Milan
25km 1:26:21 Joan Benoit (USA) 9 May 1981 Grand Rapids, Mich.
30km 1:44:25 Patti Catalano (USA) 15 Feb 1981 Ohme, Japan
20 mile 1:51:23 Grete Waitz (Nor) 26 Oct 1980 New York
50km 3:26:47 Janice Arenz (USA) 16 Mar 1980 Brooklyn Park
40 mile 5:03:49 Lesley Watson (GB) 30 Sep 1979 Westminster-Bolney (for 40 mile 83ly)
50 mile 6:02:37 Lesley Watson (GB) 3 May

1981 Lake Waramaug, Ct.
100km 7:27:22 Chantal Langlace (Fra) 6 Sep 1980 Amiens

WOMEN'S WORLD BEST PERFORMANCES AT OTHER DISTANCES
((i) = indoors)
50 yards hand timed: 5.5(i) Iris Davis (USA) 1973 and Alice Annum (Gha) 1975 auto: 5.64(i) Evelyn Ashford (USA) 1982.
50 metres hand timed: 6.0(i) Barbara Ferrell (USA) 1968 and 1969; Renate Stecher (GDR) 1971 and Annie Alize (Fra) 1977 auto: 6.11(i) Marita Koch (GDR) 1980.
60 yards hand timed: 6.5(i) by five American girls, of whom the first was Wyomia Tyus in 1966 auto: 6.54(i) Evelyn Ashford (USA) 1982.
60 metres hand timed: 6.9 Alice Annum (Gha) 1975 and Marlies Göhr (GDR) 1979. auto: 7.10(i) Marlies Göhr 1980 and Marita Koch (GDR) 1981.
This event was on the IAAF schedule until 1976. Most world records set were four by Stanislawa Walasiewicz (Pol) from her 7.6sec in 1929 to 7.3 in 1933, which was not bettered until Betty Cuthbert (Aus) ran 7.2 in 1960. At all events Cuthbert set 16 world records.
300 yards 32.63(i) Merlene Ottey (Jam) 1982
300 metres hand timed: 35.7 Irena Szewinska (Pol) 1975. auto: 35.83(i) Merlene Ottey (Jam) 1981
500 yards 1:03.3(i) Rosalyn Bryant (USA) 1977 and Janine MacGregor (GB) 1982
500 metres 1:09.9 Colette Besson (Fra) 1970
600 yards 1:17.38(i) Delisa Walton (USA) 1982
600 metres 1:23.9 (in 800m race) Anita Weiss (GDR) 1976
1000 yards 2:23.8(i) Mary Decker (USA), now married to marathon runner Ron Tabb, 1978
1000 metres 2:30.6 Tatyana Providokhina (USSR) 1978
2000 metres 5:33.5 Maricica Puica (Rom) 1979
2 miles 9:31.7 Jan Merrill (USA) 1979 in a race against men
50 yards hurdles hand timed: 6.2(i) Annelie Ehrhardt (GDR) 1975. auto: 6.20(i) Johanna Klier (GDR) 1978
50 metres hurdles hand timed: 6.6(i) Annelie Ehrhardt (GDR) 1972 auto: 6.74(i) Annelie Ehrhardt 1976 and Zofia Bielczyk (Pol) 1981.
60 yards hurdles hand timed: 7.3(i) Jane Frederick (USA) 1977, Deby LaPlante (USA) 1977 and Candy Young (USA) 1979. auto: 7.37(i) Stephanie Hightower (USA) 1982 and Candy Young (USA) 1982.

MARATHON

It is only in the past decade that marathon running by women has become widespread, following the pioneering efforts by some determined ladies, particularly in the USA, who had quite a struggle to break down prejudices against their participation. It was only as recently as 1975, that the WAAA permitted women to run long distance road races in Britain.

A Greek woman, Melopene, was reported to have run unofficially in the 1896 Olympic marathon, finishing in about 4½ hours, and Violet Piercy ran the Poly marathon course in 3:40:22 in 1926.

The first sub 3½ hour time: 3:27:45 Dale Greig (GB) Ryde, Isle of Wight 23 May 1964.

The first sub 3 hour time: 2:46:30 Adrienne Beames (Aus) Werribee 31 Aug 1971, closely followed by 2:55:22 by Beth Bonner (USA) in Central Park, New York on 19 Sep 1971.

The first championship marathon for women was that organised by the Road Runners Club of America on 27 Sep 1970, won by Sara Berman (USA) in 3:07:10. The first AAU title was won by Judy Ikenberry in 1974.

The first international race solely for women was held at Waldniel, Ger. on 22 Sep 1974, and organised by Dr Ernst Van Aaken, the notable coach. The winner was Liane Winter (Ger) in 2:50:31.4, a European best. There were 45 entries from 7 nations.

The first national marathon championship for women was that of the Federal Republic of Germany on 28 Oct 1973. The winner Christa Kofferschlager (Ger) (later Vahlensieck) (2:59:25.6) set world bests of 2:40:15.8 in 1975 and 2:34:47.5 in 1977.

Grete Waitz (née Andersen) (USA) has had a notable career as a track runner, winning European bronze medals at 1500m in 1974 and 3000m in 1978 and twice setting world records at 3000m. Yet good as it is this record scarcely begins to do her justice for she has been undoubtedly the greatest ever female long distance runner. She was unbeaten for 12 years in cross-country races and her first loss on the road occurred on 10 Mar 1981 when she was beaten by Maricica Puica.

Waitz made her marathon debut in the 1978 New York race. She finished 104th overall and her 2:32:30 was a women's world best. Since then her next three marathons have also been in the New York race. In 1979 she improved to 2:27:33, the first sub 2:30 woman's marathon and in 1980 made it three world bests in three races when her 2:25:42 placed her 74th overall. Second in 1980 was Patti Catalano (USA) in 2:29:34, the second sub 2:30.

In 1981 the New Zealander Allison Roe won both the major American marathons, first Boston in 2:26:46 and then New York in 2:25:29 for a new world best, as Waitz had to drop out due to injury halfway through the race.

The best time recorded for an 'out-and-back' course is 2:30:27 by Joyce Smith (GB) on 16 Nov 1980 in Tokyo.

The most prolific woman marathoner is Leslie Watson (GB). She ran her first, in 3:31:00 at the age of 30 in 1975 and to the end of 1981 had run 66 marathons as well as several races of longer distance such as the London to Brighton (86.1km/53½ miles) and setting world bests for 50 miles. Her best time is 2:45:40 in 1980. She was Scottish cross-country champion in 1966 and 1967.

Grete Waitz en route to a UK All-Comers 1 mile record at Gateshead.   *(G. Herringshaw)*

Avon International Marathon
First held at Atlanta, Georgia the 'Avon' has rapidly gained the status of an unofficial world championship for women.
The venues and winners have been:
1978 *Atlanta* Marty Cooksey (USA) 2:46:15;
1979 *Waldniel, Ger.* Joyce Smith (GB) 2:36:27;
1980 *London* Lorraine Moller (NZ) 2:35:11;
1981 *Ottawa* Nancy Conz (USA) 2:36:46.

80 METRES HURDLES
The standard women's hurdles distance was 80m, over seven flights of 2ft 6in hurdles from 1927 until replaced by the 100m over eight flights of 2ft 9in hurdles in 1969. From 1922 to 1927 the standard event had been 120y over ten flights of hurdles.

The 'final' record stood at 10.2sec to Vera Korsakova (USSR) at Riga on 16 Jun 1968. Korsakova had earlier that day equalled the record of 10.3, which had first been set by Irina Press in 1965. Press held the most IAAF 80m records at five (and one unratified mark), from 10.6 in 1960 to that 10.3.

The fastest ever on automatic timing was 10.39sec run by Maureen Caird (Aus) in winning the 1968 Olympic title.

The biggest ever improvement in the IAAF record was 0.3sec by Fanny Blankers-Koen (Hol), when she ran 11.0 at Amsterdam on 20 Jun 1948. Claudia Testoni (Ita) also took 0.3sec off the record with 11.3 at Garmisch-Partenkirchen on 23 Jul 1939, but she had an unratified 11.5 a week earlier.

Barrier breakers
12sec: Marjorie Clark (SA) 11.8 Pietermaritzburg 2 May 1931
11sec: Shirley Strickland (Aus) 10.9 Helsinki 24 Jul 1952.

100 METRES HURDLES
This event was added to the international programme in 1969, and the first ratified record was 13.3 run by Karin Balzer (GDR) and Teresa Sukniewicz (Pol) at the Kusocinski Memorial meeting, Warsaw on 20 June that year, although Pam Kilborn (Aus) had also run a 13.3 earlier.

Karin Balzer has the most records, with five from 13.3 to 13.0, then the first sub-13sec time, 12.9 at Berlin 5 Sep 1969, two times of 12.7 and finally a 12.6 at Berlin on 31 Jul 1971.

The current world record is 12.36sec by Grazyna Rabsztyn (Pol) on 13 Jun 1980 in Warsaw. The final hand time accepted was 12.3 by Annelie Ehrhardt (GDR) in 1973, but this was auto-timed as 12.68.

200 METRES HURDLES
Run over ten 2ft 6in hurdles, records at 200m hurdles were accepted only from 1969 to 1974. The 'final' record was 25.7sec by Pam Kilborn in Melbourne on 25 Nov 1971. Kilborn set four IAAF records at 200m hurdles out of eight in all.

400 METRES HURDLES
This event was first raced experimentally by women in 1971, Sandra Dyson (GB) winning at Bonn on 15 May in 61.1sec. Three years later it was added to the IAAF roster of events with Krystyna Kacperczyk (Pol) the first official record holder at 56.51.

The most world records set is three (unofficial) by Maria Sykora (Aut) in 1973 and two (official) by Kacperczyk, Tatyana Zelentsova (USSR) and Karin Rossley (GDR), current record holder at 54.28 in 1980.

The first major international race was in the 1977 European Cup, with Rossley the winner in 55.63, a world record for only her third race at this event. The first national championships were held in 1973 by England (WAAA), Poland, Romania, Scotland and USA.

HIGH JUMP
The greatest number of world records by an athlete at any event is the 14 high jump records of the 1.85m tall Romanian Iolanda Balas. Her first record was 1.75m/5 ft 8½ in as a 19-year-old in Bucharest on 14 Jul 1956. She lost that record to Mildred McDaniel (USA), when the latter won the 1956 Olympic title with 1.76m/5 ft 9¼ in with Balas fifth. Balas equalled the new record in 1957 only to lose it again to Cheng Feng-jung (Chi) who used a built-up shoe (see p. 53) to clear 1.77m/5 ft 9¾ in on 17 November. From 1958, though, it was all Balas with 12 successive improvements from 1.78m/5 ft 10 in on 7 Jun 1958 at Bucharest to 1.91m/6 ft 3¼ in on 16 Jul 1961 at Sofia. At that time the next best by a woman was 1.78m by Taisia Chenchik (USSR) in 1959.

The greatest domination by any athlete of any event in the history of athletics is by Iolanda Balas over the high jump. At the end of 1963 she had jumped 1.80m/5 ft 10¾ in in 72 competitions, yet it was not until 27 Sep 1964 that another woman, Michele Brown (Aus) jumped as high. On 1 Nov 1964 Brown became the second woman six-footer with a quarter of an inch to spare. By then Balas had 46 competitions at 6 ft or better. Balas was ranked number one in the world from 1958 until her retirement in 1966. She married her coach Ion Söter (Romanian men's record holder, 2.055m/6 ft 8¾ in in 1956) at the end of 1967. She won the 1960 and 1964 Olympic titles and 1958 and 1962 European titles. Her style was described as a cross between a scissors and the Eastern cut-off.

Balas's record stood for the longest time in the history of the event, 10 years 50 days, until Ilona Gusenbauer (Aut) cleared 1.92m/6 ft 3½ in in Vienna on 4 Sep 1971.

Barrier breakers
5ft: Phyllis Green (GB) 1.52m/5ft 0in London 11 Jul 1925.
1.60m: Marjorie Clark (SA) 1.60m/5ft 3in London 23 Jun 1928.
1.70m: Fanny Blankers-Koen (Hol) 1.71m/5ft 7¼in Amsterdam 30 May 1943. This was a 5cm improvement on the previous record, the best ever.
1.80m: Iolanda Balas (Rom) 1.80m/5ft 10¾in Cluj 22 Jun 1958.
6ft: Iolanda Balas (Rom) 1.83m/6ft 0in Bucharest 18 Oct 1958. This was the second of six successive records Balas set in Bucharest.
1.90m: Iolanda Balas (Rom) 1.90m/6ft 2¾in Budapest 8 Jul 1961.
2.00m: Rosemarie Ackermann (GDR) 2.00m/6ft 6¾in East Berlin 26 Aug 1977. This was her seventh and last world record. Ackermann was succeeded by her arch-rival Sara Simeoni (Ita) who cleared 2.01m/6ft 7in on her first attempt on 4 Aug 1978 at Brescia. Simeoni and Ackermann had several classic battles, most

notably at the 1978 European championships (see p. 160).

The first woman to use the 'Fosbury Flop' style to set a world record was Ulrike Meyfarth (Ger), whose 1.92m at the Olympic Games in Munich in 1972 equalled Gusenbauer's record. Since then Yordanka Blagoyeva (Bul) (1.94m) and Ackermann have been straddle jumpers and Simeoni a 'flopper'.

The first woman to use the 'flop' style effectively was the Canadian, Debbie Brill, who developed her 'Brill Bend' independently of Dick Fosbury. She won the Commonwealth title at age 17 in 1970 and although 'dropping out' for a while returned to her greatest triumph in winning the 1979 World Cup event at 1.96m/6ft 5in and improved her Commonwealth best to 1.97m/6ft 5½in in 1980, which was the 15th Canadian outdoor record she had set, as well as two improvements indoors. Her first had been 1.77m in 1974. After having a baby in 1981, she returned to set a world indoor record of 1.99m/6ft 6¼in at Edmonton on 23 Jan 1982.

Rosi Ackermann at Prague in 1978 when her second place to Sara Simeoni was only her second loss in four years.   *(M. Shearman)*

Their duels were as follows:

Date	Meet	Venue	Ackermann	Simeoni
4 Sep 1972	Olympics	Munich	7 – 1.85pb	6 – 1.85pb
11 Mar 1973	Eur. Ind.	Rotterdam	4 – 1.86	9 – 1.82
5 Aug 1973	Eur. Cup SF	Bucharest	1 – 1.87	2 – 1.82
10 Mar 1974	Eur. Ind.	Göteborg	1 – 1.90	11 – 1.75
8 Sep 1974	European	Rome	1 – 1.95WR	3 – 1.89pb
9 Mar 1975	Eur. Ind.	Katowice	1 – 1.92	4 – 1.80
28 Jul 1976	Olympics	Montreal	1 – 1.93	2 – 1.91pb
12 Mar 1977	Eur. Ind	San Sebastian	9 – 1.80	1 – 1.92pb
2 Sep 1977	World Cup	Dusseldorf	1 – 1.98	2 – 1.92
31 Aug 1978	European	Prague	2 – 1.99	1 – 2.01WR (=)
5 Aug 1979	Eur. Cup	Turin	1 – 1.99	2 – 1.94
26 Aug 1979	World Cup	Montreal	4 – 1.87	2 – 1.94
26 Jul 1980	Olympics	Moscow	4 – 1.91	1 – 1.97

(pb = personal best, WR = world record)

Dorothy Odam (later Tyler) set a world record of 1.66m/5ft 5¼in at Brentwood on 29 May 1939. This appeared on the list of records issued in 1946, but was deleted in 1957 when the IAAF ratified a 1.67m/5ft 5¾in by Dora Ratjen (Ger) from 1938. However Ratjen was then revealed to have been a man, so Tyler went back into the record books.

The greatest height a woman has jumped over her own head is 27cm/10½in by Marina Sisoyeva (USSR) who jumped 1.93m/6ft 4in in 1980.

POLE VAULT
Not an event often attempted by women, the best on record is 3.05m/10ft 0¼in by Irene Spieker (USA) in 1979. A pole vault competition is held annually at the Mason-Dixon indoor meeting at Louisville, Kentucky.

LONG JUMP
The most records is four by Tatyana Shchelkanova (USSR), from 6.48m/21ft 3¼in in 1961 to 6.70m/21ft 11¾in in Moscow on 4 Jul 1964. Her absolute best ever was a wind assisted 6.96m/22ft 10in in the Soviet championships in 1966.

Gisela Mauermayer set world records at both shot and discus. She won the 1936 Olympic discus title, but then the shot was not held.

A world record was set by a woman placed only third in a competition: This occurred on 23 Jun 1961 with Hildrun Claus (Ger) adding 2cm. to her world record with a final round leap of 6.42m/21 ft 0¾in. Ahead of her were Tatiana Shchelkanova 6.50m/21ft 4in and Valentina Shaprunova (USSR) 6.46m/21ft 2½in, but both their jumps, in the second round, were assisted by winds over the 2m/s limit.

Barrier breakers
5.50m and 18ft: Marie Kiessling (Ger) 5.54m/18ft 2¼in Munich 29 May 1921
19ft: Kinue Hitomi (Jap) 5.98m/19ft 7½in Osaka 20 May 1928. This was the first IAAF record, and added 36cm/14¼in to the previous record, the greatest ever improvement
6m and 20ft Kinue Hitomi 6.16m/20ft 2½in Seoul 17 Oct 1929 – unratified.
Stanislawa Walasiewicz (Pol) was the next to jump over 6m, with 6.04m/19ft 9¾in at Lodz on 28 Aug 1938
6.25m: Fanny Blankers-Koen (Hol) 6.25m/20ft 6in Leiden 19 Sep 1943
21 ft: Hildrun Claus (Ger) 6.40m/21ft 0in Erfurt 7 Aug 1960
6.50m: Tatyana Shchelkanova (USSR) 6.50m wind aided (as above) and 6.53m/21ft 5¼in Leipzig 10 Jun 1962
22ft: Mary Rand (GB) 6.70m/22ft 0in wind aided Portsmouth 26 Sep 1964, and 6.76m/22ft 2¼in Tokyo 14 Oct 1964
7m and 23ft: Vilma Bardauskiene (USSR) 7.07m/23ft 2½in Kishinev 18 Aug 1978. In that competition the 25-year-old Lithuanian opened with 7.07 to add 8cm to Sigrun Siegl's world record, and had further jumps of 7.07 (third) and 7.06 (fourth round). Eleven days later she improved to 7.09m/23ft 3¼in in the qualifying round of the European Championships at Prague

SHOT
The first world record ratified by the IAAF was 14.38m/47ft 2¼in by Gisela Mauermayer (Ger) on her international debut against Poland in Warsaw on 15 Jul 1934. This remained as the record for the longest period, 14 years 20 days, until surpassed by Tatyana Sevryukova (USSR), although Sevryukova had first beaten the mark nearly three years earlier in 1945, when the USSR was not a member of the IAAF. Since those days the record has been improved dramatically to the present 22.45m/73ft 8in outdoors of Ilona Slupianek (GDR) in 1980 and 22.50m/73ft 10in indoors by Helena Fibingerova (Cze) in 1977.

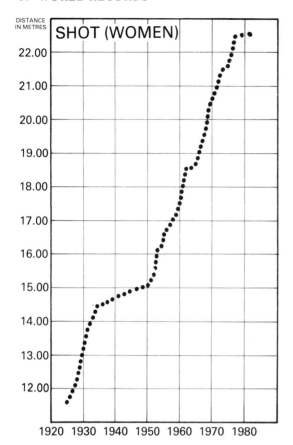

The greatest number of IAAF world records is nine by Nadyezhda Chizhova (USSR) from her first at 18.67m/61ft 3in in 1968 to her last 21.20m/69ft 6¾in and an unrecognised 21.45m/70ft 4½in in 1973.

The greatest number of improvements in all however is 15 in succession by Galina Zybina (USSR) from 15.19m/49ft 10in in 1952 to 16.76m/55ft 0in in 1956, of which eight were ratified. She improved the record by 78cm/2ft 6½in with her 16.20m/53ft 1¼in in 1953, but including her unrecognised records her best margin of improvement was 71cm that year while Tamara Press (USSR) improved by 77cm when she put 18.55m in 1962, for the fourth of her six records.

Barrier breakers
12m and 40ft: Grete Heublein (Ger) 12.85m/42ft 2in Frankfurt 21 Jul 1929
15m: Anna Andreyeva (USSR) 15.02m/49ft 3½in Ploesti 9 Nov 1950

50ft: Galina Zybina (USSR) 15.28m/50ft 1¾in Helsinki 26 Jul 1952
60ft: Tamara Press (USSR) 18.55m/60ft 10½in Leipzig 10 Jun 1962
20m: Nadyezhda Chizhova (USSR) 20.09m/65ft 11in Chorzow 13 Jul 1969
70ft: Nadyezhda Chizhova (USSR) 21.45m/70ft 4½in Varna 29 Sep 1973.

DISCUS
The greatest number of world records has been 12, including one unratified, by Faina Melnik (later Veleva, following her marriage to Bulgarian discus thrower Velko Velev). The Soviet woman succeeded Liesel Westermann (Ger) (63.96m/209ft 10in in 1969) on 12 Aug 1971 with 64.28m/212ft 8in and took the record to 70.50m/231ft 3in at Sochi on 24 Apr 1976. Her sequence was broken by Argentina Menis (Rom) with 67.32m/220ft 10in on 23 Sep 1972, and she was succeeded by Evelin Jahl (née Schlaak) 70.72m/232ft 0in in 1978.

The greatest improvement on the record is 3.43m/11ft 3in by Nina Dumbadze's 57.04m/187ft 2in at Tbilisi on 18 Oct 1952. Dumbadze (USSR) succeeded Nina Romashkova (later Ponomaryeva) but had earlier set two more IAAF records and four unofficial bests, starting with 49.11m/161ft 1½in in 1939.

Other multiple record breakers: 10 Jadwiga Wajsowna (Pol) 1932–34, 7 Gisela Mauermayer (Ger) 1935–36, 7 Halina Konopacka (Pol) 1925–28, 6 Tamara Press (USSR) 1960–65.

Barrier breakers
100ft: Halina Konopacka (Pol) 31.24m/102ft 6in 10 May 1925 Warsaw
50m: Nina Dumbadze (USSR) 50.50m/165ft 8in 29 Aug 1946 Sarpsborg
60m and 200ft: Liesel Westermann (Ger) 61.26m/201ft 0in 5 Nov 1967 Sao Paulo
70m: Faina Melnik (USSR) 70.50m/231ft 3in 24 Apr 1976 Sochi.

JAVELIN
The most world records have been set by Ruth Fuchs (GDR). Her first was in 1972 when she added 2.36m/7ft 9in with 65.06m/213ft 5in. She threw at Potsdam, but just 30 minutes earlier in Bucharest Ewa Gryziecka (Pol) had set one of the shortest lasting world records ever when she threw 62.70m. Fuchs set her sixth on 29 Apr 1980 with 69.96m/229ft 6in at Split, Yugoslavia.

The largest improvement was by Natalya Smirnitskaya (USSR) whose 53.41m/175ft 2in in Moscow on 5 Aug 1949 added 3.82m/12ft 6in to her own 11-day old official record or 3.09m/10ft 1in to the unratified record set by Klavdiya Mayuchaya (USSR) in 1947.

The longest lasting record was the 62.40m/204ft 8in by Yelena Gorchakova (USSR) in the 1964 Olympic qualifying round which stood for 7 years 238 days.

Barrier breakers
30m and 100ft: Lilian Copeland (USA) 34.28m/112ft 5½ins 9 Jul 1926 Philadelphia
40m: Mildred Didrikson (USA) 40.62m/133ft 3¼in 4 Jul 1930 Dallas
50m: Klavdiya Mayuchaya (USSR) 50.32m/165ft 1in 23 Sep 1947 Moscow
60m and 200ft: Elvira Ozolina (USSR) 61.38m/201ft 4ins 27 Aug 1964 Kiev
70m: Tatyana Biryulina (USSR) 70.08m/229ft 11in 12 Jul 1980 Podolsk. At the European Cup finals in Zagreb on 15 Aug 1981 Antoaneta Todorova (Bul) became the youngest ever javelin world record holder as she added 1.8m to the record with 71.88m/235ft 10in at the age of 18 years 37 days.

The most surprising record was Anna Pazera's 57.40m/188ft 4in at the 1958 Commonwealth Games, for her previous best was just 50.60m/166ft, set in 1956 in Warsaw as Anna Wojtasek. She claimed political asylum in Australia and was placed ninth at the Olympic Games in Melbourne. After her record she had a fair competitive record, but never exceeded 54.58m/179 ft 1in.

PENTATHLON
The composition of events for the women's pentathlon has changed four times and the order of events once. Also new scoring tables were introduced in 1954 and 1971 so the situation is a little complicated. From 1981 the Heptathlon has replaced the Pentathlon in major championships.

The first multi-events competition for women at a major Games, was a triathlon (100m, HJ, JT) held at the 1930 World Games.

Pentathlon 1928–48 (1st day: SP, LJ; 2nd day: 100m, HJ, JT) The 'final' world record (on 1971 tables) was 3992 by Aleksandra Chudina (USSR) in 1947.

Pentathlon 1948–61 (1st day: SP, HJ, 200m; 2nd day: 80mh, LJ) World record taken from 4098 by Chudina in 1949 to 4486 by Irina Press (USSR) in 1961.

Pentathlon 1961–68: the order changed to: 1st day: 80mh, SP, HJ; 2nd day: LJ, 200m. The world record was taken from 4592 in 1961 to 4702 in 1964 by Irina Press.

Irina Press (USSR) has set most pentathlon world records, eight in all between 1959 and 1964. Her 4486 (on the 1971 tables) was the first score of over 5000 points on the 1954 tables, then in use, at 5020, in Leningrad on 16/17 Aug 1961.

Pentathlon 1969–76 (1st day: 100mh, SP, HJ; 2nd day: LJ, 200m) Heide Rosendahl (Ger) set the first world record with the 100mh replacing the 80mh, with 4384. There were four further improvements including two by Rosendahl before the first one accepted by the IAAF; Liese Prokop (Aut) 4727 in Vienna on 4/5 Oct 1969. There were four more improvements, one

Burglinde Pollak won three European and two Olympic pentathlon medals and ranked in the top ten in the world from 1970 to 1980 but won no gold medals. Her best shot was 17.28m in 1978.
(M. Shearman)

by Mary Peters (GB) and three by Burglinde Pollak (GDR), culminating in the final record for these events of 4932 by Pollak at Bonn on 22 Sep 1973. However, in addition Heide Rosendahl held a world record for the shortest period ever to that date – just 1.12sec. For in the 1972 Olympic final at Munich on 3 Sep 1972, Rosendahl won the last event, the 200m in 22.96 to secure a total of 4791 which was 16 points better than Pollak's record. Mary Peters finished fourth in this race in 24.08 to win overall with a total of 4801 points.

Pentathlon 1977–81 (100mh, SP, HJ, LJ, 800m on one day). The first world record with the 800m replacing the 200m was set by Eva Wilms (Ger) at 4765 points on 24 May 1977 at Göttingen. Wilms improved further to 4823 on 18 June and on 18 Sep 1977 Nadyezhda Tkachenko (USSR) scored 4839 at Lille. In 1980 Olga Kuragina (USSR) scored 4856 on 20 June in Moscow, where there came massive improvement five weeks later in the Olympic Games, as the first three, all Soviet athletes smashed the record.

As with Rosendahl and Peters eight years earlier, the medallists finished the final race, this time the 800m, in reverse order: Olga Kuragina won in 2:03.6 to total 4875 a record for 1.2sec until Olga Rukavishnikova finished in 2:04.8 for a total of 4937. This lasted for just 0.4sec, **the shortest world record duration for any event ever**, as Nadyezhda Tkachenko ran 2:05.2 to win the gold medal with the world record score of 5083 points. Tkachenko's performances in this the first 5000 plus score under the current tables were: 100mh 13.29; SP 16.84m/55ft 3in; HJ 1.84m/6ft 0½in, LJ 6.73m/22ft 1in; 800m 2:05.2, an amazing display of versatility. Her individual performances would have been world records at each discipline as recently as 1969, 1959, 1960, 1964 and 1955 respectively!

HEPTATHLON
The pentathlon has now been extended into a heptathlon event, with the addition of two extra events, the 200m and the javelin, and this was introduced into major meetings in 1981.

The first score of over 6000 points was recorded by Yekaterina Gordienko (USSR) – 6144 on 14 Sep 1980. As might be expected there was rapid progress in 1981. After Jane Frederick (USA) 6166 and Nadyezhda Vinogradova (USSR) 6212 had made minor improvements, Ramona Neubert (GDR) took the world record to a higher plane, with 6621 in the GDR championships at Halle on 24 May and 6717 at Kiev on 28 June 1981. The latter score included 4962 for the five old pentathlon events. The addition of the javelin helped spur Tessa Sanderson (GB) to re-tackle multi-events and she set two British records, first 5906 and then 6110 in the European Cup semi-final.

WOMEN'S RELAYS
Four relay events are on the current IAAF world record schedule: 4 × 100m, 4 × 200m, 4 × 400m and 4 × 800m. The 4 × 110y, 4 × 220y, 4 × 440y and 4 × 880y were included until 1976 and 3 × 800m and 3 × 880y were dropped in 1969.

Summary of main achievements by event
4 × 100m and 4 × 110y
The first sub 50sec time was run over the slightly longer 4 × 110y by Great Britain at the World Games in Göteborg on 29 Aug 1926. The first sub 45sec times were those of 44.9 by both Australia and Germany in the heats of the 1956 Olympic Games, Australia going on to improve further in the final to 44.5 (44.65 auto).

Up to 1972, when the West German team set a record of 42.81 in winning the Olympic title, the official IAAF records had been set by the following national teams: USA 6 times, USSR 5, Germany 5, Australia 3, Holland 1. The first IAAF record, 46.4 by Germany at the 1936 Olympic Games, lasted the longest, 12 days short of 16 years. Since 1972, however the event has been dominated by the GDR, whose teams have set ten successive records, from 42.6 at Potsdam on 1 Sep 1973 to 41.60 in the Moscow Olympic final on 1 Aug 1980. Marlies Göhr (née Oelsner) has run on the last seven records. The last three, all in 1980, were achieved by the squad of Romy Müller, Bärbel Wöckel, Ingrid Auerswald and Göhr.

4 × 200m
A comparatively rarely run event, but the current record is a highly meritorious one: 1:28.15 by the GDR team of Marlies Göhr, Romy Müller, Bärbel Wöckel and Marita Koch at Jena on 9 Aug 1980. This time took 2.65sec off the previous record.

The first IAAF record was 1:45.8 by Germany in 1932. After another German team had run 1:45.3 in 1938, there was a massive improvement to 1:41.0 by a Dutch team with Fanny Blankers-Koen on the second leg in 1944. The first sub 1:40 time was run by the USSR national team with 1:39.7 in 1951.

4 × 400m

This event was added to the record lists in 1969, when it was included for the first time at a major championships – the European in Athens. Seven world records were ratified that year, the record chase culminating in the European final, when both Great Britain and France shared the time of 3:30.8, as Lillian Board just held off Colette Besson after an epic duel. Since 1969 the record has been improved five times, each time by the GDR national team. After whittling the record away to 3:28.48 in the semi-finals of the 1972 Olympic Games, GDR women made two massive improvements – first to 3:22.95 in the 1972 Olympic final and then to 3:19.23 in the 1976 Olympic final. The team on the latter occasion being Doris Maletzki (50.5), Brigitte Rohde (49.5), Ellen Streidt (49.5), Christina Brehmer (49.7). The most world records at the event is four by Helga Seidler, who ran on the first four of those GDR records.

The fastest leg ever run is 47.8 by Jarmila Kratochvilova (Cze) in a European Cup semi-final at Frankfurt on 5 Jul 1981.

3 × 800m – 4 × 800m

Teams of three ran this event until 1969, when the more conventional relay number of four took over.

The 3 × 800m record progressed from 7:37.4 in 1933 to 6:15.5 by a Dutch team in 1968, teams from the USSR setting six of the fourteen records.

The first 4 × 800m time recognised was 8:33.0 by GDR in 1969. Since then the record has improved sharply, and the first sub 8min

time, representing an average 800m of less than two minutes per woman, was the 7:54.2 by the GDR team of Elfi Zinn, Gunhild Hoffmeister, Anita Weiss and Ulrike Klapezynski in 1976. Ten days later on 16 Aug 1976 the current record of 7:52.4 was set by the USSR team of Tatyana Providokhina (1:58.4), Valentina Gerasimova (1:59.2), Svyetlana Styrkina (1:57.3) and Tatyana Kazankina (1:57.4).

WOMEN'S WALKING
Best recorded performances
Track
1500m 6:19.0 Sue Cook (Aus) 8 Nov 1980 Doncaster, Aus.
1 mile 6:47.9 Sue Cook (Aus) 14 Mar 1981 Canberra, Aus.
3000m 13:02.17 Sally Pierson (Aus) 21 Feb 1982 Melbourne, Aus.
5000m 22.45.6 Sue Cook (Aus) 24 Apr 1982 Adelaide, Aus.
10000m 47:58.2 Ann Jansson (Swe) 17 Oct 1981 Falkenberg, Swe.
15000m 1:19:49.8 Susan Liers (USA) 20 Mar 1977 Kings Point, USA
20000m 1:48:18.6 Susan Liers (USA) 20 Mar 1977 Kings Point, USA

Road
5000m 22:40.6 Lyudmila Khrushchova (USSR) 17 May 1981, Kishinyov, USSR
10000m 46:48.0 Sue Cook (Aus) 11 May 1980 Moss, Aus.
15000m 1:15:21.0 Sue Cook (Aus) 3 Feb 1980 Melbourne, Aus
20000m 1:41:41.6 Sue Cook (Aus) 3 Feb 1980 Melbourne, Aus
30000m 2:54:04 Jeanne Bocci (USA) 23 Mar 1980 Houston, USA
50000m 5:09:41 Lillian Millen (GB) 18 Jul 1981 Sleaford GB.

Barrier breakers
First sub 15min 3000m: Mary Nilsson (Swe) 14:52.6 (track) 2 May 1965 Copenhagen
First sub 25 min 5000m: May Bengtsson (née Johansson) (Swe) 24:57.4 (track) 11 Jul 1943. She won the European titles for the over-60's at 5km and 10km in 1980!
First sub 50min 10000m: 49:04.0 (road walk) Margareta Simu 22 Jun 1975 Äppelbo.

The longest distance walked in 24 hours is 197km/122½ miles by Ann van de Meer (Hol) at Rouen on 2/3 May 1981. Ann Sayer (GB) set a world best for 100 miles of 19:32:37 at Sink-Dedenrode, Holland on 31 May/1 June 1980.

The British team (from left) of Rosemary Stirling, Pam Piercy and Pat Lowe after their world record 3 × 800m relay 6:20.0 at the White City in 1967. Pat Lowe (later Mrs Cropper) set five world records, best by a British woman. *(Topix)*

WORLD ATHLETICS

Olympic Games

THE GREEK GAMES

The original Olympic Games were staged every four years at Olympia, on the Western side of Greece, about 195km/120 miles from Athens.

The first definite mention of the Games was in 776 BC and all the subsequent Games are dated from these. However, earlier celebrations had been held, perhaps dating back several hundred years, and these Games had considerable religious significance.

Gradually the Games grew in size and importance to their height of fame in the fifth and fourth centuries BC. From 776 to 724 BC there was just one event at each Games, the stade race of 190m and the first recorded winner was Coroibos, a cook from Elis. In 724 BC a two stade race, the *diaulus*, was added, followed four years later by a longer distance race, the *dolichus* of 24 stade (about 4½km). The pentathlon, comprising running, jumping, wrestling and throwing the discus and javelin was added in 708 BC. Later, boxing and chariot racing were among the events added to the Games which grew in duration from one to five days. There were also events for boys under 17 years, but women were banned from competing or even watching.

The Games provided much more than just sporting contests for they were also great artistic and cultural festivals maintaining the Greek ideal of perfection of mind and body. Great crowds were drawn from all over the Greek-influenced world to see the competitions. The athletes prepared themselves for ten months prior to the Games, and spent the last month at Olympia.

The prize for winners was a branch of wild olive, the Greeks' sacred tree, but the athletes achieved great fame and reward on returning home, which led to the emergence of specialist full-time athletes.

The final Games were held in AD 393, as the following year the Emperor of Rome, Theodosius I, decreed their prohibition.

For many years the Games had declined from their ancient glories becoming very corrupt, and incompatible with early Christian beliefs.

THE MODERN OLYMPIC GAMES

Pierre de Fredi, Baron de Coubertin, born in Paris in 1863, was the driving influence behind the revival of the Olympic Games. He believed in the value of the Greek athletic ideal and his energies were devoted to achieving his dream. In 1889 he was commissioned by the French government to form a universal sports association and he visited other European nations. He made public his views on 25 Nov 1892 at the Sorbonne in Paris. These led to the formation of the International Olympic Committee in 1894 and the staging of the first Games in Athens, which were opened on Easter Sunday, 24 Mar 1896 (5 April by the new calendar).

The first Olympic champion of the modern era was James Connolly (USA) of the Boston Athletic Association who won the triple jump on 6 Apr 1896 with 13.71m/44ft 11¾in. Connolly's first novel *Out of Gloucester* was published in 1902 and he was for many years a distinguished war correspondent. Connolly won the first final, but the first Olympic winner was Francis Lane (USA), who won a heat of the 100m about two hours earlier in 12.2 sec. Lane later came fourth in the final.

The first woman to win an athletics gold medal was Halina Konopacka (Pol) with a 39.62m/ 130ft world record in the discus on 31 Jul 1928 in Amsterdam. A little later the same day Elizabeth Robinson (USA) won the first track gold medal in the 100m, but the first women's Olympic winner was Anni Holdmann (Ger), who had won the first heat of the 100m the previous day.

The first black athletes to be placed in the first three of an Olympic final were George Poage (USA), third in the 400m hurdles, and Joseph Stadler (USA), second at standing high jump, both on 31 Aug 1904. The first black gold medallist was DeHart Hubbard (USA) at long jump in 1924. Harry Edward, born in British Guiana (now Guyana), was Britain's first black medallist, with a bronze in the 1920 100m.

Bärbel Eckert at the 1976 Olympic Games when she won the first two of her record four Olympic gold medals. *(G. Herringshaw)*

The winner of the most Olympic medals is Paavo Nurmi (Fin) with 12 (9 gold and 3 silver). In 1920 he won three gold (10000m, cross-country team and individual) and one silver (5000m). In 1924 he won five gold, a record for one Games (1500m, 5000m, cross-country team and individual, 3000m team). He won the team race in 8:32.0 but individual medals were not awarded. Including heats he won six races in six days. In 1928 he won one gold (10000m), and two silver (5000m, 3000m steeplechase). Nurmi had hoped to run the marathon, and possibly the 10000m in the 1932 Games, but was unable to do so because he was barred by the IAAF from amateur athletics for alleged professionalism.

The winner of the most Olympic gold medals if the unofficial Games of 1906 are included is Ray Ewry (USA) with ten at standing jumps – both high jump and long jump in 1900, 1904, 1906 and 1908; and the triple jump in 1900 and 1904.

The winner of the most Olympic medals at one Games is Ville Ritola (Fin) with six in 1924. He won the 3000m steeplechase, 10000m, cross-country team and 3000m team (second to Nurmi) and was second at 5000m and individual cross-country and had in all eight races in eight days including heats. In 1928 Ritola added two more medals, a gold at 5000m and a silver at 10000m, when he finished second to Nurmi for the fourth time in an Olympic final. He lived in the USA from the age of 17, and won 14 AAU titles.

The winner of the most women's Olympic medals is Shirley de la Hunty (née Strickland) (Aus) and Irena Szewinska (née Kirszenstein) seven each. Strickland: 1948 2nd 4 × 100mR, 3rd 100m and 80mh; 1952 1st 80mh, 3rd 100m; 1956 1st 80mh and 4 × 100mR. Examination of the photo-finish of the 1948 200m by statistician Bob Sparks showed that she should have been placed third rather than her official position of fourth and thus would have won a record eight medals. Szewinska: 1964 1st 4 × 100mR, 2nd 200m and LJ; 1968 1st 200m, 3rd 100m (also failed to qualify at LJ); 1972 3rd 200m (also semis at 100m); 1976 1st 400m. In 1980 she again competed at 400m.

The record number of gold medals won by a woman is four by: Fanny Blankers-Koen (Hol) – 100m, 200m, 80mh and 4 × 100mR all in 1948 (also the most medals at one Games by a woman); and by Betty Cuthbert (Aus) 100m, 200m and 4×100mR in 1956 and 400m in 1964; and Bärbel Wöckel (GDR) 200m and 4×100mR in both 1976 and 1980.

The most medals won at an event is four by: Al Oerter (USA), who uniquely won the discus at four Games in 1956–68; Viktor Saneyev (USSR) won three golds and a silver at triple jump in 1968–80; and Vladimir Golubnichiy

Hannes Kolehmainen (left) in his fourth race of the Games is about to pass Jean Bouin to win the 1912 Olympic 5000m title. Both men smashed the 15 minute barrier for the first time.

(USSR) two golds, a silver and a bronze at 20km walk 1960–72.

The most gold medals won at individual events at one Games is four by Alvin Kraenzlein (USA), who in 1900 won the 60m 7.0, 110mh 15.4, 200mh 25.4, LJ 7.18m/23ft 6¾in.

Gold medals at both track and field events have been won by Kraenzlein (above), Jesse Owens (USA) (100m, 200m, LJ, 4×100mR in 1936), Mildred Didrikson (USA) (80mh and JT in 1932) and Heide Rosendahl (Ger) (LJ and 4×100mR in 1972). Didrikson also took second place in a jump-off for the high jump in 1932.

Medals at most events have been won by Paavo Nurmi with seven (as above). Ritola follows with six and then the following at five events: Irving Baxter (USA) HJ, PV and standing HJ, LJ and TJ; Robert Garrett (USA) HJ (3rd 1896), LJ (2nd 1896), SP (1st 1896, 3rd 1900), DT (1st 1896), standing TJ (3rd 1900); Walter Tewksbury (USA) 1st 200m and 400mh, 2nd 60m and 100m, 3rd 200mh all in 1900; Hannes Kolehmainen (Fin), who won six races in nine days in 1912 to take the 5000m, 10000m and cross-country titles (he also won a team silver) and won the 1920 marathon. Including the 1906 unofficial Games Martin Sheridan (USA) won medals at six events, if we include both forms of discus throwing. In 1906 he won at discus and shot, was second at standing high jump and long jump and the weight event. In 1904 he won the discus and in 1908 both discus and Greek style discus, as well as a bronze at standing long jump. Irena Szewinska is the only woman to have won medals at five events.

Medals at three women's field events have been won by Micheline Ostermeyer (Fra): 1st SP and DT, 3rd HJ in 1948; and by Aleksandra Chudina (USSR): 2nd LJ and JT, 3rd HJ in 1952.

The most Olympic Games participated in by any athlete is six by Lia Manoliu (Rom), who competed in the discus final at each Games from 1952 to 1972.
See individual event summaries for further details for many of the above.

The only nation represented by both men's and women's teams at every Games is Australia. Greece and Great Britain have been ever-present for men and Poland for women.

THE OLDEST AND YOUNGEST MEDALLISTS

The oldest Olympic gold medallists – men

	AGE Years	Days	Name	Country	Event	Placing	Year
Any event	42	26	Patrick McDonald	USA	56lb weight	1st	1920
Sprinter	32	62	Arthur Wint	Jam	4 × 400m Relay	1st	1952
Distance	36	130	Mamo Wolde	Eth	Marathon	1st	1968
Walker	39	126	Thomas Green	GB	50km Walk	1st	1932
Jumper	31	195	Peter O'Connor	Ire	Triple Jump	1st	1906
Other throws	40	187	John Flanagan	USA	Hammer	1st	1908
Multi-event	35	314	Thomas Kiely	GB/Ire	All-round	1st	1904

The oldest Olympic gold medallists – women

	Years	Days	Name	Country	Event	Placing	Year
Any event	36	176	Lia Manoliu	Rom	Discus	1st	1968
Sprinter	31	136	Shirley de la Hunty	Aus	4 × 400m Relay	1st	1956
Distance	29	47	Lyudmila Bragina	USSR	1500m	1st	1972
Jumper	29	67	Viorica Viscopoleanu	Rom	Long Jump	1st	1968
Multi-event	33	59	Mary Peters	GB	Pentathlon	1st	1972

The oldest Olympic medallists – men

	Years	Days	Name	Country	Event	Placing	Year
Any event	48	115	Tebbs Lloyd Johnson	GB	50km Walk	3rd	1948
Sprinter	33	292	Jocelyn Delecour	Fra	4 × 100m Relay	3rd	1968
Distance	40	90	Mamo Wolde	Eth	Marathon	3rd	1972
Jumper	34	296	Viktor Saneyev	USSR	Triple Jump	2nd	1980
Thrower	45	205	Matt McGrath	USA	Hammer	2nd	1924

The oldest Olympic medallists – women

	Years	Days	Name	Country	Event	Placing	Year
Any event	37	248	Dana Zatopková	Cze	Javelin	2nd	1960
Sprinter	34	95	Karin Balzer	GDR	100m Hurdles	3rd	1972
Distance	33	24	Gunhild Hoffmeister	GDR	1500m	2nd	1976
Jumper	30	365	Tatyana Talisheva	USSR	Long Jump	3rd	1968

The youngest Olympic gold medallists – men

	Years	Days	Name	Country	Event	Placing	Year
Any event	17	263	Bob Mathias	USA	Decathlon	1st	1948
Sprinter	18	118	Johnny Jones	USA	4 × 100m Relay	1st	1976
Middle distance	19	237	Ted Meredith	USA	800m	1st	1912
Distance	20	301	Juan Carlos Zabala	Arg	Marathon	1st	1932
Walker	18	337	Ugo Frigerio	Ita	10km Walk	1st	1920
Jumper	17	360	Lee Barnes	USA	Pole Vault	1st	1924
Thrower	20	6	Richard Sheldon	USA	Discus	1st	1900

The youngest Olympic gold medallists – women

	Years	Days	Name	Country	Event	Placing	Year
Any event	15	123	Barbara Jones	USA	4 × 100m Relay	1st	1952
Individual event	16	123	Ulrike Meyfarth	Ger	High Jump	1st	1972
Individual sprints	16	343	Elizabeth Robinson	USA	100m	1st	1928
Distance	20	251	Madeline Manning	USA	800m	1st	1968
Thrower	17	86	Mihaela Penes	Rom	Javelin	1st	1964
Multi-event	21	271	Sigrun Siegl	GDR	Pentathlon	1st	1976

The youngest Olympic medallists – men
(as for gold medallists, except):

	Years	Days	Name	Country	Event	Placing	Year
Any event	17	229	Ture Persson	Swe	4 × 100m Relay	2nd	1912
Distance	19	178	Ernst Fast	Swe	Marathon	3rd	1900
Thrower	19	187	Uwe Beyer	Ger	Hammer	3rd	1964

The youngest Olympic medallists – women
(as for gold medallists, except):

	Years	Days	Name	Country	Event	Placing	Year
Distance	20	100	Inge Gentzel	Swe	800m	3rd	1928
Multi-event	21	85	Burglinde Pollak	GDR	Pentathlon	3rd	1972

Athletes who have run a lap of the track and lit the Olympic flame:

1948 John Mark, Cambridge University quarter-miler (best time 49.4).

1952 Paavo Nurmi, joined by Hannes Kolehmainen on the tower.

1956 Ron Clarke, at the time the world junior record holder for the 1 mile (4:06.8). Between 1957 and 1961 Clarke ran very little, concentrating on accountancy studies and his family, but returned to revolutionise distance running.

1964 Yoshinori Sakai, born on the day the atomic bomb was dropped on Hiroshima; second Asian Games 400m 1966.

1968 Enriqueta Basilio, the first woman to have this honour, Mexican record holder 400m (55.0) and 100m hurdles (14.1). She was eliminated in the heats of the 400m and 80m hurdles at Mexico City.

1972 Günter Zahn, 1972 West German junior 1500m champion.

Athletes who have taken the Olympic oath:

1924 Georges André, the great French all-rounder (see p. 231).

1948 Don Finlay, bronze medallist in 1932 and

The Olympic Opening Ceremony at Melbourne in 1956. The torch bearer is Ron Clarke, then world junior 1 mile record holder. *(GOPA)*

silver medallist in 1936, but who fell while leading in his heat in 1948, at the age of 39.

1956 John Landy, world 1 mile record holder, and bronze medallist at 1500m.

1960 Adolfo Consolini, competing at his fourth Games.

1968 Pablo Garrido, 26th at marathon.

1972 Heidi Schüller, the first woman to take the oath, fifth long jump.

Event by event Olympic survey

MEN
60 metres

This event was held at the 1900 and 1904 Games and won by Alvin Kraenzlein (USA) and Archie Hahn (USA) respectively, both in 7.0sec.

100 metres

The only double winner is Archie Hahn, if one counts his 1906 victory as well as that in 1904. Valeriy Borzov won in 1972 in 10.14 and was third in 1976 in the same time, behind Hasely Crawford (Tri) 10.06 and Don Quarrie (Jam) 10.07. Other double medallists include Ralph Metcalfe (USA), second in 1932 and 1936, and Lennox Miller (Jam), second in 1968 and third in 1972. Metcalfe lost by just an inch to Eddie

Tolan (USA) in 1932, as both equalled the world record at 10.3 (10.38 auto), and was a metre down on Jesse Owens 10.4 to 10.3 in 1936, although he had gained considerably from a very poor start. Other athletes who have set world records are: Francis Jarvis and Walter Tewksbury in 1900, with 10.8 in a heat and semi-final respectively, before finishing in that order in the final; Bob Hayes in 1964 with 10.0 (10.06 auto), having run the fastest time ever, 9.91 in the semi-final, but aided by a 5.28m per sec tailwind. (His 2m winning margin is a record for a 100m final); and Jim Hines in 1968 with 9.9 (9.95 auto) (all USA).

Frank Wykoff (USA) was placed fourth in 1928 and 1936, each time just a tenth of a second off a medal. However, he made up for his disappointment by winning three relay gold medals.

In 1972 Eddie Hart and Rey Robinson, who had equalled the world record of 9.9 when placed first and second in the US Trials, failed to report for the second round. The first reaction from spectators was that they were making some form of protest, but actually they had mistaken the time of the event and had by chance seen the first race on television in the Olympic village. They were rushed to the stadium by car with the third member of the US team, Robert Taylor, who just made the third race, but Robinson had missed the first race, and Hart the second. Their coach, Stan Wright, had been using an old timetable and had not checked the revised schedule. Hart won a gold medal in the sprint relay with Taylor, who was second in the 100m final, but for Robinson there was no opportunity to show what might have been.

200 metres
No man has won twice, but three winners won a second medal: Andy Stanfield (USA) won in 1952 in 20.7 (20.81 auto) and was second in 1956 in 20.7 (20.97 auto) to Bobby Morrow (USA) 20.6 (20.75 auto); Don Quarrie (Jam) added a bronze in 1980 (20.29) to his 1976 gold (20.23); Pietro Mennea (Ita) was the 1980 winner with 20.19, and is the only man to have contested three Olympic 200m finals, having been third in 1972 and fourth in 1976.

World records have been set as follows: 1960 Livio Berruti (Ita) 20.5 in both the semi-final and the final (20.62 auto); 1968 Tommie Smith (USA) 19.83, unbeaten for 11 years.

In 1928 Helmut Körnig (Ger) and Jackson Scholz (USA) finished so close that judges offered them a run-off for third place. Scholz

declined, so Körnig was awarded the medal. The photo-finish confirmed that justice had been done.

Olympic sprint doubles (100m and 200m) have been won by: Archie Hahn 1904; Percy Williams (Can) 1928; Eddie Tolan 1932; Jesse Owens 1936; Bobby-Joe Morrow 1956; Valeriy Borzov 1972. Owens and Morrow went on to win a third gold on their sprint relay teams.

400 metres
This event has had the greatest turnover of medallists. The only winner to gain another medal was Wyndham Halswelle (GB), who had served in the Boer War and was later killed in action in World War I. He was placed second in the intercalated Games of 1906 before winning in 1908 with **the only walk-over in Olympic athletics history**. He was the favourite for the event, having set a British 440y record of 48.4sec in Glasgow three weeks before the Games. He won his heat in 49.4 and improved the Olympic record to 48.4 in winning his semi-final. Three Americans won other semi-finals. The final was not run in lanes and a battle for positions resulted. As the runners came into the home straight Robbins was leading, but Halswelle and

Pietro Mennea (left) and Valeriy Borzov (right) both Olympic sprint champions in a relay semi-final at Montreal in 1976. Mennea became the oldest Olympic 200m champion in 1980, and Borzov won both 100m and 200m in 1972.

(G. Herringshaw)

John Carpenter swung out to pass him. Carpenter on the inside of Halswelle proceeded to run diagonally down the straight, giving Halswelle no chance to overtake and he slowed up before the tape. The post-race inquiry ruled that Halswelle had been obstructed and ordered a re-run, this time in 'strings', that is taped off lanes. Carpenter was disqualified and his teammates boycotted the re-run, so Halswelle was left to run over the distance on his own, which he did in 50.0sec.

Two other men have won two 400m Olympic medals: Guy Butler (GB) second in 1920 and third in 1924, when the winner was the Scotsman Eric Liddell in 47.6; and the Jamaican Herb McKenley, widely regarded as the greatest 400m runner, perhaps of all time, yet second best in Olympic finals in both 1948 and 1952, when the winners were his fellow countrymen Arthur Wint and George Rhoden respectively. In 1948 McKenley went out very fast (21.4 at 200m) but finished with 46.4 to Wint's 46.2. In 1952 he started unusually slowly as this time Wint was the early leader, but he had left his finish until too late as he just failed to catch Rhoden. The official times showed 45.9 for both men, although the automatic times, 46.09 and 46.20, showed Rhoden a metre up. Wint came fifth, and the three Jamaicans teamed up with Leslie Laing to win the 4 × 400m relay in a world record time of 3:03.9. McKenley's third leg being timed in 44.6, the fastest relay split ever.

The closest finish ever came in 1960 when both Otis Davis (USA) and Carl Kaufmann (Ger) set a new world record of 44.9. The automatic times (45.07 and 45.08) showed Davis the winner by one hundredth of a second.

Other world records have been set in 1932 by Bill Carr with 46.2, and in 1968 by Lee Evans with 43.86 (see p. 22). 13 gold medals have been won by athletes from the USA, who had clean sweeps of the medals in 1904 and 1968.

800 metres
Three men have been repeat winners. The first was Douglas Lowe (GB) 1:52.4 in 1924 and 1:51.8 in 1928. Mal Whitfield (USA) won in both 1948 and 1952, running 1:49.2 on each occasion and each time beating Arthur Wint (Jam) by about 2m. Peter Snell (NZ) won in 1960 and 1964, as a complete outsider on the first occasion and as a very firm favourite on the second. Each time Snell improved the Olympic record, in 1960 to 1:46.3 and in 1964 to 1:45.1.

World records have been set in the 800m on more occasions than in any other individual men's running event: 1908 Mel Sheppard (USA) 1:52.8; 1912 Ted Meredith (USA) 1:51.9; 1932 Tom Hampson (GB) 1:49.7; 1968 Ralph Doubell (Aus) 1:44.3 (1:44.40 auto); 1976 Alberto Juantorena (Cub) 1:43.50. Juantorena is the only man to have won the 400m and 800m Olympic double.

Phil Edwards (Can) is the only man to have run in three finals, being placed fourth, third and third respectively in 1928, 1932 and 1936. The closest winner has been Dave Wottle (USA), famous for running in a golf cap, whose margin over Yevgeniy Arzhanov (USSR) was just 0.03sec in 1972. Wottle held back and was

The 1948 Olympic 800m final. The winner was Mal Whitfield (USA – 136), second Arthur Wint (Jam – 122), third Marcel Hansenne (Fra – 151), fourth Herbert Barten (USA – 172), fifth Ingvar Bengtsson (Swe – 164).   *(BBC Hulton)*

last with 200m to go, yet he ran an even paced race and flew past the whole field as they faded. He was so overcome by his victory that he forgot to remove his cap during the national anthem at the victory ceremony and was in tears as he explained his embarrassment to pressmen afterwards.

1500 metres

James Lightbody (USA) won in both 1904 and in 1906, the only repeat winner. His time of 4:05.4 in 1904 was a new world record, the second of four winners to secure this added distinction. Charles Bennett (GB) had been the first, with 4:06.2 in 1900; Jack Lovelock (NZ) won in 1936 with 3:47.8 and in 1960 Herb Elliott (Aus) set the seal on his fabulous career to lead from halfway and win unchallenged in 3:35.6. Elliott's winning margin of 2.8sec over Michel Jazy (Fra) has only been bettered once. That came in 1968 when Kip Keino (Ken) ran an amazing 3:34.91 at the altitude of Mexico City to finish 2.9sec ahead of Jim Ryun (USA). Speculation before the meeting had centred on a winning time of around 3:40 but Keino, who had already run in both the 10000m and 5000m winning a silver medal in the latter, set a blistering pace, passing 800m in 1:55.3, 18m ahead of Ryun and ended with the second fastest time ever. Both men had suffered from serious illnesses in the months leading up to the Games, Ryun having had glandular fever and Keino gall bladder trouble. Keino's second daughter was born while he was in Mexico. She was named Olympia.

Fast finishes rather than fast overall times have been the feature of the three Olympics since then. Pekka Vasala (Fin) won in 1972 with a 1:49.0 last 800m to clock 3:36.33 with Keino half a second behind. John Walker (NZ) won in 1976 with 3:39.17, but a last 300m in 37.9 and Sebastian Coe (GB) won in 1980 with 3:38.40, a last 800m of 1:49.2 and above all a last 100m of 12.1.

5000 metres

Lasse Viren (Fin) is the one man to win twice, as he followed 10000m victories in both 1972 and 1976. On each occasion he won with a long sustained drive to the finish after a fairly slow early pace. In 1972 he ran the final 2000m in 5:06.0 to end with 13:26.42, and in 1976 he ran 13:24.76. In that year Brendan Foster (GB) ran 13:20.34 in his heat for the still-standing Olympic record, but he was placed fifth in the final (13:26.19).

Joseph Guillemot (left) and Paavo Nurmi (right). In 1920 Guillemot won the 5000m with Nurmi second and the order was reversed in the 10000m. *(BBC Hulton)*

The most medals won at 5000m is three by Paavo Nurmi (Fin). As a 23-year-old in 1920 he was second to Joseph Guillemot (Fra) clocking exactly 15min 4.4sec behind the Frenchman. In 1924 the 5000m was his fourth gold medal of the Games, and despite starting the race only 75min after winning the 1500m in an Olympic record time of 3:53.6, he won in another Olympic record time 14:31.2, a fifth of a second ahead of his American-based teammate Ville Ritola, and 30sec ahead of their arch-rival Edvin Wide (Swe). In 1928 it was Ritola's turn to win, with Nurmi second and Wide again third.

Like Nurmi, Mohamed Gammoudi (Tun) qualified for three finals, but scratched in 1964 following his silver medal in the 10000m. However, he went on to win in 1968 and was placed second to Viren in 1972.

A world record was set in 1912, the first year the event was held at the Olympics, at 14:36.6 by Hannes Kolehmainen who won by just a tenth of a second from Jean Bouin (Fra). Kolehmainen's was the first of seven Finnish gold medals, and no other nation has had more than one winner.

The fourth Finnish winner, Lauri Lehtinen set an Olympic record of 14:30.0 in 1932. The same time was given for runner-up Ralph Hill

(USA) yet Hill was most unlucky to lose for Lehtinen undoubtedly impeded him in the finishing straight. The spectators at Los Angeles were incensed by the seeming injustice to Hill, who came from San Francisco, but were quieted by the announcer Bill Henry who said: 'Remember, please, these people are our guests.' There was no protest.

10000 metres

Three of the greatest names in track and field history have won two Olympic gold medals at the 10000m: Paavo Nurmi, Emil Zatopek and Lasse Viren.

Nurmi beat Joseph Guillemot in 1920, 31:45.8 to 31:47.2, and Ville Ritola in 1928, 30:18.8 to 30:19.4. His first win may have been his least comfortable Olympic race, for Guillemot ended the race by being sick over him! The reason for this was that unbeknown to Guillemot the time of the race was brought forward from 5pm to 1.45pm at the request of the King of Belgium. The Frenchman dashed to the race directly after consuming his lunch and had difficulties during the race before it was finally too much for him.

Emil Zatopek (Cze) won by a record margin of 47.8sec in 1948 in a time of 29:59.6 and went on to win a silver behind Gaston Reiff (Bel) in the 5000m. In 1952 he won again (in 29:17.0), the first leg of his unique treble of 10000m, 5000m and marathon. All Zatopek's wins were in new Olympic record times, and Alain Mimoun (Fra) was runner-up in each 10000m and he was also in the 5000m in 1952.

Lasse Viren set a new world record of 27:38.35 with the first of his four Olympic gold medals in 1972, yet he fell during the twelfth lap! He was lying fifth at the time but got to his feet almost immediately and regained contact. He brought down Mohamed Gammoudi, who had been second in 1964 and third in 1968, and Gammoudi was soon forced to drop out. Dave Bedford (GB) led for most of the early part of the race, then a group of five runners contested the lead with Miruts Yifter (Eth) and Viren prominent. At 9000m Yifter led but Viren's powerful sprint finish took him to the tape ahead of Emiel Puttemans (Bel) 27:39.58 and Yifter 27:40.96. Four years later Viren won again, throwing in a second 5000m in 13:31.3 to finish with 27:40.38 and only the Portuguese Carlos Lopes could stay with him for second at 27:45.17. Brendan Foster was third in 27:54.92. One man who might well have caused a different result was non-starter Miruts Yifter who was prevented from competing by the

Brendan Foster tracks Lasse Viren in the 1976 Olympic 5000m. Foster was fifth as Viren completed his second double.   *(G. Herringshaw)*

African boycott of the Games, yet he had demonstrated in the Montreal warm-up meetings that he was in the form of his life. Yifter, however, had his triumph in 1980 as he kicked to victory in both 10000m and 5000m.

A World record was also set by Ville Ritola in 1924 (30:23.2).

Discontinued distance events

Team track races at distances from 3000m to 4 miles were held at six Games from 1900 to 1924. In 1906 and 1908 there were races at 5 miles and in 1912, 1920 and 1924 there were cross-country races with both team and individual medals. Finland provided all three cross-country gold medallists, Hannes Kolehmainen in 1912 and Paavo Nurmi in 1920 and 1924, and won the team title in the latter years, but were pipped by Sweden in 1912.

Standing jumps

Contested between 1900 and 1912, these events were dominated by Ray Ewry (USA), who won all ten gold medals between 1900 and 1908 including two at the unofficial Games of 1906, with best standing performances at the

Games of: HJ 1.655m/5ft 5¼in (world record) in 1900, LJ 3.476m/11ft 4¾in (world record) in 1904, TJ 10.58m/34ft 8½in in 1900. Amazingly Ewry, as a boy, had been paralysed and confined to a wheelchair. Irving Baxter (USA) won silver medals at all three standing jumps in 1900, but also won a unique Olympic double that year of 'running' high jump and pole vault.

Marathon

The Ethiopian Abebe Bikila was not only the first man to win twice but also the first to win two medals. He was unknown to the world's athletics experts when, in 1960 at the age of 28 he ran a new world best time of 2:15:16.2, running barefoot through the streets of Rome to beat the not much better known Rhadi ben Abdesselem of Morocco by 25sec. Bikila was a member of Emperor Haile Selassie's personal guard, which he had joined as a private at the age of 19. He was coached by Onni Niskanen of Sweden and had won a trial race a month before the Games in 2:21:23, a remarkable time at the high altitude of Addis Ababa.

After a Eurovean tour in 1961 Bikila only once ran outside Ethiopia, in the Boston marathon of 1963, in which he placed fifth,

Ray Ewry, winner of the most Olympic gold medals at individual events, at the standing high jump.

before the next Olympic year of 1964. Then he won the Ethiopian trial race in 2:16:18.8, just 0.4sec ahead of Mamo Wolde, but then underwent an appendix operation. Amazingly after only six weeks in which to recover he smashed the field in Tokyo and again set a new world best time 2:12:11.2. He completed his triumph by calmly going into a callisthenics routine while just over four minutes elapsed before the runners-up came into the stadium, Kokichi Tsubaraya (Jap) entered in second place but was overtaken by Basil Heatley (GB) on the final bend. Heatley ran the last 200m in 32.3sec.

Bikila ran again in the 1968 marathon, but an injured leg forced him to retire at 17km, and his team-mate Mamo Wolde won in 2:20:26.4. Wolde became the second man to win two Olympic marathon medals with his third place in 1972. Earlier he had been placed fourth at the 10000m in 1964, but made his Olympic debut at the 1956 Games in Melbourne when he was last in his heat in both the 800 and 1500m and ran in the 4 × 400mR.

The habit of repeat medals at the marathon has continued: the 1972 winner, Frank Shorter (USA) was placed second in 1976; Karel Lismont (Bel) was second in 1972 and third in 1976; and Waldemar Cierpinski (GDR) won in both 1976 and 1980. Cierpinski ran an Olympic record 2:09:55 in 1976 and 2:11:03 in hot weather in Moscow in 1980, when he sprinted the last 200m in 33.4. Behind him and Gerd Nijboer (Hol) Soviet athletes finished 3–4–5, the best 'team' performance since the Americans finished 1–3–4 in 1908 and 1–2–3 in 1904.

The narrowest margin of victory is 12.8sec by Hannes Kolehmainen (Fin), who won in 2:32:35.8, over Juri Lossman (Estonia) in 1920. In 1948 Delfo Cabrera (Arg) won in 2:34:51.6, 16sec ahead of Tom Richards (GB). Etienne Gailly (Bel) was a further 26sec behind in third place, although he had entered Wembley Stadium in first place with just a lap to run.

The greatest victory margin is 7min 13sec for the first Olympic marathon champion, Spyridon Louis (Gre) in 1896.

Two men have won in their first attempts at the distance: Emil Zatopek (Cze) in 1952 and Alain Mimoun (Fra) in 1956. The full marathon distance of 26 miles 385 yards (42195m) has been run in 1908 and each year from 1924, distances in other Games were: 1896 and 1904 40000m; 1900 40260m; 1906 41860m; 1912 40200m; 1920 42750m.

The first man to enter the stadium first and yet lose the race was Dorando Pietri (Ita) in 1908. Pietri fell to the track after entering the White City Stadium. He first turned right then was redirected left around the track. He was assisted to his feet but fell again four more times before crossing the finish line surrounded by officials, doctors and helpers. Half a minute later John Hayes (USA) finished (in 2:54:46.4) and was awarded the race as Pietri was disqualified. There was enormous popular sympathy for the unfortunate Pietri and he was awarded a special gold cup, an exact replica of that won by Hayes, by Queen Alexandra.

Practically every Olympic marathon has featured dramatic happenings. In 1904 Fred Lorz of New York after leading early in the race took a ride in a car for a while then rejoined the race and ran the last 8km. He entered the stadium 15 minutes ahead of Thomas Hicks (USA) and the AAU who did not appreciate this 'joke' banned him for life. The winner, Hicks, was sustained during the race by raw eggs laced with strychnine as well as sips of brandy. In 1968, 64 years later, a joker again led the field into the stadium and for some time this distracted the crowd from the real winner, Frank Shorter. This hoaxer was a 22-year-old student, Norbert Sudhaus.

Dorando Pietri in the lead running through Harlesden near the finish of the 1908 Olympic marathon.   *(BBC Hulton)*

3000 metres steeplechase
The first Olympic steeplechase was in 1900, when races were held at both 2500m and 4000m. Steeplechases were held at 2500m in 1904 and at 3200m in 1908, before the modern distance of 3000m was standardised in 1920.

An extra lap was run in error in 1932 when Volmari Iso-Hollo (Fin) won easily in 10:33.4 for the 3450m course. Iso-Hollo won again in 1936, this time over the correct distance in 9:03.8, becoming the only man to win two gold medals at this event.

World records have been set by three winners: Iso-Hollo (unofficially) in 1936 (see above), Horace Ashenfelter (USA) with 8:45.4 in 1952 and Anders Garderud (Swe) with 8:08.02 in 1976. Second to Garderud was Bronislaw Malinowski (Pol) in 8:09.11, also inside Garderud's previous record of 8:09.70. Malinowski, who had been fourth in 1972, when the Kenyans Kip Keino (in his first serious season at the event) and Ben Jipcho had taken the gold and silver medals, went on to win in 1980 in 8:09.70. In that race he gradually wore down the blazing pace set by Filbert Bayi (Tan). Bayi, who had passed up the chance of a possible 1500m medal, set an 8min pace, passing 1000m in 2:38.8 and 2000m in 5:20.3, but on the final lap this pace told and Malinowski overtook him at the water jump as Bayi struggled home second in 8:12.48.

When Ashenfelter beat Vladimir Kazantsev (USSR) in 1952 it was stated that 'it was the first time that an FBI agent (Ashenfelter) had deliberately let himself be followed by a Russian'.

Another man to run in three finals was the 1964 gold medallist Gaston Roelants (Bel). He was fourth in 1960 and seventh in 1968.

The 1956 winner, Chris Brasher (GB), was originally disqualified for pushing the bronze medallist Ernst Larsen (Nor). Sandor Rozsnyoi (Hun) was declared the winner, but after an appeal the jury of the IAAF reinstated Brasher, having decided that the contact was unintentional and both athletes had stated that it had not affected their running.

Chris Brasher with his hard earned gold medal flanked by Ernst Larsen third (left) and Sandor Rozsnyoi (right) second.   *(GOPA)*

110 metres hurdles
Americans have dominated this event in Olympic history more than any other track event, winning 16 of the 20 gold medals, as well as 13 silver and 13 bronze.

Lee Calhoun (USA) is the only double gold medallist, but he won by tiny margins. In 1960 he beat Willie May 13.98 to 13.99 and in 1956 he held off Jack Davis (USA) 13.70 to 13.73, as the latter collected his second successive silver medal, a feat which was emulated by Alejandro Casanas (Cub) in 1976 and 1980.

Four winners have won medals of other colours as well: Sydney Atkinson (SA) second in 1924 and first in 1928; Hayes Jones (USA) third in 1960 and first in 1964; Willie Davenport (USA) first in 1968 and third in 1976; Guy Drut (Fra) second in 1972 and first in 1976. Davenport is

the only man to have run in three finals; he was fourth in 1972, when the winner Rod Milburn (USA) ran a world record time of 13.24. Davenport also ran in the 1964 Games but was seventh in his semi-final following injury.

Apart from Milburn the only other men to set world records were Earl Thomson, a Canadian student at Dartmouth College, USA in 1920 when he won with 14.8sec, and Forrest Towns (USA) with 14.1 in his semi-final before winning the final in 14.2 in 1936.

Athletes from the USA have won all three medals at eight different Games (1900, 1904, 1908, 1912, 1948, 1952, 1956 and 1960), the most times such a clean sweep has been achieved at any event in the Olympic Games.

In 1932 Don Finlay (GB) was originally placed fourth and Jack Keller (USA) third, but the judges reversed the placings after seeing a film of the race, the first such reversal in Olympic history.

400 metres hurdles
Glenn Davis (USA) is the only double gold medallist. Davis won in 1956 in his first season of 400m hurdling with 50.1 (50.29 auto) and in 1960 with 49.3 (49.51 auto) leading home the third and fourth USA clean sweeps in this event. As with the 110m hurdles Americans have been dominant, with twelve winners, nine second places and seven third places.

World records have been set six times: 1908 Charles Bacon (USA) 55.0; 1920 Frank Loomis (USA) 54.0; 1932 Glenn Hardin (USA) 51.9; 1968 David Hemery (GB) 48.12; 1972 John Akii-Bua (Uga) 47.82; 1976 Edwin Moses (USA) 47.64. Akii-Bua had a tooth extracted on the morning of the race in 1972! Hardin's world record came in second place! The winner at Los Angeles in 1932 was Bob Tisdall of Ireland in 51.7, but Tisdall knocked down the last of the ten hurdles and according to the rules in force at the time this invalidated his achievement for record purposes. Tisdall had only raced three times at the event before the Games. His first try was a 55.0sec win in Athens in 1930, then he ran the 440y hurdles in 56.2 and 54.2 in Dublin in 1932. At Los Angeles he won his heat in 54.8 and his semi-final in 52.8 and his breakthrough was one of the greatest in Olympic history. He was later placed eighth in the decathlon but then retired. He was born in Ceylon (now Sri Lanka), and was educated at

Shrewsbury School and at Cambridge University. Glenn Hardin went on to win in 1936.

The biggest winning margin is 1.05sec by Edwin Moses over Mike Shine (USA) in 1976 and every winner has been well clear at the finish, for the narrowest margin is the 2m by which Volker Beck (GDR) 48.70 beat Vasiliy Arkhipenko (USSR) 48.86 in 1980.

200 metres hurdles
This event was on the Olympic programme in 1900 and 1904. The winners were multiple gold medallists Alvin Kraenzlein (USA) and Harry Hillman (USA) respectively, Kraenzlein won four golds in 1900 and Hillman three in 1904.

4 × 100 metres relay
The USA has been the winning team on 12 of the 15 times the sprint relay has been held since 1912. World records have tumbled frequently, 25 being set in all, at least one at each Games from 1912 to 1936 and from 1956 to 1972, when the American team set the current record of 38.19.

Frank Wykoff (USA) is the only man to win three sprint relay medals, and his were all golds and all world records. He ran the first leg in 1928 and the anchor leg in 1932 and 1936. Livio Berruti (Italy) also ran in three sprint relay finals, but the closest he came to a medal was the 0.01sec by which Nick Whitehead held him off in 1960 to gain the bronze medal for Britain.

The American team won in 1948, 40.6 to 41.3 for Great Britain, but they had been disqualified at first. They also finished first in 1960, 39.4 to 39.5 for West Germany, but this time there was no reinstatement. Ray Norton (USA) had had a disastrous Games, coming sixth and last in the finals of both the 100m and 200m despite being the pre-Games favourite. He was desperately anxious to make amends, but started running too soon on the second leg and had overrun the zone by the time Frank Budd could reach him. He ran a great leg, and an even greater one was run by Dave Sime on the final leg to start 2m down on Martin Lauer (Ger) and finish nearly 1m up, but all to no avail.

In 1964 seven of the eight finalists equalled or bettered the 1960 Olympic record (39.66 USA), and even the eighth team, Great Britain, were only 0.03sec down by automatic timing. For the winning American team Bob Hayes gave perhaps the most devastating display of sprinting ever seen as he charged down the finishing straight. He started about 3m down on

George Larner, two Olympic golds 1908. *(BBC)*

France, in fourth place. He passed all his rivals about a third of the way through his leg and won by the extraordinary margin of 3m. The winning time was 39.06.

4 × 400 metres relay
The USA have ten wins out of 15 as well as winning the medley (200m, 200m, 400m, 800m) relay in 1908. They would surely have won in 1972 as well but were unable to field a team. John Smith had torn a hamstring in the 400m final, and first and second in that race, Vince Matthews and Wayne Collett, were disqualified by the IOC from taking part in any further Olympic competition following their behaviour during the victory ceremony for the 400m. They treated the ceremony, particularly the US national anthem, in a cavalier fashion, just as they had been able to treat their rivals with disdain on the track.

Nine world records have been set, eight by the USA and one, 3:03.9 in 1952, by Jamaica. The time of 2:56.16 recorded by the US team in 1968 still stands as a world record. Individual splits for the four runners were: Vince Matthews 45.0, Ron Freeman 43.2, Larry James 43.8 and Lee Evans 44.1. Freeman's time is the fastest 400m relay leg ever run. No athlete has been on two winning teams, the best achievements being a gold and a silver, which have been won by Godfrey Rampling (GB), second in 1932 and first in 1936, Mal Whitfield (USA), first in 1948 and second in 1952, and the Kenyans Charles Asati and Hezekiah Nyamau, second in 1968 and first in 1972.

Walks
Walking events have been held at the Olympic Games at the following distances: 1500m 1906; 3000m 1906 and 1920; 3500m 1908; 10000m 1912, 1920, 1924, 1948, 1952; 10 miles 1908; 20000m each Games since 1956; 50000m each Games since 1932, except for 1976.

The most gold medals for walking is three by Ugo Frigerio (Ita). He won the 3000m (in 13:14.2) and the 10000m (in 48:06.2) in 1920, and the 10000m (in 47:49.0) in 1924. George Larner (GB) emulated Frigerio in winning two walking golds at one Olympics as he took the 3500m (14:55.0) and the 10 miles (a world record time of 1:15:57.4) in 1908. Larner, a Brighton policeman, had retired from competitive walking, but his Chief Constable gave him time off from police duties for training.

The most medals at walking events is four by Frigerio and by Vladimir Golubnichiy (USSR). Frigerio won the bronze medal at 50km in 1932. Golubnichiy is the only man to have won the 20km twice. His first success was in 1960 in 1:34:07.2. In 1964 he was placed third in 1:31:59.4 when Ken Matthews (GB) won in 1:29:34.0 and in 1968 he became the first man since Paavo Nurmi (Fin) to regain an Olympic athletics title. He just held off José Pedraza (Mex) to win in 1:33:58.4. Pedraza entered the stadium for the last lap in third place, about 45m behind Golubnichiy and 25m behind Nikolai Smaga (USSR). The Mexican passed Smaga entering the final turn and sped down the home straight (many would say stretching the walking rules to the limit or beyond) to finish just 1.6sec down on Golubnichiy. In 1972 Golubnichiy was back to win a silver medal in 1:26:56, 13sec behind Peter Frenkel (GDR). Golubnichiy was still not finished, for at the age of 40 in 1976, he came seventh as Daniel Bautista won Mexico's first Olympic gold medal in a world best time of 1:24:41. Bautista and Anatoliy Solomin (USSR) were leading the 20km in Moscow in 1980, but both were disqualified for 'lifting' between 1800m and 1500m from the finish. This left Maurizio Damilano (Ita) to win in the Olympic record time of 1:23:36.

The most medals won at 50km is three by John Ljunggren (Swe), who won in 1948 (4:41:52), dropped to ninth in 1952 (4:43:45.2) after setting the early pace, was third in 1956 (4:35:02) and improved to second in 4:25:47 at the age of 41 in 1960. He went on to take part in a fifth Olympic Games, with 16th at 50km in 1964. He also competed three times at 20km, and his third/fourth in 1956 is the best ever double at 50km/20km at one Games. In 1960 he finished 17sec behind Don Thompson (GB) after a tremendous battle. Thompson had carefully prepared for the heat of Rome by sweating it out in his bathroom at home with the temperature at 100°F/38°C.

Vladimir Golubnichiy had a 20-year career in the forefront of world walking and won a European and two Olympic titles. *(M. Shearman)*

The Olympic 50km record is 3:49:24 by Hartwig Gauder (GDR) in 1980.

The greatest winning margin at any Olympic walk is 10:03.4 by Christoph Höhne (GDR) at 50km in 1968, when he was timed in 4:20:13.6.

High Jump
The closest any man has come to winning two gold medals is the achievement of Valeriy Brumel. In 1960 as a 19-year-old he cleared the same height as the winner Robert Shavlakadze (USSR), 2.16m/7ft 1in, but had to settle for second on the count-back. He won in 1964, this time with the count-back in his favour, from John Thomas (USA), both clearing 2.18m/7ft 1¾in. Thomas had been third in 1960 at 2.14m/7ft 0¼in, when he was the world record holder.

Con Leahy (Ire) won in 1906 at 1.775m/5ft 9¾in and was second equal in 1908 with 1.88m/6ft 2in, an inch behind Harry Porter (USA).

The closest battle for medals was in 1932 when four men succeeded at 1.97m/6ft 5½in, and went to a jump-off to decide the places. The winner was Duncan McNaughton (Can), the first non-American winner, and only selected because he was already in California at college. The unlucky fourth placer was Cornelius Johnson (USA), but four years later he won at 2.03m/6ft 8in.

Stig Pettersson (Swe) had the galling experience to be placed successively fourth in 1956, fifth in 1960 and fourth in 1964, improving at each Games: 2.06m, 2.09m, 2.14m.

The only time **a world record** has been set in this event was in 1980. Gerd Wessig (GDR), a cook by profession, came into the Games with a best of 2.30m/7ft 6½in, but improved this three times, to 2.31m, 2.33m and finally the world record 2.36m/7ft 8¾in at his second attempt. Second at 2.31m/7ft 7in was Jacek Wszola (Pol) who became the third man to win a high jump gold and silver, as he had won in 1976 with 2.25m/7ft 4½in.

Pole Vault

Bob Richards (USA) is the only double gold medallist. He won in 1952 with 4.55m/14ft 11¼in and in 1956 with 4.56m/14ft 11½in. He is also the only man to have three medals, for he was placed third in 1948 with 4.20m/13ft 9½in.

World records have been achieved twice, in 1920 by Frank Foss (USA) at 4.09m/13ft 5in, when he won by the record margin of 39cm/15¼in, and in 1980 by Wladyslaw Kozakiewicz (Pol) at 5.78m/18ft 11½in.

Standards have improved dramatically on several occasions. In 1912 the first seven men bettered the 1908 Olympic record of 3.71m, with the winner Harry Babcock (USA) vaulting 3.95m/12ft 11½in.

The most Olympic records in any one Olympic competition, came in 1964, when the first nine men bettered Don Bragg's 1960 Olympic record of 4.70m/15ft 5in. The first 12 men equalled the record, then the bar went higher and higher until Fred Hansen (USA) was left the winner at 5.10m/16ft 8¾in. In all the record had been equalled or bettered 36 times during a nine-hour competition. Even more men, however, bettered the Olympic record four years later as 11 men vaulted 5.15m/16ft 10¾in or higher. This time there were 33 Olympic records. The first three all cleared 5.40m/17ft 8½in: Bob Seagren (USA), Claus Schiprowski (Ger) and Wolfgang Nordwig (GDR).

In 1972 Nordwig came first with 5.50m/18ft 0½in and Seagren second at 5.40m. Nord-wig set a standard for any event of seven Olympic records (4 in 1968, 3 in 1972) and was the first non-American to win the Olympic pole vault, though the competition was marred by the IAAF bans on certain makes of pole, which caused 14 of the 21 finalists to vault on 'new' poles. There was considerable confusion over the acceptability of the new models of Cata-poles and Sky-poles and after these had been banned and then re-allowed, a decision was taken only on the eve of the final competition. Seagren had to vault with a pole he had never even practised with, though it seems that others were allowed to use the banned poles.

The first three men in 1976 equalled Nordwig's 5.50m record, and further improvement came in 1980 when another 15 Olympic records were achieved by six men.

Two gold medals were awarded in 1908, to Edward Cooke and Alfred Gilbert who tied at 3.71m/12ft 2in.

In 1900 the leading Americans Bascom Johnson and Charles Dvorak were told that the event was not being held on the day they reported, so they left, but to their indignation it was contested later that day. Their countryman Irving Baxter was on hand to win at 3.30m/10ft 10in. The French Olympic Committee put on a special competition for the Americans, and this was won at 3.45m/11ft 3¾in by D. S. Horton, who had also not known the time of the final.

Long Jump

Ralph Boston (USA) gained a complete set of medals. He won in 1960 with 8.12m/26ft 7¾in, the first man to better Jesse Owens' winning 8.06m/26ft 5¼in jump of 1936. Boston's team-mate Bo Roberson narrowly failed to snatch victory with a last round jump of 8.11m/26ft 7¼in. In 1964 Boston jumped 8.03m/26ft 4¼in with his last attempt, but stayed 4cm behind Lynn Davies (GB) and in 1968 he was third with 8.16m/26ft 9½in.

Ahead of Boston in 1968, Bob Beamon (USA) achieved what most experts would vote the greatest single performance in athletics history. He took advantage of all the conditions in his favour, the thin air of high altitude, a wind behind him and the challenge of the great occasion, to smash the world record with his epic jump of 8.90m/29ft 2½in. Igor Ter-Ovanesyan (USSR) was a great rival of Ralph Boston, but finished behind him in three Olympics, third in 1960 (after suffering a skiing injury at the start of the year that was so severe it was thought he might be unable to jump ever

Above: Daniel Bautista (13) on his way to winning the 1976 Olympic 20km walk. Raul Gonzales (17) was fifth. Between them is Karl-Heinz Stadtmüller, who placed fourth.

Left: Daley Thompson put the shot 14.43m in the third event of the 1978 Commonwealth decathlon, when he set the highest ever first-day score of 4550 points.

Above: The Houston Astrodome, site of the largest indoor track (352y circumference) ever laid.

Heide Rosendahl (left, 2nd), Mary Peters (centre, 1st) and Burglinde Pollak (right, 3rd) after 1972 Olympic pentathlon.

Geoff Capes, undefeated by a British shot-putter from 1970 and ranked number 1 in the world in 1975, also breeds budgerigars.

again), and in 1964 and fourth in 1968. He also competed in 1956, but had three no-jumps in the final and went on to a fifth Games in 1972, when he missed qualifying for the final by one place.

Apart from Beamon the only world record in Olympic competition came not in the long jump event itself but in the pentathlon of 1924 when Robert LeGendre (USA) jumped 7.76m/25ft 5½in en route to a bronze medal. Le Gendre was not entered in the long jump, which was won by William DeHart Hubbard (USA) with 7.44m/24ft 5in. Hubbard took the world record from LeGendre the following year.

Athletes from the USA have won 17 out of 20 gold medals. In 1936 Jesse Owens improved the Olympic best four times, a record for any event other than the pole vault. His full series: 7.74m, 7.87m, 7.75m, N, 7.94m and 8.06, all with a following wind.

William De Hart Hubbard, the first black athlete to win an Olympic title – the 1924 long jump.
(University of Michigan)

Triple Jump

Viktor Saneyev (USSR) has an Olympic record second only to that of discus-thrower Al Oerter. He won three successive gold medals followed by a silver at the age of 34 in Moscow in 1980. His Olympic career started in 1968, when in the greatest triple jump competition of all-time he won with a final round world record of 17.39/57ft 0¾in. In the third round he had also set a world record of 17.23m/56ft 6½in only to see Nelson Prudencio (Bra) improve it to 17.27m/56ft 8in in the fifth round. Two further world records had been set earlier, both by Giuseppe Gentile (Ita), at 17.10m/56ft 1¼in in the qualifying round and at 17.22m/56ft 6in in the first round to gain him the bronze medal. Saneyev won again in 1972 with a wind assisted 17.35m/56ft 11in, his first jump of the competition, from Jorg Drehmel (GDR) 17.31m/56ft 9½in, and for a third time in 1976 with a fifth round 17.29m/56ft 8¾in. In 1980 he entered the competition with a season's best of 16.78m/55ft 0¾in, but demonstrated his competitive ability by jumping 16.85m, 17.04m, 17.07m and finally his best jump for four years – 17.24m/56ft 6¾in into a headwind with the last jump of the competition as Jaak Uudmae (USSR) won the gold with 17.35m/56ft 11in. Unfortunately the 1980 competition was overshadowed by some highly debatable judging decisions which ruled as no jumps, for dragging the trailing leg, leaps of around 17.50m/ 57ft 5in for Joao Oliveira (Bra) and Ian Campbell (Aus). Oliveira finished third for the second successive Games and Campbell was fifth.

Double gold medallists have been: Myer Prinstein (USA) 1900 14.47m/47ft 5¾in and 1904 14.35m/47ft 1in on the same day that he won the long jump with 7.34m/24ft 1in, the only man to have achieved the LJ/TJ double at an Olympic Games; Adhemar Ferreira da Silva (Bra) 1952 a world record 16.22m/53ft 2½in, 1956 16.35m/53ft 7¾in; and Jozef Schmidt (Pol) 1960 16.81m/55ft 1¼in, 1964 16.85m/55ft 3½in. Schmidt set Olympic records on each occasion, yet jumped even further in 1968 with 16.89m/55ft 5in when he was only seventh. Da Silva competed in two other finals, and was placed 11th in 1948 and 14th in 1960.

In addition to the six referred to above, world records have been set by the winners in: 1908 Irishman Tim Ahearne, competing for Great Britain, 14.91m/48ft 11in; 1924 Anthony Winter (Aus) 15.52m/50ft 11in; 1932 Chuhei Nambu (Jap) 15.72m/51ft 7in; 1936 Naoto Tajima (Jap) 16.00m/52ft 6in.

Ralph Rose won the Olympic shot in 1904 and 1908 and the double-handed shot in 1912. He also won medals at discus and hammer in 1904.

(BBC Hulton)

Shot

Two men have won two gold medals and a silver at the shot. Ralph Rose (USA) set a world record 14.81m/48ft 7in in 1904, won again in 1908 at 14.21m/46ft 7½in and came second in 1912 with 15.25m/50ft 0½in 9cm behind his team-mate Pat McDonald. Parry O'Brien (USA) narrowly won with his first round put of 17.41m/57ft 1½in in 1952, as his arch-rival Darrow Hooper (USA) put just 2cm less in the final round. O'Brien won easily in 1956 with 18.57m/60ft 11¼in from Bill Nieder (USA) 18.18m/59ft 7¾in. Nieder turned the tables in 1960, when he was only placed fourth in the US trials but took his place after the withdrawal of Dave Davis, to win with 19.68m/64ft 6¾in to O'Brien's 19.11m/62ft 8½in. Third was Dallas Long, who went on to win in 1964 with 20.33m/66ft 8½in from Randy Matson (USA) 20.20m/66ft 3¼in. The third American was O'Brien, who threw his furthest in the Olympics yet finished fourth at 19.20m/63ft 0in.

Randy Matson won in 1968 at 20.54m/67ft 4¾in and second was George Woods (USA), who won a second silver medal in 1972 in the closest ever Olympic throwing event. Wladyslaw Komar (Pol) was the winner with his first put of 21.18m/69ft 6in, but that throw came under tremendous pressure. The two East Germans, Hartmut Briesenick and Hans-Peter Gies each threw 21.14m and came third and fourth respectively. Woods' fourth round effort was 21.17m/69ft 5½in and in the final round his shot actually hit the marker placed for Komar's winning mark. The flight of his shot was thus impeded and measured at 21.05m/69ft 0¾in but he must be adjudged distinctly unlucky. American throwers have won fifteen gold medals and have made a clean sweep of the medals seven times, but failed to gain any medals in 1976 when the gold went to Udo Beyer (GDR) at 21.05m/69ft 0¾in. Al Feuerbach was the best American thrower with a fourth place, to add to his fifth in 1972, and Woods was seventh. In 1980 when the Americans boycotted the Games, Vladimir Kiselyev (USSR) improved the Olympic record to 21.35m/70ft 0½in.

The previous record had been set in the qualifying round in 1976 by Aleksandr Barishnikov (USSR) at 21.32m/69ft 11½in. Barishnikov was third in the final and improved to second in 1980.

World records have been set by Rose in 1904 (see above) and by John Kuck (USA) in 1928 – 15.87m/52ft 0¾in.

Discus

Al Oerter (USA) is the only athlete to win four gold medals at one event. He also improved the Olympic record on each occasion. His Olympic career began as a 20-year-old in Melbourne in 1956 when he set a personal best of 56.36m/184ft 11in on his first throw in the final.

In 1960 he improved to 58.42m/191ft 8in in the qualifying competition and again to 59.18m/194ft 2in in the fifth round of the final to overtake his arch-rival Rink Babka (USA) who had to settle for the silver medal with 58.02m/190ft 4in. Perhaps Oerter's most remarkable win came in 1964 for he had suffered from a cervical disc injury for months. On top of that he tore some cartilages in his lower rib cage just six days before the competition. Doctors had advised him not to throw, as six weeks of rest would be required. For Oerter however the Olympics came first and with his ribs heavily taped he somehow overcame the severe pain. His first round throw of 57.65m placed him second to Ludvik Danek (Cze), the world record holder. In the second round he improved to 58.34m, but slipped back to third as Dave Weill (USA) took the lead at 59.49m. Oerter could throw only 55.11m, and 54.37m in the next two rounds, while Danek regained the lead with 60.52m. In the fifth round, however, his tremendous competitive spirit overcame all the obstacles and his discus sailed out to 61.00m/200ft 1½in to win his third gold.

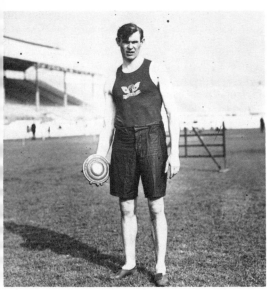

Martin Sheridan won a total of nine Olympic medals, including five in 1906. He also set five discus world records. *(BBC Hulton)*

Irish–American John Flanagan in 1908 when he won his third consecutive Olympic hammer title. *(BBC Hulton)*

In 1968 he again came into the Olympics as the underdog, for Jay Silvester (USA), fourth in 1964, had improved the world record to 68.40m/224ft 5in while Oerter's best for the year was 62.74m/205ft 10in. Silvester set an Olympic record of 63.64m/207ft 10in in the qualifying round, but in the final could manage only 61.78m/202ft 8in for fifth place. Oerter, rising as always to the great occasion, smashed his personal best and the field with 64.78m/212ft 6in in the third round, backed by a 64.04m in the sixth round to win clearly from Lothar Milde (GDR) 63.08m/206ft 11in.

Curiously Oerter never won the US Olympic trials. He was second in 1956, 1960 and 1964 and third in 1968. In his amazing comeback in 1980 he was fourth at 65.56m/215ft 1in and thus did not qualify, but the Americans had decided to boycott the Games and who can say that Oerter would not have made the squad if it had been 'for real'.

Martin Sheridan (USA) won three times – in 1904 (39.28m/128ft 10in), at the intercalated Games in 1906 (41.46m/136ft), and in 1908 (40.89m/134ft 1in). There was a throw-off for first in 1904 as both Sheridan and Ralph Rose (USA) had each recorded the same distance. Sheridan won the throw-off by about 1.5m. Clarence 'Bud' Houser (USA) won in 1924 (46.14m/151ft 4in) and in 1928 (47.32m/155ft 3in) and also won the shot in 1924.

Three medals were won by Ludvik Danek (Cze), second in 1964 and third in 1968 before winning in 1972 with 64.40m/211ft 3in. Danek competed in a fourth final in 1976 when he was ninth in the competition won by Mac Wilkins (USA) at 67.50m/221ft 5in. Wilkins set the current Olympic record of 68.28m/224ft in the qualifying round.

Two other throwers competed in four finals: Adolfo Consolini (Ita) 1948 1st, 1952 2nd, 1956 6th, 1960 17th; Jay Silvester (USA) 1964 4th, 1968 5th, 1972 2nd, 1976 8th.

The carelessness of the judges cost Jules Noel (Fra) a medal in 1932. In the first round they were watching the pole vault when he threw and failed to find a mark for his discus, yet onlookers were sure that it was close to the winning mark. He was allowed an extra throw but could not reproduce such form.

The discus is the only men's event at which a world record has not been set in Olympic competition.

Hammer

The Irish-American John Flanagan won the first three Olympic hammer gold medals. From a 9ft/2.74m circle he threw 49.73m/163ft 1½in in 1900. Then from the now-standard 7ft/2.13m circle he threw 51.23m/168ft 0½in in 1904 and improved to 51.92m/170ft 4in in 1908. All nine medals in these years were won by the Americans and the 'Irish Whales', as the Irish-Americans who dominated the event in the early years of the 20th century were known, maintained their supremacy in the Games to follow. Matt McGrath, who had been born at Nenagh, Tipperary, was second in 1908 and won in 1912 with 54.74m/179ft 7in. He was fifth in 1920 and second in 1924 at the age of 46. Patrick Ryan, who like Flanagan came from County Limerick, won in 1920 with 52.86m/173ft 5in.

Two other men have successfully defended their titles. Patrick O'Callaghan of Ireland won in 1928 and 1932 and Yuriy Syedikh (USSR) won in 1976 and 1980. In the former year Syedikh won at 77.52m/254ft 4in with team-mates Aleksey Spiridonov second and Anatoliy Bondarchuk, the defending champion and Syedikh's coach, third. In 1980 Syedikh threw first in both the qualifying round and in the final. In qualifying he upped his Olympic record to 78.22m/256ft 7in and improved further with the first throw of the final to win at 81.80m/268ft 4in, a new world record. The former record holder Sergei Litvinov (USSR) battled mightily but had five no throws following his opening 80.64m/264ft 7in. Juri Tamm came third for the second successive Soviet medal sweep.

Apart from Syedikh's 1980 throw, a world record was also set in 1952 by Jozsef Csermák (Hun) 60.34m/197ft 11in. Gyula Zsivotzký (Hun) won three medals. Following silver medals in 1960 and in 1964, he had a narrow win in 1968 over the defending champion, Romuald Klim (USSR) with 73.36m/240ft 8in to 73.28m/240ft 5in. Zsivotzký was also fifth in 1972.

Javelin
Erik Lemming (Swe) won the most gold medals for javelin, and has the unique achievement of having set new individual world records at three Games. He won in 1906 with 53.90m/176ft 10in, improving to 54.82m/179ft 10½in in 1908 and to 60.64m/198ft 11in in 1912. He won a fourth gold medal as he took the 'freestyle' javelin event on the only occasion that it was contested, in 1908, with 54.44m/178ft 7in. In 1912 he was fourth in an aggregate javelin contest for both hands. He threw 58.33m with his right hand but only 40.26m with his left. Juho Saaristo (Fin), who had been second in the main event at 58.66m, threw a world record 61.00m/200ft 1½in right-handed and 48.42m/158ft 10in left-handed.

The only other double gold medallist has been Jonni Myyrä (Fin), who won in 1920 and 1924.

World records were also set by the winners in 1956 and 1976. Egil Danielsen (Nor) threw 85.70m/281ft 2in in 1956 and twenty years later Miklos Nemeth (Hun), the son of the 1948 hammer champion, won with his first round throw of 94.58m/310ft 4in. This world record gave him a record winning margin of 6.66m/21ft 11in over Hannu Siitonen (Fin).

Two men have competed in four finals, Janusz Sidlo (Pol) and Janis Lusis (USSR). Sidlo was second in 1956, eighth in 1960, fourth in 1964 and seventh in 1968. He also competed in 1952 but did not qualify for the final. In 1960 he had the best throw of the Games, 85.14m/279ft 4in, but sadly for him this was in the qualifying round and his final best was only 76.46m, well behind the 84.64m/277ft 8in of winner Viktor Tsibulenko (USSR). Janis Lusis was third in 1964 and won in 1968 with an Olympic record of 90.10m/295ft 7in. In 1972 Lusis led with 88.88m in the first round and improved to 89.54m in the third round. Klaus Wolfermann (Ger) closed to 88.40m in the fourth round and then broke the Olympic record with 90.48m/296ft 10in. This throw 'destroyed' the

Erik Lemming took the world javelin record from 49.32m to 62.32m in 1899–1912. He won four Olympic golds and 25 Swedish titles at five events.

finalists with the exception of Lusis, who showed just why he is regarded as the greatest ever javelin thrower by responding in the last round with 90.46m, just 2cm, the smallest measurable distance behind Wolfermann's best. Lusis went on to be placed eighth in 1976.

Dainis Kula (USSR) won the 1980 title with a fourth round throw of 91.20m/299ft 2in, yet many observers considered him exceptionally lucky to have done so. He had no throws in the first and second rounds and his third throw came down tail first according to most reports, yet it was adjudged a fair throw, contrary to the rules, and this took him into the lead with 88.88m/291ft 7in. If that had been a foul he would have been out of the competition. Following the competition there was much controversy over 'cheating', but this centered on the ridiculous theory that the stadium doors were opened to assist the Soviet throwers (Kula's team-mate Aleksandr Makarov was second) rather than on the judging error.

The Nordic tradition is very strong in the javelin. Finland has much the best record with five gold, six silver and four bronze medals; Sweden has four gold, two silver and two bronze; Norway one of each variety; and the Latvian representatives of the USSR have won two gold, one silver and one bronze.

Decathlon
Two Olympic gold medals were won by Bob Mathias (USA). He was the youngest ever male Olympic gold medallist at 17½ in 1948. In just his third decathlon the high school boy from Tulare, Cal. won with 7139 points on the 1934 tables then in use (6825 on the current 1964 tables). In 1952 he won a devastating victory with the world record score of 7887 on the 1952 tables (7731 on the 1964 tables). In this, his third world record, he won by the record margin of 912 points from Milton Campbell (USA), who went on to win in 1956 with 7937 points (7708 on the 1962 tables).

Eight world records have been set at the Games. Others have been:
1912 – Jim Thorpe (USA) 8412 on the 1912 tables (6756 current). Thorpe's achievement was not ratified and he forfeited his gold medal when he was disqualified several months after the Games as a result of disclosures concerning his having received payment for playing baseball in 1909.
1924 – Harold Osborn (USA) 7720 on the 1912 tables (6668 current). Osborn also won the 1924 high jump, the only decathlon winner also to win an individual event.
1928 – Paavo Yrjöla (Fin) 8053 on the 1912 tables (6774 current). Akilles Järvinen (Fin) finished second with 7931, yet on the current tables his score of 6815 would have beaten Yrjola. Järvinen was again second in 1932, and again his score comes out higher on the current tables than that of the actual winner, Jim Bausch (USA) (7038 to 6896).
1932 – Jim Bausch (USA) 8462 on the 1912 tables (6896 current)
1936 – Glenn Morris (USA) 7900 on the 1934 tables (7421 current)
1972 – Nikolai Avilov (USSR) 8456 points
1976 – Bruce Jenner (USA) 8617 points.
    Several men who became notable coaches won decathlon medals, including Gösta Holmer (Swe), who was third in 1912 and fourth in 1920, Brutus Hamilton (USA) who was second in 1920, and Ken Doherty (USA) who was placed third in 1928.

Pentathlon
The standard pentathlon (LJ, JT, 200m, DT and 1500m) was held in 1912, 1920 and 1924. Eero Lehtonen (Fin) won the last two. In 1906 a pentathlon was held comprising a standing long jump, Greek style discus, javelin, one stade

Bob Mathias, double Olympic decathlon champion, had a 110m hurdles best of 13.8 in 1952 and was second in the NCAA 120y hurdles for Stanford University. *(Stanford University)*

(192m) and Graeco-Roman wrestling. The winner was Hjalmar Mellander (Swe).

Other throwing events
Double handed shot, discus and javelin events were contested in 1912, the throwers' bests with both right and left hands being aggregated, and other events were: 56lb/25.4kg weight in 1904 and 1906; 14.1lb/6.4kg stone in 1906 and Greek-style discus in 1906 and 1908.

WOMEN
100 metres
Wyomia Tyus (USA) is the one double winner of the 100m. In 1968 she won the final in the first official 11.0sec by a woman (11.08 auto). She beat her former co-holders of the world record Barbara Ferrell (USA), second in 11.15 and Irena Szewinska (Pol), third in 11.19. Four years earlier Tyus had equalled Wilma Rudolph's then world record in the semi-finals at 11.2 (11.23 auto), before winning the final in 11.4 (11.49 auto). Tyus shared a fifth world record at the Olympics on the winning US sprint relay team in 1968.

Two girls have won a gold and a silver at 100m and each set a world record. Stanislawa Walasiewicz (Pol), known in the USA as Stella Walsh, won in 1932 with a world record of 11.9, a time she also ran in her heat and semi-final and which was shared by runner-up Hilde Strike (Can). But in 1936, although she ran 11.7 she had to give the best to Helen Stephens, the almost 6ft/1.83m tall American teenager. Stephens was timed at 11.5, having run 11.4 and 11.5 in preceding rounds. These times were all well inside Walasiewicz's world record of 11.7, but were wind assisted. Renate Stecher (GDR) won in 1972, her time of 11.07 taking 0.01sec off Tyus's world record, but she was beaten by Annegret Richter (Ger) in 1976, 11.08 to 11.13. Richter had improved the world record to 11.01 in her semi-final.

Raelene Boyle (Aus) is the only woman to have run in three finals. As a 17-year-old in 1968 she was fourth in 11.19, improved to second in 1972 (11.23) and was again fourth in 1976 (11.23). In addition to those referred to above world records have been set as follows: 1952 Marjorie Jackson (Aus) 11.5 (11.65 auto); and 1960 Wilma Rudolph (USA) 11.3 in the semi-final. She ran a devastating 11.0 (11.18 auto) in the final but unfortunately the wind speed was just over the limit for record purposes at 2.752m/s.

Perhaps surprisingly for the shortest event on the programme there have been three wins by at least 3m margins. Fanny Blankers-Koen (Hol) in 1948, Marjorie Jackson (Aus) in 1952 and Wilma Rudolph (USA) in 1960.

200 metres
In 1980 Bärbel Wöckel (GDR) became the first double 200m winner when she set an Olympic Record time of 22.03 from lane one with 18-year-old Natalia Bochina (USSR) running a 22.19 world junior record in second place. Four years earlier, Wöckel, then Fraulein Eckert, beat the 100m winner Annegret Richter (Ger) by just 0.02 in 22.37.

Raelene Boyle (Aus) won two silver medals and on each occasion her conqueror set a world record: in 1968 Irena Szewinska (Pol) won with 22.5 (22.58 auto) to Boyle's 22.7 (22.73 auto) and in 1972 Renate Stecher (GDR) won with 22.40 to Boyle's 22.45.

Irena Szewinska is the only woman to have contested three finals, preceding her win by being placed second to Edith McGuire (USA) in 1964, 23.05 for the winner to 23.13 for Szewinska, and coming third in 1972 (22.74).

In addition to the two referred to above, world records were also set in 1952 by Marjorie Jackson (Aus), who ran 23.6 in her heat and 23.4 in her semi-final, before winning the final with 23.7.

Renate Stecher (left) beats Raelene Boyle by 0.05sec in the 1972 Olympic 200m. Both broke the previous world record.   *(E. D. Lacey)*

Fanny Blankers-Koen (Hol) holds the record for the largest margin of victory, 0.7sec in 1948, at 24.4 to Audrey Williamson (GB) 25.1. The first four women's 200m champions, Fanny Blankers-Koen, Marjorie Jackson, Betty Cuthbert (Aus) 1956 and Wilma Rudolph (USA) all won the 100m as well, as did Stecher in 1972. Blankers-Koen, Cuthbert and Rudolph also won gold medals in the sprint relay.

400 metres

First held at the Olympics in 1964, the 400m has had just one double medallist, Christina Lathan (née Brehmer) (GDR), who was second in 1976 and third in 1980. Ahead of her in 1976 Irena Szewinska (Pol) took nearly half a second off her own world record with 49.29 to win by the enormous margin of 1.22sec. In 1980 Marita Koch (GDR) improved the Olympic record to 48.88, as Szewinska closed her great Olympic career by sadly limping in last in her semi-final having pulled a muscle. Szewinska's misfortune let Linsey Macdonald (GB) into the final. There she was more than five years younger, and 14kg/31lb lighter than any other finalist, and though coming last in 52.40 rounded off a marvellous first Olympics with a bronze medal in the relay (at 16 years 171 days, Britain's youngest ever Olympic medallist).

The closest win at this event came in 1968 as Colette Besson (Fra) scored an upset win over Lillian Board (GB) 52.03 to 52.12.

800 metres

The 800m was included in the first Games to hold women's events in 1928. The winner, Lina Radke (Ger) set a world record of 2:16.8, but the event was not included again until 1960, when evidence in the change of standards was shown as Lyudmila Shevtsova (USSR) equalled the world record of 2:04.3. The third successive Olympic winner to set a world record was Ann Packer (GB), who followed her 400m silver medal with an 800m win in only her eighth race at the distance. Her home-straight-sprint took her past Maryvonne Dupureur (Fra) to a time of 2:01.1.

In 1976 the first four beat the then world record of 1:56.0. Tatyana Kazankina (USSR), who was to win her speciality the 1500m four days later, won in 1:54.94 from Nikolina Shtereva (Bul) 1:55.42, Elfi Zinn (GDR) 1:55.60 and Anita Weiss (GDR) 1:55.74.

In 1980 for the fifth time in seven Games the world record was broken. Nadyezhda Olizarenko (née Mushta), who had married

Tatyana Kazankina won her third Olympic gold medal in 1980. She is also the first woman to run 1500m faster than Nurmi.   *(G. Herringshaw)*

Soviet Steeplechaser Sergey Olizarenko after her silver medal in the 1978 European championships, broke Kazankina's world record with 1:54.85 six weeks before the Games and smashed that in Moscow by leading all the way, passing 400m in 56.2 to finish in 1:53.43. Her husband was also on the Olympic team, and qualified from the steeplechase heats but withdrew from the semi-final because of injury.

1500 metres

The 1500m was first held in 1972. The world record at the time stood at 4:06.9 to Lyudmila Bragina and had been set six weeks earlier in the heats of the Soviet Championships, the final of which she had won in 4:09.6. At the Olympics Bragina showed her style of crushing the opposition by proceeding to lead all the way in her heat to improve to 4:06.47. Then she ran 4:05.07 in her semi-final, leading for all but the first 300m. In the final she held back to start with, but took over the lead with two laps to go and held on running with a long, relaxed stride to win with an astonishing 4:01.38. Behind her six more women ran faster than the pre-Games record.

The next two Olympic finals at 1500m were won by Tatyana Kazankina (USSR). In 1976 she won a tactical race with 4:05.48, half a second ahead of Gunhild Hoffmeister (GDR), who had also been runner-up in 1972. Four years later she won with the third fastest time ever recorded, 3:56.56, but even more remarkable was her tremendous sustained finish, for she ran the last 800m in under two minutes. Twelve days later, in Zurich, she took $2\frac{1}{2}$ seconds off her own world record with one of the greatest women's athletic performances in history, 3:52.47.

80 metres/100 metres hurdles

The women's hurdles race was contested at 80m from 1932 to 1968 and at 100m subsequently. Shirley de la Hunty (née Strickland) of Australia is the only double winner, and has also won the most medals, three. She started her Olympic career with a bronze medal behind Fanny Blankers-Koen (Hol) and Maureen Gardner (GB) in 1948, and won by 2m margins in both 1952 10.9 (11.03 auto), a world record, and in 1956 10.7 (10.96 auto). Uniquely she set Olympic records in each of the three rounds. Emulating Shirley de la Hunty by running in three finals have been: Karin Balzer (GDR) 1964 1st 10.54, 1968 5th 10.61, 1972 3rd 12.90 and Pam Ryan (née Kilborn) (Aus) 1964 3rd 10.56, 1968 2nd 10.46, won by 17-year-old Maureen Caird (Aus), 1972 4th 12.98.

Close finishes have been a feature of Olympic hurdle races. In 1932 the first and second, Mildred Didrikson (USA) and Evelyne Hall (USA) both took 0.1sec off the 11.8 world record that Didrikson had equalled in her heat. In 1936 the first four were all given the same time of 11.7 with Trebisonda Valla (Ita) declared the winner, her team-mate Claudia Testoni being the unlucky fourth. In the semi-finals Valla had run 11.6 and curiously this was later ratified as a world record even though the following wind was over the limit at 2.8m/s. There were similarly close finishes in 1964: Balzer 10.54, Tereza Ciepla (Pol) 10.55, Kilborn 10.56 and Irina Press (USSR) 10.62, and in 1976 Johanna Schaller (GDR) 12.77, Tatyana Anisimova (USSR) 12.78, Natalya Lebedyeva (USSR) 12.80 and Gudrun Berend (GDR) 12.82. A further world record was set in 1972, Annelie Ehrhardt (GDR) winning by 0.25sec with 12.59. This was improved as an Olympic record in 1980 by Vera Komisova

(USSR), winner at 12.56 from defending champion Johanna Klier (GDR).

4 × 100 metres relay

The USA have been the most successful nation with five golds, two silver and one bronze medal. Three women have been on two winning teams, Annette Rogers (USA) in 1932 and 1936, and both Marlies Göhr (née Oelsner) and Bärbel Wöckel (née Eckert) were on the GDR teams of 1976 and 1980.

Lyudmila Maslakova (née Zharkova) has run on four Soviet final teams, third in 1968, fifth in 1972, third in 1976 and second in 1980. The great Australian sprinters Shirley Strickland and Raelene Boyle ran in three finals each. Just as in the men's events, more world records have been set in Olympic competition at the sprint relay than in any other event, 16 in all.

In 1964 the first three teams all beat the old world record: 1) Poland 43.69; 2) USA 43.92; 3) Great Britain 44.09. The current world and Olympic record was set in 1980 by the GDR at 41.60.

4 × 400 metres relay

This event was first held in 1972. World records were set in the 1972 and 1976 finals by the winning East German team, 3:22.95 in 1972 and 3:19.23 four years later. On each occasion the GDR team won easily, beating the USA by margins of 2.2sec and 3.6sec.

In 1980, despite a 48.3 last leg by Marita Koch, the GDR team had to yield to the USSR 3:20.2 to 3:20.4. The winning Soviet team in 1980 included two runners, Nina Zyuskova and Irina Bagryantseva, who had not run in the heats of the event. They were the two best Soviet 400m runners, and had been placed fourth and fifth in the individual event, yet they replaced Olga Mineyeva and Lyudmila Chernova, who produced medical certificates showing their inability to run. The two fresh runners ran great legs of 49.7 and 48.8 and this 'using' the rules may have made all the difference to the result.

The only double medallist at the event is Christina Lathan (née Brehmer) (GDR), who was first in 1976 and second in 1980.

High jump

Iolanda Balas (Rom) is the only double gold medallist. She first took part in 1956 when she was fifth with 1.67m/5ft 5¾in. In 1960 she totally outclassed the field, the second place went at 1.71m but Balas set new Olympic records at 1.77m, 1.81m and finally 1.85m/6ft 0¾in for the greatest margin of victory in Olympic high jump history. Four years later she was again supreme, improving first to 1.86m and then to 1.90m/6ft 2¾in to beat Michele Brown (Aus) by 10cm.

Dorothy Tyler (GB) twice won silver medals and each time cleared the same height as the winner. In 1936 as a 16-year-old, she jumped 1.60m/5ft 3in but lost the jump-off to Ibolya Csak (Hun) at 1.62m/5ft 3¾in. After missing two Olympiads through the war, she came back in 1948 with 1.68m/5ft 6in, but lost on the countback to Alice Coachman (USA). Tyler went on to be placed seventh in 1952 and concluded as she had begun with 1.60m for twelfth in 1956, thus being one of only two women to compete in Olympic finals 20 years apart.

World records have been set by four winners: 1928 Ethel Catherwood (Can) 1.59m/5ft 2½in; **1932** Jean Shiley (USA) and Mildred Didrikson (USA) 1.65m/5ft 5in. Shiley cleared 1.67m/5ft 5¾in in the jump-off, but the rules then in force did not permit a record to be set in a jump-off. Didrikson also cleared 1.67, but the judges ruled her jump invalid for going over head-first. This rule was rescinded in 1937; **1956** Mildred McDaniel (USA) 1.76m/5ft 9¼in; **1972** Ulrike Meyfarth (Ger) 1.92m/6ft 3½in.

The Olympic record stands at 1.97m/6ft 5½in to Sara Simeoni (Ita), winner in 1980.

Long jump

Only one woman has won two Olympic long jump medals: Elzbieta Krzesinska (Pol), who was first in 1956 with a world record of 6.35m/20ft 10in and second in 1964 at 6.27m/20ft 7in.

World records were also set by the winners in 1964 and 1968. Mary Rand (GB), who as Mary Bignal had led the qualifiers in 1960 at 6.33m/20ft 9¼in but failed to jump more than 6.00m/19ft 8¼in for ninth in the final, put that experience well behind her in Tokyo in 1964. She set an Olympic record of 6.52m/21ft 4¾in in the qualifying round and then had a superb series of 6.59m, 6.56m, 6.57m, 6.63m, 6.76m/22ft 2¼in, 6.61m in the final. In second place Irena Szewinska won her first Olympic medal with 6.60m/21ft 7¾in. In 1968 Viorica Viscopoleanu (Rom) jumped 6.82m/22ft 4½in in the first round.

The American Willye White competed in five finals, with her best placing coming on her first appearance as a 17-year-old in Melbourne. Her complete record: **1956** 2nd 6.09m/19ft 11¾in; **1960** 16th 5.77m/18ft 11¼in; **1964** 12th

Tatyana Kolpakova poised to win the dramatic 1980 Olympic long jump competition – her only major win of the year.

(G. Herringshaw)

6.07m/19ft 11in; **1968** 11th 6.08m/19ft 11½in; **1972** 11th 6.27m/20ft 7in.

The closest margin of victory has been Heide Rosendahl's 1cm win over Diana Yorgova (Bul) at 6.78m/22ft 3in in 1972 (Rosendahl also set an Olympic record 6.83m/22ft 5in, wind assisted, in the pentathlon).

The most dramatic competition must be that of 1980. In Moscow Tatyana Skachko (USSR) led from the first round at 6.96m/22ft 10in and improved to 7.01m/23ft 0in in the third round. The order at the start of the final round was: 1) Skachko 7.01m, 2) Brigitte Wujak (GDR) and Anna Wlodarczyk (Pol) 6.88m, 4) Tatyana Kolpakova (USSR) 6.87m. Skachko jumped 6.64m, but her lead looked assured. Then Wlodarczyk leaped 6.95m/22ft 9¾in, a personal best and she leapt into the air with joy. But on the third last jump of the competition Kolpakova, the pretty, shy, 20-year-old responded to the occasion in her first major championships with the third equal best jump of all time, 7.06m/23ft 2in. She was followed by Brigitte Wujak, now back in fourth place and she too came through with 7.04m/23ft 1¼in, and poor Wlodarczyk was out of the medals.

Shot

Tamara Press (USSR) is the only double gold medallist, each time with new Olympic records: 1960 17.32m/56ft 10in; 1964 18.14m/59ft 6¼in. Press also won the discus in 1964 after taking the silver medal in 1960. The only other shot/discus gold medallist is the French concert pianist Micheline Ostermeyer, whose winning performances in 1948 (13.75m/45ft 1¼in and 41.92m/137ft 6in) have been left well behind by succeeding generations and who also won a high jump bronze medal. Galina Zybina (USSR) set a world record when winning the 1952 title at 15.28m/50ft 1½in. She went on to compete in three more Games: 1956 2nd 16.53m, 1960 7th 15.56m, 1964 3rd 17.45m. World records have also been set by Margitta Gummel (GDR) 19.07m and 19.61m/64ft 4in in 1968, and Nadyezhda Chizhova (USSR) 21.03m/69ft 0in in 1972. Chizhova was runner-up in 1976 with 20.96m/68ft 9¼in to 21.16m/69ft 5in by Ivanka Khristova (Bul). The current Olympic record and the record margin of victory was set in 1980 by Ilona Slupianek (GDR). Slupianek's series read: 22.41m, 21.81m, 21.42m, 21.60m, 22.00m, and 21.85m. Her best 22.41m/73ft 6¼in was 99cm better than the best of runner-up Svyetlana Krachevskaya (USSR), whose 21.42m/70ft 3¼in equalled Slupianek's worst.

Dana Zatopkova, born the same day as husband Emil. Both Dana and Emil were Olympic champions and world record holders.   *(PA-Reuter)*

Discus

Nina Ponomaryeva (USSR) is the only woman to regain an Olympic title at the same event. As Nina Romashkova she won in 1952, 51.42m/168ft 8in with a record 4.34m/14ft 3in margin of victory. Then she slipped to third in 1956 at 52.02m/170ft 8in to 53.68m/176ft 1in for the winner Olga Fikotová (Cze) who made the headlines after the Games by seeking political asylum and marrying the US Olympic hammer champion, Hal Connolly. Ponomaryeva was back in 1960 to win clearly, 55.10m/180ft 9in to 52.58m/171ft 9in for Tamara Press.

A second double gold medallist is Evelyn Jahl (née Schlaak) (GDR), who set successive Olympic records of 69.00m/226ft 4in when the youngest (aged 20) individual event winner at the 1976 Games, and 69.76m and 69.96m/229ft 6in in 1980. On each occasion Maria Vergova (Bul) was runner-up, the first such repeat in women's Olympic history.

Many of the top women discus throwers have had long careers. Olga Connolly for instance went on to compete in four more Games, representing the USA, and had successive placings of 7th, 12th, 6th and 16th from 1960 to 1972. Ponomaryeva competed for a fourth Games, and came 11th in 1964, but pride of place must go to Romanian Lia Manoliu, an electrical engineer by profession, who holds the record for the most Games, of any track and field competitor, at six. Her complete record is: **1952** 6th

Maria Caridad Colon, the first Central American woman Olympic champion, won the javelin with her fifth Cuban record of 1980.   *(M. Shearman)*

42.64m/139ft 11in; **1956** 9th 43.90m/144ft 0in; **1960** 3rd 52.36m/171ft 9in; **1964** 3rd 56.96m/186ft 10in; **1968** 1st 58.28m/191ft 2in; **1972** 9th 58.50m/191ft 11in.

In 1952 the Soviet throwers took all three medals, the first ever clean sweep in women's events at Olympic track and field.

Javelin

Ruth Fuchs (GDR) won two titles with Olympic records, 63.88m/209ft 7in in 1972 and 65.94m/216ft 4in in 1976. Surprisingly she managed only eighth place in 1980 at 63.94m/209ft 9in as Maria Colon smashed the Olympic record with 68.40m/224ft 5in in the first round of the final becoming the first Cuban woman to win an Olympic gold medal.

The longest ever gap between winning an Olympic medal is 12 years. Dorothy Tyler achieved this in the high jump (1936–48) and Yelena Gorchakova (USSR) won bronze medals in the javelin in 1952 and 1964. In the latter year she set a world record 62.40m/204ft 8in in the qualifying round but in the final, won by the 17-year-old Romanian Mihaela Penes at 60.54m/198ft 7in, she only threw 57.06m/187ft 2in. In 1960 Britain's Susan Platt threw over 54m/177ft in the third round. It was the greatest throw of her career, but she was so excited by the achievement that although she had completed her throw well before the scratch line, she walked over the line so that the throw had to be ruled a foul. The gold medal went to Elvira Ozolina (USSR) 55.98m/183ft 8in and the silver to Dana Zatopkova (Cze) 53.78m/176ft 5in. Platt had to settle for seventh with 51.00m/167ft 4in and rue for ever what might have been.

Dana Zatopkova, wife of the great Emil, won that silver medal at her fourth Games. In 1948 in her maiden name of Ingrova she was seventh with 39.64m/130ft 1in. She won with 50.46m/165ft 7in in 1952, on the same day that Emil won the 5000m, and was fourth in 1956 with 49.82m/163ft 5in.

Pentathlon

First held in 1964 the Olympic pentathlon has three times been won with a world record performance. In 1964 Irina Press (USSR) scored 5246 points (4702 on the current tables) with the 80m hurdles and 200m rather than the 100m hurdles and 800m as on the 1980 schedule. Then in 1972 Mary Peters (GB) won with 4801 by the slender margin of 10 points from Heide Rosendahl (Ger). Rosendahl had held the world record for just 1.12sec, as she ran

the 200m in 22.96 as Peters came in that margin behind in 24.08. Rosendahl had also scored heavily at the long jump 6.83m/22ft 5in to 5.98m/19ft 7½in but Peters had a big lead in the shot 16.20m/53ft 1¾in to 13.86m/45ft 5¾in and in the high jump 1.82m/5ft 11½in to 1.65m/5ft 5in. In the latter event she improved her personal best by 4cm and also ran a best 100m hurdles time of 13.29 (Rosendahl 13.34) to gain a tremendous triumph at her third attempt, having been fourth in 1964 and ninth in 1968. In third place was Burglinde Pollak (GDR) with 4768 points and she was to gain another bronze medal four years later in an even closer affair. Pollak's total was 4740 when both the girls in first and second place scored 4745 points, victory going to Sigrun Siegl by her superior performances in three out of the five events over Christine Laser, in a clean sweep of the medals for the GDR.

The second successive clean sweep of the medals came in Moscow in 1980, but this time to three Soviet women, who each smashed the official world record. The result: 1st Nadyezhda Tkachenko 5083; 2nd Olga Rukavishnikova 4937; 3rd Olga Kuragina 4875. Tkachenko's individual performances were: 100mh 13.29; SP 16.84m/55ft 3in; HJ 1.84m/6ft 0½in; LJ 6.73m/22ft 1in and an amazing 2:05.2 for 800m. Pollak was sixth at 4553 points in her third Games.

GREAT BRITAIN AT THE OLYMPIC GAMES

From 1896 to 1980 British athletes won 42 Olympic gold medals. Of these just three were women, Mary Rand, long jump, and Ann Packer, 800m in 1964 and Mary Peters at pentathlon in 1972.

Britain's best event is the 800m, which has been won six times by British athletes: Alfred Tysoe in 1900, Albert Hill in 1920, Douglas Lowe in 1924 and 1928, Thomas Hampson in 1932 and Steve Ovett in 1980.

Britain's worst event is the men's javelin, at which the highest ever placing is 14th.

The most complete dominance by British athletes of any Olympic event was in the 10 miles walk in 1908, when George Larner beat an all-British field of six runners, one of whom failed to finish. That was one of two British clean sweeps of the medals, the other being in the 4000m steeplechase in 1900 won by John Rimmer. At those events currently on the schedule,

British athletes have been placed first and second three times: in the 1906 triple jump the Irishmen Peter O'Connor and Con Leahy; in the 1920 1500m Albert Hill and Philip Noel-Baker; and in the 1980 800m Steve Ovett and Sebastian Coe.

The most Olympic medals won by a British athlete is four by Guy Butler, who at 400m was second in 1920 and third in 1924 and at 4 × 400m relay was first in 1920 and second in 1924. The four other British athletes to have won gold, silver and bronze medals are Wyndham Halswelle, David Hemery, Mary Rand and Sidney Robinson.

COMMONWEALTH GAMES

The Commonwealth Games have become known as the 'Friendly Games'; even if, at the time of writing, political pressures threaten the latest celebration at Brisbane, Australia.

The first British Empire Games were held at Hamilton, Canada 16–23 Aug 1930. Eleven countries competed: Australia, Bermuda, British Guiana, Canada, Newfoundland, New Zealand, South Africa and the four British countries. England, Scotland, Wales and Ireland competed as separate teams, in order to reduce British domination, at the instigation of the Games organiser M. M. 'Bobby' Robinson, a sports reporter on the 'Hamilton Spectator'. Robinson, who had been manager of the 1928 Canadian Olympic team, had to work exceptionally hard to ensure the staging of the Games. Six sports were included, but only in swimming were there women's events. The Canadian women's athletics championships were held simultaneously, but the British women could not participate because they were committed to take part in the World Games in Prague in early September.

The idea of an Empire sporting festival had first been put forward by a young Yorkshireman, J. Astley Cooper in August 1891. In the magazine *Greater Britain* he proposed a festival 'to draw closer the ties between the nations of the Empire'. He developed this idea in a letter to *The Times* of 30 Oct 1891. Although this attracted much attention it was to be 20 years before such a gathering came about. A 'Festival of Empire' was held in 1911 in conjunction with the celebrations for the Coronation of King George V. Five athletics events were staged at the Crystal Palace, London. There were three Canadian wins, including a sprint double by F. J. Halbhaus and two British wins. Athletes from Australasia and South Africa also took part.

Venues for the Games, which became known as 'British Empire and Commonwealth Games' in 1954 and simply 'British Commonwealth Games' in 1970, with leading medallists have been:
(**G** = Gold, **S** = Silver, **B** = Bronze)

1930 Hamilton, Canada
Lord Burghley (Eng) **3G** 1st 120yh, 440yh, 4 × 440yR
Harry Hart (SA) **2G 1B** 1st SP, DT; 3rd JT (and 6th 120yh)

1934 White City, London
Eileen Hiscock (Eng) **3G 1S** 1st 100y, 220y, 440yR; 2nd 660yR
Arthur Sweeney (Eng) **3G** 1st 100y, 220y, 4 × 110yR
Harry Hart (SA) **2G 1S** 1st SP, DT; 2nd JT

1938 Sydney Cricket Ground
Decima Norman (Aus) **5G** 1st 100y, 220y, LJ, 440yR, 660yR,
This is the record number of gold medals at one Games.
John Loaring (Can) **3G** 1st 440yh, 4 × 110yR, 4 × 440yR
Cyril Holmes (Eng) **2G 1S** 1st 100y, 220y; 2nd 4 × 110yR

1950 Auckland (Eden Park)
Marjorie Jackson (Aus) **4G** 1st 100y, 220y, 440yR, 660yR.
Jackson, the 'Lithgow Flash' set the first world records in Games history, equalling both 100y (10.8) and 220y (24.3).
Shirley Strickland (Aus) **3G 2S** 1st 80mh, 440yR, 660yR; 2nd 100y, 220y.
John Treloar (Aus) **3G** 1st 100y, 220y, 4 × 110yR

1954 Vancouver (Empire Stadium)
Marjorie Nelson (née Jackson) **3G** 1st 100y, 220y, 4 × 110yR
Yvette Williams (NZ) **3G** 1st LJ, SP, DT. This equalled Decima Norman's achievement of three individual golds. Williams had also won the long jump in 1950, but the shot and discus were not then on the programme, although she was placed second at javelin.

1958 Cardiff Arms Park
Keith Gardner (Jam) **2G 1S 1B** 1st 100y, 120yh; 2nd 220y; 3rd 4 × 440yR. The only man to win four medals at one Games.
Marlene Willard (Aus) **2G 1S** 1st 100y, 220y; 2nd 4 × 110yR

Harry Hart won 31 South African titles in 1926–46 as well as four Commonwealth gold medals, two each in 1930 and 1934.

1962 Perth (Perry Lakes Stadium)
Dorothy Hyman (Eng) **2G 1S** 1st 100y, 220y; 2nd 4 × 110yR

1966 Kingston, Jamaica
Diane Burge (Aus) **3G** 1st 100y, 220y, 4 × 110yR
Ed Roberts (Tri) **1G 1S 1B** 1st 4 × 440yR (world record 3:02.8); 2nd 220y; 3rd 100y.

1970 Edinburgh (Meadowbank)
Don Quarrie (Jam) **3G** 1st 100m, 200m, 4 × 100mR
Raelene Boyle (Aus) **3G** 1st 100m, 200m, 4 × 100mR
Ann Wilson uniquely won three silver medals (HJ, LJ and Pen). She won a fourth in 1974 at the pentathlon.

1974 Christchurch, New Zealand
Raelene Boyle (Aus) **3G** 1st 100m, 200m, 4 × 100mR
Denise Robertson (Aus) **1G 1S 1B** 1st 4 × 100mR; 2nd 200m; 3rd 100m
Ben Jipcho (Ken) **2G 1B** 1st 5000m, 3000m S/C; 3rd 1500m.

Jipcho first won the steeplechase in 8:20.8, when John Davies (Wal) and Evans Mogaka (Ken) running behind him fell over each other, yet got up to be placed second and third respectively. Davies's time 8:24.8 was a new British record, although he was initially disqualified and had an agonising five hour wait before reinstatement. Then Jipcho had an epic duel with Brendan Foster (Eng) at 5000m, winning by two tenths of a second in 13:14.4 in a blazing finish. Finally Jipcho won the bronze medal in a superb 1500m, won by Filbert Bayi (Tan), who led from the gun in an awe-inspiring front-running display. Both Bayi, 3:32.16 and John Walker (NZ), 3:32.52 broke the world record and the next three, Jipcho 3:33.16, Rod Dixon (NZ) 3:33.89 and Graeme Crouch (Aus) 3:34.22 ranked 4–5–7 on the all-time list. Mike Boit (Ken) was sixth with 3:36.84 and in seventh came Brendan Foster, whose 3:37.64 was a British record, his second at the Games. Foster had been placed third at 1500m in 1970 and went on to win the 10000m and a third place at 5000m in 1978.

1978 Edmonton, Canada
Sonia Lannaman (Eng) **2G 1S** 1st 100m, 4 × 100mR; 2nd 200m
Denise Boyd (née Robertson) (Aus) **1G 1S 2B** 1st 200m; 2nd 4 × 400mR; 3rd 100m, 4 × 100mR

The finish of the 1974 Commonwealth 1500m. Filbert Bayi (613) wins from John Walker (483). Rod Dixon (453) is fourth. Third placer Ben Jipcho is obscured by Bayi.   *(E. D. Lacey)*

At other running events **double gold medallists** have been:
880y and 1mile: 1958 Herb Elliott (Aus), 1962 Peter Snell (NZ); **1 mile and 3 mile:** 1966 Kip Keino (Ken); **3 mile and 6 mile:** 1938 Cecil Matthews (NZ); **5000m and 3000m S/C:** 1974 Ben Jipcho (Ken), 1978 Henry Rono (Ken); **6 mile and Mar:** 1958 David Power (Aus).

The most gold medals won is: 7 Marjorie Jackson (Aus) **1950** and **1954** (see p. 108); 6 Pam Kilborn/Ryan (Aus): **1962** 80mh, LJ; **1966** 80mh, 4 × 100mR; **1970** 80mh, 4 × 100mR; 6 Raelene Boyle (Aus) **1970** and **1974** (see p. 109); 6 Don Quarrie (Jam): **1970** (see p. 109); **1974** 100m, 200m; **1978** 200m.

Three successive gold medals at one event have been won by: Howard Payne (Eng) HT: 1962, 1966, 1970; Pam Kilborn (Aus) 80mh: 1962, 1966, 1970; Valerie Sloper/Young (NZ) SP: 1962, 1966, 1970; Jennifer Lamy (Aus) 4 × 110y/100mR: 1966, 1970, 1974; Don Quarrie (Jam) 200m: 1970, 1974, 1978.

The most medals won is: 7 by Marjorie Jackson (Aus) (see p. 108), and the most in individual

events, by Valerie Sloper/Young (NZ), who in addition to her shot wins (above), won the discus in 1962 and 1966 and won a silver at shot in 1974 and a bronze at discus in 1958. Her 16-year medal span is a record. Raelene Boyle (Aus) won the silver at 100m in 1978 to add to her six golds and Denise Boyd (Aus) also won seven medals in 1974 and 1978 (see p. 109).

The only athletes to **win medals at four Games** are Val Young (NZ) and Howard Payne (Eng), who added a silver in 1974 to his three golds.

The greatest span of competition is 20 years by Stanley Lay (NZ), who won the javelin in 1930, was third in 1938 and was placed sixth in 1950.

Athletes to have competed at five successive Games have been: Howard Payne, who first competed in 1958 for Rhodesia, and was placed fourth at hammer before his four medals as above; Dave Norris (NZ) 1958–74 was placed successively 3–6–5–11–6 at triple jump and 8–2–7–5 at long jump at the first four; Mary Peters (NI) was placed 8–4–2–1–4 at shot, as well as winning the pentathlon in 1970 and 1974 and also competing at high jump and 100m hurdles; Robin Tait (NZ) 1962–78 was placed 4–3–6–1–4 at discus.

Family matters
As befits the 'Friendly Games' there have been several family successes. Husband and wife champions have been:
John (400mh) and Sheila (LJ) Sherwood in 1970;
Howard (HT) and Rosemary (DT) Payne won on the same day in 1970;
Lawrie (HJ 1966 and 1970) and Judy (800m 1978) Peckham.

Rosemary and Howard Payne — between them they won six Commonwealth medals, set 19 British records, made 112 international appearances and won 10 AAA/WAAA titles.
(Fionnbar Callanan)

Yvette Williams's four gold medals were followed by her younger brother Roy winning the decathlon in 1966.

Les Mills (NZ) won five medals: DT 1st in 1966, 2nd 1958 and 1970; SP 2nd in 1966, 3rd in 1970. He had also competed in 1962, but regrettably was unable to take part at Christchurch in 1974, when his wife Colleen ran in the 400m, their son Phillip ran the 110m hurdles and their daughter Donna took part in the high jump.

The oldest medallist is Jack Holden (Eng), who was aged 42 years 335 days when he won the marathon in 1950. He ran the last eight miles barefoot, although his soles were already blistered and cut from soggy, split shoes, and he was attacked by a Great Dane when he still had two miles to go.

The oldest female medallist is Rosemary Payne (Eng), who was 40 years 252 days when she was second at discus in 1974. She was also the oldest champion at 37 years 60 days in 1970.

The oldest ever track medallist is Thomas Lavery (SA), who was 38 years 53 days when he was third at 120y hurdles in 1950 just ahead of Don Finlay (Eng) who was only three months short of his 42nd birthday. Finlay had won the event in 1934 and Lavery in 1938.

The youngest medallists were both aged 15. Canadian Sam Richardson won the long jump in 1934, having earlier been placed third at long jump, and the Kenyan girl Sabine Chebichi was third at 800m in 1974.

The youngest female gold medallist is Debbie Brill (Can), winner of the high jump in 1970 at 17 years 137 days.

Tom Robinson (Bahamas) won three successive silver medals 1958–66 at 100y, but he did win a gold at 220y in 1958.

The first man to win both Commonwealth and Olympic titles was Tom Hampson (Eng) who won the 880y in 1930, two years before his Olympic victory. The first women to do so were Marjorie Jackson (Aus), Shirley Strickland (Aus) and Yvette Williams (NZ), who all followed their 1950 Commonwealth successes with Olympic titles in 1952.

The first black champion was Phil Edwards, who won the 880y in 1934 while representing his native British Guiana (now Guyana). He won five Olympic medals in Canadian colours.

The first black African to win a gold medal was high jumper Emmanuel Ifeajuna of Nigeria in 1954, when he sprang 34cm/13½in above his own head to clear 2.03m/6ft 8in.

Marjorie Jackson (p. 108) set **the first world records** at the Commonwealth Games, and the first by a man was 49.72 for 440y hurdles by Gert Potgieter (SA) in 1958.

Travel to and from the early Games was a major problem. For instance the 90 British competitors in 1938 left London in late November 1937 for a six-week boat trip to Sydney, Australia. They had to keep fit by running round a swaying deck, but they did also call on various ports and had the opportunity to train on a variety of tracks in Gibraltar, Aden and Ceylon, for instance.

The luckiest medallist might be accounted to be Canadian Donald Pettie. In 1950 he was disqualified for two false starts in the 100y final. However, he was reinstated after the race had been delayed for an hour while the officials deliberated. At the third go he was placed third behind John Treloar. The starter had correctly ruled him out, yet he was adjudged to have been ignorant of the 'two breaks and out' rule. He had also false started in his heat and semi-final!

The most memorable day in Commonwealth Games history must be the final day in Vancouver, 7 Aug 1954. At 2.30pm there was the 1 mile, featuring the long-awaited duel between Roger Bannister and John Landy, the first two four-minute milers (see p. 261). Before the race Landy had cut his foot and Bannister had a cold, but that was put behind them as the eight-man field got to their marks. Landy dashed into the lead on the second turn, and from then on the race was strictly a two-man contest. Landy passed 440y in 58.2 and 880y in 1:58.2, by then eight yards up on Bannister. But Bannister narrowed the gap steadily, three yards behind Landy's 2:58.7 at ¾ mile. As Landy looked inside on the final turn, Bannister went outside in an undeniable run for home to win, 3:58.8 to 3:59.6, the first time two men had broken the great barrier. Far behind Rich Ferguson (Can) was third in 4:04.6.

Two hours before the mile started the marathoners left the stadium in 75°F/24°C heat. The favourite Jim Peters, who had won a bronze medal at 6 miles on the first day and had won eight of his ten marathons from 1951, surged away from his team-mate Stan Cox at nine miles and built up a huge lead. On the final hill leading to the stadium Peters began to wobble, but as he entered for the final lap he had a good 20 minutes lead. The next ten minutes will be seared on the minds of all who saw it, for Peters, severely affected by heatstroke and dehydration, staggered, reeled and fell a dozen times. Eventually at the usual finishing point, but still 200 yards from the marathon finish he collapsed into the arms of Mick Mays, English team masseur, and shot champion John Savidge. He was rushed to hospital, where he spent seven hours in an oxygen tent, alongside Cox, who, similarly affected, had run into a telegraph pole at 24 miles. Joe McGhee of Scotland eventually came in to win in 2:39:36. Peters retired after the Games, but received a special gold medal from the Duke of Edinburgh, who had been present.

Canadian officials in 1954 were known as the 'Green Hornets' due to their shirts and peaked caps. Such a naming tradition was carried on at the 1976 Olympic Games in Montreal when the stewards' outfits earned them the title of 'Yellow Bananas'.

The hottest weather in Games history was that at Perth in 1962. Although there were strong winds, temperatures on the first three days were recorded as between 35°–37°C/96–100°F each day. Despite such heat Bruce Kidd, at 19, became the youngest ever winner of a distance gold medal before cooling off with a dip in the water jump. On that day the 30000 crowd were estimated to have consumed 2400 gallons of beer.

Ron Clarke won four silver medals, two each at 3 miles and 6 mile/10km. In 1962 he won a surprise silver medal at 3 miles behind Murray Halberg, who was quoted afterwards as saying 'You may not realise it in Australia but Ron is one of the finest talents in distance running today'. In the years that followed he, with Kip Keino (Ken) (11th in that 3 mile) led a revolution in distance running, yet a gold medal eluded him. In 1966 he was twice beaten by Kenyans in fast races, by Naftali Temu at 6 miles, 27:14.6 to 27:39.4 and by Kip Keino at 3 miles, 12:57.4 to 12:59.2. In 1970 he was second at 10000m, when he was surprisingly beaten by Lachie Stewart (Sco). Then in his final Commonwealth Games race he was fifth in the 5000m, in which

two Scots battled it out down the finishing straight, with the iron will of Ian Stewart taking him to victory over Ian McCafferty, 13:22.8 to 13:23.4. Keino was third.

In 1966 Jim Alder of Scotland approached the stadium to finish the marathon with a 70 yards lead. But he was misdirected and eventually entered the stadium to see Bill Adcocks of England 30 yards ahead. With supreme tenacity, however, he overcame his shock to win.

In 1970 David Hemery (Eng) won the 110m hurdles on his 26th birthday and at the victory ceremony the band followed the national anthem with 'Happy Birthday'. Also that year Marilyn Neufville, having changed allegiance from Britain, in whose colours she had won the European Indoor title, to the land of her birth, Jamaica, won the 400m in a world record time of 51.02. She was only 17 at the time, yet, sadly,

Diane Konihowski starred at Edmonton in 1978 with a Commonwealth pentathlon record 4768 to win by 546 points.   (M. Shearman)

troubled by recurring injuries, never again approached that form.

The most successful day for England in recent years was the final day in 1978 at Edmonton, when their team won seven out of nine gold medals. The two that got away were the men's relays. In the 4 × 400m relay England finished first but were disqualified because Glen Cohen cut in too quickly on Kenya's Bill Koskei on the third leg, and Scotland won the 4 × 100m relay. Stars in Edmonton were the multi-event gold medallists. Both Diane Konihowski (Can) 4768 points pentathlon and Daley Thompson (Eng) 8467 decathlon recorded the third best scores of all-time. The major upset of these Games was the marathon win by Gidemas Shahanga of Tanzania in 2:15:40. In his only previous major race he had been placed seventh in the African Games.

COMMONWEALTH GAMES MEDAL WINNERS BY COUNTRY 1930–1978

Country	MEN Gold	Silver	Bronze	WOMEN Gold	Silver	Bronze	Total Medals
England	67	57	51	29	38	28	270
Australia	40	49	39	45	30	23	226
Canada	29	34	39	10	16	29	157
New Zealand	17	14	22	9	11	9	82
South Africa (1930–58)	16	13	14	4	2	2	51
Kenya	20	8	14	–	1	1	44
Scotland	9	9	13	2	1	2	36
Jamaica	13	7	8	1	1	2	32
Nigeria	2	8	4	1	1	2	18
Ghana	4	4	5	–	2	2	17
Wales	4	4	4	–	–	1	13
Trinidad & Tobago	3	7	3	–	–	–	13
Pakistan (1950–70)	2	3	6	–	–	–	11
Northern Ireland	2	2	–	4	2	–	10
Uganda	–	3	3	–	–	1	7
Bahamas	1	4	–	–	–	–	5
India	1	2	2	–	–	–	5
Tanzania	2	1	1	–	–	–	4
Fiji	1	2	1	–	–	–	4
Rhodesia (now Zimbabwe)	–	1	2	–	–	1	4
Guyana (British Guiana)	1	2	–	–	–	1	4
Northern Rhodesia (now Zambia)	–	–	–	1	1	1	3
Barbados	–	–	2	–	–	–	2
Ceylon	1	–	–	–	–	–	1
Ireland (1930–8)	–	1	–	–	–	–	1
Bermuda	–	1	–	–	–	–	1
The Gambia	–	–	1	–	–	–	1
Swaziland	–	–	1	–	–	–	1

Analysis of medals for the leading countries at each games

		1930 M	1930 W	1934 M	1934 W	1938 M	1938 W	1950 M	1950 W	1954 M	1954 W	1958 M	1958 W	1962 M	1962 W	1966 M	1966 W	1970 M	1970 W	1974 M	1974 W	1978 M	1978 W
ENGLAND	G	9		10	6	3	1	4	1	9	–	5	3	4	3	4	1	5	2	7	3	7	9
	S	10		6	3	5	3	5	2	6	3	3	4	5	3	4	4	4	7	9	4	–	5
	B	6		9	6	–	2	1	1	4	3	4	3	3	2	4	2	10	2	3	2	7	5
AUSTRALIA	G	–		1	–	1	5	9	6	3	3	5	5	7	5	4	7	5	5	3	5	2	4
	S	3		1	–	8	3	5	3	1	2	4	2	7	5	4	4	6	3	3	4	7	4
	B	1		2	–	10	2	4	1	4	–	3	3	7	6	1	1	–	3	4	3	3	4
CANADA	G	6		4	1	7	1	2	–	1	–	–	–	1	–	2	1	2	1	–	4	4	2
	S	4		8	6	5	1	2	–	5	2	2	–	–	–	2	1	2	–	–	2	4	4
	B	9		–	1	4	2	5	1	3	4	3	2	2	–	4	5	2	5	2	4	5	5
NEW ZEALAND	G	2		1	–	3	–	1	1	1	3	1	1	3	2	3	2	–	–	2	–	–	–
	S	–		–	–	1	–	3	3	1	–	1	2	2	2	1	–	2	1	2	2	1	1
	B	–		1	–	3	2	8	4	–	–	3	1	–	2	4	–	1	–	2	–	–	–
KENYA	G	–		–	–	–	–	–	–	–	–	–	–	2	–	3	–	4	–	6	–	5	–
	S	–		–	–	–	–	–	–	–	–	–	–	1	–	1	–	1	–	2	–	3	1
	B	–		–	–	–	–	–	–	–	–	2	–	–	–	1	–	4	–	5	1	2	–

Key: M = Men W = Women G = Gold S = Silver B = Bronze

IAAF Golden Events

The Golden Mile was originally conceived as the star event of the Dubai International Track and Field Championships, with a 300000 dollars first prize. Plans were announced in 1977, but this major venture into professional athletics never got off the ground. Instead the first IAAF Golden Mile was staged on 25 Sep 1978 as part of the Eight Nations meeting in Tokyo. In 1979 the IAAF announced that eight golden events would be staged over three years as part of a sponsorship scheme in which funds for the IAAF development programme are provided by the Government of Dubai.

The Golden Mile has been staged annually and winners have been: 1978 Tokyo Steve Ovett 3:55.5; 1979 Oslo (Bislett Games) Sebastian Coe 3:48.95 (world record) from Steve Scott (USA) 3:51.11 and eight other men under 3:56; 1980 Crystal Palace Steve Ovett 3:52.84

James Sanford, the world's fastest man of 1979, when he won the World Cup and IAAF Golden 100m races. *(University of Southern California)*

with Scott again second and seven more under 3:56; 1981 Brussels (Van Damme Memorial) Sebastian Coe 3:47.33 (world record, see p. 34).

Winners of other IAAF Golden Events
1979 Javelin – Arto Harkonen (Fin) 90.18m/295ft 10in at Budapest.
Sprints – James Sanford (USA) 100m 10.15 and 200m 20.39 (2nd to James Gilkes 20.33) at the Weltklasse meeting in Zurich.
10000m – Mike McLeod (GB) 27:39.76 at the Van Damme Memorial meeting in Brussels.
1980 Pole vault – Serge Ferreira (Fra) 5.70m/18ft 8¼in at the Nikaia meeting in Nice.
1981 (Sponsored by the Citizen watch company)
5000m – Barry Smith (GB) 13:21.14 at Gateshead.
10000m – Mike McLeod (GB) 27:59.42 at Prague.
Sprints – Allan Wells (GB) 100m 10.15 (2nd to Herman Panzo 10.14) and 200m 20.15 at the ISTAF meeting in Berlin.
1982: Marathon – over the traditional Marathon to Athens course, lengthened to the standard distance – Rodolfo Gomez (Mex) 2:11:49.

Lugano Trophy

The IAAF Race Walking World Cup is contested biennially for the 'Lugano Trophy', named after the Swiss town, which was its first venue in 1961. Points are awarded for the first three walkers to finish from teams of four at both 20km and 50km, and totalled to determine the team positions.

Venues and winning teams have been as follows:

Year	venue	team	points
1961	Lugano, Switzerland	Gt. Britain	53
1963	Varese, Italy	Gt. Britain	93
1965	Pescara, Italy	GDR	117
1967	Bad Saarow, GDR	GDR	128
1970	Eschborn, West Germany	GDR	134
1973	Lugano, Switzerland	GDR	139
1975	Le Grand Quevilly, France	USSR	117
1977	Milton Keynes, England	Mexico	185
1979	Eschborn, West Germany	Mexico	240
1981	Valencia, Spain	Italy	227

Great Britain, Sweden and Italy have contested every final. The GDR have been in the first four every year since they first entered in 1965.

The closest victories were in 1961 and 1981 when Sweden and the USSR respectively finished with the same points as the winners, who were determined on the basis of their better individual placing at 50km.

The most sweeping victory was that of GDR in 1965 when they beat Great Britain by 30 points.

The most individual final victories is three by Christoph Höhne (GDR), at 50km in 1965 (4:03:14), 1967 (4:09:09) and 1970 (4:04:35.2). He was also placed third in 1973.

The walker who has competed in the most finals is Gerhard Weidner (Ger) with seven, at 50km each year from 1965 to 1979. His best placing was second in 1975 at the age of 42.

The fastest times were recorded in the 1979 finals. Daniel Bautista (Mex) sped to a world best of 1:18:49 at 20km and Martin Bermudez (Mex) recorded the second best ever 50km in 3:43:36. Raul Gonzales (Mex) who had won the 50km in 1977 and would win again in 1981 set off at a sensational pace in 1979 and had a 5min 22sec lead at 30km but the pace told and he faded to fourth at the finish.

The best British performances have come from Ken Matthews, who won at 20km in 1961 and 1963. Ray Middleton competed in a record six finals for Britain, each time from 1961 to 1973 at 50km, with a best of second in 1963.

A women's race has been held in conjunction with the Lugano Trophy races on each occasion since 1975. In 1979 the organisers presented a challenge cup, the 'Eschborn Cup' for the winning team. Great Britain was the first winner and the USSR won in 1981. Individual winners at 5km have been: 1979 Marion Fawkes (GB) 22:51 and 1981 Siw Gustavsson (Swe) 22:56.

World Championships
The IAAF recognises the athletic events of the Olympic Games as World Championships. The first full-scale World Championships outside the Olympics have been scheduled by the IAAF for Helsinki 7–14 Aug 1983. This followed a resolution by the IAAF at their congress in Puerto Rico in 1978 that they should organise such championships in the third year of each Olympiad. Three World Championships have already been held for events not on the Olympic schedule.

In 1976 the 50km walk was dropped from the Olympic Games, so a world championship at that event was held at Malmo, Sweden on 18 September. The winner was Venyamin Soldatenko (USSR) 3:54:40.

In 1980 the women's 3000m and 400m hurdles events were not on the Olympic programme although well established internationally, so world championships were held at Sittard, Holland on 14/15 August. The Soviet athletes did not compete, perhaps in retaliation against the Dutch Government's attitude to the Olympic Games, although this was denied by the Soviet Union, and this seriously weakened the events. Several other top contenders also passed up the opportunity of competing, notably the Norwegian Grete Waitz in the 3000m. Winners: 3000m Birgit Friedmann (Ger) 8:48.1 from Karolina Nemetz (Swe) 8:50.3 and Ingrid Christensen (Nor) 8:58.8; 400mh Barbara Broschat (GDR) 54.55 from Ellen Neumann (GDR) 54.56 and Petra Pfaff (GDR) 55.84. The first two 400m hurdles times were the second and third fastest times ever recorded for the event.

The World Cup
The first ever competition for the IAAF World Cup was held in Dusseldorf, Germany from 2–4 Sep 1977. The idea of having a competition between eight teams representing the top nations and continents of the world was conceived two years earlier. The combination of national and continental teams was admitted, by IAAF President, Adriaan Paulen, to be a somewhat artificial formula, but the athletics in Dusseldorf however certainly succeeded in meeting the aims of the IAAF, which were fourfold: to provide a great athletics meeting; to offer additional world-class competition for the sport's elite; to stimulate the continental areas not only in the World Cup competition itself but also by the staging of trial meetings; and to provide additional revenue for the development of athletics throughout the world.

The aggregate attendance over the three days in Dusseldorf was over 135000 and, with television fees, a profit of 1.2 million Deutsche Marks was reported.

Two years later the second World Cup was contested in the Montreal Olympic stadium, but here the three-day attendance from 24–26 August was only just over 54000 and the meeting made a loss of 50000 Canadian dollars. The IAAF obviously wish to take their competition around the world, but there can be little doubt that the biggest attendances will be found in Europe. This was borne out by the success of the third World Cup held in the Olympic Stadium, Rome from 4–6 Sep 1981, when the total attendance was 185000.

Results of the World Cup competitions, with positions and points:

Team	1977(m)	1979(m)	1981(m)	1977(w)	1979(w)	1981(w)
AFRICA	6th– 78	6th– 84	7th– 66	7th– 32	7th– 30	9th– 26
AMERICAS	5th– 92	5th– 98	5th– 95	5th– 56	5th– 68	5th– 72
ASIA	8th– 44	8th– 36	9th– 59	8th– 30	8th– 26	8th– 32
EUROPE	4th–111	2nd–112	1st–147	1st–109	3rd– 88	2nd–110
GDR	1st–127	3rd–108	2nd–130	2nd– 93	1st–106	1st–120½
WEST GERMANY	3rd–112	–	–	–	–	–
OCEANIA	7th– 48	7th– 58	8th– 61	6th– 46	6th– 47	7th– 58
USA	2nd–120	1st–119	3rd–127	4th– 60	4th– 76	4th– 89
USSR	–	4th–102	4th–118	3rd– 90	2nd– 98	3rd– 98
ITALY	–	–	6th– 93	–	–	6th– 68½

(m – men, w – women)

The European nations are selected on the basis of the first two in the European Cup of the same year, with the Europe team selected from the remaining European countries. The absence of a home team was marked in Montreal, but this problem was overcome in 1981, as the IAAF allowed Italy to compete with the addition of a ninth lane to the track in Rome.

Just one world record has been set in World Cup competition, the 4 × 100m relay in 38.03 by the USA team of Bill Collins, Steve Riddick, Cliff Wiley and Steve Williams in 1977. There have, however, been a series of **second best perform-ances ever: 1977:** Rosemarie Ackermann HJ 1.98m/6ft 6in, Irina Szewinska 400m 49.52 (see later), Edwin Moses 400mh 47.58. **1979:** Evelyn Ashford 200m 21.83, Edwin Moses 400mh 47.53, Larry Myricks LJ 8.52m/27ft 11½in. This jump, second only to Bob Beamon's 8.90 came in the final round when Myricks was lying third to Lutz Dombrowski (8.27m) and David Giralt (8.23m). It was a triumph for Myricks, who, in the same Montreal stadium had cracked his ankle during the warm-up for the Olympic final, an injury which put him out of long jumping for 19 months. **1981:** Jarmila Kratochvilova 400m 48.61. Second in 49.27 was Marita Koch, her first defeat since the 1977 World Cup. In those four years Koch had won 18 races at 400m, 14 of them sub-50sec.

Athletes to have won their event at each World Cup have been: Edwin Moses, who followed the above two 400m hurdles victories with a 47.37 in 1981, the fourth fastest ever to that date. His winning margins, 1.25, 1.18 and 1.79sec gave yet further demonstration of his outstanding superiority. Joao Carlos de Oliveira in triple jump with 16.68m, 17.02m and 17.37m successively. Udo Beyer with shot 21.74m, 20.45m and 21.40m successively.

Jarmila Kratochvilova was unbeaten in 1981 and improved by 1.48sec at 400m. She won a second European Indoor 400m in 1982. *(M. Shearman)*

The most individual victories is four by Evelyn Ashford and Miruts Yifter.

Ashford scored an upset sprint double over the GDR favourites in 1979. She beat Marlies Göhr at 100m with 11.06 to 11.17 and Marita Koch at 200m with 21.83 to 22.02. Koch's time was the third fastest ever, and she went on to run the anchor leg for GDR's winning 4×400m relay team, just two hours later, in 48.2, the fastest relay leg every run by a woman. But, running in lane one, even Koch had to yield to the beautifully smooth running of Ashford. Ashford was injured during 1980 but returned in 1981 to win the sprint double again. She first beat Jarmila Kratochvilova and Bärbel Wöckel at 200m (22.18) and then the 100m from Kathy Smallwood (British record 11.10) and Marlies Göhr in 11.02.

Miruts Yifter won the 5000m/10000m double in 1977 and in 1979. On each occasion the tiny (1.62m/5ft 4in) man from the mountains of Northern Ethiopia smashed the opposition by a devastating finishing kick, which had earlier gained him the sobriquet of 'Yifter the Shifter'. Whether the pace was fast or slow seemed to make no difference to him, for even in the 1977 5000m where he missed the world record by only 0.9sec he still ran a 53.9sec last lap.

His winning times and last 400m and 200m

```
 2 Sep 1977 10000m 28:32.3  54.3 25.1
 4 Sep 1977  5000m 13:13.82 53.9 26.5
24 Aug 1979 10000m 27:53.07 54.3 25.5
26 Aug 1979  5000m 13:35.9  53.5 25.8
```

Yifter's successes were true reward for a great career, yet he had had more than his fair share of misfortune. The first was in a 5000m race on 16 Jul 1971, the first day of the USA v Africa match at Durham, N. Carolina. Mistaking the number of laps he sprinted off with two to go, leaving Steve Prefontaine behind. He did an amazing 57.6 lap in 87°F heat and stopped as the gun, which actually indicated one lap to go, went off. Steve Prefontaine went on to win in 13:57.6. However, Yifter made up for this on the second day when he won the 10000m, running as a guest, in 28:53.2, 0.8 ahead of Frank Shorter in 91°F heat. His first international races had been in 1970 – third at 10000m in the Eastern and Central African Championships and a victory over Kip Keino at Tel Aviv in the Hapoel Games 5000m. In the 1972 Olympics Yifter won the bronze medal at 10000m behind Lasse Viren and Emiel Puttemans, but his jinx struck again as, entered in the 5000m, he could not find the entrance to the track and was left

Evelyn Ashford, world woman athlete of the year in 1981, when she repeated her 1979 World Cup sprint double.   *(M. Shearman)*

weeping as he heard the gun go for the start of his heat. In 1976 Yifter displayed impressive form in the pre-Olympic meetings in Montreal, but had to miss the Games due to the African boycott.

Thereafter he had better fortune with double wins in two World Cups, the African Championships and the Olympic Games. Yet he was one of the Ethiopian team that misjudged the laps at the 1981 World Cross-Country Championships and put in their burst a lap early. Yifter, fifth at 'his finish', started up again and ended in 15th place.

The great mystery about Yifter is that of his age. He had his first important race in 1968, a 10000m in which he finished three laps behind Abebe Bikila and Mamo Wolde and he may have been about 25 at the time. He then enlisted in the air force to give him better opportunities to train. After his World Cup triumphs in 1979 he was promoted to Captain, yet he still devotes his spare time to breeding cows. His date of birth has been officially listed in Olympic entries as follows: 1972 – 8 Jun 1947, 1976 – 28 Jun 1947, 1980 – 5 Jun 1945. In 1981 the Ethiopian National Coach, Nigusie Roba, gave his date of birth as 15 Sep 1943. Then again, another authoritative source (apparently confirmed by his passport) gives 15 May 1944 for Yifter, whose real name in Beja – his North Ethiopian language, is Yefter Mururuse. While the oldest one seems the most likely, we will never know which is right, but really that is of little consequence compared to the memories of his awe-inspiring sprint finishes.

Two classic duels highlighted the first World Cup. Each had the necessary ingredients for historic races, and each race fully lived up to expectations.

Alberto Juantorena v Mike Boit at 800 metres. In 1976 Alberto Juantorena (Cub) won the Olympic double of 400m and 800m and in winning the latter set a world record of 1:43.50. Mike Boit, however, had had the frustration of missing the Olympics after Kenya had boycotted the Games, yet he had clocked a time only 0.07sec slower than Juantorena less than a month after the Olympic final. Juantorena was unbeaten in 1976 and Boit lost just one race at 800m and in 1977 both men were in superb form. Juantorena improved his world record with 1:43.44 in Sofia at the World Student Games on 21 August, and just three days later beat Boit in their first ever clash, 1:43.64 to 1:44.64 at the Weltklasse meeting in Zurich.

By the World Cup Boit had run 13 races in under 1:46 in 1977 and five under 1:45. In his career he had run 17 sub 1:45 races out of a world total of 60, whereas Juantorena, nearly two years younger than Boit, was comparatively inexperienced, in spite of his two world records. The race itself was, for me at least, the greatest ever head-to-head clash. Both men followed Sri Ram Singh of India through a steady first lap of 52.3sec. They passed Singh entering the back straight with Juantorena pounding along in the lead with his giant strides. Boit made his move after 600m and came up to Juantorena's shoulder, seeming almost puny in spite of his 1.83m/6ft 0in height against the 1.90m/6ft 3in and 84kg/185lb Cuban. All down the home straight they ran together before Juantorena's strength and speed finally took him to a one metre victory.

Their duels:

24 Aug 1977	Zurich	1st Juantorena 1:43.64 2nd Boit 1:44.67
2 Sep 1977	Dusseldorf	1st Juantorena 1:44.04 2nd Boit 1:44.14
16 Aug 1978	Zurich	2nd Boit 1:46.03 … 6th Juantorena 1:47.06 (1st James Robinson (USA) 1:45.92)

Irena Szewinska v Marita Koch at 400 metres
Irena Szewinska has long graced women's athletics, collecting an unrivalled clutch of medals and world records, but she did not make her debut at 400m, an event to which she seemed ideally suited, until very late, at the age of 27 in 1973. The following year she became the first woman to run the distance in less than 50sec with her 49.9 on 22 June at Warsaw and a 48.5 relay leg in the European Championships. She improved that time twice in 1976, her season climaxed by an Olympic gold medal and world record of 49.29, when she beat Christine Brehmer (50.51) by 10m.

Marita Koch had made the Olympic semi-finals, and was improving fast. In 1976 she ran 50.19 and in 1977 ran in successive weeks 50.09, 49.68 and then 49.53 to win the European Cup Final. Then on 21 August she beat Szewinska over 200m at Nice 22.55 to 22.63. Finally on the first day of the World Cup Koch's 49.3 anchor leg in the 4 × 400m relay took her further away from Szewinska, who ran 49.9, although her team was well behind. In the 400m on the final day Koch blazed the first half passing 200m in 23.1, and at 300m in 35.4 she had a 3m lead. Then Szewinska's coolness, grace and determination gradually closed the gap, before her long legs took her to a 2m victory, 49.52 to 49.76. Szewinska was still the 'Queen of the Track' and fittingly received the World Cup for the winning European Select Team. For Koch, nearly 11 years younger, though beaten in this first 400m clash with Szewinska, it was the prelude to the unassailable world number one position for the next three years.

Their duels:

21 Aug 1977 Nice   200m
  1st Koch 22.55 2nd Szewinska 22.63

 4 Sep 1977 Dusseldorf   400m
  1st Szewinska 49.52 2nd Koch 49.76

22 Aug 1978 Stuttgart   200m
  1st Koch 22.18 2nd Szewinska 22.98

31 Aug 1978 Prague   400m
  1st Koch 48.94 ... 3rd Szewinska 50.40 (European Championships ... 2nd Brehmer (GDR) 50.38)

 4 Sep 1979 Turin   400m
  1st Koch 48.60 ... 3rd Szewinska 51.27 (European Cup Final ... 2nd Kulchunova (USSR) 49.63)

26 Aug 1979 Montreal   400m
  1st Koch 48.97 ... 3rd Szewinska 51.15 (World Cup Final ... 2nd Kulchunova 50.60)

Positive doping tests at earlier meetings caused subsequent adjustments of world cup scores for women in 1977 and 1979. In 1977 Ilona Slupianek won the shot with 20.93 and in 1979 Totka Petrova the 1500m in 4:06.5, but both lost their victories later (see p. 249). Slupianek was back to win the 1979 World Cup shot with 20.98m.

The highest ever Asian placing is second by Zou Zhenxian (Chn) at triple jump in 1981. His 17.34m final jump left him just 3cm behind Oliveira. The best Asian woman's placing is fourth by Esther Rot (Isr) at 100m hurdles in 1977.

The highest ever Oceania placing is Lynette Jacenko's (Aus) long jump win in 1977, and they have had three men's second places: Michael O'Rourke (NZ) javelin 1979, John Walker (NZ) 1500m 1981 and Gary Honey (Aus) long jump 1981.

The highest ever African women's placing is fifth by Sakina Boutamine (Alg) at 1500m in 1979.

British winners
1977: 1500m Steve Ovett 3:34.45 (UK record); 4 × 100mR (W) Andrea Lynch (2nd leg) and Sonia Lannaman (4th leg) for Europe – 42.51;

1979: 4 × 100mR (W) Heather Hunte (4th leg) for Europe – 42.19; **1981:** 800m Sebastian Coe 1:46.16; 100m Allan Wells 10.20; 1500m Steve Ovett 3:34.95.

The youngest ever competitor is the Kenyan Christine Chepchirchir, sixth at 3000m in 1981, at the age of 13. She had earlier run the remarkable times of 9:14.74 for 3000m and 15:53.8 for 5000m in Japan. At the age of 12 she had won the Kenyan Schools 3000m title in 9:29.6.

Early women's athletics

The first organised women's athletics meetings were probably those of Vassar College, Poughkeepsie, New York State. Vassar's first 'Field Day' was held in November 1895. In addition to the USA various women's events were held in Australia, New Zealand and South Africa in the first decade of the 20th century while in Europe several countries pioneered women's competition from 1917 when the Fédération Féminine Sportive de France was formed by Alice Milliat. Her request to the International Olympic Committee in 1919 for women's events to be added to the Olympic programme was refused. However, in spite of some strong opposition, particularly from Finland, the IOC Congress in 1926 voted 12–5 to include women's events in the 1928 Olympic Games. Those nations voting against were Australasia, Finland, Hungary, Ireland and Great Britain. Five events were duly held in Amsterdam, but at the IOC meeting there the Finnish delegate, Mr Pikhala again proposed the abolition of women's events. This time his motion was defeated 16–6.

The first multi-national women's meeting was the Monte Carlo Games held in March 1921 at which five countries, France, Great Britain, Switzerland, Italy and Norway sent teams. Several sports were contested and the British girls won six of the ten athletics events, led by Mary Lines, who set world records at 60m (8.2) and 250m (36.6) as well as winning the long jump (4.70m/15ft 5in) and running on both winning relay teams. The Monte Carlo Games were also staged in 1922 and 1923.

The first international governing body for women's athletics, the Fédération Sportive Féminine Internationale (FSFI), was founded by Alice Milliatt on 31 Oct 1921 in Paris on the day following the first match between France and Great Britain. Initially there were six countries represented, France, Britain, USA, Italy, Spain and Czechoslovakia. The International Olympic Committee had declined to include women's events at the Games so the FSFI held their own Women's Olympic Games in Paris in 1922 in the Pershing Stadium. Five nations competed: Czechoslovakia, France, Great Britain, Switzerland and the USA.

The Paris Games were the first of a series of women's meetings, held every four years, which became known as the **World Games**. The remaining venues were: Göteborg 1926, (8 nations competing), Prague 1930 (17 nations) and White City, London 1934 (19 nations).

The greatest number of individual wins in the World Games was four by Stanislawa Walasiewicz (Pol). She won a unique treble, 60m, 100m and 200m, in 1930 and won the 60m in 1934.

The most medals won was eight by Kinue Hitomi (Jap) – 1926: 1st LJ and standing LJ, 2nd DT, 3rd 100y (also 5th 60m and 6th 250m); 1930: 1st LJ, 2nd Pen, 3rd 60m and JT.

Britain's most successful athlete was Mary Lines, who in 1922 won the 300m and long jump as well as being on the winning sprint relay team. She was also second at 60m and third at 100y.

The FSFI merged with the IAAF in 1936, so that men's and women's athletics at last had one governing body.

World student games

The 'Universiade' or World Student Games has become established as one of the most important international fixtures. They are run by the Fédération Internationale du Sport Universitaire (FISU) and are entered by athletes either in or who have just completed full-time further education.

The first 'International Universities' Games was held in Warsaw in 1924 in conjunction with the annual congress of the CIE (Confédération Internationale des Etudiants). The meeting was organised at short notice and Poland had the most successful athletics team. There was no British team but Dr Arthur Porritt, of Oxford University and New Zealand, was an English delegate to the congress and was persuaded to compete; he won the 100m in 10.9 and the 200m in 22.2 and was second in the 110m hurdles in 15.8.

The first English representation came in 1928 in Paris when an athletics team of 32 placed fifth. At Darmstadt in 1930 women's events were staged for the first time, though British women first competed in Turin in 1933. From 1947 to 1962 FISU and UIE held separate Games the standard being much stronger at the Communist inspired UIE Games, known as the World Youth Games from 1954. Since the merging of the Games in 1963, standards have risen to their present status, and venues since that date have been: 1963 Porto Alegre, Brazil; 1965 Budapest; 1967 Tokyo; 1970 Turin; 1973 Moscow; 1975 Rome (unofficial); 1977 Sofia; 1979 Mexico City; 1981 Bucharest. Scheduled for 1983 Edmonton, Canada; 1985 Kobe, Japan.

The most individual victories at one event was achieved by Iolanda Balas (Rom) with the well-nigh incredible total of eight high jump victories. With the Games now held biennially and stricter rules on participation no one will be able to get close to her record. She was aided of course, by the rival Games and won the UIE organised events of 1954, 1955, 1957, 1959 and 1962 and the FISU Games of 1957, 1959 and 1961. Aleksandra Chudina (USSR) won a total of ten individual victories: 1949–HJ; 1951–80mh, HJ, LJ, Pen; 1953–HJ, LJ, JT, Pen (world record 4704 points); 1955–JT. Four individual victories in one year, which Chudina achieved twice, is also a record, though Trebisonda Valla (Ita), in 1933, and Gisela Mauermayer (Ger), in 1937, each won three individual events and shared in a relay victory. The most men's victories is five by both Janusz Sidlo (Pol) JT–1951, 1954, 1955, 1957 and 1959 and Igor Ter-Ovanesyan (USSR) LJ–1959, 1961, 1962, 1963, 1965.

Aleksandra Chudina, winner of the greatest number of USSR titles, and world record holder at high jump, pentathlon and 4 × 200m relay.

The only athlete to win the same event on three occasions since 1963 is Pietro Mennea (Ita) at 200m. He won in 1973, 1975 (unofficial) and 1979; in the latter year he set a world record of 19.72.

The most successful British athlete is Dorothy Saunders, who won three gold medals; the 80m and 200m in 1937 and the javelin in 1939. British winners of two individual event gold medals have been: Cyril Holmes 100m and 200m in 1937, Jim Alford 800m and 1500m in 1937, Peter Ward 5000m in 1935 and 1937, John Wilkinson 100m and 200m in 1947, and Kevin Gilligan 5000m in 1957 and 1959.

The most successful British athlete in recent years is Kathy Smallwood, who won the 200m in 1981 and won a silver medal on Britain's sprint relay team, as she had in 1979 when she was also second at 100m and 200m. Bev Callender (née Goddard), who was also on those relay teams, was third at both 100m and 200m in 1979 and won the 100m in 1981.

IAAF World International Cross-country Championship

The first in the series of International Cross-Country Championship races was held at Hamilton Park Racecourse, Glasgow on 28 Mar 1903. This, however, had been preceded by a match between England and France in 1898 when the French Athletic Federation challenged the first eight runners in the English Championships to a race over 9 miles 20y/ 14.5km on 20 March from Ville-d'Avray. The race resulted in a whitewash as the Englishmen swept to the first eight places, headed by Sidney Robinson, who had recently won his second successive National title.

The 1903 race was contested by the four countries from the British Isles over 8 miles/ 12.87km. England gained an easy victory with 25 points as their six scoring runners were placed 1st, 2nd, 4th, 5th, 6th and 7th. Alfred Shrubb was the individual winner, his time of 46min 22.6sec being 34 seconds clear of the runner-up. Shrubb's record-strewn career included a further International win in 1904, before he was suspended for allegations regarding expenses payments. He turned professional in 1906.

At the post-race dinner in 1903 Fred Lumley of Edinburgh offered to present an annual trophy, the Lumley Shield and the following year on 26 March the inaugural meeting of the International Cross-Country Union, which was

to govern the race for nearly 70 years, was held at the Moseley Hotel, Manchester. At this meeting it was proposed that the race should be open to the world, but in fact there were no entrants from outside the British Isles until 1907, when France (where the First national championships were held in 1887) entered for the first time.

The main milestones in the development of the race since then: **1908** First race outside the British Isles – at Colombes, near Paris. **1911** First non-English individual winner – Jean Bouin of France. Bouin won again in 1912 and 1913 to become the first man to win three successive titles. He was killed in action at the age of 25 on 29 September 1914 right at the start of the Great War.

1922 First non-English team winner – France
1923 Belgium competed for the first time
1929 Race distance fixed at 9 miles/14,484m. Record entry of ten nations with 88 runners at Vincennes Racecourse, Paris.
1940 Despite the state of war, the first international junior race was held on 24 March in the Bois de Boulogne, Paris, contested by France (1st), England (2nd) and Belgium (3rd). The individual winner was Frank Aaron (Eng), who ten years later twice improved the British 6 mile record and was fourth in the European 10000m. Dr Aaron was English national cross-country champion 1949–51 and had a highest international placing of fourth in 1950.
1953 Jubilee year for the international race. Yugoslavia competed for the first, and to date, only time, and provided the individual winner in Franjo Mihalic.
1961 Junior race revived; England won both team and individual events (Colin Robinson)
1967 First women's race at Barry, Wales contested by four teams: in order England, Ireland, Scotland and Wales; but there were two individual runners from the USA, including individual winner Doris Brown, who won by 37sec from Rita Lincoln (Eng).
1973 IAAF took control of the race from the International Cross-Country Union. It is now recognised by them as the official World Cross-Country Championships.

The first women's race in the current series was in 1967, but the first ever international cross-country for women was held at Douai in 1931 when the teams finished in the following order: England, France and Belgium. Gladys Lunn (Eng) was the individual winner.

The first African competitor was Ahmed Djebellia of Algeria who represented France in 1912 when he failed to finish. The following year another Algerian Allemamen Arbidi was 12th. Séghir Beddari (Alg) was the first African to finish in the first three, second in 1927 and third in 1928, while the first African winner was yet another Algerian running for France, Alain Mimoun in 1949. In 1958 Tunisia became the first non-European team to enter.

The first Oceanic team to enter was New Zealand in 1965, the first American, the USA in 1966 and the first Asian: Iran, Syria and Saudi Arabia in 1975.

The progressive number of competing nations completing a team:
Men 1903–4, 1907–5, 1924–6, 1929–10, 1963–11, 1965–15, 1973–18, 1975–23, 1981–27.
Women 1967–4, 1968–5, 1969–7, 1971–10, 1973–12, 1977–17.
Juniors 1961–6, 1962–8, 1965–9, 1971–10, 1972–12, 1974–13, 1976–15, 1978–16, 1980–17, 1981–19.

The lowest winning scores
Men: 21 points by England in both 1924 and 1932 when they placed the first six men home, in each case from five other teams. The 1924 winner was William Cotterell and the 1932 win-

ner was Tom Evenson. The lowest winning score since the race has been under IAAF jurisdiction, is 90 by England in 1976: 2) Tony Simmons, 3) Bernie Ford, 15) David Slater, 16) Grenville Tuck, 26) David Black, 28) Mike Tagg.
Women: (four to score): 15 USSR 1980. Their scorers were 2) Irina Bondarchuk, 3) Yelena Sipatova, 4) Giana Romanova, 6) Svyetlana Ulmasova. England scored less points, 13, in 1967, but this was after excluding the winner, Doris Brown (USA), as the USA did not finish a team. England's scorers: 2) Rita Lincoln, 4) Joyce Smith, 5) Pam Davies, 6) Joy Jordan.
Juniors: (four to score): 12 Ethiopia 1982, when the individual winner was Zurubachev Gelaw, and the other Ethiopian scorers were placed second, fourth and fifth. Their dominance was underwritten by their non-scorers finishing ninth and tenth.

The most finishers: men 228 in 1981; women 116 in 1981; junior 102 in 1981.

The largest winning margins
Men: 56sec Jack Holden (Eng) in 1934
Women: 40sec Grete Waitz (Nor) in 1980
Junior: 25sec Ian McCafferty (Sco) in 1964

The youngest senior champion is Lewis Payne (Eng) who was aged 19 in 1927. He retired later the same year.

The youngest competitor to be placed in the first three is Eileen Claugus (USA), second in 1972 at 16.

SUMMARY OF ALL THE PLACINGS IN THE FIRST THREE TEAMS

Country	MEN 1st	2nd	3rd	WOMEN 1st	2nd	3rd	JUNIORS 1st	2nd	3rd	First Year
England	45	15	7	6	2	3	11	4	2	1903
France	14	24	10	–	–	–	–	–	–	1907
Belgium	7	7	16	–	–	–	1	4	–	1923
Ethiopia	2	–	–	–	–	–	1	–	–	1981
New Zealand	1	1	2	–	3	1	–	–	–	1965
Ireland	–	9	5	–	1	1	–	2	–	1903
Scotland	–	7	17	–	–	3	–	2	4	1903
Wales	–	1	2	–	–	–	–	–	–	1903
Spain	–	1	3	–	–	–	2	3	5	1929
Morocco	–	1	1	–	–	–	–	2	4	1959
USSR	–	1	3	5	1	–	1	–	1	1973
USA	–	1	–	4	6	4	5	1	1	1966
Yugoslavia	–	–	1	–	–	–	–	–	–	1953
Kenya	–	–	1	–	–	–	–	–	–	1981
Romania	–	–	–	1	–	–	–	–	–	1978
Italy	–	–	–	–	3	1	1	2	3	1929
Finland	–	–	–	–	1	1	–	–	–	1971
Canada	–	–	–	–	–	–	–	1	2	1969
Tunisia	–	–	–	–	–	–	–	1	–	1958

Left to right: Mike McLeod (fifth), Mohamed Kedir (first) and Alberto Salazar (second) in the 1982 world cross-country. *(M. Shearman)*

England have only twice been out of the first three in the men's event. Those falls from grace were in 1973, the first year that the race was run under IAAF jurisdiction, and 1981, when they came fifth and sixth respectively. Obviously the competition is now more intense than in the earlier years of the race, but nonetheless England's harrier tradition persists for from 1974 to 1980 they were placed successively: 2nd, 2nd, 1st, 2nd, 3rd, 1st, 1st. In the women's race, too, England lead the way and here their worst ever placing was sixth in 1981.

Individual records – men's race
The most wins is four by Jack Holden (Eng), Alain Mimoun (Fra), and Gaston Roelants (Bel).

The most placings in the first three is seven by Gaston Roelants, followed by six for Jack Holden, Alain Mimoun and Frank Sando (Eng).
The most placings in the first ten is ten by Jack Holden, followed by nine for Frank Sando and Gaston Roelants and eight by Mariano Haro (Spa).
The above five men have easily the most outstanding records in the race. Their complete race records are as follows:
Holden 1929–18, 1930–7, 1931–6, 1932–2, 1933–1, 1934–1, 1935–1, 1936–2, 1937–dnf, 1938–6, 1939–1, 1946–6.
Mimoun 1949–1, 1950–2, 1952–1, 1954–1, 1956–1, 1958–2, 1959–6, 1960–18, 1961–24, 1962–26, 1964–18.
Sando 1952–9, 1953–2, 1954–4, 1955–1, 1956–2=, 1957–1, 1958–3, 1959–2, 1960–8.
Roelants 1959–27, 1960–2, 1961–11, 1962–1, 1963–2, 1964–dnf, 1965–dnf, 1967–1, 1968–31, 1969–1, 1970–2, 1971–12, 1972–1,

1973–8, 1974–14, 1975–10, 1976–13.
Haro 1961–3 Junior race, 1962–dnf, 1963–3, 1964–11, 1965–32, 1967–79, 1968–6, 1969–10, 1971–8, 1972–2, 1973–2, 1974–2, 1975–2, 1976–11, 1977–13.
(dnf = did not finish).

Jack Holden sealed his career, which included 'National' titles in 1938, 1939 and 1946, with a fantastic year in 1950, when he ran and won five marathons, including the Commonwealth and European titles, his fourth successive AAA title and his third successive Poly marathon.

Alain Mimoun-o-Kacha, born in Algeria, was aged 28 when he ran and won his first International title. He was five times runner-up to Emil Zatopek in major races (three Olympic and two European) before winning the Olympic marathon. He went on running, with many world age records, including 10000m in 32:14.0 and a 2:34:36.2 marathon at age 51 in 1972. He was 64th, one place behind Gillian Adams (GB), the first woman to finish, in the 1980 Paris marathon at the age of 59.

Alain Mimoun, most capped French athlete and winner of most French titles, runs at Hamilton Park, Glasgow in 1952.   *(H. W. Neale)*

Frank Sando also had a fine track career, if overshadowed by contemporaries such as Gordon Pirie and Chris Chataway. At the 1952 Olympics he was fifth at 10000m, yet he had lost a shoe on the third lap. He won three medals in 1954: at the Commonwealth Games he was second at the 6 mile and third at the 3 mile; at the European Games he was third in the 10000m. In the AAA 6 mile he was third in 1952, then runner-up for four successive years.

Gaston Roelants set world records at the steeplechase and at longer distances, yet he was at his best over the country. In 1972 one of his shoes was dislodged about a third of the way through the race. He lost about 50sec, yet worked his way back to beat Haro by about 100m to equal the record of four wins.

Mariano Haro who holds the unenviable record of being placed second for four successive years, and in the last three years he lost by a second or less each time, the closest being Pekka Paivarinta's one metre victory in 1973.

The most race appearances is 20 by Marcel Van de Wattyne (Bel) in successive years from 1946 to 1965. His best placing was second in his first race in 1946, again in 1952 and again in 1962.

The most appearances for other leading nations is **France** 14 Noel Tijou 1963–75, 1977 (best, 5th 1969 and 1970); **Scotland** 14 Jim Alder 1962, 1964–76 (best, 15th 1965); **Spain** 14 Mariano Haro (above); **Wales** 14 Danny Phillips 1922, 1924, 1926–37 (best, 17th 1930); **England** 12 Jack Holden (above).

The closest race was in 1965, when on Ostend racecourse, Jean Fayolle (Fra) was adjudged to have beaten Mel Batty (Eng) although most observers were unable to separate them after an elbow-to-elbow duel. England and France tied on points for the team title, but England were the winners on the basis of the best placed sixth man – 13th to 19th.

The best record in the Junior race is that of Scotland's Jim Brown, successively third, second and first, 1971–3. He followed that remarkable series with a fourth place in the senior race in 1974. Thom Hunt (USA) was second in 1976 and first in 1977 and John Treacy (Ire) also had two successive years in the top three third in 1974 and 1975. Treacy next ran and won the senior races of 1978 and 1979. Franco Fava (Ita) was placed four times in the

Junior top ten – tenth in 1970 at the age of 17, sixth in 1971, third in 1972, and fourth in 1973. In the senior race, he has five top ten placings headed by a fourth in 1977.

Athletes to have won both Junior and Senior events have been Mike Tagg (Eng) (junior 1966, senior 1970) and David Bedford (Eng) (junior 1969, senior 1971).

Individual records – women's race
The most wins is five by Doris Brown (USA) and four by Grete Waitz (Nor).

Doris Brown won the race by a big margin in each of the first five years it was staged, from 1967 to 1971. Later she ran in 1973–15th, 1975–17th and 1976–17th. Lack of longer distance track races gave this Seattle housewife few opportunities in other major events, although at 800m she twice won silver medals in the Pan-American Games (1967 and 1971) and was placed fifth in the 1968 Olympic Games.

Grete Waitz won by 30 seconds in 1978, 26 seconds in 1979, and 40 seconds in 1980 (three of the four greatest winning margins), and by 15 seconds in 1981. Her third place in 1982 was her first ever defeat in a cross-country race. Romanians Maricica Puica and Fita Lovin were first and second.

The most placings in the top ten have been six by Rita Ridley (née Lincoln) (Eng): 2nd 1967 and 1970; 3rd 1972 and 1974; 4th 1973 and 10th 1971; and by Joyce Smith (Eng): 1st 1972; 2nd 1973; 3rd 1971; 4th 1967; 7th 1974 and 9th 1978. with additional placings of 14th in 1969 and 16th in 1970 Smith's eight runs in the race are the most by an English woman.

The most appearances in the race have been made by Margaret Coomber (née MacSherry) of Scotland who competed in every race from the first in 1967 until 1980 (best 5th 1972) and Jean Lochhead of Wales who competed each year from 1967 to 1979 and also in 1981 (best 6th 1973).

Arab Games and Championships
The first Pan-Arab Games were held at Alexandria, Egypt 27–31 Jul 1953.
  The Arab Athletics Championships are held biennially. The first was at Damascus in 1977, followed by Baghdad in 1979 and Tunis in 1981. Women's events were held for the first time in 1981. The Kuwaiti Mohamed Al-Zinkawi won the shot on each occasion and also won Asian titles in 1979 and 1981.

Maccabiah Games
The World Maccabiah Games, for athletes of the Jewish faith, were first held in Tel Aviv, Israel, 29 Mar–6 Apr 1932, when teams of men and women from 20 countries participated. The idea was put forward in 1929 by Joseph Yekutieli, a Russian-born Jew who settled in Palestine. The Games were named after Judah Maccabeus, an Israelite hero who drove the Assyrians out of the Temple in Jerusalem in 165BC.
  The USA team was seen off by New York Mayor Jimmy Walker with the quip 'You bring home the bacon – and I'll eat it'. Since the War they have been held every four years. By the Tenth Games in July 1977 there were a record 33 countries represented. The American contingents have traditionally been the largest and the strongest. However, in the 1935 celebration there was an unusually large contingent from Germany – many of whom did not return home.
  Esther Rot (Isr) holds the record of 11 wins, eight individual and three relay, in the 1969, 1973 and 1977 Games. the most wins by a man is five by walker Shaul Ladany (Isr) in 1969, 1973 and 1977, and five by Mike Herman (USA) in 1957 and 1961.

Mediterranean Games
These Games were first held at Alexandria in Egypt from 6–10 Oct 1951, when the most notable achievements were doubles by two North African athletes running for France – Patrick El Mabrouk (800m and 1500m) and Alain Mimoun (5000m and 10000m). They are held every four years.
  The 1963 Games were not deemed as official by the IAAF, due to the fact that Albania, Israel and Libya were not invited to Naples, neither were the 1971 Games when Israel was not invited to Izmir, Turkey.
  Women's events were included for the first time in 1967 in Tunis.
  Pietro Mennea (Ita) won gold medals at three successive Games: 200m in 1971, 100m and 200m in 1975 and 100m in 1979.
  Mohamed Gammoudi (Tun) first made his presence felt internationally at the 1963 Games when he set new Tunisian records to win at 5000m (14:07.4) and 10000m (29:34.2). He repeated this double in 1967.

AFRICAN ATHLETICS

Africa

The earliest African nations to have national athletics federations were South Africa 1894, Zimbabwe (then Rhodesia) 1901, Egypt 1910 and Uganda 1925.

The earliest to compete in the Olympic Games were South Africa 1904, Egypt 1906 and then no others until Ghana and Nigeria in 1952.

Apart from South Africans the earliest African successes were obtained by athletes from French colonies and protectorates who were eligible to compete for France before their nation's independence. Of these nations the earliest to develop was Tunisia, whose Track and Field Sports Committee was formed in 1908.

The first African Olympic medallist was Reggie Walker of South Africa in 1908 (see p. 129), while the first from the rest of the continent was Boughera El Ouafi, winner of the 1928 marathon, who was born at Ould Djileb, Algeria, worked at the Renault factory and represented France. Alain Mimoun O'Kacha, with a gold and three silver medals, was the most successful of all French African Olympians. The first African-based woman to win an Olympic gold medal was Micheline Ostermeyer (Fra) at both shot and discus in 1948; she originated from Tunisia. Abdou Seye from Senegal was third at 200m in 1960.

African Games

African Games had been planned during the 1920s, originally for Algiers in 1925, but for a variety of reasons not least the hostility to the idea of the colonial powers, England and France, these plans were not progressed. Alexandria in Egypt had been mooted for 1929, but this venue had to wait for a major Games until the first Mediterranean Games were staged in 1951. Friendship Games, originally for the French-speaking African nations, but in which some English-speaking nations joined, were staged in Tananarive, Madagascar in 1960; Abidjan, Ivory Coast in 1961 and Dakar, Senegal in 1963. These paved the way for IAAF recognition of the first African Games for 1965. These were held at Brazzaville, Congo, opening on 18 Jul 1965. Ten sports were contested, including athletics in the Revolution Stadium.

Subsequent Games have been held at Lagos, Nigeria in 1973 and at Algiers in 1978 and are scheduled to be held in Kenya in 1982. The most successful nations at the first three Games have been: Nigeria 23 gold – 23 silver – 12 bronze; Kenya 20–19–18; Ghana 13–10–11; Uganda 8–10–13; Ivory Coast 6–2–7; Egypt 6–1–3; Algeria 4–7–7; Ethiopia 3–5–6; Senegal 3–5–5; Mali 3–2–0.

One world record has been set at these Games: Ben Jipcho (Ken) 3000m steeplechase in 8:20.69 in 1973. Jipcho won a second gold by winning the 5000m from the 10000m champion Miruts Yifter (Eth) and at the same Games there was an upset win for the 20-year-old Filbert Bayi (Tan) in the 1500m over Kip Keino (Ken) 3:37.18 to 3:39.58. The previous month Bayi had improved his best by 6.1sec to 3:38.9 to win the East and Central African title.

The most gold medals won at individual events is five by Modupe Oshikoya (Nig). She won the 100m hurdles (14.2), high jump (1.71m) and long jump (6.15m) in 1973 and the high jump (1.77m) and long jump (6.32m) in 1978. Alice Annum (Gha) won the long jump in 1965 and both 100m and 200m in 1973. The men's record is three golds by Namakoro Niare (Mali) with the discus in 1965, 1973 and 1978. He is the only athlete to have won medals at all three Games, and joins Oshikoya as having won a record five individual medals with second places at shot in 1973 and 1978 to Nagui Assad (Egy).

African Championships

The first African Championships, which as opposed to the quadrennial African Games are for athletics only, were held at Dakar from 2–5 Aug 1979. Nagui Assad won the shot to add to his two African Games titles.

The second Championships were due to be staged in Lagos in August 1981, but these were cancelled by the withdrawal of the athletes after top 400m-runner Dele Udo (Nig), second at the 1978 African Games and home from the University of Missouri, USA, was shot and killed at a checkpoint by a policeman in Lagos.

East and Central African Championships

The youngest ever champion at an international championships is Elizabeth Onyambu who won the 1500m in Mombasa on 7 Jul 1979 in a time of 4:25.0 at the age of 12.

These championships emanated from the annual match between Kenya and Uganda, the first of which in 1934 was the first inter-African nation duel.

Central African Games

These Games have been held in 1976 at Libreville, Gabon and in 1979 in Luanda, Angola.

Egypt

Nagui Assad set his first African shot record at 18.95m/62ft 2¼in in 1969 and steadily improved this to 20.71m/67ft 11½in in 1972. He stayed a world-class athlete for the next decade, yet must be accounted one of the unluckiest athletes ever, for he missed three successive Olympic Games due to political boycotts: the Egyptian boycott of the Games with the Arab protest over Israeli policies in 1972, the African boycott over New Zealand's sporting links with South Africa in 1976 and the Muslim boycott over the Soviet Union's intervention in Afghanistan in 1980.

Ethiopia

The national federation was formed in 1949, Ethiopia joined the IAAF in 1950 and first competed in the Olympic Games in 1956. In that Games Mamo Wolde was last in the heats of the 800m and 1500m. After being placed fourth at 10000m in 1964 he went on to win two Olympic medals in 1968 (1st Mar and 2nd 10000m) and another in 1972 (3rd Mar). But Ethiopia's athletes were first brought to world attention by Abebe Bikila with his double Olympic marathon triumph in 1960 and 1964.

Ghana

Ghana's first Olympic participation was in 1952. Christina Boateng won the national women's 100y title at the age of 13 in 1957, the year Ghana (formerly the Gold Coast) gained independence.

Kenya

The Kenya athletics federation was founded in 1951 and the first Kenyan Olympic representation was in 1956. Nyandika Maiyoro presaged the Kenyan distance running triumphs of recent years with seventh and sixth places at the Olympic 5000m in 1956 and 1960 respectively, after being fourth in the 1954 Commonwealth Games 3 miles. The first Kenyan medals at the Commonwealth Games came in 1958 with bronze medals for Arere Onentia (6m) and Bartongo Rotich (440yh).

The Kenyans really burst onto the Olympic scene in 1968 with eight medals including golds for Kip Keino (1500m), Naftali Temu (10000m) and Amos Biwott (3000m, S/C). Since then the Kenyans, their distance runners in particular, have never failed to make a big impact on all the major events at which they have competed. Kip Keino leads their medallists with two gold and two silver Olympic medals and three gold and one bronze at the Commonwealth Games. At both 800m and 4 × 400m relay the Kenyans have taken the gold medals at all three Commonwealth Games between 1970 and 1978.

Kip Keino, world record holder at 3000m and 5000m, won two African Games, two Olympic and three Commonwealth golds. *(M. Shearman)*

To date Kenya is the only nation apart from the USA to have broken 3 minutes for the 4 × 400m relay, with an Olympic second place in 1968 (2:59.64) and victory in 1972 (2:59.83), when Julius Sang, individual bronze medallist, ran an extraordinary anchor leg in 43.5sec.

Kenyan women have yet to make as much impact on their track as their men, but Sabine Chebichi won their first major medal, with a third in the 1974 Commonwealth 800m.

Morocco
Moroccan athletes first competed in the Olympic Games under their national colours in 1960, when Rhadi Ben Abdesselam won the marathon silver medal.

Nigeria
The first black African athlete to win a Commonwealth medal was Josiah Majekodunmi, equal second at high jump in 1950. At the same event four years later Emmanuel Ifeajuna won the first gold medal by a Nigerian. Their first woman commonwealth champion was Modupe Oshikoya at long jump (6.46m) in 1974. Oshikoya was also second at pentathlon and third at 100m hurdles.

Nigeria's best placed Olympic competitor is Wariboko West, fourth at long jump in 1964. Prince Adegboyega Adedoyin competed for Britain at the 1948 Olympics, and was placed fifth at long jump. He was studying at Queen's University, Belfast.

South Africa
The South African AAU was founded on 26 Mar 1894, the year in which national championships for men were first held. Women's championships were first staged in 1929.

The winner of the most South African titles has been Harry Hart, with 31 between 1926 and 1946 (13 at SP also a record for one event, 9 DT, 4 PV, 3 JT and 2 HT). He set national records at 220y hurdles (26.0 in 1929), pole vault (best 3.50m in 1930), shot (best 15.72m in 1931, a record which stood for 25 years), discus (44.96m in 1931, stood for 21 years), and javelin (62.36m in 1932).

The most women's national titles is 18 by: Marjorie Clark between 1929 and 1935, (100y – 3, 220y – 3, 80mh – 5, HJ – 6, LJ – 1); and 18 by Sonja Laxton (née Van Zyl) between 1971 and 1978 (800m – 1, 1500m – 6, 3000m – 6, cross-country – 5).

The oldest South African champion is Luther Jurgenson, aged 50 years 50 days when he won at 50km walk in 1964. Another walker George Hazle became the oldest to set a national record at 43 years 206 days, when he clocked 23:16.4 for the 5000m walk on 27 Apr 1968.

The oldest women's champion is Anne McKenzie who won the 1966 880y title at 40 years 255 days. She was also the oldest to set a national record at 41 years 357 days with 4:36.0 for the 1500m on 20 Jul 1967.

The greatest number of South African records also stands to Anne McKenzie, who set 24 in all (between 1962 and 1967), two each at 1500m and 1 mile and 20 at 880y or 800m, a record for any one event. Born Anne Joubert on 28 Jul 1925, her great-uncle had been Daniel Joubert, world 100y record holder in 1931. Married in 1950, she was provincial champion at shot, discus and javelin, but didn't train seriously until aged 35. She ran her first half mile two years later in 2:33.0 and a week later equalled the

Anne McKenzie (left) holds off Pam Piercy for second in the 1967 WAAA 880y. Her 2:07.4 is still an over-40 age record.   (H. W. Neale)

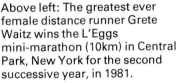

Above left: The greatest ever
female distance runner Grete
Waitz wins the L'Eggs
mini-marathon (10km) in Central
Park, New York for the second
successive year, in 1981.

Above right: Brendan Foster leads
Nick Rose in the 1976 AAA 5000m.
They finished first and second
respectively. Both have won the
5000m at European Cup finals.

Below right: Alberto Juantorena
wins Cuba's first Olympic athletics
gold medal with the 800m in 1976.
Second was Ivo van Damme (103),
third Rick Wohlhuter (red vest),
fourth Willi Wülbeck (450), fifth
Steve Ovett (on Wülbeck's right)
and sixth Luciano Susanj (behind
Ovett).

Above: Iolanda Balas was unbeaten at the high jump for 10½ years. She set 14 world records.

Right: Udo Beyer in Prague in 1978 when he added the European shot gold medal to the Olympic gold he had won in 1976.

Matthews Motshwaretu (100) wins at 3000m in 1978 in the third race of his career from Victor Liebenberg (62) and Bernard Rose (58).

national record of 2:24.8. Over the next five years she steadily whittled that time down to 2:06.5 for 800m and 2:07.4 for 880y for second place in the WAAA championships on 1 Jul 1967. She has continued to compete and set age records, including 2:23.1 for 800m and 4:54.5 for 1500m at the age of 50 in 1975. Sonja Laxton also set 24 national records at distances from 1000m to marathon between 1971 to 1980.

The most records by a South African man is 19, all at hammer by Adam Barnard, from 62.18m/204ft 0 in in 1970 to 73.86m/242ft 4in in 1976.

The youngest national champion and record holder is Esther van Heerden (later Brand). She won her first high jump title in 1938 at 14 years 2 months and was 15 years 203 days when she set her first national record at 1.61m/5ft 3½in on 20 Sep 1939. On 29 Mar 1941 she set a world record of 1.66m/5ft 5¼in and won nine South African high jump titles as well as three at discus and one at shot, a total that would have been higher but for the war years. She capped her career by becoming the first South African women's Olympic champion and incidentally their oldest Olympic competitor in 1952 at 1.67m/5ft 5¾in.

The youngest men's champion and record holder is Emile Rossouw, also a high jumper, who was a record holder with 2.08m/6ft 10in at

16 years 32 days in 1970 and champion at 17 years 103 days in 1971 with 2.185m/7ft 2in which remained his best ever as injuries terminated his career.

South Africa first competed officially at the Olympic Games in 1908, when 19-year-old Reggie Walker won **the first African gold medal** at 100m. Walker ran the first world best (11.4 for 120y in 1908) by a South African. However two black South Africans, Lentauw and Yamasani, who worked as casual labourers at the St Louis World's Fair competed in the marathon at the 1904 Olympic Games, **the first African Olympic competitors**. Lentauw finished ninth after being chased nearly a mile off course by an angry dog and Yamasani was 12th. Most Olympic medals have been won by Bevil Rudd who won a complete set in 1920, gold at 400m, silver 4 × 400mR and bronze 800m. South Africa's oldest Olympian has been distance runner Len Richardson, aged 43 in 1924 and he has been the only South African to take part in three Games.

South Africa competed at each Olympic Games from 1904 to 1960, but since then have not been invited by the IOC due to apartheid policies. In 1968 the IOC had promised them re-admittance provided an integrated team was selected, however this invitation was withdrawn on the threat of a boycott by 39 nations. The South African AAU was expelled in 1976 from the IAAF (227 votes to 145) which has meant that their athletes have since been barred from international competition. However black South Africans at American Universities have been able to compete in limited competition, notably Sydney Maree, who became an American citizen in 1981, and Matthews Motshwarateu, who ran a 27:48.2 10000m in 1979 and on 4 Oct 1980 became the first man to win a TAC Grand Prix road race for the first prize of 10000 dollars, which later had to be refunded. He burst onto the scene in 1978, winning the South African 5000m title in only his second race and clocking a world-class 13:29.6 in his seventh race, just three weeks after his first.

The first black South African to set a national record was Humphrey Khosi who set the first of three 880y records with 1:48.9 on 25 Apr 1964.

Tanzania

In 1954 the national federation was formed and the first national championships held. The first

Olympic representation was in 1964, and silver medals were won by Suleiman Nyambui at 5000m and Filbert Bayi at 3000m steeplechase in 1980. Bayi was the first Tanzanian world record holder, with his 1500m victory at the 1974 Commonwealth Games.

Tunisia

After independence from France Tunisian athletes first took part at the Olympic Games in 1960. Their most successful athlete has been Mohamed Gammoudi, Olympic 5000m champion in 1968.

Uganda

John Akii-Bua won Uganda's first gold medal at a major championships in superb style at the 1972 Olympic Games.

Akii-Bua was one of 43 children born to his father's eight wives. An elder brother, Lawrence Ogwang, had been placed sixth at the triple jump at the 1954 Commonwealth Games. After 53.7sec for the 440y hurdles in his debut season of 1968, Akii-Bua came to world prominence with a fourth placing in the 1970 Commonwealth 400m hurdles in 51.14. He improved to 49.0 in 1971 before his world record

Bruce Kennedy who missed three Olympic Games due to politics.
(University of California)

47.82 at the Olympics when he finished so elated that he continued to hurdle through the finish and around the back straight.

A national hero, Akii-Bua fled from Uganda in the turmoil at the end of Idi Amin's rule in 1979. He was jailed in Kenya for a month before being recognised and freed. He then made his way to Germany. In 1980 he had a best of 50.16 on his return to the track, far from his best, but as he said it was 'for joy'.

Zimbabwe

The national governing body was founded, as the Rhodesia Amateur Athletic Union, in 1901.

Men's national championships (at 100y and 440y) were first held in 1902, when both events were won by W. H. Trott.

The most men's titles won is 21 by George Baker between 1943–54 (100y – 4, 220y – 7, 440y – 10).

Women's national titles were introduced in 1930 at 100y and high jump, both being won by Mollie Bragge.

The most women's titles won is 25 by Andrea Nadalet (née Davies) between 1964–75 (100m – 2, 200m – 6, 400m – 5, 800m – 6, 1500m – 3, 3000m – 1, LJ – 2). She also set the most national records, 20, which encompassed the same events, thus showing a remarkable range from sprinting to long distance.

Rhodesia competed in the Olympic Games of 1960 and 1964. Entered in 1968 for the Games, the teams visas were 'mislaid' by the Mexican government. In 1972 a team of ten athletes (six black, four white) went to Munich but were not allowed to compete (see p. 242). Bruce Kennedy, who at the age of 17 had become the youngest ever male Rhodesian international in 1968, was one of those ten in 1972 and was again selected in 1976, when again Rhodesia was not allowed to compete. Kennedy moved to the USA in 1969 to study at the University of California, improving his national javelin record by over 27ft in his second competition in 1970. He married an American and became an American citizen in 1977. In 1980 he was second in the US Trials and was thus again selected for the Olympic Games, this time for the USA, but as the Americans boycotted the Games, yet again he did not fulfill his ambition of actually competing in the Olympics.

AMERICAN ATHLETICS

Canada

Origins of athletics in Canada include snowshoe races held in Montreal from 1840, and in Montreal an 'Olympic Games' was held on 28/29 Aug 1844. The Montreal AAA ran national championships from 1880 to 1886.

The Canadian AAU was formed on 11 Apr 1884, and the first national championships were staged on 27 Sep 1884. Women's championships were first held in 1925.

George Gray was the first Canadian to set a world record with a 13.76m/45ft 2in shot put on 24 May 1889. In all he set six world records, with a best of 14.75m/48ft 4¾in in 1898.

Canada first took part at the Olympic Games in 1900, when George Orton, at 2500m steeplechase, won their first gold medal. Their first women's Olympic champion was the beautiful Ethel Catherwood at high jump in 1928. On the same day their sprint relay team, who included three 100m finalists headed by silver medallist Fanny Rosenfeld, also won. Rosenfeld won four Canadian championships in 1926 (Standing LJ, SP, DT, JT) and three in 1928 (LJ, SP, DT).

Abigail Hoffman is the only Canadian to have competed at four Olympic Games, 1964–76, twice making the final of the women's 800m.

Etienne Desmarteau was the only non-US athlete to win a 1904 Olympic title, at 56lb weight. A Montreal policeman, he died the following year of typhoid and a park was named after him.

Caribbean and Central American Nations

Cuba

The first Central American Olympic competitor was Cuba's Felix Carvajal at the 1904 marathon. He was placed fourth, having raised money for the trip by running exhibitions in Havana's main square. He lost all his money gambling in New Orleans, but hitch-hiked to St Louis. He turned out for the marathon, his first attempt at the distance, in his ordinary clothes, and the start was delayed while these were 'tailored' by Martin Sheridan. He clowned throughout the race, and might have won but for suffering cramp possibly induced by eating green apples.

Cuba's first Olympic medallist was Enrique Figuerola, who was second at 100m in 1964. Their first gold medallist was Alberto Juantorena in 1976, at both 400m and 800m. Cuba's national federation was formed in 1922.

Haiti

The one Haitian athlete to have achieved top world class is long jumper Silvio Cator, the first man to exceed 26ft. That same year, 1928, he won the Olympic silver medal behind Ed Hamm (USA). He also captained the Haitian soccer team.

The three longest standing national track records in the world are those of Haitian sprinters: André Théard 100m in 10.5 and 200m in 22.0 in 1926, and oldest of all E. Armand's 110m hurdles of 16.6 in 1924.

More recently Haitian athletes achieved some notoriety of a more doubtful kind with the worst series of performances in Olympic history. In 1972 all their athletes finished last in their heats with such poor times as: 100m 11.50, 200m 22.97, women's 100m 13.84. In 1976 a slightly larger team did even worse, women's 100m, 200m, and 400m times were 13.11, 28.19 and 73.27. The men's 800m 2:15.26 and 1500m 4:23.41 added to the embarrassment, but worst of all were 5000m in 18:50.07 by Dieudone Lamothe, more than five minutes behind the second from last man, and 10000m in 42:00.11 by one Olmeus Charles, just under 14min after Carlos Lopes had won the heat.

Jamaica

Jamaica was first represented in the Olympic Games in 1948, when Arthur Wint won the 400m. This was the first of four gold medals that Jamaicans have won at the Games.

Mexico

They were first represented at the Olympic Games in 1924 and their national federation was formed in 1933. Mexican walkers have been outstanding with their first Olympic medal going to José Pedraza, who was second at 20km in 1968, and the first gold to Daniel Bautista at 20km in 1976.

Panama
They were first represented at the Olympic Games in 1948, when Lloyd La Beach, third at 100m, won their one medal.

Trinidad and Tobago
First represented in 1948, Trinidad's first Olympic medals were won by Ed Roberts, third at 200m, Wendell Mottley, second at 400m and the 4 × 400m relay team, which was third, all in 1964. Their first gold medallist was Hasely Crawford at 100m in 1976.

CENTRAL AMERICAN AND CARIBBEAN GAMES (CAC)
These Games were first staged in 1926 in Mexico City. They have been held approximately every four years since then with the exception of 1942. Women's events were first included in 1938 in Panama City. The 14th Games were held in 1982.

The statue outside the National Stadium Kingston, Jamaica is a composite of McKenley, Rhoden and Wint. *(Jamaican High Commission)*

The most gold medals won by any athlete is five by three Cuban sprinters: Rafael Fortun won the 100m in 1946 (10.4sec), 1950 (10.3w) and 1954 (10.5), the 200m in 1946 (21.6) and was on the winning sprint relay team in 1950; Silvio Leonard won the sprint double in both 1974 and 1978 (10.49/20.99 and 10.10/20.49) and won a relay gold in 1974; and Miguelina Cobian won the women's 100m in 1962 (12.0), 1966 (11.7) and 1970 (11.4w) and the 200m in 1970. Cobian also won three silvers making a record eight medals by a woman.

The most medals by an individual is ten by George Rhoden (Jam) during 1946–54. In both 1950 and 1954 he won four medals equalling the record for one Games set by his team-mate Herb McKenley in both 1946 and 1950. These two comprised half the Jamaican gold medal team at 4 × 400m at the 1952 Olympic Games. Their two colleagues on that team had barely less distinguished CAC careers, for Arthur Wint won five medals (four gold) during 1938–46 and Les Laing six during 1950–4. Curiously the four never competed together at the CAC Games as a relay team. In 1954 another Jamaican, Keith Gardner, also won four medals, first in both relays, second at 110m hurdle and third at long jump. McKenley (Boston and Illinois), Rhoden (Morgan State), Laing (Fresno State) and Gardner (Nebraska) all attended Universities in the USA, while Wint spent most of his career in Britain after arriving in 1944 to complete his RAF training. Wint's career had begun with Jamaican under-13 sprint titles in 1931 and 1932. Very tall at 1.94m/6ft 4½in, Wint was one of the greatest and most popular athletes in Britain in the immediate post-war era. He represented Britain in five international matches, and won both 400m and 800m against both France and Yugoslavia in 1951. A medical student and member of Polytechnic Harriers his presence and awe inspiring strides were greatly missed by the British public when he returned to Jamaica in 1952, but he came back to London in 1974 as Jamaican High Commissioner, and in 1975 he was appointed Ambassador to Sweden.

The most CAC medals won at one event is four by high jumper Teodoro Flores (Gua), winner in 1959, 1962 and 1966 and second in 1974, and by women's discus thrower Carmen Romero (Cub) who followed her third place in 1966 with wins in 1970, 1974 and 1978. Maria Betancour (Cub) was runner-up to her on each occasion. Another instance of the same winner and runner-up at three successive Games came in the pole vault in 1959, 1962 and 1966 when the winner each time was Rolando Cruz of Puerto Rico with his brother Ruben second.

Central American and Caribbean Championships are held biennially. The first was at Jalapa, Mexico in 1967.

Pan-American Games

The first Pan-American Games was held in Buenos Aires from 27 Feb–5 Mar 1951. There was a crowd of about 100000 in the River Plate Stadium when the Games were opened by the Argentinian President, Juan Peron. In addition to Track and Field Athletics, the Games, which have been held every four years since 1951, embrace 19 other sports. The venues have been: 1955 Mexico City; 1959 Chicago; 1963 Sao Paulo; 1967 Winnipeg; 1971 Cali, Colombia; 1975 Mexico City; 1979 San Juan, Puerto Rico. Open to all North and South American nations, the Games have been dominated by the USA, who have won 129 of the 186 gold medals to date. Even so, the USA have not always been at full strength and they have been challenged by Cuba who won seven golds in 1975 and six in 1979.

The official series, originally scheduled to start in 1942, was preceded by the Pan-American Exposition Games held at the Dallas Cotton Bowl in 1937. The highlight of these Games was the '800 metres' won by the 1936 Olympic champion John Woodruff (USA). The 1.89m/6ft 2½in tall Woodruff, known as 'Long John' was however deprived of a world record. Six days earlier Elroy Robinson had set world records for 800m and 880y when he was timed at 1:49.6 for the longer distance. Woodruff beat Robinson by 7m at Dallas in a time of 1:47.8, but the course on a five lap to the mile, clay track was re-measured and found to be about 5ft/1.52m short. Woodruff's time was equivalent to about 1:48.0 for the full 800m.

The most Pan-American gold medals won is four by Joao Carlos de Oliveira, winner of the long jump/triple jump double in both 1975 and 1979, and by Osvaldo Suarez (Arg), winner of the 5000m and 10000m in 1955, the 10000m in 1959 and the 5000m in 1963. Oliveira smashed the world triple jump record at the high altitude of Mexico City in 1975 with his second round jump of 17.89m/58ft 8½in. This was a 1.15m/3ft 0¼in improvement over the 21-year-old

Joao Carlos de Oliveira at Moscow in 1980 when judges' decisions may have cost him the triple jump gold medal. *(M. Shearman)*

Brazilian Army Corporal's previous personal best and a 45cm/1ft 5¾in increase in the world record. Suarez also won silver medals at 5000m in 1959 and 10000m in 1963, for a record total of six medals, a feat he shares with Miguelina Cobian, the Cuban sprinter.

Abigail Hoffmann (Can) uniquely won medals at four Games. She won the 800m at the age of 16 in 1963 and after being placed third in 1967 regained this title in 1971. In 1975 she was second at 800m and third at 1500m.

Three gold medals at one event have been won by: Adhemar Ferreira da Silva (Bra) at triple jump in 1951, 1955 (world record 16.56m) and 1959; Al Hall (USA) at the hammer 1959, 1963 and 1971; and Carmen Romero (Cub) the women's discus 1971, 1975 and 1979.

The 1955 Games at Mexico City was the first major athletics meeting to be held at high altitude. At the time the effects of altitude, benefiting the sprinters and horizontal jumpers, and adversely affecting the distance runners had not been fully appreciated, but eyes were opened by world records in the triple jump (above) and at the 400m in which Lou Jones

(USA) improved from 46.4 to 45.4 to take 0.4sec off George Rhoden's record. There was also great long jumping, with Rosslyn Range, 8.03m/26ft 4¼in and John Bennett, 8.01m/26ft 3½in, both USA, moving to third and fourth on the all-time list in the first ever competition with two men jumping over 26ft.

There were two more world records at Cali in 1971, where although only half as high above sea level as Mexico City, the 1003m/3290ft altitude again helped the 'explosive' events. Don Quarrie ran the 200m in 19.86 and there was a sensational breakthrough by Pedro Perez Duenas (Cub) at the triple jump. Perez had improved fast, from 15.78m in 1969 to a world junior record 16.38m/53ft 9in in 1970, to 16.86m earlier in 1971, but few can have predicted his series of 16.92m, 17.40m/57ft 1in, 14.92m, 17.04m, 17.12m, 17.19m. Only 19 years old, Perez's 17.40m added 1cm to Viktor Saneyev's world record. He was coached by Leonid Shcherbakov, the Russian former world record holder.

Alberto Juantorena (Cub) won four silver medals at the Pan-American Games, two in both 1975 and 1979. In the latter year Julie Brown (USA) won silver medals at 800m, 1500m and 3000m despite intense heat.

In 1979 the Virgin Islander Wallace Williams, running in the marathon, reached the stadium well behind the other runners to find the gates locked. A public address announcement had to be made for the doors to be opened so that he could finish the race.

The first Pan-American Junior Championships were held at Sudbury, Canada 29–31 Aug 1979. Competitors, both men and women, had to be born in 1961 or later.

South America

Chile was the only South American nation to be represented at the first Olympic Games in 1896. They were followed in 1924 by Brazil, Ecuador and Argentina, for whom Luis Brunetto won the silver medal at the triple jump with 15.42m/50ft 7in, a tremendous 78cm improvement on his South American record.

The first Olympic gold medal won by a South American was at the 1932 marathon by Juan Carlos Zabala (Arg).

The best Olympic results by South American women have been silver medals by Noemi Simonetto (Arg) for long jump in 1948 and Marlene Ahrens (Chi) at the javelin in 1956.

The earliest national federations to be formed were: Brazil 1914, Chile 1917, Peru and Uruguay 1918.

SOUTH AMERICAN CHAMPIONSHIPS

The first official South American Championships were held at Montevideo, Uruguay from 11–13 Apr 1919. Since then they have been held regularly every two or three years, so that the 31st Championships were held at La Paz, Bolivia in November 1981. Eight unofficial championships have also been staged, from the first at Buenos Aires in 1918. Santiago de Chile has staged the most championships with six official as well as three unofficial. Montevideo has also had six official and two unofficial championships, followed by Lima (Peru) and Buenos Aires (Argentina) with five each. Women's events were held for the first time in 1939 at Lima.

Team victories have been: Brazil 13 men/13 women: Argentina 10/5; Chile 6/3; Venezuela 2/0.

The most men's individual victories at one event is six by Ricardo Heber (Arg) at the javelin 1947, 1949, 1952, 1956, 1958 and 1961. He did not compete in 1954, and went on to be placed fourth in 1963 and 1965. In his best season of 1951, he twice improved the South American record, on the first occasion when winning the Pan-American title with 68.08m/223ft 4in and later with 71.04m/233ft 1in.

The most women's individual victories at one event is also six by Wanda dos Santos (Bra) who won the 80m hurdles at successive Championships 1949, 1952, 1954, 1956, 1958 and 1961.

The most individual titles won at all events is 11 by Osvaldo Suarez (Arg) and Manuel Plaza (Chi). Suarez won treble victories at the 5000m, 10000m and the half marathon in both 1956 and 1958, doubles at the 5000m and 10000m in 1961 and 1963 and also won the 10000m in 1967. Suarez also set a record number of 11 South American men's track records (six at 5000m, five at 10000m). Plaza won treble victories at the 5000m, 10000m and the cross-country in 1924, 1926 and 1927, in which years he was also placed first in the team 3000m event. He returned to win the cross-country and 32km road race in 1933.

SOUTH AMERICAN COUNTRIES

Argentina

National championships were first held in 1920 for men and 1939 for women. The most titles won is 22 by Ingerborg Mello, ten shot, nine discus and three javelin, in 1940–62. Her ten shot put wins shares the record for the most at one event with Juan Fuse at the hammer between 1933–57 and Ricardo Heber at the javelin between 1946–60.

Brazil

Amateur athletics in Brazil dates from 1872 when the first meeting was held in Rio de Janeiro.

The first world record by a South American athlete was Adhemar Ferreira da Silva's 16.00m/52ft 6in triple jump at Sao Paulo on 3 Dec 1950. He followed this with four more world records and was emulated as world record holder by his countrymen Nelson Prudencio 17.27m/56ft 8in in 1968 and Joao Carlos de Oliveira 17.89m/58ft 8½in in 1975. At the Olympic Games da Silva won two gold medals, Prudencio a silver and a bronze and Oliveira two bronze medals. They also won three, four and four, respectively, South American triple jump titles.

Chile

Manuel Plaza was second in the 1928 Olympic marathon for Chile's first medal.

Chile was team winner at the first two South American Championships in 1919 and 1920.

Guyana

Formerly British Guiana, for whom Phil Edwards won their first Commonwealth gold medal at 800m in 1934. He won five Olympic medals in Canadian colours, as his home nation first entered the Olympic Games in 1948.

Venezuela

Venezuela first entered the Olympic Games in 1948. In 1952 Arnoldo Devonish was third at the triple jump.

Bolivar Games

First held at Bogota, Colombia in 1938, these Games are now held every four years and are contested by the nations liberated by Simon Bolivar – Bolivia, Colombia, Ecuador, Panama, Peru and Venezuela.

Sao Silvestre Race at Sao Paulo

This famous race, watched annually by vast crowds is contested over major roads in Sao Paulo, Brazil. It starts before midnight on New Year's Eve to finish a few minutes after the turn of the New Year.

The first race was held in 1925 with 60 runners and organised by Casper Libero, a Brazilian newspaper publisher. The race's appeal grew until in 1936 a record 4636 runners entered. Thereafter the numbers were reduced by the introduction of qualifying races. Foreign athletes were first invited in 1947, and since then many great names have raced amidst the fireworks and excitement of the crowds. The course has varied in length but is now of about 8200m, a little over 5 miles.

The most wins is four by Gaston Roelants (Bel) (1964/5, 1965/6, 1967/8, 1968/9) and by Victor Mora (Colombia) (1972/3, 1973/4, 1975/6, 1981/2). In 1953/4 Emil Zatopek broke the record for the 7300m course (the distance until 1965) by the huge margin of 68sec.

British winners have been: Ken Norris 1955/6; Martin Hyman 1961/2. A separate women's race was held for the first time in 1975/6.

United States of America

The premier club in the early days of athletics in the USA was the New York Athletic Club (NYAC), founded on 8 Sep 1868 at a meeting at the Knickerbocker Cottage, Sixth Avenue following some get-togethers of athletes organised by John C. Babcock, William B. Curtis and Henry E. Buermeyer. The rules of London AC

The pioneers of the New York A.C. William B. Curtis is third from left and Henry Buermeyer on the extreme right. *(BBC Hulton)*

were read out and taken as the basis of the NYAC constitution and laws. On 11 Nov 1868 the club staged the first ever indoor track meeting in the USA at a building which was being constructed by Babcock for the Third Avenue Railway Company as the Empire City Skating Rink. To this meeting the club also invited athletes from the New York Caledonian Club. The track on a clay surface was of an eighth-of-a-mile circumference with very sharp bends. There were some 2000 spectators with a 42-piece band to entertain them as well as six track and eight field events. Seven years later the Intercollegiate Association of Amateur Athletes of America (ICAAAA or IC4A) was formed, mostly by the Atlantic Seaboard colleges, to foster track and field athletics in the colleges. The IC4A have staged annual championships every year from 1876 (20–21 July at Saratoga), with the exception of 1917.

The NYAC organised the first three USA championships in New York in 1876, 1877 and 1878. Then from 1879 to 1888 championships were organised by the National Association of Amateur Athletes of America. In the latter year the Amateur Athletic Union of America

Pat McDonald throwing the hammer in 1925; eight years later he became the oldest ever US champion. *(Topical Press)*

(AAU) was founded to promote the spirit of amateurism and combat the corrupt practices of promoters of professional sports. Fifteen athletic clubs were founder members on 21 Jan 1888. The AAU speedily rose to prominence, organising championships from that summer and taking on national responsibility for a wide range of sports. The great name of the early days of the AAU was James E. Sullivan, secretary-treasurer from 1889 to 1906, when he became President for three years, and again from 1909 until his death in 1914. In 1979 The Athletics Congress of the USA (TAC) replaced the AAU as the governing body.

USA NATIONAL TITLES (AAU/TAC)
The greatest collection of AAU titles is 65 by Ron Laird at walking events, between 1958 when he won his first at the age of 20 to his 5000m walk win in 1976 in an American record 21:09.4. In 1976 he won all six AAU walk titles. The previous record was held by another walker Henry Laskau with 43. Excluding the walks, where many titles are held each year, the record number is 41 by Stella Walsh between 1930 and 1954. Her total is made up as follows: 8 indoors (60y 1, 200m/220y 6, basketball throw 1); 33 outdoors (100y/100m 4, 200m/220y 12, LJ 11, DT 2, Pen 5).

The most men's track and field titles is 15 by Lawrence Myers (6 at 440y 1879–84; 4 at 220y 1879–81, 1884; 3 at 880y 1879–80, 1884; 2 at 100y 1880–81). His quadruple effort in 1880 is unparalleled and he followed it by winning the same events for four Canadian (Montreal AAA) titles within a week. Myers won six more Canadian titles and crossed the Atlantic to win AAA titles at 440y in 1881 and both 440y and 880y in 1885. After the latter he became the first athlete to be given New York's traditional 'ticker-tape' reception on his return. A testimonial meet for him at Madison Square Garden on 17 Oct 1885 raised 4000 dollars which enabled him to set up in business as a bookmaker. As a professional he continued his series of races against Walter George. Racing at 880y, ¾ mile and 1 mile, they first met as amateurs in 1882, when Myers won at 880y but George won the other two races. In 1886 Myers won all three races indoors in New York, and in Australia in 1887 Myers again won the 880y but George won the other two.

The oldest champion is Pat McDonald who won the 56lb weight at 56 years 339 days in 1933. Matt McGrath won at the hammer in 1926 aged

50 and competed at the 56lb weight aged 57 in 1933.

Bruce Kidd (Can) is the **youngest distance event winner** at 17 years 214 days, when he won the indoor 3 mile in 1961 and Bob Mathias was just eight days older when he won the 1948 decathlon.

The most men's titles won by event:
100y/100m 3 Malcolm Ford 1884–6; Bernie Wefers 1895–7; Ralph Metcalfe 1932–4; Harold Davis 1940, 1942–3; Barney Ewell 1941, 1945, 1948; Arthur Bragg 1950, 1953–4; Bobby Morrow 1955–6, 1958; Bob Hayes 1962–4. **200m/220y** 5 Ralph Metcalfe 1932–6. **400m/440y** 6 Lawrence Myers 1879–84. **800m/880y** 5 Mel Sheppard 1906–8, 1911–12; Mal Whitfield 1949–51, 1953–4; James Robinson 1976, 1978–81. **1500m/1 mile** 8 Joie Ray 1915, 1917–23. **3 mile/5000m** 5 Gregory Rice 1938–42. **6 mile/10000m** 7 Louis Gregory 1929–31, 1933, 1939, 1943. **Marathon** 8 John J. Kelley 1956–63. **2 mile/3000m steeplechase** 9 Joseph McCluskey 1930–3, 1935, 1938–40, 1943. **120y/110m hurdles** 5 Hayes Jones 1958, 1960–1, 1963–4. **400m/440y hurdles** 5 Arky Erwin 1941, 1943–6. **High jump** 5 Irving Baxter 1897–1900, 1902; Cornelius Johnson 1932–6; Dave Albritton 1937, 1945–7, 1950; Charles Dumas 1955–9; Dwight Stones 1973–4, 1976–8. Albritton also tied for first in 1936 and 1938 but lost in jump-offs. From 1936 when he was Olympic runner-up to Johnson, Albritton's AAU record was five firsts, two seconds, three thirds and one fourth with just one year (1948) unplaced before his 15th place in 1951. **Pole vault** 9 Robert Richards 1948–52, 1954–7. **Long jump** 6 DeHart Hubbard 1922–7; Ralph Boston 1961–6; Arnie Robinson 1971–2, 1975–8. **Triple jump** 8 Daniel Ahearn 1910–11, 1913–18. **Shot** 10 George Gray (Can) 1887–94, 1896, 1902. **Discus** 6 Fortune Gordien 1947–50, 1953–4; Al Oerter 1957, 1959–60, 1962, 1964, 1966; Mac Wilkins 1973, 1976–80. **Hammer** 9 James Mitchell 1889–96, 1903; Harold Connolly 1955–61, 1964–5. **Javelin** 6 George Brodner 1914–19; Franklin Held 1949, 1951, 1953–5, 1958. **Decathlon** 5 Bill Toomey 1965–9. **All-around** 5 Bill Urban 1961, 1963–5, 1967. **56lb weight** 11 James Mitchell 1888, 1891–7, 1900, 1903, 1905. Pat McDonald won 10 titles: 1911, 1914, 1919–21, 1926–9, 1933.

The most women's titles won by event: (women's events first held in 1923)
50y/50m (1923–59) 5 Alice Coachman 1943–7.

100y/100m 4 Stella Walsh 1930, 1943–4, 1948; Wilma Rudolph 1959–62. **200m/220y** 11 Stella Walsh 1930–1, 1939–40, 1942–8. **400m/440y** 2 titles by seven women. **800m/880y** 6 Madeline Manning 1967–9, 1975–6, 1980–1. **1500m/1 mile** 7 Francie Larrieu 1970, 1972–3, 1976–7, 1979–80. **3000m** 3 Jan Merrill 1976–8. **80mh/100mh** 5 Helen Filkey 1925–9; Nancy Phillips (née Cowperthwaite) 1943, 1946–7, 1951, 1953. **200mh** (1963–72) 4 Pat Hawkins 1969–72. **400mh** 2 Debbie Esser 1975, 1978. **High jump** 10 Alice Coachman 1939–48. **Long jump** 11 Stella Walsh 1930, 1939–46, 1948, 1951. Willye White won 10 titles: 1960–2, 1964–6, 1968–70, 1972. **Shot** 11 Maren Seidler 1967–8, 1972–80. **Discus** 6 Frances Kaszubski 1945, 1947–51. **Javelin** 11 Dorothy Dobson 1939–49. **Pentathlon** 8 Pat Connolly (formerly Daniels, Winslow and Bank) 1961–7, 1970.

US Indoor Championships
These were first held in 1906 at New York's Madison Square Garden, although an unofficial championships had been held there on 21 Nov 1888. Women's championships were first held in 1927 at 40y, high jump and shot.

The most indoor titles at one event is ten by Henry Dreyer at 35lb weight 1934–5, 1939, 1941–7 and by Henry Laskau at 1 mile walk in 1948–57. In those years Laskau also had ten successive wins at 3000m/2 mile walk.

The most indoor titles won at one women's event is seven at shot by both Rema McDonald 1927, 1929–34 and by Maren Seidler 1968–9, 1972, 1974, 1977–8 and 1980. Thus in all Seidler won 18 USA shot titles, a record for one event.

The men's record for US titles indoors and out at one event is 17 by shot-putter Parry O'Brien who added nine indoor titles, 1953–61, to his eight outdoors and by pole vaulter Robert Richards who won eight indoor titles 1948, 1950–3, 1955–7 as well as nine outdoor titles. He also won three decathlon titles outdoors, and O'Brien won an outdoor discus title. Joseph McCluskey also won 17 steeplechase titles, with eight indoors 1932–6, 1938, 1940–1 as well as his nine outdoors.

US Cross-Country Championships
The AAU cross-country was first held in 1890.

The most individual titles won is seven in succession by Don Lash from 1934 to 1940. Lash's team, Indiana University, had a perfect score in

Parry O'Brien in the Los Angeles Coliseum. In these USC colours he won two NCAA titles and went on to win a record 17 AAU titles.   *(USC)*

winning the 1936 team title, as behind Lash, Tom Deckard, Jim Smith, Mel Trutt and Applegate filled the next four places. The following year running in the order Trutt, Smith, Deckard, Lash they set a world record at 4 × 1 mile relay.

The AAU women's cross-country was first held in 1964, when Marie Mulder, at the age of 14, became the youngest ever US champion.

British athletes to have won US titles:
Outdoors women's 440y Christine McKenzie 61.6 in 1958; 6 mile Gordon Minty (later a US citizen) 27:20.8 in 1973; 440y David Jenkins 44.93 in 1975.
Indoors women's LJ Mary Rand 6.20m/20ft 4in in 1965; triple jump Keith Connor 17.04m/55ft 11in in 1982.
Cross-country Nick Rose in 1977, Adrian Royle in 1981.

Mildred Didrikson won the 1932 AAU women's team title on her own for her club, Employers' Casualty of Dallas. At Evanston she took part in eight events, missing only the 50y and 220y. She won the 80m hurdles, shot, javelin, baseball throw, long jump, was first equal at high jump, fourth at discus and was third in a

semi-final of the 100y for a total of 30 points. Second was the 22-strong team of Illinois Women's AC with 22 points. Didrikson had won the javelin in 1930, the long jump and 80m hurdles in 1931 and baseball throw in both years at the previous AAU championships.

Jim Beatty set US records in five successive meetings in 1962: 9 Aug Oslo 1500m 3:39.4; 15 Aug Avranches 3000m 7:54.2; 18 Aug London 1M 3:56.5; 21 Aug Helsinki 1M 3:56.3; 24 Aug Turku 5000m 13:45.0 (and 3M 13:19.2).

INTERNATIONALS
The first dual meeting contested by the USA with a full team was a 122–92 men's win over Germany on 13–14 Aug 1938 in the Berlin Olympic Stadium. However this had been preceded by the USA *v* British Empire Relays meetings after each Olympic Games from 1920, two contests by a 14-man USA team in Japan in 1934 (a USA win in Tokyo and a loss to Japan at Osaka 75½ to 77½) and victories in Paris over Sweden and France in 1920 and over France and Japan in 1936.

The first USA v British Empire Relays were held at the Queen's Club, London on 4 Sep 1920. The event was held in front of the largest crowd ever to gather at Queen's and was organised by the newly formed Achilles Club. The result of the match contested at five relays, a 2 mile team race, 120y hurdles, 440y hurdles, high jump and long jump was a tie, five wins each. Subsequent results in the series, always decided by event wins were: 1924 USA 11–3; 1928 USA 8–6; 1932 USA 6–4; 1936 USA 11–3; 1948 USA 11½–3½; 1952 USA 11–5; 1956 USA 13–5; 1960 USA 14–3.

Women's events were included from 1948 but did not count in the match. Many world relay records were set in the series. In 1964 after the Olympic Games a match was held against both the British Commonwealth and Japan in Osaka.

After the 1938 match against Germany, the USA next met and beat Scandinavia in Oslo in 1949 by 238½ to 224½ in a men's match, but it was not until 1958 that the USA started a regular programme of dual internationals with matches for both men and women against the USSR.

USA v USSR
The first battle of the super powers was on 27–28 Jul 1958 in Moscow. The teams met annually to 1965 with the exception of 1960,

but the series was then beset by political problems. The USSR withdrew at short notice from the scheduled Los Angeles fixture in 1966 ostensibly in protest at the escalation of the Vietnam war and the series was not resumed until 1969. In the seven matches from 1958 to 1965, 16 world records were set but in the nine outdoor contests since 1969 only four world records have been set as the matches have declined somewhat in importance particularly to the Americans, whose teams at times have been below full strength.

The first USA v USSR indoor international was held at Richmond, Virginia on 17 Mar 1972 and further indoor contests were held annually until 1977 and again in 1979.

Summary of results
Outdoors: **men** USA won 12 (1958–9, 1961–4, 1969, 1971, 1974, 1976, 1978, 1981); USSR won 4 (1965, 1970, 1973, 1977). Largest margin of victory: USA 139–97 Los Angeles 1964; USSR 129–89 Kiev 1975. **women** USSR won 15 (1958–9, 1961–5, 1970–1, 1973–8, 1981), with the largest margin 75–28 at Moscow 1963, while the USA won once, 70–67 at Los Angeles 1969.
Indoors: **men** USA won 4 (1972, 1975, 1977, 1979) to USSR 3 (1973–4, 1976). **women** USA won 4 (1972–3, 1975, 1977) to USSR 3 (1974, 1976, 1979).

On a combined basis, as the Soviets like to score the match the USA have won just thrice outdoors, in 1964, 1969 and 1978 with the 1971 match tied, but lead 4–3 indoors.

USA v USSR multi-event (decathlon and pentathlon) matches have been held six times from 1974 to 1981. The USSR lead 4–2 men and 6–0 women. Indoor septathlon/pentathlon contests were held in 1979 and 1980 for men (one win each) and 1979 for women (USSR won).

USA v USSR Junior internationals have been held since 1972. USA leads 7–3 for men and USSR 7–2 for women. **The greatest performance** in this series must be the world high jump record of 2.33m–7ft 7¾in by Vladimir Yashchenko (USSR) at Richmond on 3 Jul 1977. The 18-year-old Ukrainian broke the world junior record, which had been set by Valeriy Brumel at 2.25m/7ft 4½in 16 years earlier, three times, and added 1cm/½in to Dwight Stones' senior record. He said afterwards that he had no idea that he could break the record, hardly surprisingly for he went into the competition with a best of 2.26m indoors and 2.22m outdoors.

Elzbieta Krzesinska (right) and Willye White were first and second in the 1956 Olympic long jump. White went on to compete in a further four Olympic Games. *(GOPA)*

The most USA v USSR appearances is 11 by Willye White (USA), each match from 1959 to 1974. At long jump she was: first in 1969 and 1971; second in 1961, 1962, 1964, 1970, 1974; third in 1963, 1965 and fourth in 1959 and 1973. The most appearances by a man is ten by Janis Lusis (USSR) at the javelin, who won in five matches from 1962 to 1969, was second in 1971, 1973 and 1976 and third in 1970 and 1974. Soviet long jumper Igor Ter-Ovanesyan competed at each match from 1958 to 1971, except for 1964, and was second on all nine occasions. Ralph Boston (USA) beat him four times.

The most individual event wins is 11 by Tamara Press (USSR) (6 SP and 5 DT during 1959–65). The most wins at one event is eight by Faina Melnik (USSR), who won the discus at each match from 1971 to 1978 with a ninth win as a guest in 1970.

The youngest international is Mary Decker, who was third at 1 mile indoors against USSR on 16 Mar 1973, aged 14 years 224 days. Later in the year, still two weeks before her 15th birthday, she won the 800m against the USSR in 2:02.9 and a month earlier won the Pacific Conference 800m. She set a world indoor record for 880y at 2:02.3 in 1974, but missed the next four years through injuries. However she made a magnificent comeback and ran world indoor and outdoor 1 mile records in 1980.

Summary of USA international matches against other teams between 1958–81

Against	MEN	WOMEN	Years
Poland	6–0	2–4	1958–75
West Germany	9–0	1–7	1961–77
West Germany (indoors)	2–0	2–0	1965–9
Great Britain	4–0	0–3	1961–9
Great Britain (indoors)	1–0	1–0	1965
British Commonwealth	2–0	1–1	1967–9
Italy	3–0	2–0	1967–77
Spain	1–0	–	1967
France	1–0	–	1970
Romania	–	1–0	1970
World All-Stars	1–0	1–0	1971
Africa	3–0	3–0	1971–5
Canada	–	1–0	1972
Switzerland	–	1–0	1973
Bulgaria	–	1–0	1975
Czechoslovakia	1–0	1–0	1975
Europe (indoors)	0–1	0–1	1978

Although not regarded as a full international, the USA's most devastating victory was over Canada by 121 points to 20 on 3 Aug 1946 at McGill University, Montreal. The USA athletes came first and second in all 13 men's events and a clean sweep was marred only by Meyers of Canada being placed second at 100y in one of the three women's events.

Olympic Games
The USA men won the highest total of medals by any nation at each Olympic Games until 1976. The women have fared less spectacularly but still won the most medals in 1932.

The US Olympic Committee voted in favour of President Carter's proposed Olympic boycott by 1604 votes to 797 on 12 Apr 1980. So, to the bitter disappointment of many of the athletes, the USA were unrepresented in Moscow.

The most Olympic appearances by a US athlete is five by long jumper Willye White. Six men competed in four Games: Matt McGrath (HT 1908–24), Parry O'Brien (SP 1952–64), Al Oerter (DT 1956–68), Harold Connolly (HT 1958–68), George Young (3km S/C, 5000m and marathon 1960–72), Willie Davenport (110mh 1964–76).

USA Olympic Trials
From 1928 the US Olympic team has primarily been selected from Final Trials meetings. With, in most cases, the first three at each event being automatic choices for Olympic places, these meetings have produced competitions of the highest standard and tension. Indeed some events have proved, such has been American strength in depth, of higher standard than even the Olympics. From 1908 regional trials had been held.

The only athletes to win the same event at four Final Olympic Trials have been Madeline Manning (800m) and Maren Seidler (SP) who both won in 1968, 1972, 1976 and 1980, although of course in 1980 they could not compete at the Games. George Young won the 3km steeplechase in 1960, 1964 and 1968 and the marathon in 1968 and Earlene Brown went one better by winning the women's shot in 1956, 1960 and 1964 and the discus in 1960 and 1964. Other three-time winners: Ira Davis triple jump 1956–64; Olga Connolly women's discus 1964–72, after being second in 1960 and, of course, representing Czechoslovakia when she won the Olympic title in 1956.

Athletes to win three events in one year: Mildred Didrikson women's 80mh, HJ, JT 1932; Jesse Owens 100m, 200m, LJ 1936. Willye White was fifth in the 1976 long jump, after being placed 2–1–1–2–2 from 1956 and both Harold Connolly and Al Oerter went close to making five teams. Connolly was fifth in 1972 and Oerter was fourth in 1980.

Frank Shorter won both the 10000m and marathon in 1972 and again in 1976.

The biggest crowd was 62000 at Palo Alto, Cal. 2 Jul 1960. 29 **world records** have been set at the Trials with a peak of seven (in five events) in 1956, but none in 1928 or 1980. None have been set by women.

N.C.A.A. CHAMPIONSHIPS
The first National Collegiate Athletic Association Track and Field Championships were held in 1921 at the University of Chicago. They have long been established as the premier competition for athletes attending colleges and universities in the USA.

NCAA outdoor Track and Field Championships The most team wins is 27 by the University of Southern California (USC). USC, the 'Trojans', have been by far the most successful university in the USA. Their athletes have set more than 60 world records, since the first one and USC men have won 19 individual and 10 relay Olympic gold medals.

The next most successful teams are: 5 UCLA (the Bruins), 5 Illinois (the Fighting Illini), 4 Oregon (the Ducks), 4 UTEP, the University of Texas at El Paso, (the Miners). USC's traditional supremacy has been strongly challenged in the past decade by both UCLA and UTEP. From 1970 to 1981 the tally of first three placings: UTEP 4–3–1; UCLA 3–4–1; USC 2–2–2.

UTEP's successes have been based on a strong squad of foreign athletes. In 1981 their winning score of 70 points was gained solely by non-Americans, including a record 26 points for one event, the 10000m, in which their African runners placed 1–2–3–5.

The most individual wins is 8 by Jesse Owens (Ohio State), who in both 1935 and 1936 won a record four events – 100y, 220y, 220yh and LJ.

The most individual wins at one event is 4 by Steve Prefontaine (Oregon) 3M/5000m 1970–3 and Scott Neilson (Washington and Canada) HT 1976–9.

Two men have won two different events three times: Ralph Metcalfe (Marquette) – 100y/100m and 220y/200m in 1932, 1933 and 1934 (he also won both AAU titles all three years) and Gerry Lindgren (Washington State) – 3M/5000m and 6M/10000m in 1966, 1967 and 1968. Fred Wolcott (Rice) came close as he won the 220yh in 1938, 1939 and 1940 and the 120yh the first two years only to be placed second to Ed Dugger in 1940. Mel Patton (USC) won the 100y/100m in 1947, 1948 and

The Canadian hammer thrower Scott Neilson won a record four NCAA titles as well as the 1979 Pan-American title. *(Washington University)*

1949 and the 200m/220y in 1948 and 1949, but he withdrew from the longer event in 1947 to favour a muscle strain. 32 other men have won three titles at one event. Perhaps the luckiest was David Albritton (Ohio State) as he tied for first at high jump in 1936, 1937 and 1938. He also won AAU titles each year, tying twice! Others to have won both NCAA and AAU titles in three successive years: Al Blozis, who was undefeated in his university career, (Georgetown) SP 1940–2; Ralph Mann (Brigham Young) 440yh 1969–71.

Athletes to have won NCAA and AAU titles both indoors and outdoors in the same year are: Renaldo Nehemiah (60yh/110mh) and Larry Myricks (LJ) both 1979.

NCAA indoor Track and Field Championships were first held in 1965.

The most team wins is 7 by UTEP 1974–6, 1978, 1980–2. In 1980 and 1981 they scored a record 76 points.

The most individual wins is 7 by Suleiman Nyambui (UTEP and Tanzania) – 1M 1979–82, 2M 1979–80, 1982. He was edged out by 0.06sec by Doug Padilla in the 1981 two miles. Eleven other men have won titles in three successive years, including three who have also achieved this feat outdoors: Charlie Greene (Nebraska) 60y (100y outdoors) 1965–7; Karl Salb (Kansas) SP 1969–71; John Ngeno (Washington State) 3M 1974–6 (outdoor 3M 1975), 6M/10000m 1974–6; Scott Neilson 35lb weight 1977–9 (outdoor HT).

NCAA cross-country championships were first held in 1938.

The most team wins is 8 by Michigan State. UTEP won in 1975–6, 1978–81.

The most individual wins is 3 Gerry Lindgren 1966–7, 1969; Steve Prefontaine 1970–1, 1973; and Henry Rono (Washington State) 1976–7, 1979. Sandwiched between Rono's wins is one of the most amazing results in athletics history, for in 1978 he finished 237th of 241 finishers! In extreme cold (19°F/−7°C) he was with the leaders early on, but after a brief detour off the course near the 2 mile mark, he slipped gradually backwards, 50th at halfway, and finally with a sore ankle and a touch of unaccustomed frostbite he jogged in. The next year he got his revenge as he beat the 1978 winner, Alberto Salazar, into second place.

The most NCAA titles overall is 13 by Suleiman Nyambui who won five outdoor (10000m 1979–81, 5000m 1980–1), seven indoor and the 1980 cross-country. He is followed by Gerry Lindgren who won six outdoor, three cross-country and two indoor (2M 1966–7) titles. His only loss was in the 1968 indoor 2 mile when he was second to Jim Ryun.

In 1978 at Eugene, Henry Rono smashed the meet records in both the 3000m steeplechase and 5000m on one day for probably the finest one day distance double ever with times of 8:18.63 and 13:21.79 – yet these were in the heats! A joyous demonstration of pure running ability. He returned two days later to win the steeplechase final in 8:12.39 but withdrew from the 5000m.

NCAA women's championships were first held in 1981 at cross-country – the first champions were Betty Springs (individual) and the University of Virginia (team). The first track and field championships were held in 1982.

AIAW CHAMPIONSHIPS
These national women's intercollegiate championships were first held in 1969.

The most titles at one event is four by Debbie Esser (Iowa State) 400mh 1976–9.

The most team titles is three by Cal State Northridge 1978–80. Three titles in one year were won by Andrea Bruce (Prairie View) with 100m hurdles, high jump and long jump in 1974.

Julie Brown (UCLA) in 1977 ran in five different events. On the first day she had heats of 1500m, 800m and 4 × 440yR, on the second day she won the 800m and was fourth at 5000m and on the third day she was fourth at 1500m, won the 3000m and ran on two winning Northridge State relay teams.

ICAAAA CHAMPIONSHIPS
The most titles won is 12 by Barney Ewell (Penn State), a record nine outdoors with a treble at 100y, 220y and long jump 1940–2 as well as indoor titles at 60y in 1940 and long jump in 1940 and 1942.
    The most successful University is Villanova with 13 outdoor, 16 indoor and 9 cross-country championships, *all* coached by Jumbo Elliott, coach from his graduation in 1935 until his death in 1981. Elliott, who had been a 47.4 quarter-miler in 1935, coached 25 Olympians,

Gerry Lindgren won the 10000m for the USA v USSR at age 18 in 1964 and went on to win 11 NCAA titles.   *(Washington State University)*

yet was always a part-timer at Villanova, making his money from his heavy-equipment sales company, but giving his heart to his beloved college.

NAIA CHAMPIONSHIPS
These were first held in 1952. Four consecutive wins at one event have been achieved by John Camien (Emporia State) 1M/1500m 1962–5 and Rod Milburn (Southern) 120yh/110mh 1970–3.
    Tommy Fulton (Texas Southern) ran eight distance races in three days at the 1971 championships at Arkadelphia, Arkansas. He preceded this by winning 880y, 1M, 3M and 6M at the NAIA District 8 meeting in *one* day with the 6M in the morning, an 880y heat in the after-

noon and the three further victories in the evening. At the NAIA his programme was: *23 May* 7.45pm 1st 1M heat (4:08.3), 9.20pm 1st 880y heat (1:50.2), 10.30pm 1st 3M heat (13:58.2); *24 May* 8.40pm 1st 880y semi 1:50.2, 9.20pm 1st 3M 13:33.4; *25 May* 7.45pm 1st 1M 3:57.8, 8.45pm 2nd= 880y 1:48.8, 9.15pm 2nd 6M 28:55.2. Texas Southern duly won the team title with 81 points, including 35 from Fulton, whose series is surely unprecedented for its quality.

The greatest dual meet rivalry in the USA must be that between USC and UCLA. They first met at the Los Angeles Coliseum in 1934, when USC began a run of 33 successive victories in the series. UCLA first won (86–59) in 1966, although in 1956 UCLA won the Pacific Coast Conference meeting to hand USC its first conference beating since 1928. In 1962 USC lost to Oregon for its first dual meet loss since 1945 after 103 wins and one tie.

Since UCLA's 1966 win honours have been shared and the score in the series to 1981 reads: USC 39 UCLA 10. USC's most decisive victory was 120–11 in 1950 and UCLA's 107–47 in 1981. Among the many world class performances recorded in the series perhaps the best was Mel Patton's wind assisted double in 1949 of 9.1 for 100y, 0.2sec inside the world record, but with the wind over the limit at 2.9m/s (6.5mph), followed by 20.2 for 220y straight to take a tenth off Jesse Owens' 12-year-old world record. This time the wind was under the limit at 1.5m/s. A year earlier Patton had become the first man to run a world record 9.3 for 100y.

JUNIOR CHAMPIONSHIPS

For many years the AAU organised such championships, but the term referred to athletic experience rather than to age. From 1972, however, Junior Championships have been staged with the age qualification, men under-19 and women under-18 in the year of competition.

The most titles won is 5 by Carol Lewis – LJ 1978–9 and 1981; 100mh 1980–1. The most titles at one event is four by Cathy Sulinski at javelin 1974–7. She was aged 19 when she won her fourth title, which would make her over age by the current ruling.

MAJOR MEETINGS – USA (Names, venues and dates first held)
Outdoor
Tom Black Classic, Knoxville, Tennessee, 1972
Brooks Invitational (formerly Brooks Meet of Champions), Berkeley, Cal., 1979.

California Relays – Modesto, 1942.
Coliseum Relays – Los Angeles, 1941. Had a peak crowd of 59661 in 1948. Combined with Compton Invitational in 1969, and became Von's Classic in 1972–3.
Compton Invitational – Compton, 1935 by Herschel Smith, its director until 1969.
Dogwood Relays – Knoxville, Tenn. on Tom Black track, 1967.
Drake Relays – Des Moines, Iowa 1910.
Florida Relays – Gainesville at Percy Beard Stadium, 1939.
Bruce Jenner Classic – San José, Cal., 1979, named after the Olympic decathlon winner.
Jumbo Elliott Memorial – Philadelphia, 1981, named after the great Villanova coach.
Kansas Relays – Lawrence, 1923.
Martin Luther King Freedom Games – various venues: Philadelphia (Villanova) 1969–72, Durham, NC 1973, Oslo 1974, Kingston, Jamaica 1975, Atlanta, Georgia 1976, (not held 1977–8), Philadelphia 1979, Stanford 1980–2.
Mount San Antonio Relays – Walnut, Cal., 1959.
Penn Relays – Philadelphia at Franklin Field, 1895, the largest and oldest of all the relays meets, with over 10000 competitors annually.
Pepsi Invitational – Westwood, Cal (UCLA's Drake Stadium), 1978.
Prefontaine Classic – Eugene, Oregon, 1976, named in memory of Steve Prefontaine.
Princeton Invitational – Princeton, NJ, 1934–40, of short duration, about an hour, with the 1 mile usually the main event, revived in 1980. After the 1937 mile, the six fastest times ever had been run at Princeton.
Texas Relays – Austin, 1925.
West Coast Relays – Fresno, Cal., at the Ratcliffe Stadium, 1927.

Indoor
Los Angeles Times Games – Inglewood, Cal. from 1968, previously at the Los Angeles Sports Arena from 1960.
Mason-Dixon Games – Louisville, Kentucky, 1961.
Millrose Games – Madison Square Garden, New York from 1914; but first held in 1908 for employees of the John Wanamaker store.
Philadelphia Classic – 1968, but previously as the Philadelphia Enquirer Games 1945–67.
Sunkist Invitational, Los Angeles, 1970.
Toronto Star – Maple Leaf, 1963 as the Telegram Maple Leaf Games.

The longest lasting major meeting was the Boston AA Games, held annually from 1890 to 1971.

Asia

The first Asian federation was formed in 1906 in the state of Perak, now in Malaysia. In that year the Ipoh Athletic Sports were first held; winners were considered as national champions of Malaya.

National federations followed: 1911 Phillipines and Japan, 1922 Sri Lanka, 1924 China.

The first Asian team to compete at the Olympic Games was that of Japan in 1912 with two athletes. However, Norman Pritchard of India had taken part in the 1900 Games as an individual while holidaying in Europe and he won two silver medals, at 200m and 200m hurdles.

The first Asian Olympic gold medallist was Mikio Oda of Japan at triple jump in 1928 with 15.21m/49ft 10¾in. For many years a top athletics official Oda also set a world record of 15.58m/51ft 1½in at Tokyo on 27 Oct 1931. This together with Chuhei Nambu's long jump of 7.98m/26ft 2¼in at the same meeting were the first Asian world records by men. Injury prevented Oda from being at his best in the 1932 Olympics as he was 12th in the triple jump final, won by Nambu, who had earlier been placed third at the long jump.

Oda is also the man to have set most Asian records: 21 including seven at long jump (6.90m in 1923 to 7.38m in 1928); ten at triple jump (14.27m in 1923 to that 15.58m); and four at decathlon (5324 in 1924 to 6003 in 1926).

The greatest number of Asian records set by a woman is 44 by Chi Cheng of Taiwan between 1964 and 1970. Born in Hsinchu on 15 Mar 1944, Chi's first record came in 1964 at 100y (11.1). She moved to the USA to study physical education at California Polytechnic College in Pomona, where she was coached by Vince Reel, whom she later married. At the 1968 Olympic Games in Mexico City she won a bronze medal at 80m hurdles in 10.4 (auto 10.51) and was seventh at 100m (11.5).

Following the 1968 Games Chi had two amazing seasons, for she won 153 out of 154 competitions, losing only in a disputed verdict to Barbara Ferrell at 100y as both girls ran 10.4 at the Southern Pacific AAU Championships. In 1970 she won all 83 competitions at distances varying from 50y to 440y, 80m to 200m hurdles, long jump and relays. In that year she set 23 Asian records and eight world records, culminating in her best ever times of: 100y–10.0, 100m–11.0, 200m–22.4, 220y–22.6, 100mh–12.8, 200mh–26.2. In addition to the above world records she also held Asian records at 440y of 52.5 and pentathlon with 4844 points, the latter in 1968. Indoors, in five meetings in early 1970, she had 21 competitions (17 sprints, 4 LJ) in which she set or equalled personal best performances 17 times, including two world bests.

Sadly injuries restricted her further participation, but Chi had made an indelible mark in the record books and had delighted athletics enthusiasts with her style, grace and sheer competitive ability.

The first Asian athlete to set a world record and the first Asian woman to win an Olympic medal was the great all-rounder Kinue Hitomi. She set world records at long jump (officially with 5.98m/19ft 7½in in 1928, but she jumped a better 6.07m/19ft 11in in 1929) and at pentathlon (3841 in 1930). Her first major international appearance was in 1926 at the age of 18 at the second World Games, where she won both running and standing long jumps, was second at discus, third at 100m and fifth at 60m. In 1928 she was second in the Olympic 800m in 2:17.6, only 0.8sec behind Lina Radke's world record, and went on in 1929 and 1930 to establish her claim as the greatest woman athlete in the world. At the third World Games in 1930 she again won the long jump and backed this with a second and two third places. After these Games she took part in 20 events in seven days: first for Japan against Poland at Warsaw she took part in seven events scoring 23 out of Japan's 36 points in a 54–36 defeat, then six days later she did another six events against Belgium, and finally seven events against France.

Hitomi set Asian records at ten standard

events: 100m, 200m, 400m, 800m, 80mh, HJ, LJ, DT, JT, Pen as well as at 60m, 100y and 220y for an unmatched demonstration of versatility. She died of tuberculosis at the age of 23 in 1931.

The greatest number of improvements to an Asian record at one event is the 13 new records set by Ni Chih-Chin (Chn) from 2.11m in 1961 to the world record 2.29m/7ft 6¼in at Changsha on 8 Nov 1970. As China was not affiliated to the IAAF the latter was not able to be ratified officially. Ni had ranked number one in the world in 1966 at 2.27m/7ft 5¼in, but then the machinations of the 'Cultural Revolution' put an end to organised athletics in China. Nothing more was heard of Ni until 1970. It was reported that Ni was exhorted to his record by 80000 spectators chanting quotations from Chairman Mao. Ni commented: 'If my jumps were as high as the thoughts of Chariman Mao, I would need a fireman's ladder to measure them'.

Mikio Oda wins the long jump with 7.34m/24ft 1in for Waseda University v Achilles at Stamford Bridge in 1928.   *(BBC Hulton)*

Far Eastern Games

The first international meetings in Asia were the Far Eastern Games, ten of which were held between 1913 and 1934. The first Games were held at Wallace Field, Manila, Philippines, from 3–7 Feb 1913. They were also staged in China and Japan, and these three nations dominated, particularly Japan. At the 1930 Games held in the Meiji Jingu Stadium, Tokyo, all but two of the events were won by the Japanese.

The most individual wins was nine by Fortunato Catalon (Phi), 100m and 200m in 1917, 1919, 1921 and 1923 and 100m in 1925. He won three more gold medals for the sprint relay. Mikio Oda won the long jump in 1923 and 1927, the triple jump in 1923, 1925, 1927 and 1930, and the decathlon in 1927.

Asian Games

The first Asian Games were held in the National Stadium, New Delhi, India from 8–11 Mar 1951. Ten nations took part and the number increased to 17 for the second Games in 1954 in Manila. Subsequent Games have been held in: 1958 Tokyo, 1962 Djakarta, 1966 Bangkok, 1970 Bangkok (after the South Koreans had withdrawn from staging the Games), 1974 Teheran, 1978 Bangkok, and in 1982 they are scheduled for New Delhi.

The 1962 Games were declared unofficial by the IAAF as the Indonesian government had prohibited entries by Israel and Taiwan. For this

Indonesia was suspended by the IAAF and the IOC. The 1978 Games were not granted a permit by the IAAF as the Asian Games Federation Council did not invite Israel to compete. 21 nations took part and as a result these nations were suspended by the IAAF for three months. It was decided, however, that individual athletes would be reinstated after just one month.

Japan has been by far the most successful nation, but their dominance was matched in 1978 when China, taking part for the second time, won 12 gold medals to Japan's ten, both nations taking 35 medals in all. The tally for the eight Games up to 1978 is: Japan 123 gold, 131 silver, 72 bronze; India 44–41–40; China (1974 and 1978 only) 17–19–20.

The only athlete to win the same event at three Games is Shigenobu Murofushi (Jap) who won at the hammer with 67.08m in 1970, 66.54m in 1974 and 68.26m in 1978. With second in 1966 he also holds the record for the most medals. In 1981 he improved his own Asian record from 71.14m in 1971 first to 71.36m then 71.72m after a ten-year gap.

The most individual gold medals is five by Esther Rot (née Shakhamurov) (Isr). She won at pentathlon (3946) and 100m hurdles (14.0) in 1970 as well as being placed second at long jump. In 1974, in her first competition since the birth of her first baby five months earlier, she won at 100m (11.90), 200m (23.79) and 100mh

(13.31). She was prevented from adding to her total by the refusal of the organisers to invite Israel to the 1978 Games. Anat Ratanapol (Tha) also won five gold medals; three individual sprint titles and two for Thailand's sprint relay team in 1970 and 1974. Yang Chuan-kwang (Tai) won the decathlon in 1954 and 1958, and in the latter year won three more medals: second at long jump and 110m hurdles and third at 400m hurdles.

A link between the old Far Eastern Games and the modern Asian Games was provided by pole vaulter Shuhei Nishida (Jap). He won the Far Eastern title in 1930 at 4.00m, 10cm less than his Asian record and went on to win Olympic silver medals in 1932 (4.30m) and 1936 (4.25m). At the age of 41 he returned to be placed third at the first Asian Games in 1951 with 3.61m.

Asian Track and Field Championships

In addition to the Asian Games, Asian Championships are staged biennially. The first was at Marakina, near Manila, Philippines on 18–23 Nov 1973. Subsequent championships have been held at: 1975 Seoul, S. Korea; 1979 and 1981 Tokyo. The latter two were styled Asian Invitation Championships as due to the exclusion of Israel full championship status could not be granted by the IAAF.

Japan has been the dominant nation with 19 golds in 1973, 15 in 1975, 20 in 1979 and 19 in 1981. India has won respectively 4, 9, 2 and 5 golds and China has made a strong showing with 7 golds in 1979 and 11 in 1981.

The most individual gold medals is four by Anat Ratanapol (Thailand) who won both 100m and 200m in 1973 and 1975. Shigenobu Murofushi followed his three Asian Games hammer titles with championship wins in 1979 and 1981.

SEAP GAMES

The South East Asia Peninsular Games were first held in Bangkok, Thailand in December 1959. They have been held biennially ever since with the exception of 1963. Nine nations now take part.

The most individual victories is 13 by Jennifer Tin Lay (Bur). She won eight successive shot titles from 1967 to 1981 and five discus titles, between 1973–81. The most by a man is 12 by Jimmy Crampton (Bur) between 1969 and 1979 (800m–4, 1500m–6, 5000m–2).

Asian Countries
China

The first Chinese international participation was at the Far Eastern Games in 1913. The national federation was formed in 1924 and Chinese athletes competed at the Olympic Games in 1932 and 1948. China withdrew from the IAAF in protest at the admittance thereto of Taiwan (the Republic of China), but was readmitted to international competition in 1978, and to the IOC in 1979. The first major stadium, seating 40000, was built at Shanghai in 1935. The first national championships were held in 1910 for men and 1959 for women.

China have yet to reappear at the Olympic Games, for they joined the 1980 boycott, but their athletes have made a strong impression since their return to international competition following the years of non participation during the Cultural Revolution. There were 11 Chinese in the 1981 Asian world cup team.

China (Taiwan)

As the Republic of China, Taiwan competed at five Olympic Games from 1956, winning two medals – Yang Chuan-kwang was second at decathlon in 1960 and Chi Cheng was third at the women's 80m hurdles in 1968.

Cheng Feng-jung, after setting the first world record by a Chinese athlete, a 1.77m/5ft 9¼in high jump in 1957.

Hong Kong

Annual military sports in Hong Kong dated back to at least 1868. The Hong Kong AAA was founded in 1951, in which year national championships were held for the first time for men. Women's events were first contested in 1960.

Hong Kong has once sent a team to the Olympic Games, four athletes in 1964.

India

Although Norman Pritchard had won two silver medals in 1900 the first official Indian team to compete at the Olympic Games was in 1920. This team was sponsored by Sir Dorabji Tata and the entry was permitted despite the fact that India did not then have a National Olympic Committee. The first Indian Games were staged in 1924, and these national championships were subsequently held in 1927, 1928 and then biennially to 1949 and annually since.

India's first international match was against Ceylon in 1940. India first entered a team at the Commonwealth Games in 1954, and their first medallist was Milkha Singh, 440y champion (46.6) in 1958. Singh made a tremendous impression with his majestic smooth running style and flowing black hair. He was placed fourth at the 1960 Olympics with his best of 45.73.

The first organised athletics meeting in India was that of Temalpore Cricket Club in January 1868.

Indonesia

After their suspension by the IAAF, Indonesia hosted the first GANEFO (Games of the New Emerging Forces) Games in Djakarta in 1963. The highlight was Shin Geum Dan's 400m and 800m victories in 51.4 and 1:59.1 respectively, both better than the IAAF world records.

Indonesia first competed in the Olympic Games in 1956.

Japan

Japan has for long been the most powerful athletics nation in Asia. Their peak international successes came in the 1930s, when they won four Olympic medals in 1932 and seven in 1936. National championships were first held in 1914 and women's events were first held in 1925.

Their first international against China was held in 1975, when Japan won both men's and women's matches.

Europeans in Japan had organised athletics meetings as early as 1872 and the University of Tokyo held its first meeting in 1898.

Korea

The first governing body was the Chosun Amateur Athletic Association formed in 1920 while the country was under Japanese rule. The Korean Amateur Athletic Federation was affiliated to the IAAF in 1947.

The greatest Korean successes have come from their marathon runners. The first Korean Olympic competitors were two marathon runners, in 1932 Un-bae Kim who was placed sixth and in 1936 Kee Chung Sohn (or Kitei Son as he was known in Japanese) who won the Olympic marathon, after setting a world best time of 2:26:42 the previous year, and another Korean, Sung-yong Nam was third. These men ran for Japan but the tradition was maintained after Korea regained its independence in 1945. At the Olympic Games fourth places were gained by Yoon Chil Choi in 1952 and Chang-Hoon Lee in 1956. At the Boston Marathon Koreans won in 1947 (Yun Bok Suh) and 1950 when Kee Yong Ham headed a Korean 1–2–3, the first overseas clean sweep. Fittingly Kee Chung Sohn was their trainer.

Since the partition of Korea into North and South, marathoners from the north in particular have maintained the national tradition.

Philippines

Two Philippine athletes have won Olympic bronze medals: Simeon Toribio at high jump in 1932 and Miguel White 400m hurdles in 1936. National championships were first held in 1911.

Sri Lanka

The first Ceylonese athlete to reach world class was Duncan White, who at the age of 30 won the 1948 Olympic silver medal at 400m hurdles. This was an amazing breakthrough for his previous best was 53.0, yet he ran 51.8 in the final. Two years later he won the Commonwealth title.

The next Ceylonese star was Nagalingam Ethirveerasingam, a 2.03m/6ft 8in high jumper. He went to the USA to study at UCLA, where his announcer's nightmare of a name was shortened simply to 'Ethir'. His younger brother, also at UCLA, also gave some problems, his name – Nagalingam Pararajasinyam. In the 1954 Ceylon championships Bob Richards, the 'vaulting vicar', put in a guest appearance and carried off six titles (PV, 110mh, DT, JT, LJ, SP), with one second place in eight events entered.

The national federation was formed in 1922.

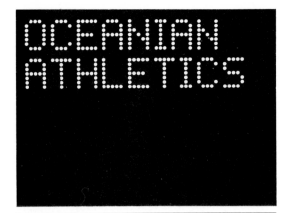

OCEANIAN ATHLETICS

Australia

The first properly organised athletics club was Sydney Harriers (later AAC) in 1872. The Australian Athletic Union was formed in 1897, ten years after the first State's governing body, that of New South Wales. Further States' AAAs followed, Victoria in 1891, Queensland in 1895, Tasmania in 1902, South Australia in 1905, Western Australia in 1905.

The first Australasian Championships were held in Melbourne in 1893 with competitors from New South Wales, Victoria and New Zealand. The latter nation continued to take part until 1927. It has only been since 1947 that the championships have been held annually.

The Australian Women's Athletic Union was founded in 1932, three years after Queensland and Victoria had been the first States to have women's governing bodies. The Australian National Games of 1928 included a women's 100m and full championships were first held in 1930, though they have been annual only since 1962.

Olympic Games

Australians have the unique achievement of being the only nation to be represented at both men's and women's events at each Olympic Games. The first Australian to win a gold medal was Edwin Flack who, in the colours of the London AC won both the 800m and 1500m in 1896. The first woman to compete was 100m semi-finalist Edith Robinson in 1928. Shirley Strickland was the first woman medallist, in 1948, and in 1952 Marjorie Jackson won the first gold medals.

National titles

The most titles at one event is 12 by Richard Leffler at the hammer 1959–67, 1969–70, 1973. His nine successive titles is also a record.

Ron Clarke leads in the 1967 AAA 3 miles, when he won his third consecutive title in less than 13min. *(Sport & General)*

Leffler was also second in 1968 (the first Australian), third in 1971 and second in 1972. The women's record is 8 Jean Roberts at shot 1963–70.

The most titles overall is 18 by Warwick Selvey – 7 shot and 11 discus between 1960 and 1973. The women's record is 17 by Pam Ryan (née Kilborn) (80mh–7, LJ–3, Pen–3, 100mh–2, 100y–1, 200mh–1) between 1963 and 1972. She also ran on seven winning relay teams. Kilborn's 80m hurdles victories were in successive years, 1963–9, while other athletes to win seven times in succession have been Hec Hogan, 100y 1952–8 and Lawrie Peckham at high jump 1969–75 (as well as three further wins 1965–7).

Pole vaulter Don Baird won the 1974 Commonwealth title and at various times the national titles of France, West Germany and USA as well as Australia.

Fiji
Affiliated to the IAAF 1949, Fiji was the first South Pacific country to have an athlete compete at the Olympic Games, as discus thrower Mesulame Rakuro was placed 15th at Melbourne in 1956.

The first Fijian athlete to achieve international success was Mataika Tuicakau, who at the 1950 Commonwealth Games won the shot and was second in the discus. Saimoni Tamani achieved the best Fijian performance in world terms with his 400m time of 45.82 for third in the 1970 Commonwealth Games.

New Caledonia
The most distinguished athletes from New Caledonia have achieved international success representing France: Arnjolt Beer (SP), Paul Poaniewa (HJ), Christian Kaddour (TJ) all of whom have won French championships.

The Wallis and Futuna Islands have a population of only about 15000, yet they have produced four top French javelin throwers! The main activity of the islanders is fishing, especially with harpoons, and obviously this skill has been readily transferred to javelin throwing.

Petelo Wakalina represented France in 15 internationals, was French champion in 1966 and 1968 and had a best of 80.16m/263ft 0in. Lolesio Tuita had 19 internationals, was French champion in 1970, 1972, 1973 and 1976 and had a best of 81.70m/268ft 0in. Penitio Lutui had 17 internationals to the end of 1980, was French champion in 1977, 1978 and 1979. Jean-Paul Lakafia set a French record of 83.56m/274ft 2in in 1980.

New Zealand
One of the pioneering nations in organised athletics, the Wellington AA club was founded in 1875, the New Zealand AA formed in July 1887 and the first national championships were staged in 1888. The first womens' championships, at 100y, were held in 1926.

National championships
The most titles won is 37 by Valerie Young (née Sloper) 17 shot (1956–66, 1972–4, 1979–81), 18 discus (1957–8, 1961–6, 1972–3, 1975–82), and two pentathlon (1958, 1963). She won her first title at the age of 18 in 1956 and was still going strong at the age of 44 in 1982, and might have won even more titles but for a six-year retirement in the middle!

The most titles at one event is 18 by Dave Norris at the triple jump (1957–71, 1974–5, 1977). His 15 successive titles is also a record. Norris also won eight long jump titles (1960–1, 1963–4, 1966, 1968, 1970–1) and two 220yh (1961–2) for 28 in all, a men's record although Peter Munro's total is 31, if four are included at which he did not win the event but was recognised as champion for being the first New Zealander. These were made up by 12/14 shot, 13/14 discus and 2/3 javelin between 1920–35.

The champion at the most different events is Yvette Williams, at 5 events, who in all won 21 titles between 1947 and 1954: SP–8, LJ–7, DT–4, JT–1, 80mh–1.

The youngest champion ever was Joe Scott who as a 12-year-old won an unofficial professional 2 mile walking race on 1 Jan 1875.

The Olympic Games
Two New Zealanders, Harry Kerr and H. Murray, competed for the Australasia team at the 1908 Games. Kerr won a bronze medal at 3500m walk. The first New Zealand team competed in 1920, with one athlete, George Davidson, who was fifth at 200m. Arthur Porritt, later Governor General, was third at the 100m in 1924.

The most successful New Zealand Olympian is Peter Snell, winner of the 800m in 1960 and both the 800m and 1500m in 1964.

The first New Zealander to set an official world record was Jack Lovelock at 1 mile with 4:07.6 at Princeton, NJ on 15 Jul 1933. Lovelock went

Peter Snell wins the 1964 Olympic 800m. Second was Bill Crothers (57), third Wilson Kiprugut (386) and fourth George Kerr (375).   *(M. Shearman)*

on to win the 1936 Olympic 1500m title with another world record 3:47.8. For nine years the victim of double vision following a riding accident Dr Lovelock tragically fell to his death under a subway train in New York on 29 Dec 1949, at the age of 39.

The most appearances at major Games by a New Zealander was achieved by thrower Les Mills, with four each at Olympic and Commonwealth Games. He was also placed second in the 1966 New Zealand heavyweight weightlifting championships and was selected for the 1966 Commonwealth Games, but missed the event due to injury, although he won the discus and was second at shot. Discus thrower Robin Tait competed in a record five Commonwealth Games, winning his event in 1974.

PACIFIC CONFERENCE GAMES
These are held every four years. The venues to date have been: 1969 Tokyo, 1973 Toronto, 1977 Canberra, 1981 Christchurch. The Games are contested by those nations bordering the Pacific Ocean, principally Australia, New Zealand and USA.

The most individual victories have been by Denise Robertson (now Boyd) the 200m and 4 × 100m relay in 1973; and the 100m, 200m, 4 × 100m relay and 4 × 400m relay in 1977.

SOUTH PACIFIC GAMES
The first South Pacific Games were held in Suva, Fiji in 1963. Subsequent Games have been staged in New Caledonia, Papua New Guinea, Tahiti, Guam and the sixth Games back in Suva in 1979. They are now scheduled for every four years.

A most remarkable achievement, probably without parallel in distance running history, was set by Alain Lazare of New Caledonia in 1979, for he won all five distance running events at the Games: 1500m–3:54.38, 5000m–14:47.3, 10000m–32:00.9, 3000m steeplechase–9:22.3, marathon–2:30:57. He also won the marathon in 1975.

The most individual gold medals is seven by Usaia Sotutu (Fiji) 1969–75, and seven by Arnjolt Beer (New Caledonia) 1966–75.

SOUTH PACIFIC CHAMPIONSHIPS
The championships, as opposed to the Games, were first held in Noumea, New Caledonia in 1976. Lazare won four gold medals, the 1500m, 5000m, 10000m and marathon.

European records

The greatest number of European records, as recognised by the European Athletics Association, is 14 by Iolanda Balas (Rom) at women's high jump, from 1.75m in 1956 to 1.91m in 1961. The most for men is ten by Matti Järvinen (Fin) at javelin from 71.57m in 1930 to 77.23m in 1936, and ten by Valeriy Brumel (USSR) at high jump, from 2.17m in 1960 to 2.25m in 1963.

The greatest time span of record breaking is 14 years 44 days by Adolfo Consolini (Ita) at the discus from 53.34m in 1941 to 56.98m in 1955. The women's record span is 12 years 63 days by Herma Bauma (Aut) at the javelin from 45.71m in 1936 to 48.63m in 1948.

Paavo Nurmi (Fin) set 13 records in all at eight different events – the most for any athlete.

Bengt Nilsson (Swe) improved the high jump record three times in 14 minutes at Göteborg on 15 Jul 1954, as he cleared 2.06m, 2.08m and 2.10m.

European Championships

The first European Championships were held in Turin, at the Stadio Communale 7–9 Sep 1934. These were for men only, and neither Great Britain nor the Soviet Union took part. The Hungarian, Szilard Stankovits was the leading advocate for these championships and the decision to stage them was taken at a meeting of the newly formed European Committee of the IAAF in Budapest on 3 Nov 1932.

Great Britain first took part in 1938 and the Soviet Union in 1946, when women's events were held jointly for the first time. The first women's championships had been held separately in 1938.

The Championships are now organised by the European Athletic Association, formed in 1970 to succeed the IAAF's European Committee. They are held at four-yearly intervals, although there was a break in this pattern in 1969 and 1971.

The venues have been: 1934 Turin; 1938 Paris (men), Vienna (women); 1946 Oslo; 1950 Brussels; 1954 Berne; 1958 Stockholm; 1962 Belgrade; 1966 Budapest; 1969 Athens; 1971 Helsinki; 1974 Rome; 1978 Prague; 1982 Athens. The venue for 1986 will be Stuttgart.

The winner of the most gold medals is Irena Szewinska (née Kirszenstein) of Poland with six. She has also won the most medals, ten, and uniquely has won medals at four different individual events as well as in both relay events. Her complete record is: 1966 – 1st 200m, LJ, 4 × 100m R; 2nd 100m. 1971 – 3rd 200m, 5th LJ, 6th 100m. 1974 – 1st 100m, 200m; 3rd 4 × 100m R; 4th 4 × 400m R (a 48.5 leg!). 1978 – 3rd 400m, 4 × 400m R; 5th 4 × 100m R.

Four medals at one Championships have been won by Irena Szewinska in 1966 (see above) and by Stanislawa Walasiewicz (Pol) in 1938, 1st 100m and 200m, 2nd LJ and 4 × 100m R, and by Fanny Blankers-Koen (Hol) in 1950, 1st 80mh, 100m and 200m, 2nd 4 × 100m R. Blankers-Koen had also won gold medals at 80m hurdles and 4 × 100m relay in 1946, when she was also placed fourth at high jump, and with bronze medals at 100m and 200m in 1938, she won eight medals in all.

The East German sprinter Renate Stecher also won eight medals, and her team-mate Petra Vogt (1st in 100m, 200m and 4 × 100m R in 1969) emulated Blankers-Koen and Szewinska by winning three gold medals at one Championships.

The most titles obtained at one event is four by Janis Lusis (USSR), for javelin in 1962, 1966, 1969 and 1971, and by Nadyezhda Chizhova (USSR), for women's shot in 1966, 1969, 1971 and 1974.

The most medals won at one event is five by Igor Ter-Ovanesyan (USSR) at long jump. He was first in 1958, 1962 and 1969 and second in 1966 to Lynn Davies (GB) and in 1971 to Max Klauss (GDR).

The oldest gold medallist is Jack Holden (GB), 1950 marathon winner at 43 years 163 days. He beat the Finn Veikko Karvonen, who later succeeded him as champion, by 32 sec in 2:32:13.2.

The oldest medallist is Väino Muinonen (Fin), who followed a marathon win in 1938 with a second behind his compatriot Mikko Hietanen in 1946 at 46 years 235 days.

The oldest female medallist is Dana Zatopková (Cze), 1958 javelin champion at 35 years 334 days. She had scratched when due to compete in 1946, was fifth in 1950 and then won in 1954 at

Igor Ter-Ovanesyan set six European long jump records, and won three outdoor and two indoor European titles. *(M. Shearman)*

52.91m/173ft 7in and 1958 at 56.02m/183ft 9in, the latter her second European record of the year. Her husband Emil won the 5000m in 1950 and the 10000m in 1950 and 1954.

The oldest European competitor was the Norwegian Edgar Bruun who, at 49 years 23 days, was ninth at 50km walk in 1954. Sixteen years earlier he had won a bronze medal and in 1939 set a world record of 25263m/15M 1228y for the 2 hours walk.

The youngest gold medallist is June Foulds (later married to Olympic fencer Raymond Paul) who was 16 years 75 days old when she ran on Britain's winning sprint relay team in 1950. Two days earlier she became the youngest ever medallist with 12.4 for 100m behind Fanny Blankers-Koen's 11.7. Blankers-Koen was just ten days short of twice her age.

The youngest men's gold medallist is François St Gilles, who was 18 years 260 days when he ran on the winning French 4 × 100m relay team in 1969.

The youngest men's individual event winner is David Jenkins, 400m champion at 19 years 80 days when he stormed round the outside lane to win the 400m title at Helsinki in 1971. His time 45.45, just 4/100sec ahead of the Italian South African-born rugby player Marcello Fiasconaro. Jenkins went off fast, passing 200m in 21.1 and 300m in 32.4. Such a pace took its toll, and even Jenkins thought that he had been caught at the line. Jenkins's pre-Helsinki best was 46.4 and this fantastic improvement seemed to presage a great career. In 1974 he was second in the European and fourth in the Commonwealth Games. A great relay runner, many of his finest performances came on the anchor leg for Britain, including a gold medal at the 1974 European 4 × 400m relay. He also won another gold medal on Scotland's 4 × 100m relay team at the 1978 Commonwealth Games. In his best year of 1975, Jenkins won both the American 400m title and the European Cup Final 400m. At the Olympic Games however, he has perhaps disappointed his fans, failing to make the final in 1972 and was placed seventh in both 1976 and 1980.

The youngest male medallist is the Scot, Alan Paterson, second at high jump in 1946 at 18 years 73 days. His 1.96m/6ft 5in best was 3cm behind Anton Bolinder (Swe). Paterson went on to win in 1950, again clearing 1.96m.

Jack Holden, the oldest European champion, in the Heysel Stadium, Brussels in 1950, in which year he won all his five marathons *(AP)*

The most medals won by an athlete without winning a gold is four by East German discus thrower Lothar Milde, third in 1962, 1966 and 1969 and second in 1971. A major title escaped Milde, but he also won an Olympic silver medal in 1968.

The most Championships at which an athlete has competed is six by Czech discus thrower Ludvik Danek and Italian walker Abdon Pamich. Their complete records are:
Danek: 1962 – 9th 52.12m; 1966 – 5th 56.24m; 1969 – 4th 59.30m; 1971 – 1st 63.90m; 1974 – 2nd 62.76m; 1978 – 15th 58.60m.
Pamich: at 50km walk: 1954 – 7th 4:49:06.4; 1958 – 2nd 4:18:00.0; 1962 – 1st 4:19:46.6; 1966 – 1st 4:18:42.0; 1969 – did not finish (and 6th at 20km walk 1:34:15); 1971 – 8th 4:14:36.2.

Athletes who have competed in five championships:
Gaston Roelants (Bel): *3km Steeplechase* 1962 – 1st 8:32.6, 1966 – 3rd 8:28.8. *10000m* 1966 – 8th 28:59.6, 1969 – 5th 28:49.8, 1971 – dnf. *marathon* 1969 – 2nd 2:17:22.2, 1971 – 5th 2:17:48.8, 1974 – 3rd 2:16:29.6.
Jean-Claude Nallet (Fra): *200m* 1966 – 3rd 21.0. *400m* 1969 – 2nd 45.8. *400m hurdles* 1971 – 1st 49.2, 1974 – 2nd 48.94, 1978 – 6th 50.19. *4 × 400m relay.* 1966 – 4th, 1969 – 1st, 1971 – 6th, 1974 – 3rd.
Igor Ter-Ovanesyan (USSR): *long jump* 1958 – 1st 7.81m, 1962 – 1st 8.19m, 1966 – 2nd 7.88m, 1969 – 1st 8.17m, 1971 – 2nd 7.91m.
Vilmos Varju (Hun): *Shot* 1958 – 7th 16.77m, 1962 – 1st 19.02m, 1966 – 1st 19.43m, 1969 – 7th 18.78m, 1971 – 4th 19.99m.
Adolfo Consolini (Ita): *discus* 1938 – 5th 48.02m, 1946 – 1st 53.23m, 1950 – 1st 53.75m, 1954 – 1st 53.44m, 1958 – 6th 53.05m.
Consolini's span of 20 years is the greatest of any competitor.
Gyula Zsivotzky (Hun): *hammer:* 1958 – 3rd 63.68m, 1962 – 1st 69.64m, 1966 – 2nd 68.62m, 1969 – 4th 69.68m, 1971 – 11th 64.94m.
Janusz Sidlo (Pol): *javelin* 1954 – 1st 76.35m, 1958 – 1st 80.18m, 1962 – 7th 75.01m, 1966 – 7th 78.86m, 1969 – 3rd 82.90m.
Gergely Kulcsar (Hun): *javelin* 1958 – 3rd 75.26m, 1962 – 5th 76.89m, 1966 – 3rd 80.54m, 1969 – 4th 81.14m, 1971 – 15th 76.48m.
Janis Lusis (USSR): *javelin* 1962 – 1st 82.04m, 1966 – 1st 84.48m, 1969 – 1st 91.52m, 1971 – 1st 90.68m, 1974 – 6th 83.06m.
John Ljunggren (Swe): *50km walk:* 1946 – 1st 4:38:20, 1950 – 2nd 4:43:25, 1954 – 4th 4:38:09.6, 1958 – 9th 4:42:40.8, 1962 – 5th 4:30:19.8.
Vittorio Visini (Ita): *50km walk* 1966 – 8th 4:26:22.4, 1969 – did not finish, 1971 – 15th 4:20:45.8, 1974 – 4th 4:05:43.6, 1978 – 6th 3:57:42.8.
Lia Manoliu (Rom): *women's discus* 1954 – 7th 43.86m, 1962 – 14th 45.02m, 1966 – 13th 49.44m, 1969 – 4th 57.38m, 1971 – 13th 52.26m. Manoliu is the only woman to have competed in five European Championships, over a 17-year time span as she missed the 1958 Championships. An electrical engineer, she improved steadily over the years and achieved her best throw of 62.06m/203ft 7in in 1962 at the age of 40. She also competed at a record six Olympic Games.
Of the many athletes who have achieved the

notable feat of representing their countries at four Championships, a dubious record of being perhaps the least successful belongs to the French hammer thrower Jacques Accambray, who from 1969 was placed successively 15th, 16th, 20th and 17th, each time failing to qualify for the final.

The first ever clean sweep of all three medals by athletes of one nation was achieved by the East German discus throwers, Detlef Thorith, Hartmut Losch and Lothar Milde in 1966.

AN EVENT BY EVENT SURVEY – including most wins and most medals for each event and major records.

MEN
100 metres
Valeriy Borzov (USSR) won three times – 1969 (10.4sec), 1971 (10.26) and 1974 (10.27). He is also the only man to compete in four 100m finals, but his last appearance in 1978 was a sad end to a great career for he tailed off last in 10.55, well behind Pietro Mennea (Ita) 10.27 Mennea had set a championship best of 10.19 in a heat.

200 metres
Pietro Mennea is the only double winner – 20.60 in 1978 and a championship best 20.16 in 1978. The only other double medallist is Martinus Osendarp (Hol), in 1934 and 1938 when he also won the 100m. Osendarp served an eight year prison sentence, for 'collaborating' during the war. Jiri Kynos (Cze) competed four times, but only once made the final.

Athletes to have won both 100m and 200m are Christian Berger (Hol) 1934, Martinus Osendarp 1938, Heinz Fütterer (Ger) 1954, Valeriy Borzov 1971, Pietro Mennea 1978. Mennea won six European medals in all, the most for a man, and ran in a record nine finals.

400 metres
No man has won twice but three winners have won second medals: Derek Pugh (GB) 1st 1950, 3rd 1946; Stanislaw Gredzinski (Pol) 1st 1966, 3rd 1969; and David Jenkins 1st 1971, 2nd 1974. Jenkins was Britain's fifth winner, the best national record. The championship best was set by Karl Honz (Ger) with 45.04 in 1974.

800 metres
Manfred Matuschewski (GDR), a master tactician, is the only double winner – 1962 (1:50.5)

and 1966 (1:45.9). He was also third in 1969, when the winner was Dieter Fromm (GDR) 1:45.9. There was a fourth East German winner in 1978 when Olaf Beyer ran the race of his life to take two seconds off the championship best with 1:43.84. The race had seemed to be between Sebastian Coe, who set a devastating pace, 49.3 at 400m and 1:16.2 at 600m, and Steve Ovett, but Coe's pace told as Ovett launched his kick only to find Beyer too strong. Coe was third and Ovett set a British record 1:44.09 and won his second silver medal, for he had run 1:45.76 as an 18-year-old in 1974 behind the 1:44.07 of Luciano Susanj (Yug).

The 1958 winner Mike Rawson (GB), was disqualified and Audun Boysen (Nor) presented with the gold medal. After a three-hour sitting, the Jury of Appeal reinstated Rawson, who had been pushed off the track on the first bend.

1500 metres
Three men have won two medals: Luigi Beccali (Ita) won in 1934 and was third in 1938; Michel Jazy (Fra) won in 1962 and was second to Bodo

David Jenkins, European champion at 19, was Britain's top 400m man for a decade. His best, 44.93 won the 1975 AAU title. *(M. Shearman)*

Tümmler (Ger) in 1966, when he won the 5000m; Henryk Szordykowski (Pol), after eighth in 1966, was third in 1969 behind John Whetton (GB) and Frank Murphy (Ire) and second in 1971 to Francesco Arese (Ita) 3:38.4. Szordykowski also ran in 1974 but did not make the final. The championship best of 3:35.59 was set by Steve Ovett in 1978. Ovett's devastating burst over the final 200m left his rivals trailing, finishing 2–3–4 were Eamonn Coghlan, Dave Moorcroft and Thomas Wessinghage.

5000 metres
Emil Zatopek (Cze) won by a record margin of 23sec in 1950 with a Czech record of 14:03:0. He had also set a national record at 14:25.8 in 1946 when he was fifth.

In 1954 he was third in 14:10.2 to Vladimir Kuts (USSR) 13:56.6 a world record and Chris Chataway (GB) 14:08.8. That was Kuts' first world record and he went on to run three more at 5000m and one at 10000m.

The only other man to win two 5000m medals is Kazimierz Zimny (Pol), second in 1958 and 1962 respectively to Zdzislaw Krzyszkowiak (Pol) and Bruce Tulloh (GB). The latter ran barefoot. The championship best was set at 13:17.21 by Brendan Foster (GB) in hot and humid conditions in Rome in 1974, when he led from the gun and broke away from the field with a 60.2 eighth lap.

The winner in 1946 was Sydney Wooderson (GB), the only man to win European titles before and after the war as he had won the 1500m in 1938.

10000 metres
Double winners have been: Ilmari Salminen (Fin) 1934 and 1938, Emil Zatopek 1950 and 1954, Jürgen Haase (GDR) 1966 and 1969. Haase, second in 1971 is the one man to win three medals. In that race Juha Väätäinen (Fin) unleashed an amazing 53.8 sec last lap to win in 27:52.78 to Haase's 27:53.36, times bettered to that date only by Ron Clarke and Dave Bedford. The latter led at the bell as he had for most of the race but was unable to match the sprinters and ended sixth in 28:04.33. That championship best was smashed in 1978 when six men bettered 27:40. The tall (1.91m/6ft 3½in) Finn, Martti Vainio won in 27:30.99 from Venanzio Ortis (Ita) 27:31.48, Aleksandr Antipov (USSR) 27:31.52, Brendan Foster 27:32.65, Dave Black (GB) 27:36.27, Gerard Tebroke (Hol) 27:36.64.

The 5000m/10000m double has been won by:

Vladimir Kuts ran a world record 13:56.6 from the front to win the 1954 European 5000m and won by 100m. He went on to double Olympic victory at 5000m and 10000m in 1956. He died of a heart attack on 16 Aug 1975.   *(E. D. Lacey)*

Emil Zatopek 1950, Zdzislaw Krzyszkowiak 1958 and Juha Väätäinen 1971.

Marathon
Ron Hill is one of seven men to have won two medals, but the only man to have run four times. He did not finish in 1962, was 12th in 1966, won in 1969 in 2:16:47.8 and was third in 1971. Second to Hill in 1969 was Gaston Roelants (Bel), who went on to fifth in 1971 and third in 1974 behind Ian Thompson (GB) and Eckhard Lesse (GDR).

The largest winning margin is 5min 33.6sec by Sergey Popov from Asiatic Russia, whose 2:15:17 in 1958 was a world best.

The current championship best is 2:11:57.5 by Leonid Mosseyev (USSR) in 1978, but he won by just 1.5sec from Nikolay Penzin (USSR), with 1971 winner Karel Lismont third in 2:12:07.7. Aurele Vandendriesche (Bel) was second twice to British runners, Brian Kilby in 1962 and Jim Hogan in 1966.

3000 metres steeplechase
Bronislaw Malinowski (Pol) won in 1974, a championship best 8:15.04, and 1978, 8:15.08.

Leonid Shcherbakov competes in the 1954 Spartakiade. He was twice European champion and lost only once in 1951–4.   *(Associated Press)*

In 1974 he beat Anders Garderud (Swe) by just 0.37sec, and was placed fourth at 10000m in 1974 and eighth at 5000m in 1971. Gaston Roelants (see p. 153) is the only other man to have won two medals. The event was first held in 1938, and the obstacles in the early days were much more severe than today. In 1946 Harold Abrahams, writing in *Athletics Weekly* described them as 'like barricades for the siege of Stalingrad'.

110 metres hurdles
Eddy Ottoz (Ita) won in 1966 (13.7) and 1969 (13.5). Asked about his appearance Ottoz once said 'Italian men and Russian women don't shave before a race'.

Three other men have won two medals. Hakan Lidman (Swe) was second to Don Finlay (GB) in 1938, when the latter equalled Lidman's European record of 14.3, and came back after the war to win in 1946 with 14.6. Anatoliy Mikhailov (USSR) was third in 1958 and first in 1962 as well as fourth in 1966. Alan Pascoe (GB) was third in 1969 and second in 1971, before winning the 400m hurdles in 1974.

The championship best was set at 13.40 by Guy Drut (Fra) in 1974.

400 metres hurdles
Yuriy Lituyev (USSR) is the closest to being a double winner. He won in 1958 after second places in 1950 and 1954. In 1962 Salvatore Morale (Ita) won in 49.2, one of only two world records for men's track events set in European championships. His winning margin of 1.1sec was bettered in 1978 when Harald Schmid

(Ger) won by 1.21sec in a championship best of 48.51.

4 × 100 metres relay
The most wins have been three by France in 1966, 1969 and 1974. Jiri Kynos (Cze) and Zenon Nowosz (Pol) both ran in four finals, each winning one gold medal, Kynos in 1971 and Nowosz in 1978 when Poland ran a championship best of 38.58.

4 × 400 metres relay
The most wins have been five by Germany in 1934, 1938 and as the Federal Republic in 1962, 1971 and 1978. They set a championship best of 3:02.03 in 1978. Horst-Rüdiger Schlöske (Ger) won the most individual medals, with a third in 1969, a first in 1971 and a second in 1974.

High jump
Kestutis Sapka (USSR) is one of five double medallists, but is closest to two wins. In 1971 he won with 2.20m/7ft 2½in, a height also cleared by the other medallists, and in 1974 was second to Jesper Törring (Den) as both cleared 2.25/7ft 4½in, Törring winning on fewer failures. In 1978 that championship best was bettered by four men, headed by Vladimir Yashchenko (USSR) 2.30m/7ft 6½in

Pole vault
Wolfgang Nordwig (GDR) won in 1966 – 5.10m, 1969 – 5.30m and 1971 – 5.35m. Eeles Landström (Fin) won in 1954 and 1958. Three men have competed four times: Christos Papanikolaou (Gre) was second in 1966 and the other two had a sorrier record. Both Francois Tracanelli (Fra) 1969–78 and Mike Bull (GB) 1966–74 twice failed to clear a height, and had best placings of seventh. The championship best was set at 5.55m/18ft 2½in by Vladimir Trofimenko (USSR) in 1978.

Long jump
Igor Ter-Ovanesyan won three times and was second twice (see p. 153). He competed against Lynn Davies (GB) four times. Davies was 11th in 1962 in his first senior international for Britain, but beat Ter-Ovanesyan in 1966 with 7.98m/26ft 2¼in on his last leap as the Soviet star had led throughout with 7.86m and responded to Davies with a great jump, but he fell back and it was measured at 7.88m. In 1969 Ter-Ovanesyan regained his title with a wind aided 8.17m/26ft 9¾in to 8.07m for Davies. There was the closest ever final in 1971 with just 7cm

covering the first six. Max Klauss (GDR) won with 7.92m/26ft 0in, 1cm ahead of Ter-Ovanesyan with Davies fourth. Davies' 1966 victory made him the only man to win Olympic, Commonwealth and European titles. Wilhelm Leichum (Ger) won in 1934 and 1938 and one other man, Nenad Stekic (Yug) competed four times between 1969–78, and was placed second in 1974 and 1978. In the latter year Jacques Rousseau (Fra) won with 8.18m/26ft 10in, second best in championship history to Ter-Ovanesyan's wind aided 8.19m/26ft 10½in in 1962.

Triple jump
Viktor Saneyev's European record is almost as remarkable as his Olympic one: 1969 – 1st 17.34m/56ft 10¾in (wind aided) with four jumps better than the runner-up; 1971 – 2nd 17.10m, 6cm behind Jörg Drehmel (GDR); 1974 – 1st 17.23m; 1978 – 2nd 16.93m, as Milos Srejovic (Yug) came through in the last round to an upset win by just 1cm. There have been two other double winners: Leonid Shcherbakov (USSR) 1950 and 1954 and Jozef Schmidt (Pol) 1958 and 1962.

Shot
The best record is that of Vilmos Varju (Hun) who competed five times (see p. 153) and won twice. There have been two double winners: Gunnar Huseby (Ice) 1946 and 1950 and Hartmut Briesenick (GDR) 1971 and 1974. The championship best is 21.08m/69ft 2in to Briesenick in 1971 (at the time a European record) and Udo Beyer (GDR) in 1978. Wladyslaw Komar (Pol) was third in 1966 and 1971, fourth in 1962 and sixth in 1974. In 1971 Heinfried Birlenbach (Ger) could not compete in the final as he injured his arm in a fight with police and stadium officials after he had been prevented from crossing a barrier between the athletes' enclosure and the spectators' area. In 1978 Geoff Capes was disqualified for failing to wear a number on his chest in an incident which seemed to owe over much to officiousness.

Discus
Adolfo Consolini (Ita) won three times in five competitions. His complete record as well as those of Ludvik Danek and Lothar Milde appear on page 153. Giuseppe Tosi finished runner-up to his countryman Consolini in 1946, 1950 and 1954. He was six months older and much larger, 1.93m and 119kg to Consolini's 1.83m and 100kg, but he was also beaten by Consolini at the Olympics in 1948 (1st and 2nd) and 1952 (2nd and 8th). The championship best was set by Wolfgang Schmidt (GDR) with 67.20m/220ft 6in in the qualifying round in 1978. He won the final at 66.82m. In 1969 Ricky Bruch (Swe) had three no throws in the qualifying round, but subsequently the judges deemed one of his throws to have been valid. So he advanced to the final, where he placed second to Hartmut Losch (GDR)

Hammer
Gyula Zsivotzky (Hun) (see p. 153) and Reinhard Theimer (GDR), who was second in 1971 and third in 1969 and 1974, each won three medals. World records have been set twice, in 1954 by Mikhail Krivonosov (USSR) with 63.34m/207ft 9in the first of his six records, and in 1969 by Anatoliy Bondarchuk (USSR) 74.68m/245ft 0in. Romuald Klim (USSR) won in 1966, was second in 1969 and was fourth in 1971, when the winner was Uwe Beyer (Ger). The championship best was set at 77.28m/253ft 6in by Yuriy Syedikh (USSR) in 1978, but he only beat Roland Steuk (GDR) by 4cm with Karl-Hans Riehm (Ger) a further 22cm away.

Javelin
Janis Lusis (USSR) won four times, 1962, 1966, 1969 and 1971, and he was sixth in 1974. He threw a championship best 91.52m/300ft 3in in 1969. Also competing five times were Janusz Sidlo, who won twice, and Gergely Kulcsar, who twice came third (see p. 153). The other man to win twice was Matti Järvinen (Fin), who went one better than Lusis or Sildo in setting a world record of 76.66m/251ft 6in in 1934. He threw farther still, 76.87m/252ft 2in, in 1938 but nine days earlier Yrjö Nikkanen (Fin) had improved the record to 77.87m/255ft 5in. In the championships, however Nikkanen came second to his older rival.

Decathlon
Vasiliy Kuznyetsov (USSR) is the only man to win three medals, winning in 1954, 1958 and 1962. In his final year he beat Werner von Moltke (Ger) by just four points 8026 to 8022. These were scored on the 1952 tables, but on the 1962 tables, brought into use later, von Moltke's performances scored higher 7786–7770. However von Moltke won with 7740 in 1966. Joachim Kirst (GDR) won twice, with 8041 in 1969 and 8196 in 1971. In 1978 Aleksandr Grebenyuk (USSR) set a championship record 8340 points ahead of Daley Thompson (GB) 8289.

Edgar Bruun (disqualified) leads winner John Mikaelsson in the 1938 AAA 7 miles walk. Bruun was the oldest European competitor in 1954.

10000 metres walk
This event was contested three times. On the first two occasions the medallists were identical: 1946 – 1st John Mikaelsson (Swe), 2nd Fritz Schwab (Swi), 3rd Emile Maggi (Fra); 1950 – 1st Schwab, 2nd Maggi, 3rd Mikaelsson. Roland Hardy and Lawrence Allen (both GB) finished second and third in 1950, but were disqualified for 'lifting'.

20000 metres walk
Vladimir Golubnichiy (USSR) won most medals. He was third in 1962 and second in 1966. He then missed the next two championships before winning in 1974, to collect his third medal. The best performance was set in 1978 by Roland Wieser (GDR) at 1:23:11.5.

50000 metres walk
There have been two double winners, Abdon Pamich (Ita) 1962 and 1966, and Christoph Höhne (GDR) 1969 and 1974. Pamich competed at a record six championships (see p. 153) and won a third medal in 1962. Three medals were also won by: Höhne who was second in 1971; Venyamin Soldatenko (USSR), who won gold, silver and bronze in 1971, 1978 and 1969 respectively; and by Peter Selzer (GDR) who was second in 1969 and third in both 1971 and 1974. Otto Bartsch (USSR) was placed fourth three times, in 1969, 1971 and 1978, but won

the silver medal in 1974. The fastest time was 3:53:30 achieved by Jorge Llopart in 1978 for Spain's first ever European title.

WOMEN
100 metres
There have been no double winners, but three winners have won a second medal. Fanny Blankers-Koen (Hol), third in 1938, won in 1950 with 11.7 by the record margin of 0.6sec, after failing to finish in the 1946 semi-finals. Renate Stecher (GDR) was first in 1971 and second in 1974 to Irena Szewinska (Pol) who had been second in 1966. Szewinska's championship record of 11.13 in 1974 was equalled by Marlies Göhr (GDR) in 1978.

200 metres
Irena Szewinska (Pol) has been the one double winner, with times of 23.1 in 1966 and 22.51 in 1974, both new championship records. She was also third in 1971 with 23.32 to the 22.71 of Renate Stecher (GDR), the only other woman to win three medals (second in 1969 and 1974).

100m/200m sprint doubles have been won by Stanislawa Walasiewicz (Pol) in 1938, Yevgeniya Sechenova (USSR) in 1946, Fanny Blankers-Koen (Hol) in 1950, Petra Vogt (GDR) in 1969, Renate Stecher (GDR) in 1971 and Irena Szewinska (Pol) in 1974. Third gold medals were won by Vogt at sprint relay and Blankers-Koen at 80m hurdles. Walasiewicz's 200m best of 23.8 in 1938 remained unbeaten until 1962, the longest span for any European championship best at any event.

400 metres
This event was first held in 1958, when it was won by Maria Itkina (USSR). She won again in 1962, when she equalled her own world record of 53.4, and she is the only double 400m medallist. New world records were set in 1969, when the French girls Nicole Duclos and Colette Besson were timed at 51.7 (51.72 and 51.74 respectively on automatic timing), and in 1978 when Marita Koch (GDR) did 48.94. Koch won by the massive margin of about 12m from Christina Brehmer (GDR) 50.38 and Irena Szewinska (Pol) 50.40. Koch later ran her anchor leg in the 4 × 400m relay in 48.21 with the benefit of a flying start.

800 metres
Vera Nikolic (Yug) won in 1966 and 1971 and also holds the record for the most medals as she won a third, a bronze, in 1969. In that year the

first four girls, headed by Lillian Board (GB) 2:01.4 broke Nikolic's 1966 championship best of 2:02.8. After a 10m win in this race Board went on to win a gold medal in a thrilling finish to the 4 × 400m relay, overhauling Colette Besson on the line as both Britain and France set a new world record of 3:30.8. For Lillian Board these were the last medals of a brilliant career tragically terminated by cancer – she died on Boxing Day 1970 in Munich.

The winning time continued to improve each year: Nikolic ran 2:00.0 in 1971, Lilyana Tomova (Bul) 1:58.11 in 1974 and Tatyana Providokhina (USSR) 1:55.82 in 1978.

1500 metres

This event was first held in 1969, when the first six all bettered Mia Gommers' (Hol) world record of 4:15.6. The surprise winner was Jaroslava Jehlickova (Cze) in 4:10.7 and Gommers was second in 4:11.9. That world record was further improved in the 1971 race, when Karin Burneleit (GDR) ran 4:09.6 and Gunhild Hoffmeister (GDR) was second in 4:10.3. Hoffmeister went on to win in 4:02.3 in 1974 and is the only double medallist to date. Further rapid improvement came in 1978 as Giana Romanova (USSR) won in 3:59.01 and Natalia Marasescu (Rom) was second in 3:59.77.

3000 metres

This event was first held in 1974, when it was won by Nina Holmen (Fin) in 8:55.10. That time was beaten four years later by the first nine contestants; Svyetlana Ulmasova (USSR) won in 8:33.16 from Natalia Marasescu (Rom) 8:33.53 and Grete Waitz (Nor) 8:34.33.

Marita Koch, the supreme 400m runner from 1978 until beaten by Jarmila Kratochvilova in the 1981 World Cup.   (M. Shearman)

80 metres/100 metres hurdles

Run at 80m from 1938 to 1966 and at 100m subsequently, the most gold medals is three by Karin Balzer (GDR). She won at 80m in 1966 (10.7sec) and at 100m in 1969 (13.3) and 1971 (12.94). Balzer also won a silver medal in 1962 in the closest women's track event final ever when the first four – Teresa Ciepla (Pol), Balzer, Maria Piatkowska (Pol) and Erika Fisch (Ger) – were all timed in 10.6, with the last two tying for third. Fanny Blankers-Koen (Hol) won twice, in 1946 with 11.8 and in 1950 with 11.1. The world record was equalled in 1938 when Claudia Testoni (Ita) ran 11.6. The championship best for 100m is 12.60 set in the 1978 semi-finals by Grazyna Rabsztyn (Pol). The final featured a pile-up as Rabsztyn hit the last hurdle hard, veered into the adjoining lane and brought down Nina Morgulina (USSR). Meanwhile the Olympic champion Johanna Klier (GDR) won in 12.61. The race was re-run without the disqualified Rabsztyn and was again won by Klier, this time in 12.62. The silver and bronze medallists Tatyana Anisimova (USSR) and Gudrun Berend (GDR) both kept the same places.

400 metres hurdles

A new event in 1978, this was won by Tatyana Zelentsova (USSR) with a new world record of 54.89.

4×100 metres relay

The USSR has been the most successful nation with three wins, in 1954, 1958 and 1978. The championship record of 42.51 set by the GDR in 1974 is one of three European records set by winning teams, the others being 44.5 by Poland in 1962 and 43.3 by West Germany in 1971. Two women have won two gold medals, Vera Krepkina (USSR) in 1954 and 1958 and Renate Stecher (GDR) in 1969 and 1974. Stecher also won a silver medal in 1971.

4 × 400 metres relay

This event was first held in 1969, when it was won by Great Britain, as their team of Rosemary Stirling, Pat Lowe, Janet Simpson and Lillian Board ran a world record 3:30.8, equalled by France in second place. The GDR team won each of the next three titles, with 3:29.3 (world record) in 1971, 3:25.2 in 1974 and 3:21.20 in 1978.

High jump

Iolanda Balas (Rom) won two gold medals and a silver. After being placed second in 1954 when she was 17 years old with 1.65m to the 1.67m / 5ft 5¾in of Thelma Hopkins (GB), Balas won in 1958 with 1.77m / 5ft 9¾in and in 1962 with 1.83m / 6ft, each time by the record margin of 7cm.

The most finals at this event is four by Dorothy Shirley (GB), who jumped 1.67m in 1958 and 1962, 1.65m in 1966 and 1.74m in 1969, and was placed respectively third, fourth, eighth and eleventh. The closest finish was in 1974 when the first four all cleared 1.83m.

The championship best was set in 1978 by Sara Simeoni (Ita) at 2.01m / 6ft 7in to equal her own 27-day-old world record. She had a classic duel with Rosemarie Ackermann (GDR) who cleared 1.99m / 6ft 6¼in. Four years earlier Ackermann had won with the then world record of 1.95m / 6ft 4¾in. An earlier 'world record' had been made in 1938 when Dora Ratjen (Ger) jumped 1.70m / 5ft 7in, but was disqualified immediately after the championships, initially as an alleged professional. Later it was confirmed that Ratjen was a man, and thus the world record stayed at 1.65m / 5ft 5in and the

Nadyezhda Chizhova won a record four European titles and won a complete set of Olympic medals at the shot. *(Novosti)*

title went to Ibolya Csak (Hun) at 1.64m / 5ft 4½in.

Long jump

Vilma Bardauskiene (USSR) set a world record of 7.09m / 23ft 3¼in in the qualifying round in 1978, before winning the final at 6.88m / 22ft 7in.

Only one woman has won two medals, Elzbieta Krzesinska (Pol) who was third in 1954 and second in 1962. Four women have competed in four championships: Helga Hoffman (Saar 1954 and West Germany 1958, 1962 and 1966), Diane Yorgova (Bul) and Sheila Sherwood (GB) both in 1962, 1966, 1969 and 1971, and Meta Antenen (Swi) in 1966, 1969, 1971 and 1974. Yorgova and Antenen each won one silver medal and Hoffman won a bronze, while Sherwood's best placing was fourth in 1971 at 6.62m.

Shot

Nadyezhda Chizhova's (USSR) record four titles included a world record of 20.43m / 67ft 0½in in 1969, when all her six puts were better than the person placed second, a unique level of field event superiority in European Championships. She improved this championship best to 20.78m / 68ft 2¼in in 1974, but by then her world record was 21.45m / 70ft 4½in. Her first two titles were won with 17.22m / 56ft 6in in 1966 and 20.16m / 66ft 1¾in in 1971.

Two East German women won three medals each, all behind Chizhova; Margitta Gummel second in 1966 and 1969 and third in 1971 and Maritta Lange third in 1966 and 1969, and second in 1971. This occurence of the same medallists at three successive championships is unique in major Games. Lange was also sixth in 1974. Others to have competed four times are: Ivanka Khristova (Bul), whose best placing was fourth in 1969 and 1974; Helena Fibingerova (Cze), who was tenth in 1969 (15.22m) and 12th in 1971 (15.73m) before improving mightily to 20.33m for third in 1974 and 20.86m for second in 1978 when Ilona Slupianek (GDR) set the championship best of 21.41m / 70ft 3in. The best record of all four-time competitors is that of Galina Zybina (USSR): 1950 – 4th, 1954 – 1st 15.65m, 1962 – 3rd 16.95m (behind the 18.55m / 60ft 10½in world record of Tamara Press (USSR)), 1966 – 4th. Zybina also won bronze medals at discus in 1954 and javelin in 1950. In 1958 she was dropped from the Soviet team for 'egotistical, uncomradely conduct', having refused to collect her second place medal at the Soviet championships.

Kenya's Henry Rono and Joel Cheruiyot training in the hills near Washington State University, USA, where they were studying.

Right: Lutz Dombrowski wins the 1980 Olympic long jump with 8.54m/28ft 0¼in, a new European record.

Below: Ruth Fuchs at Prague in 1978 when she won her second European javelin title. She was ranked No. 1 in the world for eight successive years 1972–9.

Discus
The first double gold medallist was Nina Dumbadze (USSR), who won with huge margins: by 4.06m with 44.52m/146ft 1in in 1946 and by 5.78m with 48.03m/157ft 7in in 1950. Tamara Press (USSR) won in 1958 and 1962, when she also won the shot (a unique double). A third woman to win two titles was Faina Melnik (USSR). In 1971 Melnik threw 64.22m/210ft 8in, the first of her 11 world records and in 1974 a championship best of 69.00m/226ft 4in. She was placed fifth in 1978. Lia Manoliu (Rom) competed five times (see p. 153).

Javelin
Dana Zátopková (Cze) (see p. 153) and Ruth Fuchs (GDR) have each won twice, but Fuchs won a third medal. Fuchs was third in 1971 with 59.16m/194ft 1in, and won in 1974 with a world record 67.22m/220ft 6in and in 1978 with a European record 69.16m/226ft 11in.

Pentathlon
Galina Bystrova (USSR) is the only double winner (1958 and 1962) and she also won the 80m hurdles in 1966. Burglinde Pollak (GDR), with second places in 1971, 1974 and 1978, is the only triple medallist. Gold medals proved elusive for Pollak, who also won two Olympic bronze medals, but she had the satisfaction of setting three world records. She also competed in the 1969 European championship, when she came eighth. Heide Rosendahl (Ger) featured in the two closest competitions. In 1966 she lost by just 22 points to Valentina Tikhomirova (USSR), then she had to miss the 1969 competition, when she was the clear favourite, due to the withdrawal of the West German team. Eventually she won in 1971, when she overtook Pollak in the final event, the 200m, to win by 24 points.

The heptathlon succeeded the pentathlon in 1982.

Great Britain at the European Championships
The most gold medals won is two by Sydney Wooderson (1500m in 1938, 5000m in 1946), Derek Pugh (400m and 4 × 400m relay 1950), John Wrighton (400m and 4 × 400m relay 1958) David Jenkins (400m 1971 and 4 × 400m relay 1974) and Alan Pascoe (400m hurdles and 4 × 400m relay 1974) for men, and Jean Desforges (4 × 100m relay 1950 and long jump 1954) and Lillian Board (800m and 4 × 400m relay 1969) for women.

The most medals won is four by: Derek Pugh (gold as above, silver 4 × 400m relay and bronze 400m in 1946); Dorothy Hyman (silver at 4 × 100m relay in 1958, and gold, silver and bronze respectively at 100m, 200m and 4 × 100m relay in 1962); and Alan Pascoe (gold as above, and bronze and silver at 110m hurdles in 1969 and 1971 respectively).

The most championships contested is four by: Lynn Davies; Ron Hill and Sheila Sherwood (all 1962–71); Mike Bull (1966–74); and by Alan Pascoe (1969–78).

The most gold medals won in a year is eight in 1950.

The most medals won in a year is 17 in 1950, 1958 and 1969.

Britain's least successful year was 1966, when the only medals won were the golds for Lynn Davies (long jump) and Jim Hogan (marathon). This is the only major Games contested by Britain at which no track medals were won.

Britain's most successful events have been the 400m, 1500m and marathon for men, with five gold medals won at each. A record ten medals have been won at the marathon.

Britain's least successful men's events have been the 3000m steeplechase, javelin and discus at which the highest placings have been eighth, ninth and tenth respectively. Among women's events, with the exception of the 400m hurdles which has only been contested once, the worst event has been the discus, where eighth is the best position.

European Cup
The European Cup is contested biennially, with each team entering one athlete per event and one team in each relay. In 1981 26 countries took part in the men's event and 25 in the women's.

The European Committee of the IAAF dedicated the Cup to the memory of Dr Bruno Zauli, its President, who died suddenly on 7 Dec 1963, eight months after the decision had been taken to start the competition.

The venues for the finals have been: 1965 Stuttgart (men), Kassel (women); 1967 Kiev; 1970 Stockholm (men), Budapest (women); 1973 Edinburgh; 1975 Nice; 1977 Helsinki; 1979 Turin; 1981 Zagreb.

The GDR have been **the most successful team**, winning the men's cup five times and the women's six. They have also had **the largest winning margins** as follows: **Men's final** 14 points in 1977 (winning 8 events)
Women's final 20 points in 1973 and 1975 (winning 9 out of 13 each time)
Any round – men 42 points (150–108) over France in Geneva on 30 Jun / 1 Jul 1979 (winning 14 events).
Any round – women 23 points (77–54) over Bulgaria in Sofia on 12 Jul 1975 (winning 12 of the 13 events).

The closest final was in 1967 for men. There were three teams in contention, with the USSR leading by three points, before the final event, the 4 × 400m relay. This event was won by Poland from West Germany and GDR with the USSR only fifth, but that was just enough. The final result was 1st USSR 81, 2nd GDR 80, 3rd West Germany 80.

European Cup Final records by individuals

The most wins in one year is three, two individual events and a relay on four occasions. The 100m / 200m / 4 × 100mR sprint treble was achieved by Eugen Ray (GDR) in 1977 and by Renate Stecher (GDR) in women's events in 1973 and 1975. The greatest treble, however, must be that of Harald Schmid (Ger) in 1979. On the first day he won the 400m hurdles in 47.85 to better David Hemery's 11-year-old European record and improve his own best by 0.58sec. Behind him Vasiliy Arkhipenko (USSR) 48.35 and Volker Beck (GDR) 48.58 both set national records. Just 59 minutes later Schmid returned to win the 400m with 45.31. Next day the powerful, mustachioed 21-year-old ran a comfortable 45.7 anchor leg on the winning 4 × 400m relay team.

The most wins is seven by Renate Stecher (GDR), who in addition to trebles in 1973 and 1975, won the 200m in 1970.

The highest individual events points scorers (scoring 8 for first to 1 for eighth) are:
Women 73 **Irena Szewinska** (Pol) (100m – 25, 200m – 27, 400m – 14, LJ – 7).
In her maiden name of Kirszenstein she ran in the first ever cup final in 1965 and continued through to 1979 (a record span), although missing those of 1970, when she paused in her athletics career to have a baby, and 1973 when Poland did not qualify. Her complete record is: 1965 – 2nd LJ, 1st 4 × 100mR; 1967 – 1st 100m and 200m, 6th 4 × 100mR; 1975 – 1st 400m, 2nd 200m, 3rd 100m, 4th 4 × 100mR; 1977 – 1st 200m, 3rd 100m and 4 × 400mR, 4th 4 × 100mR; 1979 – 3rd 400m, 5th 200m, 6th 100m and 4 × 400mR. 47 **Renate Stecher** (GDR) (100m – 23, 200m – 24). 45 **Ruth Fuchs** (GDR) (JT).
Men 37 **Pietro Mennea** (Ita): 1975 – 1st 200m, 2nd 100m; 1977 – 2nd 100m; 1979 – 1st 100m and 2nd 200m when he was beaten 20.31 to 20.29 for Allan Wells (GB), his first loss to a European athlete at 200m for six years.

The most wins at one event is four by Ruth Fuchs at women's javelin. After being placed third in 1967, she won in 1970 with 60.60m (the first ever 60m throw by a German), set a world record 66.10m / 216ft 10in in 1973, threw 64.80m in 1975 and narrowly missed another world record with 68.92m / 226ft 1in in 1977. In 1979 she was beaten by Eva Raduly (Hun) 66.28m to 65.46m.

Three wins at one event have been achieved by six other women: Nadyezhda Chizhova (USSR) SP 1967, 1970, 1973; Renate Stecher (GDR)

COMPLETE RECORD OF ALL FINALISTS (6 until 1973, 8 thereafter)

	MEN								WOMEN							
Nation	1965	1967	1970	1973	1975	1977	1979	1981	1965	1967	1970	1973	1975	1977	1979	1981
GDR	4	2	1	2	1	1	1	1	2	2	1	1	1	1	1	2
USSR	1	1	2	1	2	3	2	2	1	1	3	2	2	2	2	2
W. Germany (GFR)	2	3	3	3	5	2	3	4	4	3	2	4	3	4	6	3
Great Britain	6	3sf	3sf	4	4	4	5	3	3sf	5	5	5	7	3	4	4
Poland	3	4	4	3sf	3	5	4	6	3	4	4	3sf	4	5	7	1B + 6
France	5	5	5	6	7	1B + 6	7	1B + 7	4sf	4sf	4sf	3sf	8	3B	3B	5sf
Italy	4sf	4sf	7	3sf	8	8	6	5	5sf	5sf	4sf	4sf	5sf	2B	8	3B
Hungary	3sf	6	4sf	4sf	4sf	7B	4B	2B	5	6	6	3sf	3sf	4B	2B	7
Bulgaria	5sf	5sf	6sf	6sf	6sf	8B	6B	5sf	5sf	4sf	3sf	3	6	1B + 7	3	5
Finland	4sf	6sf	3sf	5	6	7	5B	4B	–	–	6sf	4sf	3sf	8	4B	6B
Romania	4sf	5sf	6sf	5sf	3sf	3B	2B	–	3sf	4sf	3sf	6	5	6	1B + 5	4B
Sweden	3sf	3sf	6	4sf	4sf	2B	6sf	6sf	4sf	3sf	4sf	5sf	5sf	6sf	7B	5sf
Yugoslavia	5sf	6sf	5sf	4sf	4sf	6B	1B + 8	8	4sf	5sf	5sf	5sf	6sf	6sf	8B	8

B = position in 'B' final, introduced in 1977 (winners qualifying for the final)

200m 1970, 1973, 1975; Faina Melnik (USSR) DT 1973, 1975, 1977; Rosemarie Ackermann (GDR) HJ 1975, 1977, 1979; Marlies Göhr (GDR) 100m 1977, 1979, 1981; Marita Koch (GDR) 400m 1977, 1979, 1981. Ilona Slupianek (GDR) was also placed first three times, 1977, 1979 and 1981, but in 1977 was subsequently disqualified after a positive doping test.

Men to have won their event three times: Harald Norpoth (Ger) 5000m 1965, 1967, 1970 (also 3rd at 5000m in 1973 and 5th at 1500m in 1970); Wolfgang Nordwig (GDR) PV 1965, 1967, 1970; Viktor Saneyev (USSR) TJ 1967, 1973, 1975 (also 2nd 1970); Guy Drut (Fra) 110mh 1970, 1973, 1975; Karl-Hans Riehm (Ger) HT 1975, 1977, 1979 (also 2nd 1981); Wolfgang Schmidt (GDR) DT 1975, 1977, 1979; Udo Beyer (GDR) SP 1977, 1979, 1981. Brendan Foster (GB) won the 5000m in 1973 and 1975 and the 10000m in 1979. Jean-Claude Nallet (Fra) is the only athlete to have won at three different events: 200m and 400m in 1967 and 400mh in 1970 (also 2nd at 400m in 1970).

World records have been set in European Cup competitions on nine occasions – all by women. These have been: 1965 Irina Press (USSR) 80mh in 10.4 and her sister Tamara SP 18.59m/61ft 0in. 1973 Faina Melnik (USSR) DT 69.48m/227ft 1in, Ruth Fuchs (Ger) JT 66.10m/216ft 10in. 1977 Karin Rossley (GDR) 400mh 55.63, Rosemarie Ackermann (GDR) HJ 1.97m/6ft 5½in. 1979 Marita Koch (GDR) 400m 48.60, GDR team (Christine Brehmer, Romy Schneider, Ingrid Auerswald, Marlies Göhr) 4×100mR 42.09. 1981 Antoaneta Todorova (Bul) JT 71.88m/235ft 10in.

Although the standard of competition is very high indeed, the essence of the competition is the scoring of points and this has resulted in many tactical races. Especially at 5000m some of these have been very slow. The 'worst' winning time of 15:35.6 was run by Derek Graham (GB) in the 1965 semi-final in Zagreb, and the slowest in the final has been 15:26.8 by Harald Norpoth (Ger) in 1967. Norpoth was the master of such races and won this race, in which the pace had dropped to 84/85sec laps, with a final 800m in 1:53.4! His victories in 1965 and 1970 came with last laps of 53.8 and 53.7 respectively after slow paces.

However such tactics are not the only way to win European Cup 5000m races as Brendan Foster and Nick Rose of Britain showed in the next three finals. The 1973 race started at the usual slow pace with Lasse Viren (Fin) leading at 400m in 75.2, but Foster smashed his rivals with a 60.2 eighth lap and won in 13:54.8. He repeated those tactics in even more devastating fashion in Nice in 1975, when after a two lap dawdle he threw in laps of 59.4 and 61.3. That left him 50m in the lead and he cruised on to win by 20sec in 13:36.18. In 1977 it was Nick Rose's turn as after 5½ laps he ran 60.9, 62.7 and 63.7. Karl Fleschen (Ger) stayed with him for a while, but had to give way, and at the bell Rose had a 50m lead. Rose won in 13:27.84 but frantic sprint finishes by Enn Sellik (USSR) 13:29.20 and Fleschen 13:29.44 had narrowed the gap to about 10m.

The record number of British final victories is six by the men in 1975. First-day winners were Alan Pascoe 400m hurdles 49.00, David Jenkins 400m 45.52 and Geoff Capes shot 20.75m. Second day winners were Steve Ovett 800m 1:46.55, Brendan Foster 5000m 13:36.18 and the 4×400m team of Glen Cohen, Jim Aukett, Bill Hartley and David Jenkins. Ovett had been uncertain whether to run. After the race he dismissed his win as of little importance in spite of having beaten four of his fellow finalists from the previous year's European 800m final.

The second day at Meadowbank in 1973 must rank as one of the most exciting ever for British track followers. Frank Clement had won the 1500m impressively, with a 1:53.6 last 800m, the previous day and on the Sunday, the team seemed to rise to exceptional heights urged on by the enthusiastic crowd. Alan Pascoe won the 400m hurdles in 50.07 and then Andy Carter scored an upset win at 800m in 1:46.44 over the favourites, both former European champions, Yevgeniy Arzhanov (USSR 1:46.70 and Dieter Fromm (GDR) 1:46.71. Carter was cool enough to deliberately false start to put his rivals on edge, before making a cautious start. However he led by 3m at 600m from Fromm and 6m clear of Arzhanov. The latter unleashed his renowned kick and when this took him past Carter the race seemed over, but somehow Carter found extra reserves to edge back into the lead in the last 20m. Further British triumphs came with an unexpected 200m win by Chris Monk and finally Foster's 5000m victory.

The most appearances by a British athlete in Finals is five by Verona Elder each year from 1973 to 1981 at 4×400m relay as well as 5th at 400m in 1973.

The most appearances by a British athlete in all rounds is nine by Elder and eight by Geoff Capes, who won the shot a record five times, in the semi-finals each year from 1973–9 and in the 1975 final. Five wins in European Cup competition have also been achieved by Steve Ovett, in all his 800m races, both semi-final and final in 1975 and 1977 and at 1500m in the 1981 semi-final. In the latter year he withdrew from the final due to a calf injury.

EUROPEAN CUP OF COMBINED EVENTS
First held in 1973 and staged biennially, the Cup is contested by teams of decathletes (men) and pentathletes / heptathletes (women), with three to score for each team.
Finals have been held as follows:
1973 – Bonn, West Germany; 1975 –Bydgoszcz, Poland; 1977 – Lille, France; 1979 – Dresden, GDR; 1981 – Birmingham, England
The only individual to win a final on more than one occasion is the East German pentathlete Burglinde Pollak, who set a world record of 4932 points in 1973 and won again with 4672 in 1975. Nadyezhda Tkachenko (USSR) was second in 1973, fourth in 1975 and first in 1977 with a world record 4839 points, but could not compete in 1979 as she had been suspended for taking drugs.

No athlete has taken part in all five finals, but those who have contested four are:
Margit Papp (Hun) – pentathlon 1973–9, best place fifth in 1979. Guido Kratschmer (Ger) – decathlon 1975–81, best place second in 1979. Rainer Pottel (GDR) – decathlon 1975–81, winner in 1981. Siegfried Stark (GDR) – decathlon 1975–81, winner in 1979.
Cup record scores were set by the 1981 final winners, Rainer Pottel (GDR) decathlon 8311, and Ramona Neubert (GDR) heptathlon 6391.

Ramona Neubert dominated the new heptathlon event in 1981, setting three world records and winning the European Cup.   *(M. Shearman)*

EUROPEAN CUP FOR MARATHON
The first European Cup marathon race was held at Agen, France on 13 Sep 1981. The men's team competition was won by Italy, with the USSR second and Poland third. The individual winner was Massimo Magnani (Ita) 2:13:29 from Waldemar Cierpinski (GDR) 2:15:44. The women's race was won by Zoia Ivanova (USSR) in 2:38:58, but there was no women's team competition.

THE COMPLETE RECORD OF ALL FINALISTS

Nation	Decathlon					Pentathlon / Heptathlon (1981)				
	1973	1975	1977	1979	1981	1973	1975	1977	1979	1981
Poland	1	2	6	5	3	–	7	–	–	–
USSR	2	1	1	3	4	2	2	1	2	3
GDR	3	4	3	1	2	1	1	–	1	1
France	4	7	4	6	–	6	6	3	–	–
West Germany	5	5	2	2	1	4	3	2	3	2
Sweden	6	3	5	–	–	–	–	–	–	–
Switzerland	7	–	–	–	6	–	–	–	–	–
Czechoslovakia	8	–	7	–	–	–	–	–	–	–
Bulgaria	9	–	–	–	5	3	–	6	–	4
Austria	10	–	–	–	–	7	4	–	–	–
Hungary	–	–	–	–	–	5	5	7	5	5
Yugoslavia	–	–	–	–	–	8	–	–	–	–
Finland	–	6	–	4	–	–	–	–	–	–
Great Britain	–	–	8	–	–	–	–	4	6	6
Netherlands	–	–	–	–	–	–	–	5	4	–
Belgium	–	–	–	–	–	–	–	8	–	–

The final of the European Indoor 60m in 1981 at Grenoble. The winner (white vest) is Marian Woronin of Poland, the third of his four consecutive sprint titles.   *(M. Shearman)*

European Indoor Championships

European Indoor Games were held for the first time on 27 Mar 1966 at the Westfalenhalle in Dortmund. From 1970 they received IAAF sanction as the European Indoor Championships.

The Venues have been: 1966 Dortmund; 1967 Prague; 1968 Madrid; 1969 Belgrade; 1970 Vienna; 1971 Sofia; 1972 Grenoble; 1973 Rotterdam; 1974 Göteborg; 1975 Katowice; 1976 Munich; 1977 San Sebastian; 1978 Milan; 1979 Vienna; 1980 Sindelfingen, 1981 Grenoble; 1982 Milan.

World indoor bests have been a regular feature of the championships with 44 set in all up to 1982, the most in one year being seven in 1970. Eddy Ottoz (Ita) three times ran a world best of 6.4 for 50m hurdles in 1967 and he is joined as the most prolific record breaker by Karin Balzer (GDR), who ran 50m hurdles in 1967 and 1968 (heat) and 60m hurdles in 8.2 in 1970.

Perhaps the finest performance was the world high jump best indoors or out by the 19-year-old Ukrainian Vladimir Yashchenko in 1978. His 2.35m / 7ft 8½in came on his 20th jump of a competition which he had begun 4 hours 2 minutes earlier. This was Yashchenko's first senior international, although he had set the outdoor world record of 2.33m the previous summer for the USSR junior team against the USA juniors. In Milan 14 of the 18 competitors cleared 2.15m / 7ft 0¾in and seven cleared 2.21m / 7ft 3in. Aleksandr Grigoryev (USSR) went out after clearing 2.25m, and Wolfgang Killing (Ger), who had equalled Grigoryev's European indoor best of 2.28m / 7ft 5¾in a few days earlier, ended third at 2.27m. That left two straddlers Yashchenko and Rolf Beilschmidt (GDR). Both cleared 2.29m / 7ft 6in for a new European best, but from then on, Yashchenko was on his own, getting better as the bar rose. Earlier he had been inconsistent failing several heights on his first jump, but he soared over 2.31m, 2.33m and 2.35m, the latter two being world indoor bests.

The most gold medals won at individual events is seven by Valeriy Borzov (USSR). He was second at 50m to Zenon Nowosz (Pol) in 1969, then he embarked on a marvellously consistent series of wins: at 60m in 1970 – 6.6, 1971 – 6.6, 1974 – 6.58, 1975 – 6.59, 1976 – 6.58, 1977 – 6.59; and at 50m in 1972 – 5.75. He did not run in 1973.

The most gold medals at individual women's events is five by Karin Balzer (GDR), Nadyezhda Chizhova (USSR) and Helena Fibingerova (Cze). Balzer won at 50m hurdles in 1967 – 6.9, 1968 – 7.0, 1969 – 7.2 and at 60m hurdles in 1970 – 8.2, 1971 – 8.1. Chizhova won the shot in 1967 – 17.44, 1968 – 18.18, 1970 – 18.60, 1971 – 19.70, 1972 – 19.41, was second in 1974 – 20.62 and third in 1966 – 16.95. Fibingerova won the shot in 1973 – 19.08, 1974 – 20.75, 1977 – 21.46, 1978 – 20.67, 1980 – 19.92, and second in 1975 – 19.97, 1981 – 20.64 and 1982 – 19.24. The big improvement in women's shot putting is indicated by the fact that the winning marks in 1970, 1971 and 1974 were all world indoor bests.

The most wins at each event (including all three-time winners): **MEN 50m/60m** 7 Valeriy Borzov (see p. 167), 4 Marian Woronin (Pol) 1979–82; **400m** 2 Andrzej Badenski (Pol) 1968, 1971, Alfons Brijdenbach (Bel) 1974, 1977; **800m** 3 Noel Carroll (Ire) 1966–8; **1500m** 4 Henryk Szordykowski (Pol) 1970–1, 1973–4, 3 John Whetton (GB) 1966–8, 3 Thomas Wessinghage (Ger) 1975, 1980–1; **3000m** 2 Ian Stewart (GB) 1969, 1975, Emiel Puttemans (Bel) 1973–4, Karl Fleschen (Ger) 1977, 1980, Markus Ryffel (Swi) 1978–79; **50mh/60mh** 3 Eddy Ottoz (Ita) 1966–8, Thomas Munkelt (GDR) 1977–9; **High jump** 3 Istvan Major (Hun) 1971–3; **Pole vault** 4 Wolfgang Nordwig (GDR) 1968–9, 1971–2; **Long jump** 3 Hans Baumgartner (Ger) 1971, 1973, 1977; **Triple jump** 6 Viktor Saneyev (USSR) 1970–2, 1975–7; **Shot** 3 Hartmut Briesenick (GDR) 1970–2, Reijo Stahlberg (Fin) 1978–9, 1981; **WOMEN 50m/60m** 4 Renate Stecher (GDR) 1970–2, 1974, 4 Marlies Göhr (GDR) 1977–9; **400m** 3 Verona Elder (GB) 1973, 1975, 1979; **800m** 2 Nikolina Shtereva (Bul) 1976, 1979; **1500m** 2 Natalia Marasescu (Rom) 1975, 1979; **50mh/60mh** 5 Karin Balzer (above); 3 Grazyna Rabsztyn (Pol) 1974–6; **High jump** 4 Sara Simeoni (Ita) 1977–8, 1980–1, 3 Rita Kirst (GDR) 1968–9, 1972, Rosemarie Ackermann (GDR) 1974–6; **Long jump** 2 Jarmila Nygrynova (Cze) 1977–8; **Shot** 5 Nadyezhda Chizhova and Helena Fibingerova (see above).

In 1982 men's 200m and women's 3000m events were added to the programme.

The most medals won is eight by Valeriy Borzov and Helena Fibingerova and seven by five athletes: Chizhova (see above); Meta Antenen (Swi) (1969–75, including one win, women's long jump in 1974); Grazyna Rabsztyn (Pol)

(1972–80); Viktor Saneyev (USSR) with a second in 1968 to add to his six triple jump wins, and Thomas Wessinghage (Ger), who has been second four times (1974, 1976–8) at 1500m. Antti Kalliomaki (Fin) shares a record four silver medals with Wessinghage; he won the pole vault in 1975 and was second in 1972, 1974, 1976–7.

Wladyslaw Komar (Pol) won five shot medals (three silver and two bronze), the most without a gold, and his span of gaining medals, 1967–78, is also a record.

European Junior Championships

European competitions for Juniors were first held unofficially in 1964. Games recognised as official by the European A.A. were staged in 1966 and 1968 as 'European Juniors Games' and since 1970 have been known as the 'European Championships for Juniors'. Junior men must not reach 20, and junior women must not reach 19, during the year of competition.

Venues have been as follows:
1964 Warsaw 1966 Odessa 1968 Leipzig 1970 Paris 1973 Duisburg 1975 Athens 1977 Donetsk 1979 Bydgoszcz 1981 Utrecht.

British teams did not take part until 1970. A team was due to participate in 1968 in Leipzig, but withdrew at the last minute due to the political crisis in Eastern Europe, engendered by the Soviet invasion of Czechoslovakia. In 1968 only 11 nations took part, although 19 had competed in 1966 and 14 in 1964. The Championships have now become established as a very high class meeting, with many future Olympic and European champions gaining their first major successes therein.

The GDR have established by far the **greatest national record** at these Championships, winning 21 gold medals in 1973, but bettering even that in 1981, when they won 22 gold, 13 silver and 7 bronze medals at the 38 events.

The only athletes to win **individual titles in two Championships** are Ari Paunonen (Fin) and Thomas Schröder (GDR). Paunonen won the 1500m in 3:44.8 in 1975, when Sebastian Coe (GB) was third, and again in 1977 with 3:41.6. Paunonen set European Junior records at 1500m, 3:38.1, and 1 Mile, 3:55.7 in 1977. Both these records were to be beaten by Graham Williamson (GB) who succeeded him as European Junior champion in 1979. Thomas

Schröder won a record five medals. He won the 100m (10.41) and was second to Mike McFarlane at 200m in 1979, and in 1981 won both 100m (10.14w) and 200m (20.69) as well as a silver in the sprint relay.

World Junior records were set in 1964 by Anders Garderud (Swe) in the 1500m steeplechase 4:08.0 and Nadyezhda Chizhova (USSR) – women's shot 16.60m in 1964. Since then individual world indoor bests have been: 1970 Aleksandr Blinyayev (USSR) 7632 decathlon; 1973 Frank Baumgartl (GDR) 5:28.2 2000m steeplechase, Ilona Schoknecht (GDR) 17.05m women's shot Evelin Schlaak (GDR) 60.00m women's discus, Bärbel Muller (GDR) 4519 women's pentathlon; 1979 Gaetano Erba (Ita) 5:27.5 2000m steeplechase, Sabine Everts (Ger) 4594 women's pentathlon; 1981 Sylvia Kirchner (GDR) 56.41 women's 100m hurdles.

There have also been 11 world junior relay records, ten of them by the GDR. The 1973 championships set the highest standards for record breaking, with 14 European, including seven world junior records. Amongst the record breakers were Udo Beyer (GDR) (shot – 19.65m) and Bärbel Eckert (GDR) (200m – 22.85), who like Schoknecht (later Slupianek) and Schlaak went on to win Olympic gold medals.

Three gold medals in one year have been won by 11 athletes, all with two individual wins and one relay win. Those to have won at 100m, 200m and 4 × 100m relay: men – Valeriy Borzov (USSR) 1968, Klaus-Dieter Kurrat (GDR)

Kathy Smallwood at the 1980 Olympic Games, where she was sixth at 100m, fifth at 200m and won a relay bronze. *(G. Herringshaw)*

1973; women – Lyudmila Zharkova (USSR) 1968, Petra Koppetsch (GDR) 1975, Bärbel Lockhoff (GDR) 1977, Kerstin Walther (GDR) 1979.

Christine Brehmer (GDR) won at 400m and both relays in 1975; and the following all also won at 4 × 100m: Valeriy Podluzhniy (USSR) LJ and TJ 1970; Irena Kirszenstein (Pol) 200m and LJ 1964; Bärbel Eckert 200m and 100mh 1973; Katrin Böhme (GDR) 100m and 100mh 1981.

Others to have won two individual events: 1964 Jürgen Haase (GDR) 1500m, 3000m; Geja Fejer (Hun) SP,DT. 1966 Meta Antenen (Swi) 80mh, Pen. 1968 Mikhail Bariban (USSR) LJ, TJ. 1970 Franz-Peter Hofmeister (Ger) 100m, 200m. 1975 Werner Bastians (Ger) 100m, 200m. 1977 Kristine Nitzsche (GDR) HJ, Pen. 1981 Thomas Schröder (GDR) 100m, 200m.

British winners have been
Men: 1970 Peter Beaven 400m 47.11, Berwyn Price 110m hurdles 14.21. **1973** Steve Ovett 800m 1:47.53. **1975** Micky Morris 2000m steeplechase 5:34.8, Aston Moore triple jump 16.16m. **1977** Nat Muir 5000m 13:49.1, Daley Thompson decathlon 7647. **1979** Mike McFarlane 200m 20.89, Graham Williamson 1500m 3:39.0, Steve Cram 3000m 8:05.2, Steve Binns 5000m 13:44.4. **1981** Todd Bennett 400m 47.18, Paul Davies-Hale 2000m steeplechase 5:31.12. **Women: 1970** Helen Golden 200m 24.34. **1973** Sonia Lannaman 100m 11.73. **1979** Fatima Whitbread javelin 58.20m.

The only British athlete to have won three medals is Kathy Smallwood who won bronze medals at 100m, 200m and sprint relay in 1977.

Balkan Games

Following experimental Games at the Averoff Stadium in Athens on 22–29 Sep 1929, the first official Balkan Games were contested by Greece, Yugoslavia, Bulgaria and Romania on 5–12 Oct 1930 at the same venue. Turkey competed the following year and since then the Games have been held annually from 1930–41 and since 1953. Unofficial games, including women's events were held in 1941 and 1947, but women joined officially in 1957. Albania also competed on six occasions.

The most individual titles won is 21 by Christos Mantikas (Gre): 200m 1931; 400m 1935–6; 110m hurdles 1930–7, 1939–40; 400m hurdles 1930–1, 1933–8.

The most titles won at an event is ten by Mantikas at 110m hurdles and by Ivanka Khristova (Bul) at women's shot 1963, 1966–73 and 1975. Iolanda Balas (Rom) won nine successive women's high jump titles 1957–65 and Stanko Lorger (Yug) won nine successive 110m hurdles titles 1953–61.

Austria

The national federation (Osterreichischer Leichtathletik-Verband) was founded on 21 Sep 1900. In 1981 there were 214 clubs with 6200 athletes affiliated.

The first official Austrian championships were held in Vienna on 1 Oct 1911 at eight men's events, although various clubs had staged so-called championships at isolated events before then. The first women's championships were held in Vienna on 29–30 Jun 1918 at six events.

The most national titles won is 36 by Emil Janausch between 1923 and 1939: hammer 11; discus 7; shot 6; and the discontinued events of discus (both hands) 8 and shot (both hands) 4. Adolf Gruber has the most wins at one men's event with 12 marathon titles in succession 1952–63 and his overall total of 29 is the most at events on the current list. His final win, at the 25km road race in 1965 at the age of 45 made him the oldest Austrian champion. The women's record is held by Karoline Käfer with 28 up to 1981, 22 outdoor (100m 7, 200m 8, 400m 7) and 6 indoor (60m 2, 200m 2, 400m 2).

The most titles won at an event is the 15 javelin wins by Herma Bauma between 1931 and 1952. Bauma won her first title at the age of 16 in 1931, when she made her international debut and set the first of 14 national javelin records 36.31m after just a month's training. She won the silver medal at the 1934 World Games and made her Olympic debut in 1936 with fourth place. After the war, in 1948, she won the first ever Austrian Olympic gold medal and set a world record of 48.63m. She won the European silver medal in 1950 and concluded her career in 1952, when she was placed ninth at the Olympics.

The youngest champion is Margit Danninger, who won the women's high jump title in 1964 with 1.69m at the age of 13 years 35 days, which is the youngest for any European national champion.

The most national records is 20 by Ferdinand Friede at events ranging from 300m to 3000m between 1913 and 1926 and a 4 × 1500m relay record in 1930.

The most records at one event is 15 by Heinrich Thun at hammer between 1957–63.

The youngest Austrian record holder is Elfriede Geist who was $15\frac{1}{4}$ when she ran 60m in 7.6sec in 1954. The youngest male record holder is Karl Mladek, aged 16 when he ran 200m in 21.8 in 1941. Just after his 16th birthday in 1940 he became the youngest male champion at 100m.

Internationals

Austria first competed at the Olympic Games in 1900 and their first international match was against Hungary in 1912. Austria's men's team has had little success, losing all 14 contests against Hungary since then, and with only one win to 13 losses against Switzerland, and 3 to 15 against Czechoslovakia. The Austrian women have done better, however: 3–8 v Hungary; 7–13 v Italy; 9–5 and one tie v Switzerland; 4–6 v Czechoslovakia.

Hans Potsch (HT, SP, DT) made 21 international appearances, over a 26-year span, 1956–81. He won the World Veterans' title three times between 1977–81.

The Sykora sisters, Liese (later Prokop) and Maria set a total of 47 Austrian records (Liese 24 in Pen, SP, 100mh, HJ, LJ; Maria 23 in 400m, 800m, 200m, 100mh, 200mh, 400mh) and won 37 national titles (Liese 21 and Maria 16). Liese set a world pentathlon record of 4727 points in 1969 and won the European title at that event in 1969 as well as the 1968 Olympic silver medal. Maria won the 1970 European Indoor 800m, was third in the 1969 European 400m and won the 1970 World Student Games 400m.

The family Haidegger must be amongst the most successful in the world, with 34 national titles: Rudolf 5; his son Rudolf 7; his daughter Lotte 4; Rudolf junior's wife Trude 4; Lotte's husband Felix Würth 14.

Erwin Pektor set five Austrian javelin records 1940–2. His best of 70.68m/231ft 11in remained the national record until his son Walter broke it in 1964, the first of ten records. Walter's best of 82.16m/269ft 7in in 1968 is still the Austrian record, so the latter has been a family preserve for over 40 years.

Austria's main stadium is Vienna's Prater Stadium, opened in 1931 for the Second Worker's Olympiad and also used for the 1938 Women's European Championships. The record attendance was 20000 in 1947 at the 'Amerikaner Meeting'.

Belgium

The Fédération Belge des Societés de Courses à Pied was formed in 1887. From 1889 the governing body was the Ligue Royale Belge d'Athlétisme (Koninklijke Belgische Atletiek Bond), but in 1978 this body split into two linguistic groups – VAL (Vlaamse Atletiek Liga) and LBFA (Ligue Belge Francophone d'Athlétisme).

National championships were first held in 1889 for men and 1921 for women.

Gaston Roelants dominates the list of Belgian record breakers. He won the most national titles, 32 between 1959 and 1972 at distance events. He also made a record 86 international appearances for Belgium, including four Olympic Games and five European Championships, between 1959 and 1977, when at 40 years 151 days he was the oldest ever. He set 30 Belgian records, beginning with his 3000m steeplechase in 8:56.6 in 1959. At the steeplechase he won the 1964 Olympic and 1962 European titles and set world records at 8:29.6 in 1963 and 8:26.4 in 1965. He later turned to longer distances up to the marathon, at which he won two European medals, and his final records were new world marks at 20km and 1 hour of 57:44.4 and 20784m respectively in 1972. He also met with great success at cross-country (see p. 123).

Roger Moens also set 30 national records, between 1952 (400m in 48.6) and 1960 (1500m in 3:41.4). He also set national records at 600m and 1000m and world records at 4 × 800m relay and 800m, the latter with his celebrated 1:45.7 at Oslo in 1955 to break Harbig's 16-year-old record. His first national 800m record was 1:51.4 in 1953 before he made a 2.6sec improvement to 1:48.8 that year.

The record number of Belgian titles and records at one event is 17 and 23 respectively by hammer thrower Henri Haest between 1947 and 1964. He became Belgium's oldest ever champion in 1964 at 37 years 9 months and his best throw was 55.33m in 1957.

The most women's titles won is 21 by Simone Saenen between 1953 and 1965, eleven at shot and ten at discus. At 35 years 171 days in 1965 she is the oldest ever women's champion. She set 18 national discus records and became the oldest women's record breaker with 13.77m for the shot in 1962. The oldest women's international was Rita Beyens at 37 years 53 days in 1979 on her record 42nd appearance.

The youngest Belgian record breaker is Sonja Desmet with a club 4 × 400m relay record in 1974 at 14 years 267 days. The youngest international is Karin Verguts at 15 years 47 days in 1976 and the youngest Belgian champion is Rosine Wallez at 16 years 113 days at 200m in 1973.

Roger Moens beats Brian Hewson in the British Games 800m in 1956. Through injury he missed the Olympic Games that year. *(BBC Hulton)*

Belgium first competed in the Olympic Games in 1900 and their first medallist was Gaston Reiff, winner of the 5000m in 1948. Reiff was also the first Belgian world record holder with 5:07.0 for 2000m in 1948, to which he later added world records at 3000m and 2 miles.

Belgium indoor championships have been held in France and in Germany, as Belgium has no indoor facilities. They were first held in Paris in 1978 and in 1981 were held in Dusseldorf.

Bulgaria

Bulgaria is a late comer to the ranks of the world's top athletics nations. The first organised meeting was held as recently as 24/25 May 1924 at Sofia in response to the invitation to Bulgaria to send a team to the Olympic Games that year.

Bulgaria are now consistently the strongest nation at the annual Balkan Games, yet only three Bulgarians were winners in the pre-war Games. Their first international match was a 39–35 win over Turkey at Istanbul in 1927, the second in 1942 and the third, including women for the first time, against Czechoslovakia in 1949.

National championships were first held at Plovdiv in 1926 for men, and women's events were added in 1938. Snezhana Kerkova has won most titles at all events 20 (4 at 100m, 4 at 200m, 10 at 80mh and 2 at Pen) between 1957 and 1967. She also set 29 Bulgarian records (100m – 4, 200m – 2, 80mh – 19, Pen – 4), the country's second highest number. The most titles won at one event is 14 by Dmitriy Khlebarov at pole vault between 1955 and 1971 and by Stoyan Slavkov who won 14 successive decathlon events from 1951–64.

Ivanka Khristova won 13 national shot titles from 1961 to 1974 excluding 1967 when she had recently given birth to a son. She competed in four European Championships with a highest placing of fourth in 1969 and 1974, and four Olympic Games. At the Olympics she improved at each Games from 1968 with a tenth, a sixth, and a third before winning Bulgaria's first Olympic gold medal in 1976. Khristova set the extraordinary number of 36 national shot records including one tie, taking the record from 15.42m/50ft 7¼in in 1962 to 21.89m/71ft 10in, her second world record, at Belmeken on 4 July 1976.

Gaston Reiff wins the 1948 Olympic 5000m from Emil Zatopek, although the latter gained 30m in the last 300m. *(BBC Hulton)*

Yordanka Blagoeva also competed at four Olympic Games, from 1968 to 1980, being placed second in 1972 and third in 1976 at high jump. She became Bulgaria's first world record holder with 1.94m/6ft 4½in on 24 Sep 1972.

Diane Yorgova shares Kristova's record of four European Championships appearances and won Bulgaria's first Olympic medal, second in the 1972 long jump when her 6.77m/22ft 2½in was just 2cm behind Heide Rosendahl's winning jump. Yorgova set 22 national records, from 5.58m/18ft 3¾in in 1959 to that 6.77m in 1972. She was married in the Olympic village in Tokyo in 1964 to a member of the Bulgarian gymnastics team.

Dr Virginia Mihailova improved the women's discus record 24 times from 38.78m/127ft 3in in 1953 to 56.70m/186 ft 0in in 1964 for fourth place at the Tokyo Olympic Games. She also won 11 national titles.

Georgi Stoikovskiy was Bulgaria's first man to achieve major championship success with the 1966 European triple jump title.

The most men's records have been set by Dmitriy Khlebarov, 19 pole vault improvements from 4.02m/13ft 2¼in in 1954 to 4.96m/16ft 3¾in in 1965. Georgi Kaburov also set 19 records at 110m hurdles but only nine improvements from 15.6 in 1954 to 14.4 in 1958.

Czechoslovakia

Formerly part of Austria-Hungary, Czechoslovakia achieved independence in 1918. It joined the IAAF in 1919 and the first national championships were staged in 1920.

The oldest club, AC Praha, was formed in 1890 and the AAU of Bohemia was established in 1897. Bohemian athletes competed at the Olympic Games of 1900, 1908 and 1912, although the first Czech Olympic medal can be attributed to Alajos Szokolyi, who was third at 100m in 1896 representing Hungary. For Bohemia, Frantisek Janda-Suk, a pioneer of the modern rotational technique, was second in the 1900 discus. The first national championships (of 'The Czech Crown Territories') were held in Prague on 7 Jul 1907 and women's events were held as early as 1914.

Janda-Suk set the first world best by a Czech, 39.42m/129ft 4in at discus in 1901, but the first IAAF records came from Frantisek Douda, 16.04m in 1931 and 16.20m in 1932 at shot. The first women's record was 50m in 6.6 by Marie Mejzlíková I on 20 Jun 1920. The latter's namesake Marie Mejzlíková II set 11 world records in 1922–23.

The most national titles by a woman is 27 by Olga Davidová (née Modrachová) between 1949 and 1960 (100m – 2, 200m – 3, 80mh – 2, HJ a record 12 in succession, LJ – 1, Pen – 7.) The most men's titles was 26 by Jaroslav Knotek between 1935 and 1950 (SP 4, DT 9, HT 13). These 13 titles are also a record by an individual for one event, shared with Dana Zatopková with 13 women's javelin wins between 1946 and 1960. Zatopková won the first Olympic gold medal by a Czech woman in 1952, following the example of her husband, who had won the only previous Olympic gold by a Czech athlete.

Emil Zatopek set 18 world records in all at distances from 5000m to 30000m. At the Olympic Games he won four gold medals and a silver, and at the European Championships, three golds and a bronze. His hard training ushered in a new era of distance running as he drastically revised the concepts of what was possible. He broke 60min for 20000m when only four men had run half the distance in half the time and in 1954 set world records at 5000m and 10000m on successive days. If you watched his face his running seemed an agony throughout as his head wobbled, he puffed and blew and grimaced, but his legs swept out a rhythm that made him one of the track's immortals.

Zatopek was born at Koprivnice on 19 Sep 1922, curiously the same birthdate as his wife Dana. He set the first of his three national records at 3000m in 8:34.8 on 16 Sep 1944, and his first world record came at 10000m on 11 Jun 1949. At 2000m Zatopek set five Czech records, with a best of 5:20.5 in 1947, and at 3000m nine records headed by 8:07.8 in 1948. His major championship career started at 5000m, when in his ninth race at the distance he set his fourth Czech 5000m record for fifth place in the 1946 European Championships with 14:25.8 to 14:08.6 for the winner, Sydney Wooderson. He set a Czech record in his first 10000m – 30:28.4 on 29 May 1948 in Budapest, and three weeks later at his second attempt ran 29:37.0 in Prague.

Emil Zatopek leads Gordon Pirie at 10000m in the London v Prague match in 1955. Pirie won from Ken Norris (behind Pirie) and Zatopek.

(H. W. Neale)

SUMMARY OF ZATOPEK'S CAREER AT 5000M AND 10000M

Year	Best	5000m Races	Wins	Czech Records	Best	10000m Races	Wins	Czech Records
1942	16:25.0	1	1					
1943	15:26.6	1	1					
1944	14:55.0	2	1	1				
1945	14:50.8	2	2	1				
1946	14:25.8	5	4	2				
1947	14:08.2	12	12	1				
1948	14:10.0	11	9	–	29:37.0	5	5	2
1949	14:10.8	10	10	–	29:21.2	11	11	2(WR)
1950	14:03.0	19	19	2	29:02.6	7	7	1(WR)
1951	14:11.6	12	12	–	29:29.8	3	3	–
1952	14:06.4	15	13	–	29:17.0	6	6	–
1953	14:03.0	9	9	1	29:01.6	4	4	1(WR)
1954	13:57.2	12	9	1(WR)	28:54.2	7	6	1(WR)
1955	14:04.0	11	5	–	29:25.6	7	5	–
1956	14:14.8	3	2	–	29:33.4	1	1	–
1957	14:06.4	9	6	–	29:25.8	10	5	–

(WR = world record)

Zatopek won his first 38 races at 10000m from 1948 until he was pipped by Jozsef Kovács (Hun) on 3 Jul 1954 at Budapest 29:09.0 to 29:09.8 in the match between the two nations. His previous 10000m race had been his best, the world record of 28:54.2 at Brussels on 1 June. Zatopek gained his revenge over Kovács at the European Championships but from that year he was no longer invincible.

1949–51 he ran and won 69 successive races. Zatopek had four great track races over longer distances, setting ten world records, and ran the marathon just twice, winning the 1952 Olympic title and was placed sixth in 1956. His final race, 16 years after his first, was a 5000m victory in Prague on 28 Oct 1957. In 30 international matches or championships he won 36 out of 46 races. In all from 1941 to 1957 he ran 334 races, winning 261 of them.

Czechoslovakia's first international match was a 41–34 women's victory over France in Paris on 21 May 1922 and the first men's match was against Poland and Yugoslavia on 6 Aug 1922.

The most internationals is 50 by Jirí Skobla between 1950 and 1967. Skobla, son of the 1932 Olympic heavyweight weightlifting champion, set eight European shot records between 1952–7. He won the 1954 European title and bronze medals at the 1956 Olympic and 1958 European Games. Ludvik Danek had 47 internationals.

The most women's internationals is 41 by Dana Zatopková during 1946–64, followed by 40 for Olga Davidová and Stěpánka Mertová (nee Richterová).

Denmark

The oldest athletics club, the Kobenhavns Idraets Forenug was formed in 1892. The Danish Sports Federation and the Danish Athletics Federation were formed in 1896 and 1907 respectively.

In 1814 Denmark had been the first country in the world to pass an act of education which made physical education for boys compulsory.

Danish athletes competed in the first Olympic Games in 1896. Their first medallist was Ernst Schultz, third in the 1900 400m, and best placer Henry Petersen, second in the 1920 pole vault. Two Danish athletes have won European titles. The first was Niels Holst Sörensen, first at 400m and second at 800m in 1946. Winner of 18 Danish titles, Holst Sörensen became a member of the IOC in 1977 after a distinguished military career, ending as a Major-General. Dr Jesper Törring won the 1974 European high jump title with his best ever jump of 2.25m/7ft 4½in, after a pre-1974 best of 2.15m. A multi-talented athlete Törring won 23 national titles from 1969 to 1980, six at 110m hurdles, eight at high jump and nine at long jump (1969–77 inclusive). He set 21 national records at: 400m (47.6), 110mh (best 13.7), 200mh (23.4) HJ (2.25m), LJ (7.80m/25ft 7¼in).

Danish championships were first held in 1894. The greatest number of titles is 34 by distance runner Thyge Tögersen from 5000m to marathon between 1951 and 1968.

Karen Inge Halkier won 32 women's titles, including the most at one event, 16 at shot 1956–69, 1971–2. She won the discus in 1957–60, 1962–8 and 1970–1 and the high jump in 1958, and competed in a record 39 internationals. Nina Fahnöe (née Hansen) won

Lasse Viren is tracked by young Finnish fans with their national flag after winning the Olympic 10000m in Munich in 1972. *(A. Huxtable)*

30 titles at 100m, 200m, 80m hurdles, long jump and pentathlon during 1959–68 (as well as several more relay titles) and set more than 40 national records.

Finland

Finland can justifiably claim to have had the greatest athletics success per capita of any nation. With a population of less than five million, there are about 250000 athletes. It is still a major contender in world athletics, even though no longer as dominant as in the golden days of Finnish athletics from 1912 to 1939.

Finland's total number of Olympic athletics medals (102) is bettered only by the USA, USSR and UK and they finished second to the USA in the medals tables at each Games from 1912 to 1936, the best years being in 1920 (16 medals including 9 gold, to 29 medals and 9 golds for USA) and 1924 (17 including 10 gold, to 32 medals and 12 gold for USA). Yet only one Olympic medal has been won by a woman (Kaisa Parviainen second 1948 javelin). Although Finland only gained independence from the USSR in 1917, its national sports federation, Suomen Urheilulitto, was founded in 1907 and Finland first competed at the Olympic Games in 1906 and 1908. Its first medals were won by Werner Järvinen at discus, gold (greek style) and bronze in 1906 and bronze (greek style) in 1908. Six golds were won in 1912, the first by Hannes Kolehmainen at 10000m on 8 July. He was followed by many more great runners in the 1920s and 1930s and the tradition of these men was revived in the 1970s by Pekka Vasala, Juha Väätäinen and Lasse Viren.

Finland has long had great field event traditions, and the javelin is practically a national sport. Overall Finland is by far the leading nation in Olympic history at 5000m, 10000m and javelin.

Medal totals are:

Event	1st	2nd	3rd
Javelin	5	6	4
	(and all three medals at both hands JT 1912		
10000m	7	4	4
5000m	7	5	1

The Finn to have competed at most Olympic Games is Elmer Niklander, with four from 1908 to 1924. In 1920 he won the discus and was second at the shot. The first Finnish championships were held at Tampere in 1907. Women's championships were first held in 1913.

The winner of most individual championships

is Erik Vilen with 28 including the most at one event – 12 at 400mh 1918–20, 1923–8, 1930–32. He also won 7 at 110mh, 6 at 400m, and one each at 100m, 200m and 800m, and a further 19 relay titles. Twelve individual victories at one event was also achieved by Sirkka Norrlund at women's high hurdles from 1961 to 1972 successively (80mh to 1968, then 100mh).

Finnish records
The greatest collection of men's national records is that amassed by the 'Flying Finn', Paavo Nurmi with 35 (33 individual and two relay) ranging in distance from 800m to 20000m. His first was an 8:36.2 for 3000m on 28 May 1920 and his last at 4 × 1500m relay on 27 Jun 1933. Most of these were also world records (see p. 14).

Even Nurmi's total was bettered by Mona-Lisa Pursiainen (née Strandvall) at 39, although her score included 19 relay records (10 at 4 × 100mR and 7 at 4 × 400mR). She set nine at 100m, taking the record from 12.0 to 11.0 (11.19 auto); ten at 200m (24.6 to 22.39) and three at 400m (52.53 to 51.27). Pursiainen also won 24 national titles between 1967 and 1977, while her greatest international success was a sprint double at the 1973 World Student Games.

The most records at one event is 15 at shot by Matti Yrjölä. His first was 16.61m/54ft 6in in 1958. This record was then beaten no less than 11 times by other men before Yrjölä regained it with 18.16m/59ft 7in in 1964. His final record was 20.49m/67ft 2¾in in 1973, although after Reijo Stahlberg became the first Finn to exceed 21m, Yrjölä set his best ever of 20.84m/68ft 4½in in 1976.

The Helsinki Olympic Stadium, originally intended for the 1940 Olympic Games, was completed in 1938. The first athletics meetings were held there in 1939, in which year the first of many world records set on the track came from Taisto Mäki (5000m in 14:08.8, 3 mile in 13:42.4) on 16 Jun.
Major meetings include: 1952 Olympic Games, 1971 European Championships, 1977 European Cup Final. The Stadium will host the first World Championships in 1983.

France
The first athletics meeting in France was held at St Servan, Brittany in September 1866. A runners' club was formed and held its first meeting on 20 Apr 1875 in Paris. The famous Racing Club was formed on 20 Apr 1882, adopting the name of Racing Club de France in 1885.
The first French championships were held at five events in 1888, organised by the Union des Sociétés Françaises des Sports Athlétiques. This body looked after various sports; in 1920 the Fédération Française d'Athlétisme took over sole responsibility for athletics. The first women's championships were held in 1918. Cross-country championships were first held in 1889 for men and in 1919 for women.

The most men's titles won is 32 by Alain Mimoun – 5000m in 1947, 1949, 1951–56; 10000m in 1947, 1949–59; marathon 1958–60, 1964–66; cross-country 1950–52, 1954, 1956, 1959.

The most titles won at one event is 15 by Guy Husson in succession at the hammer 1954–68.

The most women's titles won is 33 by Lucienne Velu – 60m 1934–6; 80m 1927, 1931–3; 200m 1927–30; shot 1928, 1930–5, 1937; discus 1925–30, 1932–7, 1939, 1942. Her 14 discus wins is the women's record for one event.

France's first international match was against Belgium in Brussels on 1 Sep 1912.

The most internationals is 84 for Alain Mimoun, who had 32 victories at 10000m, a record for one event, and 12 at 5000m; 67 for Michel Bernard, 65 for Guy Husson, 62 for Pierre Alard and 61 for Pierre Colnard. The women's record is 48 by Sylvie Telliez.

The most French records have been set by Michel Jazy with 49 between 1959 and 1966. They comprised: 800m–6, 880y–1 1000m–4, 1500m–9, 1 mile–7, 2000m–7, 3000m–3, 2 mile–2, 3 mile–1, 5000m–6, 6 mile–1, 4 × 1500m R–2. He is also the Frenchman to have set most European (17) and most world (9) records. His most hectic spell was when he set five European records in nine days in 1965: *2 Jun* Saint-Maur 1 mile 3:55.5; *6 Jun* Lorient 5000m 13:34.4; *9 Jun* Rennes 1 mile 3:53.6 (world record); *11 Jun* Paris 5000m 13:29.0 (and 3 mile 13:05.6). In all in June 1965 he set nine European records, of which four were also world records. Jazy made 59 international appearances for France, with 38 victories.

The most French women's records set is 19 by Micheline Ostermeyer (SP–10, DT–4, Pen–3, 80mh–1, HJ–1).

The longest lasting record was Jean Bouin's 1 hour run of 19021m (11 mile 1442y) on 6 Jul 1913 in Stockholm. It was a world record for 15 years 93 days, until beaten by Paavo Nurmi, and a French record for 42 years 115 days until Alain Mimoun ran 19078m (11 mile 1503y) in 1955.

The first French Olympic medallist was Alexandre Tuffère, second in the 1896 triple jump and their first gold medallist was Michel Theato, who won the marathon in Paris in 1900. A baker's roundsman, Theato had first-hand knowledge of the route through the streets of Paris and coped with the heat (up to 39° C/102° F).

Alain Mimoun has won most Olympic medals for France with four, second to Zatopek at 10000m in 1948 and 1952 and at 5000m in 1952, before winning the marathon in 1956.

Jules Ladoumègue set a world record at 1500m in the middle of a Rugby match. This was a time of 3:49.2 on 4 Oct 1930 at the Stade Jean Bouin during the game between Racing Club de France and Rugby Club Toulonnais. He also set world records at 1000m in 1930 and at 2000m and ¾ mile in 1931, but was disqualified in 1932 for professionalism.

> When asked why his country seemed unable to produce great athletic teams in the way it produced great wines, Michel Lourie, French national sprint coach, said 'Perhaps it is precisely because of our great wines that we do not produce great track teams'.

Four American athletes won the national titles of France, England (AAA) and USA in the same year, 1974. They were Steve Williams (100m), James Bolding (400mh), Dwight Stones (HJ) and John Powell (DT). Mike Tully (USA) completed the same feat, but in different years, having won the AAA title in 1976, before winning French and American titles in 1977.

Germany

Amateur athletics dates from at least 4 Jun 1862, when English residents at Bonn held a meeting at which a number of titled and distinguished students of the University competed. Early German athletics was stimulated by Englishmen, who formed cricket, soccer and rugby clubs. The first such club to cater for athletics was Arminia Frankfurt/Main, founded in 1876.

The first major meeting took place in Hamburg-Horn on a horse racing track on 6 Jun 1880. On 12 Aug 1888 there was a match between Hamburger Sport Club and South London Harriers. The first specifically athletics club, the Berliner Sportclub, was founded in 1896.

The first German championships were held in Berlin on 23 Aug 1891, when both events were won by Englishmen: Alec Hyman the 100y in 10.6 and J. Swait the 1 mile in 4:34.6. The Deutsche Sportbehörde für Leichtathletik was formed in 1898, and from then annual championships were held until 1943. The first women's championships were held in 1920 at 100m, long jump, shot and 4 × 100m relay: Marie Kiessling won all three individual events and ran on the winning relay team. Following World War II the German Republic recommended holding championships in 1946 and the Eastern Zone, later the German Democratic Republic, staged separate championships from 1948 (see later). In this section the German and West German details are combined.

The most titles won is 36 by Harald Norpoth in 1962–73. He won 27 outdoor: *1500m 3, 5000m 8* in succession 1966–73, *cross-country 7, 3 × 1000m relay 3, 3 × 1500m relay 3, cross-country team 3*; and 9 indoor: *1500m 4, 3 × 1000m relay 5.*

The most titles won by a woman is 31 by Ellen Wessinghage during 1970–81. She won 27 out-

Heide Rosendahl wins the 1972 Olympic long jump title with 6.78m in Munich. *(E. D. Lacey)*

doors, including 8 track and 11 cross-country individual wins, and 4 indoors. 27 were won by Heide Rosendahl during 1966–73. She won 15 outdoor: *100m hurdles* 1, *long jump* 5, *pentathlon* 5, *4 × 100m relay* 4; and 12 indoor: *long jump* 7, *50m hurdles* 1, *relay* 4. Also 27 by Annegret Richter during 1970–80 who won 15 outdoor: *100m* 4, *200m* 5, *4 × 100m relay* 6 and 12 indoor: *50m/60m* 8, *200m* 2, *relay* 2.

The most individual event titles won outdoors is 20 by Gisela Mauermayer at women's events in 1934–42: shot 7, discus 9, pentathlon 3 and sling ball throwing 1. Her nine discus titles in succession shares the record at one event with Karl Hähnel who won the 50km walk nine times between 1922 and 1935 and Ralf Reichenbach who won nine shot titles 1972–5 and 1977–81. Michael Sauer won eight outdoor (1963–5, 1967–71) and ten indoor (1963–72) triple jump titles as well as the 1968 indoor long jump title.

The youngest national champion ever is Hans Müller (born 1899) who won 100m and 200m titles in 1915. He was killed in action in 1918.

The most national records set at one event is 19, including one tie, by Eva Wilms, who took the women's shot record from 17.53m in 1975 to 21.43m/70ft 3¾in two years later. This rapid improvement included four records in one competition at Helsinki on 7 Jun 1975. Wilms also set three pentathlon records, two of which were also world records, for a total of 22 German records. 22 records were also set by Ingrid Mickler (née Becker): 100m 7, 4 × 100mR 6, HJ 3, LJ 4, Pen 2. Hubert Houben set 25 records, but these included 13 times of 10.5 at 100m and one

Manfred Germar (right) beats Dave Sime at 100m in London. This was Sime's return after injury put him out of the US Olympic Trials and was only his second loss in 1956 after twice equalling the world record for 100y at 9.3. *(Associated Press)*

of 10.4, all equalling the record. He also set two at 200m and nine at 4 × 100mR (1922–8). Mickler's records at five events was bettered by Käthe Krauss, whose six events comprised 100m, 200m, 4 × 100m relay, long jump, discus and pentathlon between 1931–7. The prize for **versatility** must however go to Hanns Braun who was killed flying on the Western Front on 9 Oct 1918, shortly before his 32nd birthday. He set records (1907–12) as follows: 100m 10.8; 200m 22.4; 400m 48.3 (2nd 1912 Olympics); 800m 1:53.1; 1500m 4:14.6; 110mh 16.2; 4 × 400mR 3:28.5. A memorial prize was founded in his honour in 1921 and an annual Hanns Braun meeting is held in Munich, his birthplace.

The most improvements on a record in one competition came in Mexico City on 16 Oct 1968 when Klaus Schiprowski won the Olympic silver medal at pole vault. With a previous best of 5.18m three weeks earlier, Schiprowski successively succeeded at 5.20, 5.25, 5.30, 5.35 and 5.40m/17ft 8½in to lose only on countback to Bob Seagren. Truly a case of peaking at the right time for Schiprowski never again bettered 5.21m/17ft 1¼in!

Robert Pasemann set records at high jump 5, pole vault 9 and long jump 3 between 1909–13, with bests of 1.92m/6ft 3¾in, 3.79m/12ft 5¼in and 7.10m/23ft 3½in respectively.

The longest time for a record to stand is 43 years for Hermann Müller's 3km walk performance of 12:37.6 in 1911.

The first German international match was on 4 Sep 1921 against Switzerland in Basle. The first women's matches were held in 1928, against France and Britain.

The most international appearances is 62 by Gerhard Weidner. Weidner, a walker, was aged 32 when he made his first appearance in 1965 and at 47 in 1980 he is the oldest ever German international. He is also the oldest German Olympic athlete – aged 43 years 130 days in 1976 when he was 18th at 20km walk. His highest placing in a major international event was second in the 1975 Lugano Trophy 50km walk. Others to have made more than 50 appearances are: 57 Hein-Direk Neu; 56 Klaus Lehnertz; 54 Manfred Kinder, Michael Sauer; 53 Helmut Janz; 52 Manfred Germar (Germar ran 123 races at the sprints); 51 Liesel Westermann (women's record, 1963–76); 50 Harald Norpoth.

Olympic Games

German athletes took part in the first Games in 1896, when Fritz Hofmann was second at 100m and third at 400m. Surprisingly, however, Germany's first gold did not come until 1928, when Lina Radke won the women's 800m. The first men's gold was won by Hans Wöllke at shot in 1936. Ulrike Meyfarth, high jump winner in 1972, is the youngest ever German Olympian. Also an Olympic champion in 1936 was Karl Hein with the hammer. He competed in German championship finals over a 20-year span (1936–56), winning five times. He set a world record 58.24m in 1938 and in 1964 became the oldest man (age 56) to exceed 50m. In all he bettered 50m in 26 different years.

German Democratic Republic (GDR)

The first official GDR championships were held at Halberstadt on 22/23 Jul 1950, but these had been preceded by Eastern Zone championships in 1948 and 1949. The standard in these early meetings was not particularly good, but with the emphasis on sporting participation and high quality scientific preparation the growth in the GDR's sporting successes in recent years has been phenomenal, especially considering that its population is only about 17 million. In 1980 the governing body the Deutscher Verband für Leichtathletik der DDR had 167,123 athlete members. The GDR has been a member of the IAAF since 1956, in which year its athletes competed for the first time at the Olympic Games. In 1956, 1960 and 1964 there were combined East and West German teams, but from 1968 the GDR and GFR have competed as separate nations. Since 1956 GDR athletes have won 97 medals at the Olympic Games and since 1958, when they first competed, have won 148 medals at the European Championships. The table shows their breakthrough to being firmly established with the USA and USSR as one of the three super-powers of athletics.

The first GDR athlete to win an Olympic medal was Christa Stubnick, second at 100m (and 200m) in 1956. Karin Balzer won the first gold medal in 1964 at 80m hurdles.

The most GDR titles won is 39 by Gisela Birkemeyer (née Kohler): 100m 6, 200m 5, 80mh 9 (a record for successive titles, 1953–61), Pen 5, 4 × 100mR 9, 4 × 200m 5.

The most GDR titles won at one event is 11 by Ruth Fuchs at javelin in 1967, 1970–3, 1975–80. The men's record is nine 800m titles by Manfred Matuschewski, 1959–66 and 1969. Eight titles have been won by Manfred Preussger (PV), Wolfgang Nordwig (PV), Manfred Stolle (JT), Gunhild Hoffmeister (womens 1500m as well as six 800m titles).

The record total of GDR records is 28 set by Siegfried Herrmann. His first was 3:57.0 for 1500m on 3 Jul 1952 and his last 13:30.0 for 5000m on 11 Aug 1965. He set 4 at 800m, 3 at 1000m, 12 at 1500m, 1 at 2000m, 5 at 3000m and 3 at 5000m (including unratified marks).

The greatest number of records at events on the current schedule is 20 by Johanna Lüttge (née Hübner) at women's shot. She took the record from 13.77m/45ft 2¼in in 1955 to 16.70m/54ft 9½in in 1960. The men's record is 18 improvements in the pole vault record by Manfred Preussger, from 4.25m/13ft 11¼in in 1955 to 5.15m/16ft 10¾in in 1964.

The oldest GDR champion and record holder is Max Gebhardt, 46 years and 146 days when he won in 33:10.0 in 1950. Rita Schmidt (later Kirst) is the youngest to have set a record at 16 years 269 days, with a 1.76m/5ft 9¼in high jump on 16 Jul 1967, the first of ten records. She was also GDR champion that year, but the youngest ever champion is Ingrid Zander, 16 years 66 days when she won the 400m in 55.5 in 1967.

OLYMPIC GAMES					EUROPEAN CHAMPIONSHIPS			
Year	Gold	Silver	Bronze		Year	Gold	Silver	Bronze
1956	–	4	–		1958	–	1	4
1960	–	4	3		1962	1	6	1
1964	1	3	–		1966	8	3	6
1968	2	3	1		1969	11	7	7
1972	8	7	5		1971	12	13	7
1976	11	7	9		1974	10	12	5
1980	11	8	10		1978	12	10	11

The GDR's first international match won against Poland in 1951, when they won the women's match but lost the men's. The men's team was usually beaten by Poland for the next 20 years, but since being defeated by both Finland and Poland in 1970, they have been undefeated except by the USSR. The GDR women have an even more impressive record as apart from three defeats by the USSR in the 1970s and two by the Russian SFSR in the 1960s one must go back to 1958 for their last defeat (by Poland).

The most internationals is 55 by Karin Balzer 1955–72. Balzer shares with walker Hans-Georg Reimann the distinction of having competed at four Olympic Games, and both share the GDR record of four European Championships appearances with six others. Siegfried Herrmann competed in 41 internationals between 1952 and 1966, the men's GDR record.

The GDR constitution was promulgated on 9 Apr 1968. Its article 18 guarantees the right of GDR citizens to take part in sport, the first nation so to do. Article 25 includes the statement that 'state and society encourage participation of the citizens in cultural life, physical culture and sport'.

Greece
The host nation for the first Olympic Games, Greece, has been represented at every subsequent Games at men's events. Their first female representation was in 1936. Spyridon Louis won the 1896 marathon and became a national hero, but the only subsequent Greek champion has been Constantis Tsiklitiras at standing long jump in 1912.

National championships were first held in 1895, and the first club was formed in 1886.

The George Karaiskakis Stadium in Athens was built for the 1969 European Championships and further improved for their return in 1982.

Three Greek athletes have won European medals, the best being Christos Papanikolaou's pole vault second place in 1966.

Hungary
The oldest club is the Magyar Athletikai Club, founded in 1883. The national federation was formed in Budapest on 21 Mar 1897.

The first national championships were held in Budapest on 11 Oct 1896 at 100y and 1 mile,

but a full programme of events was not instituted until 1903. Women's events were first held in 1932.

The most titles won at one event is 20 by Jozsef Várszegi at javelin 1932–43 and 1945–52. Two years later Várszegi made his final international appearance, Hungary's oldest athlete at 44 years.

The most women's titles won is 24 by Olga Gyarmati between 1941 and 1956 (100m 3, 200m 2, 80mh 7, HJ 2, LJ 8, Pen 2).

The most national records is 24 by Olga Gyarmati, at a total of six events, and by Judit Bognár, with three at discus and 21 at shot, the most at any event. Bognár took the record from 14.36m in 1957 to 18.23m in 1972.

The most men's records set at one event is 17 by Vilmos Varju, who improved the shot best from 16.63m in 1958 to 20.45m in 1971. Varju also won 13 national titles, being placed in the first three for 18 consecutive years, 1957–74. This was one better than Gyula Zsivotzky's 17 at the hammer 1956–72, but Zsivotzky won a record 13 successive titles, 1958–70.

Laszlo Tabori leads Sandor Iharos at 2 miles at White City. Iharos won in 8:33.4, one of seven world records he set in 1955. *(H. W. Neale)*

The youngest champion and international is Vera Neszmelyi, aged 15, when she was fifth in the European 100m in 1954.

Hungary's first Olympic participation was in 1896, and their first gold medallist was Rudolf Bauer in the 1900 discus.

The most international appearances have been made by Gergely Kulcsar with 56 at javelin 1955–72. The women's record is 36 by Maria Feher at shot 1947–58.

The Nepstadion in Budapest, opened in 1953, has a capacity of about 100000. It staged the 1965 World Student Games and 1966 European Championships.

Iceland

Iceland's one Olympic medallist is Vilhjalmur Einarsson, second at triple jump in 1956. Three European gold medals have been won: Gunnar Huseby (SP) 1946 and 1950 and Torfi Bryngeirsson (LJ) 1950. Huseby had a perennial drinking 'problem'. He disappeared for a while after his first win, reappeared, but after improving his national record to 16.41m in 1949 celebrated too heavily and was banned. He was reinstated in time to take his second European win in 1950, but in 1951 was again in trouble for his part in a violent robbery. However he continued to compete occasionally and topped the Icelandic rankings in 1962, 22 years after he had first done so.

Icelandic championships were first held in 1927.

The youngest champion is Stefan Th. Stefansson aged 14 in 1977, at high jump.

The oldest champion is Valbjörn Thorlaksson who won the 110m hurdles at age 46 in 1980. Thorlaksson had won his first Icelandic title at pole vault in 1955.

Iceland's first international victory was a 108–90 defeat of Denmark in 1950. They were first represented at the Olympic Games in 1912.

Ireland

Irish athletes played a notable part in the early days of athletics, with their field event men in particular, dominating the AAA championships in the 1880s and 1890s.

There had been races at Trinity College, Dublin and from 1857 and in 1873 the first inter-varsity championships and first national championships (knows as 'Tests') were staged. The Irish AAA was founded on 24 Feb 1885, a year after the Gaelic Athletics Federation.

Thomas Kiely won seven Gaelic AA titles on one day, 10 Sep 1892, the long jump, 120y hurdles, hammer, shot at 16lb, 7lb and 28lb and finally the triple jump! In all he was credited with 53 Irish titles, including 18 at the hammer. He set world records at the hammer and 56lb weight, but was past his best when he won the American all-around titles in 1904 and 1906, the former of which also counted as the Olympic title. Kiely was the first Irishman to win an Olympic title, and was followed by Con Leahy (high jump, at which his elder brother Patrick had been placed second in 1900), Peter O'Connor (TJ) in 1906 and Timothy Ahearne (TJ) in 1908.

The above medals however were won when Ireland was part of Britain, so the first Olympic gold medallist to represent Ireland was Dr Patrick O'Callaghan, winner of the hammer in 1928. Four years later he successfully defended his title, but only came through in the final round with 53.92m/176ft 11in to overtake Ville Pörhölä (Fin). His problem was that he only had a pair of shoes with long spikes which hindered his ability to turn in the circle. He filed away at them throughout the competition until at the end only manageable stumps were left.

The longest standing national record for any nation is Peter O'Connor's long jump of 7.61m/24ft 11¾in at Ballsbridge, Dublin on 5 Aug 1901, still an Irish record at the time of going to press. This, O'Connor's fifth improvement on the world's best within a year, was apparently made from a board runway, but was recognised as the first official world record by the IAAF in 1913 and was unbeaten until 1921. Although not recognised as either a World or Irish record as he knocked over a hurdle (contrary to the rules then in force for records), Robert Tisdall's 51.66 time when he won the 1932 Olympic hurdles title has also not yet been surpassed by an Irish athlete.

The first known competition in Ireland by women was in 1891 but events were few and far between for more than 50 years, and it was not until 1965 that national titles were first contested, although over the border the Northern Ireland WAAA had staged championships since 1950. The first All-Ireland women's international match was against Belgium in 1963.

Robert Tisdall gives an exhibition of hurdling at Croke Park, Dublin in 1932 after his Olympic victory in only his sixth 400m/440yh race.
(BBC Hulton)

The current governing body for athletics in Ireland, the Bord Lúthchleas Na hÉireann (BLE) was formed in 1967.

The most BLE women's titles won is 15 by Claire Walsh in 1968–73 (4 at 100m, 6 at 200m, 4 at 400m and 1 at Pen), and by Ann O'Brien in 1967–71 (1 at 440y, 4 at 800m/880y, 5 at 1500m/1 mile, 1 high jump and 4 cross-country).

Maeve Kyle born 6 Oct 1928 won a record 41 titles at all the Irish and Northern Irish championships between 1955 and 1975. She would undoubtedly have won many more if there had been organised athletics in her younger days, for her greatest successes in athletics came in her 30s, and she continued to grace the sport with outstanding success into her 40s and 50s, smashing dozens of world age bests, well after she had retired from hockey at which she won a record 58 Irish caps. She competed in the Olympic Games of 1956 (the first Irish woman), 1960 and 1964, was placed sixth at 400m in the 1962 European championships and won a bronze medal at 400m in the 1966 European Indoor Games.

Italy

The first Italian national body, the 'Union Podistica Italiana' was formed in 1896. This was succeeded in 1906 by the Federazione Podistica Italiana, and the current governing body, the Federazione Italiana Di Atletica Leggera (FIDAL) was constituted in 1926.

National championships were first held in Milan in 1906 for men and in Bologna in 1927 for women. The walker Abdon Pamich has won most titles with 40 in all: 14 consecutive 10km track walk wins 1956–69, 12 consecutive 20km road walk wins 1958–69, 14 consecutive 50km road walk wins 1955–68. Pamich, born at Fiume, now in Yugoslavia, also holds Italian records for having competed in the most European Championships (6) and Olympic Games (5).

The most titles won at an event is by Angiolo Profeti at shot (1938–42, 1945–54) and 15 by Adolfo Consolini at discus (1939, 1941–2, 1945, 1949–50, 1952–60).

The winners of the most track and field titles are Donata Govoni with 19 between 1961 and 1975: 7 at women's 100m, 7 at 400m, 5 at 200m; and Claudia Testoni with 19 in 1932–40: 7 at women's LJ, 5 at 80mh, 3 at 100m, 2 at 200m, 1 each at 60m, 80m.

The first Italian international match was against Czechoslovakia in Prague on 30 May 1925. The Czechs won 74–55. The first women's match was a loss 24–56 to France in Milan on 11 Sep 1927.

The most international appearances is 65 by Vittorio Visini (walks) 1965–80. 52 by Sergio Liani 1965–79, 50 by Adolfo Consolini 1938–60. Women: 50 by Sara Simeoni 1970–80, 49 by Donata Govoni 1961–75.

The most Italian records set at one event is 21 by Sara Simeoni at high jump, 17 improvements in height and four equalling jumps. Her first record was 1.71m/5ft 7¼in on 9 May 1970 at Padua, and her final two were both world records at 2.01m/6ft 7in on 4 Aug and 31 Aug 1978, the latter when winning the European title in Prague.

The most Italian records in total is 23 by Eddy Ottoz. He set 19 at 110m hurdles, including 4 improvements, and 4 at 200m hurdles. Ottoz,

Sara Simeoni displays the gold medal she won at the 1980 Olympics. The Italian national anthem was not played in Moscow but Italians sang it from the stands. *(G. Herringshaw)*

1966 European champion and 1968 Olympic bronze medallist, took the 110m hurdles from 13.9 in 1964 to 13.4 in 1968 (13.46 auto). Renato Dionisi set 18 pole vault records, with perhaps surprisingly only one tied mark in taking the record from 4.50m/14ft 9in in 1964 to 5.45m/17ft 10¾in in 1972.

The first Italian Olympic representation was in 1900. Italy's first medallist was Emilio Lunghi, second in the 1908 1500m, and the first gold medals were the pair won by walker Ugo Frigerio first at 10000m and then 3000m in 1920. Frigerio added a third gold at 10000m in 1924 and won a bronze medal at 50km in 1932.

The first woman Olympic medallist was Trebisonda Valla, winner at 80m hurdles in 1936.

Adolfo Consolini was unbeaten by a European discus thrower from his loss to Giuseppe Tosi in the Italian championships on 29 Sep 1951 until 25 Jun 1955 in Moscow when Consolini's 52.90 was 26cm behind Otto Grigalka (USSR). Despite missing opportunities due to the war, Consolini competed at four Olympic Games

winning gold and silver medals, and five European Championships, winning three golds. He set four world discus records, all at Milan between 1941–8. His first important title was the AAA discus in 1938.

Liechtenstein

The only Liechtenstein athlete to have made a European final is Oscar Ospelt, 15th and 8th at discus and javelin in 1938. He also has the distinction of still holding national records at those events, the third and fourth longest lasting national records for a European country.

The first Olympic participation by Liechtenstein and the formation of their national federation was in 1936.

Luxembourg

The most famous Luxembourg athlete is undoubtedly Josy Barthel, the unexpected winner of the 1952 Olympic 1500m. Coached by Woldemar Gerschler, Barthel had set his first national records in 1946. By June 1952 he had improved to 3:48.5, but took 3.4sec off that time in the Olympic final. In recent years he has been a Cabinet Minister in the Luxembourg government.

The national long jump record still stands to François Mersch at 7.44m in 1938, one of the very few national records for any country to have been set more than 40 years ago.

The first Olympic participation by Luxembourg was in 1912 and the national federation was formed in 1909. The first athletics club was the Racing Club de Luxembourg, which was founded in 1906. National championships were first held in 1910.

Netherlands

The first athletics meetings were staged by Amsterdamer SC in 1886. The Nederlandsche Athletiek-Bond was formed in 1896 and was followed in 1901 by the founding of the present governing body, the Nederlandsche Athletiek-Unie.

The first national championships were held in 1910, and the first women's championship, at 80m, was held in 1921.

The most national titles by any women athlete for any nation is Fanny Blankers-Koen's 58 Dutch titles, won between 1936 and 1955. By event her list comprises: 100m (13) 1937–40,

1942–4, 1946–9, 1951–2; 200m (12) 1936–40, 1944, 1946–8, 1950–2; 80mh (11) 1940, 1944, 1946–54; HJ (10) 1936–7, 1939–40, 1946–51; LJ (9) 1939–40, 1942, 1944, 1946–8, 1950–1; SP (2) 1947, 1955; Pen (1) 1937.

Born Francina Koen on 26 Apr 1918 in Baarn in central Holland, Fanny set her first national record at 800m on 22 Sep 1935 with a 2:29.0. She married her coach, Jan Blankers, who had won the 1931 and 1933 AAA triple jump titles, and gave birth to her first son in 1942. At the time she held seven Dutch records, but went on to greater fame, for later that year she set the first of her 12 world records, 11.3 in Amsterdam on 20 Sep 1942 in only her second major hurdle race!

In 1943 she added world records at 100m (11.5, but unrecognised by the IAAF as she raced against men), high jump (1.71m/5ft 7¼in) and long jump (6.25m/20ft 6in). She gave birth to a daughter in 1945 and the following year won the European 80m hurdles title, with a second gold on the Dutch sprint relay team and was fourth at high jump, to add to the two bronze medals (100m and 200m) she had won in 1938.

In 1948 she was the great star at the Olympic Games, collecting four gold medals (100m, 200m, 80mh and 4 × 100m R), running and winning 11 races in total – all this while pregnant which meant that she passed the opportunity of competing at high or long jumps for which she still held the world records.

In 1950 she added three more golds at the European Championships, 100m, 200m and 80m hurdles and a silver at 4 × 100m relay.

Fanny Blankers-Koen (right) wins the first of her four golds at the 1948 Olympics – the 100m, with Dorothy Manley (GB – 691) second, and Shirley Strickland (Aus – 668) third. *(BBC Hulton)*

Unfortunately at her final major event, the 1952 Olympic Games, she was troubled by boils, although she made the final of the 80m hurdles. She closed her career at the age of 37 in 1955 with the national shot title. In the early 1950s she held 12 out of 15 recognised national records including *all* the running events! Her bests at these events were: 60m–7.5 in 1938; 100y–10.8 in 1944; 100m–11.5 in 1948 and 1952; 200m–23.9 in 1952; 220y–24.2 in 1950; 800m–2:29.0 in 1935; 80mh–11.0 in 1948; HJ–1.71m in 1943; LJ–6.25m in 1943; both 4 × 100m and 4 × 200m relay teams; Pen–4692 points in 1951. She had set world records at: 100m, 100y, 220y, 80mh, 4 × 110y R, 4 × 200m R, HJ, LJ and Pen.

The first Dutch team at the Olympic Games was in 1908. Their first medals were won by the 1924 men's 4 × 100m relay team (third). Blankers-Koen has won the only gold medals.

The greatest domination of the Dutch men's records was that of Jos Hermens, who in the 1970s held all the distance running records from 2000m to 1 hour. In 1975 he set ten records in 14 races, including world records at 10 mile, 20km and 1 hour, bettering the latter two in 1976. In all from 1971–8 he set 31 national records.

Norway

The national federation (Norsk Idraetsforbund, since 1928 Norges Fri-idrettsforbund) was formed on 1 May 1896, in which year the first Norwegian championships were held in Oslo. In 1897 Norway became the first nation to hold a national marathon championship. Women's championships were first held in 1947. In 1980 there were 1204 clubs with 112553 members affiliated to the federation. The first Norwegian

Olympic participation was in 1900 and their first gold medal was won by Ferdinand Bie at the pentathlon in 1912.

The most national records at one event is 21 by hammer-thrower Sverre Strandli, who improved the record from 50.82m/166ft 9in in 1949 to 63.88m/209ft 7in in 1962. He set world records at 61.25m in 1952 and 62.36m in 1953.

The most records overall is 39 individual and 5 relay by Berit Berthelsen (née Toien), the European Indoor long jump champion 1967–8. She set records at: 100m 3, 200m 3, 400m 8, 100mh 2, LJ 19, Pen 4.

Bjørn Bang Andersen set 17 shot records, taking it from 16.34m/53ft 7½in in 1961 to 19.29m/63ft 3½in in 1972 and continued to rank in Norway's top two at the event until 1981. He has appeared in most internationals, 89, and this is the greatest number by any athlete in the world.

Charles Hoff has the most remarkable collection with records at 200m, 400m, 800m and long jump as well as his speciality, the pole vault. At the latter event he set four IAAF world records in 1922–5 culminating in 4.25m/13ft 11¼in. In a tour of the USA in 1926 he improved the indoor pole vault world best 12 times and also excelled at sprints and long jumping. However on 8 May 1926 he was barred by the AAU for professionalism. A pioneer of the 'fly-away' style, he vaulted 14ft several times as a professional.

Hoff would have been the clear favourite for the 1924 Olympic pole vault title, but an ankle injury prevented him from competing. However he was able to run, and undaunted by his misfortune made the 800m final, being placed eighth, and narrowly failed to make a second final with fourth place in his 400m semi-final. He returned as a reinstated amateur to win the Norwegian pole vault title in 1933, but after the war was convicted for high treason as a collaborator with the occupying Nazis.

National championships
The most titles won is 20 by Martin Stokken 1946–53 (5000m 4, 10000m 6, 3000m steeplechase 4, cross-country 6). The most titles won by a woman is 34 by Berit Berthelsen during 1962–74 (100m 5, 200m 8, 400m 4, 80mh 1, LJ 11, Pen 1, cross-country 4).

The most titles won at one event is 12 by Bjørn Bang Andersen at the shot between 1961–74.

The longest time span between winning championship medals is 33 years by Erling Wage with third places at standing long jump in 1913 and hammer in 1946. He became one of the world's biggest shipowners.

The Bislett Stadium, Oslo was opened on 8 Oct 1922 and used for the 1946 European Championships. The first world record set on the track was Adriaan Paulen's 63.8 for 500m in 1924 and the total reached 39 (31 on the current schedule) with Sebastian Coe's 2:12.18 for 1000m in 1981. Included in this number are many of the most significant performances in athletics history, including: Jack Torrance 17.40m SP, Forrest Towns 13.7 110mh, Roger Moens 1:45.7 800m, Terje Pedersen 91.72m JT, Ron Clarke 27:39.4 10000m, John Walker 4:51.4 2000m, Henry Rono 7:32.1 3000m and most recently four world records by Sebastian Coe and two by Steve Ovett.

Capacity crowds of about 22500 attend the annual Bislett Games.

Poland

The Polish athletics federation – Polski Zwiazek Lekkiej Atletyki (PZLA) was founded in Cracow on 11 Oct 1919, exactly one month before Poland achieved independence!

The first national championships for men were held in July 1920 in Lvov and women's events were first contested in October 1922 in Warsaw. Poland was first represented at the Olympic Games in 1924, but the first Pole to compete was Wladyslaw Ponowski who competed for Austria at 400m in 1912.

Poland's first Olympic gold medallist was Halina Konopacka in the 1928 women's discus and Poland has risen to become a major athletics power for the past twenty-five years.

Two names dominate Poland's list of record holders – Irena Szewinska and Janusz Sidlo the only Polish athletes to compete at five Olympic Games and their main achievements are detailed separately (see pp. 188–9) – but others include:

The most national titles won at all events is 27 by Stefan Kostrzewski between 1923 and 1937 at events ranging from 4 × 100m relay to 5000m, including seven at 400m hurdles.

Janusz Kusociński was the first Polish male athlete to win an Olympic gold medal, with the 10000m in 1932 when he led from the start and held off the challenge of Volmari Iso-Hollo

Janusz Kusocinski, the 1932 Olympic 10000m champion. He was killed in World War II and an annual meeting is held in his honour.

(Fin) to clock the second fastest time ever of 30:11.4. Earlier that year he set the first world record by a Polish man with 3000m in 8:18.8 and in all set 23 Polish records (more than any other man) from a 15:41.0 5000m in 1928 to 14:24.2 in 1939. He demonstrated his versatility with a Polish championship win at 800m in 1:56.6 in 1932. A great patriot, he was shot by the Gestapo on 21 Jun 1940 for refusing to betray his colleagues, members of the Resistance.

Jadwiga Wajs-Marcinkiewicz won ten women's discus titles, 1932–7 and 1945–8. She has been Poland's oldest woman national champion and Olympian (age 36 when fourth in 1948) and at 37 the oldest international a year later.

Wladyslaw Komar is the oldest international. He was 39 on his final appearance in 1979 and 38 when he won his final national title. Surprise Olympic shot champion in 1972, he had a long, successful but stormy career. Stories about him are legion and he had many brushes with authority, including suspension for excess drinking and on two occasions following incidents in which people died. He is now famed as a night-club singer.

Komar's mother, Wanda Jasienska was Polish shot record holder and four times champion and his father was a Latvian high jump champion. Before concentrating on shot putting he showed his all-round ability by setting a national decathlon record of 6813 points in 1963.

The greatest number of national records set at one event is 18 by hammer thrower Tadeusz Rut from 56.04m/183ft 10in in 1954 to 67.04m/219ft 11in in 1964 and Jaroslawa Jóźwiakowska-Bieda holds the women's record with 15 successive high jump records from 1.62m/5ft 3¾in in 1958 to 1.75m/5ft 8¾in in 1958.

The youngest international is Anna Cieślewicz at 14 (women's shot in 1947), and youngest national champion and Olympic competitor is Gertruda Kilos at 16 (800m in 1928). Jacek Wszola was 17 years 200 days when he became the youngest men's champion, at high jump in 1974. He also became Poland's youngest male international that year and went on to win the 1976 Olympic title at the age of 19. Gertruda Kilos is the youngest record holder, aged 15 in 1927 when she set her first 800m record.

IRENA SZEWINSKA

Irena Szewinska has won more major titles than any other athlete in the history of the sport. But all the myriad statistics that one can attribute to her can only begin to trace her greatness, for she has graced the tracks of the world over two decades as truly the 'Queen of the sport'. Her career as a top class athlete started in 1964, when at the age of 18 she won a gold and two silver medals at the Tokyo Olympic Games following a double triumph at the European Junior Games. Perhaps the summit of her career came in Dusseldorf in 1977 when, as captain, she stepped forward to receive the Cup for the winning Europe team at the first World Cup. In that competition she had won both 200m and 400m, sweeping to victory in the latter over the 11-year younger Marita Koch. Koch went on to supremacy at women's 400m running but even though Szewinska had to yield to a new generation she continued to demonstrate those qualities of modesty and ability that set a standard for all to follow.

Summary of achievements

Born on 24 May 1946 in Leningrad, USSR, as Irena Kirszenstein, she began her athletics career at school in Warsaw at the age of 14. She married her coach Janusz Szewinski (a 53.4 400m hurdler) on 25 Dec 1967 and gave birth to a son Andrzej in 1970.

World Junior Records

200m: 23.5 19 Sep 1964, 23.13 19 Oct 1964; LJ: 6.39m 6 Sep 1964, 6.39m 13 Sep 1964, 6.60m/21ft 7¾in 14 Oct 1964.

World records

100m: 11.1 9 Jul 1965, 11.1 14 Oct 1968; 200m: 22.7 8 Aug 1965, 22.7* 1 Jul 1967, 22.58 18 Oct 1968, 22.21 (22.0 hand timed) 13 Jun 1974; 400m: 49.9 22 Jun 1974, 49.75 22 Jun 1976, 49.29 29 Jul 1976.
*= unratified.

World bests at other distances:

60m (indoors): 7.1 10 Feb 1974; 300m: 35.7 22 Jun 1974.

Olympic Games: 1st–3, 2nd–2, 3rd–2 (equal most medals ever – see p. 83).

Irena Szewinska won more major titles than any other athlete in the history of the sport in a brilliant 17-year career. *(M. Shearman)*

European Championships: 1st–5, 2nd–1, 3rd–4 (a record ten medals – see p. 151 for full list).
European Junior Games: 1964 – 1st 200m, 1st LJ.
European Indoor Championships: 1969 – 1st 60m and LJ; 1971 – 2nd LJ; 1974 – 3rd 60m; 1975 – 3rd 60m.
World Cup: 1977 – 1st 200m and 400m, 2nd 4 × 400m R; 1979 – 3rd 400m, 4th 4 × 400m R.
European Cup Final: 1st–5, 2nd–2, 3rd–3, 4th–2, 5th–1, 6th–2 (see p. 164 for full list).
World Student Games: 1965 – 1st 100m and 200m.

Irena Szewinska has set more Polish records (38), made more international appearances (48 from 1963–80) and won more national titles than any other Polish woman. Her Polish titles include 100m – 1966–8, 1972–4, 1979; 200m – 1966, 1968, 1971–5, 1979; 400m – 1978; LJ – 1965, 1971–2.

Janusz Sidlo ranked in the world's top ten javelin throwers each year from 1953 to 1970. On 2 Oct 1953 he set his first national record, sensationally improving that by 6.88m to 80.15m/262ft 11in, also a European record. On 30 Jun 1956 he set a world record at 83.66m/274ft 5in, and his final national record came 17 years after his first, with 86.22m/282ft 10in in 1970. Sidlo competed in five Olympic Games (1952–68) and five European Championships (1954–69) (see pp. 100 and 153). He appeared in a record 61 internationals for Poland between 1951 and 1970 and won a record 14 national titles at one event.

Stanislawa Walasiewicz held all the recognised Polish running records as well as those for long jump and pentathlon from the late 1930s to the early 1950s. Her bests: 60m 7.3, 80m 9.6, 100m 11.6, 200m 23.6, 800m 2:18.4, 1000m 3:02.5, 80mh 12.2, LJ 6.04m, Pen 369 pts.
She was also on the 4 × 100m R and 4 × 200m R record teams. She won a total of 16 Polish titles between 1934–47 (100m–4, 200m–4, 80mh–2, LJ–2, JT–1, Pen–3), which if added to her 41 AAU titles in the USA gives her a total of 57 national titles, just one behind Fanny Blankers-Koen's all-time record for a woman. She competed in just seven internationals for Poland, but at 33 events.

Portugal

The first recorded athletics meeting was in Oporto in 1869, but the national federation was not formed until 1921.

National championships were first held in 1910 for men and 1937 for women. A record 42 titles were won by Georgette Duarte between 1946 and 1968 (60m 1, 100m 8, 150m 2, 200m 4, 80mh 11, HJ 3, LJ 9, Pen 4). Manuel Silva won a record 29 men's titles between 1941 and 1958 (SP 9, DT 12, HT 8).

Portugal's first Olympic participation was in 1912, and their only athletes to have won medals at major championships have been Carlos Lopes, second in the 1976 Olympic 10000m and winner of the 1976 world cross-country (he was also second in 1977), and Fernando Mamede, third in the 1981 world cross-country event before he went on to set a European record (27:27.7) for 10000m.

Romania

The national federation was founded in 1912 and Romanian athletes first participated in the Olympic Games in 1928.

The first Romanian championships were held in 1921 (men) and 1925 (women). The first men's international was a loss to Yugoslavia in 1922 and the first women's a loss to Hungary in 1932.

Iolanda Balas won Romania's first European (1954) and Olympic (1956) medals, winning two titles at each. She established the greatest domination of her event of any athlete in history. On a domestic front she won 16 successive high jump titles from her first at the age of 14 in 1951, to 1966. This feat was, however exceeded by Anna Salagean, who won 17 successive women's shot titles 1954–70, before being placed second in 1971 and 1972.

The greatest number of national titles won is 50 by Cristea Dinu from 1935 until 1958, when he won the marathon at the age of 47.
   Lia Manoliu competed in a record six Olympic Games (see p. 84), and won 13 national discus titles between 1952 and 1970.

The only Romanian man to win an Olympic medal is Gheorghe Megelea, third at javelin in 1976, after which he sought political asylum in Canada, as in previous years had his teammates Csaba Dosza, second in the European high jump 1971 and Carmen Ionescu, who won the 1978 Commonwealth women's discus title for her new country in 1978. Megelea is now not listed by Romania amongst their Olympic medallists!

The first Romanian to win a European medal was Zoltan Vamos. He had been placed fifth at 1500m at the 1960 Olympics, but made his steeplechase debut with a national record 8:41.2 on 12 Aug 1962. His second 3000m steeplechase was in a heat and his third was in the final of the European Championships, when he was placed second in 8:37.6 to Gaston Roelants, just 35 days after his first race at the event.

The '23rd August' stadium in Bucharest has a capacity of about 74000 and staged the 1981 World Student Games.

Spain

The first Spanish Championships were held in San Sebastian in 1917 as Spain made quite a late start in athletics. Women's championships were first held in 1931. Spanish athletes first competed in the Olympic Games in 1920 in which year the Spanish athletes federation was formed, but it was not until 1964 that they had their first finalist, Luis Filipe Areta sixth at long jump. Areta made 16 improvements (and one tie) to the Spanish triple jump record, the most at any event, taking it from 14.54m/47ft 8¼in in 1959 to 16.36m/53ft 8¼in in 1968, and also set four long jump records. Mariano Haro has been Spain's most successful Olympian, with fourth and sixth places at 10000m in 1972 and 1976 respectively. He has also won most Spanish cross-country titles with 11 between 1962 and 1977. The first cross-country championships for men were held in 1916 and for women in 1965.

Spain's first medallist at major championships was Jorge Llopart, winner of the 50km walk at the 1978 European Championships.

The most national records by one athlete is 25 by Ana Maria Molina, with 13 at shot, ten at pentathlon and two at 80m hurdles between 1967 and 1974.

The most national titles at one event is 13 in the javelin by Pedro Apellaniz from 1944 to 1958, missing out only in 1949 and 1956.

The most titles overall is 18 by Felix Errauzquin with nine each at shot and discus between 1932 and 1949. Errauzquin pioneered the 'Spanish Style' of javelin throwing, whereby the javelin was thrown discus fashion, and reached 74.32m/243ft 10in on 7 Oct 1956, at the age of 49. Reports of 90m/300ft throws with this very dangerous style were heard, but the IAAF banned it in 1957, ruling that the thrower could not turn his back on the direction of the throw. On 10 Aug 1957 Marjorie Larney (USA) had a competition throw in Cleveland of 57.20m/187ft 8in using the 'Spanish Style', well in excess of the then women's record. Errauzquin had got the idea from the Basque sport of throwing the 'Barra', a 3.5kg metal bar.

Spain's first international match was a 51–30 victory over Portugal on 24/25 Oct 1925 in Madrid.

Felix Errauzquin throws by greasing his hand with water and letting the javelin slide through it after rotating. *(Associated Press)*

Sweden

The national federation, Svenska Idrottsförbundet, was formed on 30 Oct 1895, and the name changed to Svenska Fri-idrottsförbundet in 1949. A separate women's federation existed between 1925 and 1927, but subsequently there has been just the one federation, except for a different body to administer walking.

National championships were first held for men in 1896 and for women in 1927.

Erik Lemming, Sweden's first Olympic gold medallist, has won the most individual titles – 25 between 1899 and 1917 (JT 10, SP 6, HT 5, DT 3, PV 1). He was fourth in the 1900 Olympic pole vault before going on to a hat-trick of javelin titles (see p. 100), but missed the opportunity to add to his collection in 1904 as this is the only Olympic Games at which Sweden has not been represented.

Lennart Strandberg won 23 individual titles (100m–11 and 200m–12 in succession 1934–45), and also won 16 relay titles, 13 at 4 × 100m R and 3 at 4 × 400m R, for a record grand total of 39 Swedish titles.

Ruth Svedberg won 23 individual titles for the women's record. Her six discus wins included both the first ever championship in 1927 and a victory in 1949 at the age of 46, the oldest ever Swedish champion.

The most titles at one event is 16 at the old Swedish event of slingball by Majken Aberg, successively 1937–52. Birger Asplund won 15 successive hammer titles 1954–68. He also holds the record for the most national records at 17 from 57.19m in 1955 to 66.37m/217ft 9in in 1964. Ingrid Almqvist won 15 women's javelin titles between 1947 and 1964 and set 16 national records at the event (the most by a woman) with a best of 52.32m/171ft 8in in 1964.

The oldest male champion is Erik Östbye who was 44 years 259 days when he won the marathon in 1965.

The youngest Swedish champion has been Ann-Louise Skoglund who was 12 years 345 days when she ran on the winning 4 × 400m relay team in 1975. Her first individual title came soon after her 16th birthday in 1978 when she set a world junior record of 57.57 for 400m hurdles. She improved this record to 56.68 in 1980.

Sweden's first international match was a win against Belgium in Brussels in 1913.

The men's record for international appearances is held by Birger Asplund with 74, while the women's is 45 (including 10 indoors) by Linda Haglund, European 100m silver medallist in 1978 and European Indoor 60m champion in 1976.

The youngest Swedish international is Siv Thuresson, aged 12¾ years when she competed at the Postal Walk International in 1969. The youngest man is Christer Gullstrand at 16 years 171 days in 1975.

The record attendance at an athletics meeting in Sweden is 35069 at Ullevi stadium, Göteborg on 28 Aug 1958 when the star attraction was the 1500m. Herb Elliott won the race in 3:36.0 to take 2.1sec off the world record. Behind him the third, fourth and sixth fastest times ever to that date were clocked by Stanislav Jungwirth 3:39.0, Murray Halberg 3:39.4 and István Rózsavölgyi 3:40.0 with the Swedish star Dan Waern fifth in 3:40.9.

Waern reached the peak of his fame in 1959 when in a nine-week period from 26 July to 30 September he ran 36 races from 800m to 3000m, winning 32, being placed second four times and setting seven Swedish records and two world 1000m records (2:18.0 and 2:17.8). After a fourth place in the 1960 Olympic 1500m, Waern was suspended by the IAAF in 1961 for excessive expenses following a tax assessment board demand for £16000 income tax. The Swedish federation had originally only cautioned him and this was only the second time that the IAAF had acted on its own initiative in suspending an athlete for 'professionalism', the first being Nurmi in 1932. In other cases, such as Waern's famous Swedish predecessors Hägg and Andersson (see p. 26) the national federation had acted first. Waern's final race had been a 3:58.9 mile in Stockholm on 1 Sep 1961 in which he had run the final lap in 51.9, the fastest ever in a sub-four-minute-mile.

The Olympic stadium, Stockholm, purpose built for the Olympic Games, was first used in May 1912. The track was designed and prepared by Charles Perry, London AC groundsman, who had also laid out the tracks at Athens in 1906 and the White City, London in 1908. As well as the 1912 Olympics it was also used for the 1958 European Championships. Originally 385m to a lap it was enlarged to 400m in 1958. From 1912 to date there have been more world records set there than at any other stadium in the world. To the end of 1981 there have been 52 world records (50 men's, 2 women's) at current events and a further 14 at events previously on the schedule.

Switzerland

The first Swiss governing body was the 'Commission des Courses à pied et des Sports athlétiques'. Its German name 'Athletischer Ausschuss des Schweizerischen Fussball-Verbandes' shows its footballing connections.

The first recorded athletics meeting was that staged by English students in Lausanne on 13 Apr 1872.

The first Swiss championships for men were held in 1906 and for women in 1934. However a so-called women's championships had been held in 1929, but only ten athletes, all from one club, Stade Lausanne, had competed.

Urs Von Wartburg won 22 javelin titles, probably the greatest number of national titles at one event by any athlete. Born on 1 Mar 1937 he won his first title in 1957 and from then until 1980 his winning run was interrupted by second places only in 1968 and 1977. He also won three pentathlon and one decathlon title. Von Wartburg turned 40 in 1977 and, finding a new forum for his talents, has so far won three titles at the biennial World Masters Championships.

Three women have won more than 30 Swiss titles each: Gretel Bolliger 41 in 1938–58 (SP 14, DT 13, Pen 6, 80mh 3, LJ 3, HJ 2); Fry Frischknecht 34 in 1957–68 (SP 10, JT 9, 80mh 4, LJ 4, DT 4, Pen 3); Meta Antenen 32 in 1964–76 (LJ 7, Pen 7, 100m 5, 100mh 5, 80mh 3, HJ 2, 4 × 100mR 3).

Antenen was much the most successful internationally. She won European Junior titles at 80m hurdles and pentathlon in 1966 and the European indoor long jump in 1974. She was second in the 1969 pentathlon and second in the 1971 long jump in four European Championships appearances. She set 16 Swiss records at long jump from 5.64m in 1964 to 6.73m in 1971 as well as nine at 100m hurdles, 8 at pentathlon, 4 at 100m and one at 200m.

16 records at one event were also set by Edy Hubacher at men's shot in 1964–70.

The first Swiss international matches were held in 1921 against France and Germany and Swiss athletes first competed at the Olympic Games in 1908.

The most internationals won is 74 by Urs Von Wartburg from 1957 to 1977, including five Olympic Games. Antenen holds the women's record with 30.

The prime candidate for the greatest name in Swiss athletics must be Dr Paul Martin, who competed at all five Olympic Games during 1920–36. His best placing was second (the first of five Swiss Olympic silver medals) at 800m in 1924 when he was just beaten by Douglas Lowe in a desperate finish. He won 17 Swiss championships (400m–3, 800m–10, 1500m–4) and set Swiss records at 1000m as well as those three distances. He won four World University Games titles and had 14 wins (11–800m, 3–1500m) in 14 international matches.

Dr Martin wrote two books: 'Au dixième de seconde' and with his Olympic memories 'Le sport et l'homme'. Dr Martin was still running at the age of 80, when he competed in the 17.4km Morat to Fribourg race and in the Engadine run-ski marathon in 1980.

Turkey

Turkish athletes first took part at the Olympic Games in 1912 and the national federation was formed in 1922. The one major championship medallist has been Ruhi Sarialp, who was third in the 1948 Olympic triple jump.

USSR

The first Russian athletics meeting was held in Leningrad in 1867. The first Russian championships were held in Leningrad in 1911 and a team of 47 athletes contested the 1912 Olympic Games. In 1913 (in Kiev) and 1914 (in Riga) 'All-Russian Olympic Games' were contested.

Following the Revolution, **the first USSR championships** were held in 1920 for men and 1922 for women. The Soviet All-Union Track and Field Federation was not a member of the IAAF between the wars and Soviet athletes did not compete at the Olympic Games again until 1952 (rejoining the IOC in 1951). Despite not joining the IAAF until 1947 Soviet athletes were re-admitted to international competition at the 1946 European Championships, though they had been invited to join the IAAF in 1945 and had not responded.

Vladimir Kuts wins the 10000m at the 1956 USSR Spartakiade, the tenth of thirteen successive victories at 10000m in 1955–7. *(Associated Press)*

The first World Workers Spartakiade was held in 1928, when athletes from a dozen nations, including Britain took part. Subsequent Spartakiades (People's Games of the USSR) have taken place in 1956, 1960, 1964, 1968, 1972, 1975 and 1979.

The first international match contested by the USSR was a win against Hungary in Budapest in 1950. Their first defeat was by West Germany at Augsburg in 1958.

Since 1952, when the first Soviet Olympic gold medal was won by Nina Romashkova (later Ponomaryeva) in the women's discus, the USSR has been consistently at the top of world athletics with the USA and, more recently, the GDR. In 1980 it was estimated that there were a claimed 6.2 million active athletes in the USSR, by far the highest number of any nation.

The greatest number of Soviet championships won by any athlete is 31 outdoor and 5 indoor by Aleksandra Chudina between 1945 and 1956; outdoor: 400m 1945; 80mh 1949–51; HJ 1946–7, 1949–51, 1953–4; LJ 1947–51, 1953–4; JT 1948, 1953, 1955–6; Pen 1946–51, 1953–5; indoor: HJ 1951; LJ 1954; Pen 1951, 1953–4.

The most titles at one event is 12 by Igor Ter-Ovanesyan at long jump in 1957, 1959–60, 1962–9, 1971 (also 2nd 1958) and by Janis Lusis at javelin in 1962–6, 1968–73, 1976 (also 2nd 1967, 3rd 1961 and 1974, 5th 1975, 6th 1960). Vasiliy Kuznyetsov won ten decathlon titles, 1953–60, 1962–3.

The most titles won at one event by a woman is ten at discus by Faina Melnik in 1970, 1972–7, 1979–80. Tamara Press won nine shot titles, 1958–66, Nina Ponomaryeva nine at discus, 1951–9 and Chudina nine at pentathlon, 1970, 1972–7, 1979–80.

The oldest Soviet record holder is Aleksandr Chistyakov, aged 47 when he threw the hammer 39.08m in 1928.

Nikolay Ozolin set his first Soviet record at 3.80m in 1928 and topped the Soviet ranking lists on a record 17 occasions up to 1950, when he won his final Soviet title at the age of 43. He became Europe's first amateur 14ft vaulter in 1938 and his best was 4.30m/14ft 1¼in a year later. He won the silver medal at the 1946 European championships.

Estonia, Latvia and Lithuania were each independent republics from 1918 until incorporated into the USSR in 1940. **Estonia** entered teams at each Olympic Games from 1920 to 1936. Their first medallist was Juri Lossman, second in the 1920 marathon. For the USSR, Estonian Olympic gold medallists have been Juri Tarmak 1972 high jump and Jaak Uudmäe 1980 triple jump. European gold medals were won at shot by Arnold Viiding in 1934 and Aleksandr Kreek in 1938.

The greatest number of Estonian championships and records have been won by Helgi Parts who at women's shot won nine titles and set seven records and at discus won 18 titles and set 21 records between 1962 and 1980.

Latvia entered Olympic teams from 1924 to 1936. Janis Dalins won their first medal with a second at the 50km walk in 1932, and also won

their one European gold at the 50km walk in 1934. For the USSR the most notable Latvian athletes have been the husband and wife javelin team of Janis Lusis and Elvira Ozolina.

Lithuania contested just one Olympic Games, in 1928. No medals were gained in Lithuanian colours at Olympics or European Championships but in Soviet teams, Lithuanians have included European champions Kestutis Sapka, 1971 high jump, and Vilma Bardauskiene, 1978 long jump.

The first Russian to set a world best performance was Louis Junker who competed in London as a member of LAC in 1877 and 1878. He ran 150y in 15.0sec in 1877 and 120y in 12.0 in 1878, both at Stamford Bridge, and also won the 1878 AAC 100y title before returning to his native Moscow.

The Luzhniki Sports Complex, Moscow was opened in July 1956. At its centre is the Lenin Central Stadium, with a seating capacity for 103000. Major events to have been held there include the 1980 Olympic Games and 1973 World Student Games.

Yugoslavia

The first Yugoslav championships were held in 1920, and a year later the national federation was formed. Two Serbian athletes competed in the 1912 Olympic Games, before the founding of the combined nation. To date no Yugoslav has won an Olympic gold medal, the highest placing being second by both Ivan Gubijan (hammer 1948) and Franjo Mihalic (marathon 1956).

European gold medals have been won by Vera Nikolic (women's 800m 1966 and 1971) and Luciano Susanj (800m 1974).

The most national records is 30 by Zvonko Sabolovic with 17 individual and 13 relay in 1947–52. Milka Babovic (later the top Yugoslav television sports commentator) holds the most by a woman, 27 again including 13 relay records. The most for individual events is 25 by Franjo Mihalic, including 15 at 10000m, the most at one event as he reduced the record from 32:59.0 in 1946 to 29:37.6 in 1954.

The greatest number of national titles is 20 by Ivo Buratovic at hurdles, jumps and decathlon in the 1920s and 1930s. Srecko Stiglic won 15

Vera Nikolic (319) leads in the European 800m at Athens in 1969. She finished third as Lillian Board (98) won in 2:01.4.   *(All-Sport/Tony Duffy)*

consecutive hammer titles from 1966 to 1980.

The first Yugoslav world record holder was Draga Stamejcic, who equalled the women's 80m hurdles time of 10.5 in 1964. She was followed by Vera Nikolic with a 2:00.5 for 800m in winning the 1968 WAAA title from Lillian Board. Nikolic was favourite for the 1968 Olympic gold but, overcome by the pressure, she stepped off the track in a semi-final.

Major Meetings – Europe

There has been a proliferation of international invitation meetings in recent years, with the world's top athletes seeming to run here, there and everywhere. The following lists most of the best established:

Bislett Games, Oslo.
Hanns Braun Sportfest, Munich; first held 1930.
Budapest Grand Prix, Nepstadion; first 1978.
Cologne International.
DN Gala, Stockholm; first 1966.
Florence International; first 1976.
Golden Spike Meet, Ostrava, Czechoslovakia; 1961.
Helsinki World Games, 1961, biennial.
Internationale Stadionfest (ISTAF), West Berlin. First held in 1921 in the 1916 Olympic stadium, revived with an 80000 crowd on 1 Aug 1937 in the 1936 Olympic stadium.
Koblenz International, West Germany.
Kusocinski Memorial, in memory of Janusz Kusocinski; first held 1954 in Żabrze, now usually held in Warsaw.
Lausanne International.
Narodna Mladej Memorial, in Bulgaria, usually Sofia, first 1955.
Nikaia in Nice, first 1976.
Paavo Nurmi Games in Turku, Finland.
Olympische Tag, usually East Berlin; first 1963.
Oslo Games, first 1975.
Pravda Cup, Moscow.
Pravda Televizia Slovnaft (PTS), Bratislava, Czechoslovakia first 1957.
Evzen Rosicky Memorial, Prague; first 1947.
Romanian International Championships, Bucharest, 1947.
Sport 2000, Paris.
Ivo van Damme Memorial, Heizel Stadium, Brussels; first 1977; maximum attendance 45000.
Weltklasse, Letzigrund Stadium, Zurich; first 1962; maximum attendance 27000.
Znamenskiy Brothers Memorial, Moscow, 1949. In memory of Serafim and Georgiy Znamenskiy, the top Soviet distance runners, killed in the war.

One should also note the following important venues on the European circuit: Copenhagen, Formia, Furth, Göteborg, Dusseldorf, Malmö, Milan, Nijmegan, Rieti, Viareggio.

International Matches

There was a match between Scotland and England at St Andrews in 1530 won by the Scots, that consisted of running, jumping, shot put, wrestling and archery.

In 1876 there was a match between England and Ireland in Dublin, although Ireland was at the time under British rule, and a return match in 1877.

The first international match of importance was held at Manhattan Field, New York, USA on 21 September 1895 between New York AC and London AC. The Americans won all 11 events and the standard of performance was extremely high. World records were achieved by Bernie Wefers 100y in 9.8 and 220y in 21.6, Charles Kilpatrick 880y in 1:53.4, Stephen Chase 120y hurdles in 15.4 and Michael Sweeney high jump in 1.97m/6ft 5⅝in.

The first international inter-university match had preceded the above match by over a year. Oxford University beat Yale University 5½ events to 3½ on 16 Jul 1894 at Queen's Club, Kensington, London. Amongst the Oxford winners was the great all-rounder Charles Fry (see p. 229) who ran the 100y in 10.4sec. Yale met Cambridge University at Manhattan Field, New York on 5 Oct 1895, winning 8 events to 3 and the first of the celebrated series of matches between the combined Oxford/Cambridge and Harvard/Yale Universities took place on 22 Jul 1899 at Queen's Club. The English team won 5–4. This series has continued to the present day as has the series of fixtures between Oxford/ Cambridge and Princeton/Cornell, the first of which was contested at Travers Island, New York on 28 Jul 1921. Edwin Gourdin set a world record at long jump of 7.69m/25ft 3in for Harvard/Yale in the Harvard Stadium at Cambridge, Mass. on 23 Jul 1921. A combined Oxford and Cambridge team beat McGill University in Montreal, Canada 7–1 in 1901.

The first inter-nation match was held on 29 Jul 1911 in Rotterdam, when Belgium won an 8-event match against Holland 60 points to 30. A year later France beat Belgium and Hungary beat Austria. The first women's international match was contested by Belgium and France in Brussels on 28 Aug 1921, with the French girls winning every event.

The first full-scale indoor international was held at Wembley, London on 6/7 Apr 1963 between Great Britain and The German Federal Republic. Britain won the men's match and Germany the women's.

Summarised results of matches between leading European nations (not including European Cup matches or other internationals with five or more teams) – note that each series of matches is shown once only. (*T = tie*). (See p. 216 for GB)

USSR v	men	women
GDR	9–2	3–7
GFR	8–1	7–2
Poland	11–0	10–1
France	5–0	1–0
Finland	3–1	3–0
Italy	2–0	1–0

GERMANY (pre 1945) v		
Poland	2–0	3–0
France	13–0	2–0
Finland	2–1	–
Italy	4–0	2–0
Sweden	1–4	–
Czechoslovakia	1–0	–
Romania	3–0	–

F.R. GERMANY v		
Poland	3–5(2T)	7–3(IT)
– indoors	0–1	1–1
France	11–1	3–0
– indoors	2–1	1–0
Finland	7–3	2–0
Italy	6–0	5–0
Sweden	6–1	1–0
Czechoslovakia	3–1	5–0
Romania	–	7–1

GDR v		
Poland	6–11	16–2(IT)
Finland	3–1	1–0
Sweden	4–1	5–0
Romania	4–0(IT)	6–0
Bulgaria	14–0	15–0

POLAND v		
France	6–1	3–0
Finland	6–1	2–0
Italy	6–3(IT)	4–1
Hungary	4–1	4–3
Sweden	2–0	3–0
Czechoslovakia	8–2	14–3
Bulgaria	6–0	5–1
Romania	2–0	6–1

FRANCE v		
Finland	8–14(2T)	3–2
Italy	5–7	9–10
Sweden	5–9	3–0
Czechoslovakia	7–1	5–4
Romania	2–2	1–2
Hungary	3–2	1–1

FINLAND v		
Sweden	28–13	9–22
Hungary	6–6	0–1
Czechoslovakia	2–3	1–0
Italy	3–4	0–2

ITALY v		
Hungary	8–6	4–4
Sweden	4–3	2–0
Czechoslovakia	5–4	2–3
Romania	9–0	2–10
Bulgaria	3–0	–

HUNGARY v		
Sweden	5–10	4–0
Czechoslovakia	13–16(IT)	18–8(2T)
Romania	3–0	10–1(IT)

SWEDEN v		
Czechoslovakia	2–6	0–6

In the 1980s many athletes put greater store by the major invitational meetings, rather than the traditional international matches, with the result that the importance of these fixtures has declined somewhat. One international that retains its predominant importance, however, is that between Finland and Sweden. This was first contested in 1925 in Helsinki. Now the venue alternates between the two nations and that fixture has been held annually from 1953. Large crowds are the regular feature, up to 90000 in the Helsinki Olympic Stadium.

Right: Debbie Brill wins the silver medal at the 1978 Commonwealth Games, narrowly failing to regain the title she had won as a 17-year-old in 1970.

Below: John Akii-Bua won the 1972 Olympic title and set a world record of 47.82 for 400m hurdles.

Above: Pirjo Häggman, one of the first two women elected to the International Olympic Committee in 1981 leaves the track after her fourth place in the 1976 Olympic 400m.

Left: Steve Ovett has just won the Olympic 800m title.

GREAT BRITAIN

British Records

In this section I have taken the term British record to mean a best performance set under record conditions made anywhere by a UK athlete. This has been the definition of a UK National record since 1 Jan 1960. From 1887 until then British records were the best performances made in the UK by athletes from anywhere in the world, but these are now defined as UK All-Comers' records.

The greatest number of British records at one event is 17 by Bill Tancred at discus, from 57.26m/187ft 10in in 1968 to 64.94m/213ft 0in in 1974. This tally, as with others in this section, includes unratified performances. Geoff Elliott also set 17 records at pole vault, but this includes 11 times on which he tied the existing mark. He took the record from 4.11m/13ft 6in in 1952 to 4.30m/14ft 1¼in which he achieved five times in 1954–9. Elliott also set two decathlon records to tie the greatest number of records set by one athlete at Olympic events – 19 also by two women, Suzanne Allday (11 SP and 8 DT) and Mary Rand (11 LJ, 6 Pen and 2 80mh). Gordon Pirie set 22 individual records, although all but four of these were at non-Olympic events. His tally: 5 each at 3000m and 3 miles, 4 at 6 miles, 2 each at 2000m, 2 miles, 5000m and 10000m, between 1952 and 1961. Four of these were world records, with a fifth at 4 × 1500m relay.

The greatest number of indoor and outdoor records have been set by Brian Hooper and Geoff Capes. Hooper improved the outdoor pole vault best 16 times from his 5.29m/17ft 4¼in in 1976 to 5.59m/18ft 4in in 1980 and the indoor best a record 14 times, including one tie, from 5.10m/16ft 8¾in in 1975 to 5.50m/18ft

0½in in 1981. His 5.59m in the 1980 AAA championships at the Crystal Palace was the climax of a competition in which he bettered the national record four times, 5.54m, 5.56m, 5.58m and 5.59m and Keith Stock three times, 5.52m, 5.55m and 5.57m for seven successive improvements on the record, by far the most in any one competition at any event.

Geoff Capes set 16 outdoor shot records and 11 indoor shot bests between 1972 and 1980.

The greatest number of women's records at one event is 12 by Rosemary Payne at discus between 1964 and 1972.

The longest standing British record at a regularly held event was George Larner's 2 mile walk of 13:11.4 set on 13 Jul 1904, a record for 56 years 3 days (and a world record for 38 years 340 days). This is followed by 48 years 296 days for Alfred Shrubb 1 hour in 18742m/11m 1137y 5 Nov 1904: 44 years 92 days for Willie Applegarth 220y 21.2sec 4 Jul 1914 (and 44 years 49 days for 200m); 44 years 87 days Marshall Brooks HJ 1.89m/6ft 2½in 7 Apr 1876.

Of even longer standing, however, was Peter O'Connor's long jump of 7.61m/24ft 11¾in set in Dublin on 5 Aug 1901. O'Connor was an Irishman but at the time Ireland was part of Britain so this was regarded as a British record. This mark, a world record for 20 years, was not bettered by a British athlete until 26 Nov 1962 when Lynn Davies jumped 7.72m/25ft 4in, 61 years 143 days later, although John Howell had jumped 7.63m/25ft 0½in into a pit below the level of the runway on 14 Aug 1960.

Geoff Elliott in Woodford Green colours wins his third AAA pole vault title at 4.11m/13ft 6in in 1955. *(H. W. Neale)*

The longest standing women's records have been 22 years 43 days Nellie Halstead, 440y – 56.8 on 9 Jul 1932, and 21 years 363 days for Muriel Cornell (née Gunn), long jump 5.85m/19ft 2½in on 26 Jul 1930.

The oldest British record still standing is Mary Rand's women's long jump record of 6.76m/22ft 2¼in in winning the 1964 Olympic title on 14 Oct 1964, her 11th British long jump record and third of that competition. Before Tokyo her record was 6.58m/21ft 7¼in and her series at the Games was 6.59m, 6.56m, 6.57m, 6.63m, 6.76m, 6.61m.

The youngest British record holder is Dorothy Tyler who was 16 years 39 days when she high jumped 1.65m/5ft 5in on 1 Jun 1936. The youngest male record holder is high jumper Alan Paterson who was 17 years 338 days, when he jumped 1.95m/6ft 5in on 15 May 1946.

The oldest British record holder, if one includes the marathon as an official event, is Joyce Smith, aged 44 years 195 days when she won the London marathon for women in 2:29:43 on 9 May 1982, her seventh win in ten marathons.

The greatest number of world records set by a British athlete (on current IAAF schedule) is eight by Sebastian Coe (see p. 33).

The greatest range of British records is held by Walter George at all distances from 880y to 1 hour 1884–7, and Alfred Shrubb, all distances from 1½M to 1 hour 1904–1936.

The British 4 × 1 mile relay record was improved to 16:17.4 in 1980 by the University of Western Kentucky at the Drake Relays in Des Moines, USA. All four runners were from Bristol AC (Erwin 'Swag' Hartel, Chris Ridler, Tony Staynings, Nick Rose)!

National Championships

AAC CHAMPIONSHIPS
The first ever national championships were those of England, held at Beaufort House, Welham Green, London on 23 Mar 1866. They were staged by the Amateur Athletic Club (AAC), which had been founded in 1865. The championships were held annually on the Monday following the University Boat Race until 1879, first at Beaufort House and after 1869 at Lillie Bridge in West London.

Dorothy Tyler clears 1.60m/5ft 3in to win the 1956 WAAA title. She first won this event in 1936 and in all won eight times.

The most AAC titles at one event are five by Walter Slade for 1 mile 1873–7.

The most AAC titles overall: 11 Robert Mitchell 1868–71 (3 each at HJ, PV, LJ and 2 SP). In 1873 Charles Lockton won the long jump with 5.89m; he was aged 16 years 227 days, still the youngest ever British male champion.

Clashes between the AAC and London Athletic Club (LAC) weakened the championships, which in 1877 attracted just 26 athletes (compared to 61 in 1866) for 12 events, and in 1879 LAC held rival championships at Stamford Bridge. The chaos that was threatened in the sport was avoided by the founding of the Amateur Athletic Association (AAA) on 24 Apr 1880, as the first national governing body of athletics in the world. Three young men from Oxford were responsible for the inception of the AAA: Clement Jackson, record holder for 120yh at 16.0sec; Bernhard Wise, AAC 1 mile champion 1879, and Montague Shearman, AAC 100y champion 1876. They invited representatives of the Northern Counties AA, Midland Counties AA and the leading southern clubs to a meeting at the Randolph Hotel, Oxford and the 28 delegates agreed to the proposals drawn up by the Oxford trio and set up the AAA.

AAA CHAMPIONSHIPS
The first AAA Championships were held at Lillie Bridge on 3 Jul 1880. Championships have been held annually with the exception of the war years 1915–18 and 1940–5 ever since. Venues have been: Lillie Bridge 1880, 1883;

Birmingham 1881, 1884, 1890; Stoke-on-Trent 1882; Southport 1885; Stamford Bridge 1886, 1889, 1892, 1895, 1898, 1900, 1902, 1905–06, 1909–14, 1919–31; Stourbridge 1887; Crewe 1888; Manchester 1891, 1897, 1907; Northampton 1893, 1896, 1903; Huddersfield 1894, 1901; Wolverhampton 1899; Rochdale 1904; White City 1908, 1932–9, 1946–70; Crystal Palace 1971–date.

After settling at Stamford Bridge for most of the early part of the 20th century, the cinder track was being increasingly used for speedway, so the AAA decided in 1932 to switch to the White City, which had been used for the 1908 Olympics. A new track was laid and the stadium shared with the Greyhound Racing Association. This arrangement continued until 1970, when after several years of declining attendances, with a nadir of 4721 spectators over the two days that year, athletics was held there for the last time and the venue switched to the Crystal Palace National Sports Centre, which cost the AAA considerably less to hire.

Emmanuel McDonald Bailey won a record number of AAA titles before a short spell as a professional rugby league player. *(H. W. Neale)*

The most individual titles are 14 by Emmanuel McDonald Bailey, 7 each at 100y and 220y 1946–47, 1949–53. Bailey, born in Trinidad, first competed in the championships as an 18-year-old in 1939 when he reached the 220y semi-finals. A beautifully smooth sprinter he dominated British sprinting in post-war years and represented Britain at the Olympic Games of 1948 and 1952. He was sixth at 100m in 1948 and in 1952 third at 100m and fourth at both 200m and 4 × 100m relay. He won a 15th AAA title as a member of the Polytechnic Harriers' 4 × 110y relay team in 1952.

The most AAA titles at one event are 13 by Denis Horgan for shot 1893–9, 1904–05, 1908–10, 1912. He was second in 1900 to Richard Sheldon (USA) who went on to win the Olympic title that year. Horgan was said to warm up by consuming a dozen eggs in a pint of sherry. His best championship distance was 14.03m/46ft 0½in in 1899 and his personal best 14.88m/48ft 10in at Mallow, Ireland in 1904, a distance no British athlete bettered until 1949. He won the Olympic silver medal in 1908 just a year after he had his skull broken by a shovel while trying to stop a fight in New York, where he was a policeman. He also won 17 Irish titles and the 1900 AAU shot.

The most placings in the first three at one event are 15 by Howard Payne with the hammer. He finished as the first British athlete on 13 occasions. His complete AAA record: first in 1964, 1969–71, 1973; second in 1961–2, 1967, 1972, 1974; 3rd 1960, 1963, 1965. Mike Ellis had beaten him while winning his four consecutive titles from 1957 to 1960, but then no British athlete beat him at the championships until Barry Williams won in 1972. Payne had been Victor Ludorum at school in Johannesburg in 1948, but then dropped out of athletics until 1954, when he set a Northern Rhodesia discus record. He started hammer throwing in 1955 at the age of 24. Before coming to England he won eight Rhodesian titles (SP and HT 1956–7, DT 1955–8) and the South African hammer title in 1956.

The most successive placings in the first three are for Bill Tancred at discus 1964–75 (first 1966–70, 1972–3; second 1974–5; third 1964–5, 1971); and 11 for Albert Cooper 2 miles walk 1929–39, David Travis javelin 1965–75 and Geoff Capes at shot 1970–80.

The most placings without a win is ten by Robert

Robert Howland took the English record from 14.02m in 1929 to 14.86m in 1935. *(BBC Hulton)*

'Bonzo' Howland, who was second nine times and third once in the shot between 1929 and 1939. On each occasion, however, he was the first British thrower. He was also twice second at the Empire Games.

The most titles at each event

100y/100m: 7 McDonald Bailey 1946–7, 1949–53
200m/220y: 7 McDonald Bailey 1946–7, 1949–53
400m/440y: 6 David Jenkins 1971–6
800m/880y: 4 Brian Hewson 1953–4, 1958–9
1500m/1 mile: 5 Sydney Wooderson 1935–9
5000m/3 mile: 3 Bruce Tulloh 1959, 1962–3; Ron Clarke (Aus) 1965–7; Brendan Foster 1973–4, 1976. Foster's 1973 win in 13:23.8 was his first serious 5000m (his only previous race was a 14:36.0).
10000m/6 mile: 5 David Bedford 1970–4
10 mile (held 1880–1939, 1947, 1958–72): 5 Ron Hill 1965–9
Marathon: 6 Donald McNab Robertson 1932–4, 1936–7, 1939
3000m Steeplechase: 8 Maurice Herriott 1959, 1961–7*
110mh/120yh: 8 Donald Finlay 1932–8*, 1949 (third in 1929!)
220yh (1952–62): 2 Peter Hildreth 1952, 1954; Paul Vine 1955–6
400mh/440yh: 7 Harry Whittle 1947–53*
High Jump: 6 Howard Baker 1910, 1912–13, 1919–21
Pole Vault: 7 Thomas Ray 1881–2, 1884–8
Long Jump: 6 Peter O'Connor 1901–6
Triple Jump: 6 Willem Peters (Hol) 1927–30, 1935, 1937

Dave Bedford revitalised British athletics in the early 1970s. Here he wins the third of his five successive AAA 10000m titles. *(G. Herringshaw)*

Shot: 13 Denis Horgan 1893–9*, 1904–5, 1908–10, 1912
Discus: 7 Bill Tancred 1966–70, 1972–3
Hammer: 6 Thomas Nicolson 1903–5, 1907, 1909, 1912
Javelin: 7 David Travis 1965, 1968, 1970–4
Decathlon: 4 Leslie Pinder 1951–4
3000m/2 mile walk: 9 Roger Mills 1969, 1972–4, 1976–9, 1981
4 mile walk (1894–1900): 6 William Sturgess 1895–1900
10000m/7 mile walk: 5 Roland Hardy 1950–3, 1955; Ken Matthews 1959–61, 1963–4; Brian Adams 1975–9
   *These four men and Albert Cooper, 2 mile walk 1932–8, share the record of seven successive titles.

Titles at four different events have been won by:
Walter George 1M and 4M in 1880 and the four events 880y, 1M, 4M and 10M in 1882 and 1884. William Snook 1M, 4M, 10M and steeplechase in 1885, those first three events in 1883 and the steeplechase in 1884. Harry Whittle 220yh in 1953, the 440yh 1947–53, the long jump in 1947 and 1949, and the decathlon 1950. George and Snook each won three titles on one day and the ten mile two days later when they won four titles in one year. In 1882 George ran only a token lap to win the four miles as there was no challenger.

The first dead heat was at 120y hurdles in 1883 between Samuel Palmer and William Pollock in 16.6sec. Palmer won a re-run in 16.2.

Harry Edward won three titles within an hour in 1922, the 100y, 220y and 440y.

The first overseas athlete to win a AAA title was 'Lon' Myers (USA) at 440y in 1881.

There have been 12 official IAAF world records set at the AAA championships in addition to the many unofficial ones that were set before such recognition was introduced (all GB unless noted):
220y – 21.2 Willie Applegarth 1914
880y – 1:51.6 Otto Peltzer (Ger) 1926
3 mile – 13:32.2 Freddie Green and Chris Chataway 1954; 12:52.4 Ron Clarke (Aus) 1965 (12:52.26 auto)
6 mile – 28:19.4 Gordon Pirie 1953
10000m – 27:30.80 Dave Bedford 1973
10 mile – 47:47.0 Basil Heatley 1961 (at Hurlingham); 47:26.8 Mel Batty 1964 (at Hurlingham); 47:02.2 Ron Hill 1968 (at Leicester)

Thirteen AAA titles between them – Bert Cooper leads Harry Churcher. *(BBC Hulton)*

440yh – 54.2 Lord Burghley 1927
Pole vault – 5.10m/16ft 8¾in John Pennel (USA) 1963

The greatest ever attendance at the AAA championships was in 1952 when there were 45373 paying spectators over the two days of 20/21 June at the White City. They saw British records by Gordon Pirie (6 mile), Harry Whittle (440y hurdles), and Roland Hardy (7 mile walk), the best ever 2 miles steeplechase – 9:44.0 by John Disley, and victories by such other great names as McDonald Bailey, Roger Bannister, Chris Chataway, John Savidge and Arthur Wint. The previous year, 1951, had a two-day attendance of 42362, confirming the early 1950s as the vintage period for athletics crowds in Britain.

The problems of holding athletics in a greyhound racing stadium were highlighted at the 1968 AAA championships at the White City. The pole vault competition had started at 2pm, but by the contracted close of the meeting, 5.30pm, was still a long way short of completion. In fifth place Martin Higdon vaulted 4.59m/15ft 0¾in, the best ever by an Englishman. The greyhounds were due to start racing at 7.30pm, there was a loudspeaker announcement for people to leave, but the 500 or so spectators ignored that as the competition progressed. Mike Bull, who a month earlier had become the first British man to vault 16ft, cleared that height again, and was second as Renato Dionisi (Italy) went higher still at 16ft 6in/5.03m. Eventually announcer Bob Sparks' microphone was disconnected and Dionisi had to finish after just one attempt at 16ft 11in after 7pm.

The first AAA indoor championships at Wembley Pool and Sports Arena in 1935. Robert Howland won the shot, in contrast with his record outdoors, and went on to win a further title in 1938.
(BBC Hulton)

The first AAA Championships to be sponsored were those of 1911 by the Carborundum Co. Ltd. In 1962 the Daily Herald sponsored the revived indoor championships and Bovril Ltd sponsored the WAAA championships. Subsequent outdoor championships' sponsors have been: AAA – Pepsi-Cola 1963–9, Nationwide Building Society 1972–80, Robinson's Barley Water 1981–; WAAA – Bovril 1962–9, Birds Eye Foods 1971–6, Sunsilk 1977–81, Trustee Savings Bank 1982.

AAA Indoor Championships
These were first held at the Empire Pool, Wembley from 1935 to 1939. They were revived at Wembley 1962–4 and since 1965 have been held annually at Cosford.

The most individual titles are eight by Mike Bull with pole vault 1967–72, 1974, 1977. Bull also won five outdoor AAA pole vault titles (1966–7, 1969, 1971–2). Geoff Capes won six AAA indoor shot titles (1971–2, 1974–5, 1977–8). Together with his seven AAA outdoor titles (1972–3, 1975–9) and two AAA Junior shot titles (1966–67) this gives him a record 15 AAA titles in all at one event.

The most successive AAA indoor titles are six by John Whetton, winner of the 1500m 1963–7 and the 1 mile in 1968. He also won at 1000y in 1964.

AAA Junior Championships
These championships have been held annually, with the exception of the war years 1940–5, since 1931, at various venues.

Since 1973 the age classification has been under 20 in the year of competition. Previously juniors had been defined as those who had reached their 17th but not their 19th birthday on 1st September in the calendar year of competition.

The most titles at one event are four by Milton Palmer at high jump 1974–7. Paul Buxton is the only junior to have won three titles, the shot, discus and hammer, in one year, 1975.

AAA Youth Championships

These have been held annually since 1968. Youths are defined under AAA rules as those who have reached their 15th but not their 17th birthday on 1st September in the calendar year of competition. Fourteen youths have won two successive titles at the same event. Of these Tony Zaidman is unique in having gone on to add two junior titles, winning youths in 1977–8 and junior 1980–1, all at the shot.

AAA National Road Relay (12-stage)

First held in 1967 at Whetstone, Leics, this event is now staged annually at Sutton Park, Sutton Coldfield. There are alternate long (5M 900y) and short (3M 100y) stages, for which the fastest recorded times are 24:27 David Moorcroft (Coventry) 1982 and 13:36 Barry Smith 1981 for Gateshead Harriers, winners in 1975–7 and 1979. Their four wins have been matched by Coventry Godiva 1967–70 and Tipton Harriers 1972, 1974, 1978 and 1981. The fastest overall time is 4:00:37 by Bristol in 1980.

AAA 6-stage road relay

First held in 1969, the record number of victories is four by City of Stoke-on-Trent AC 1969–72.

English Championships restricted to native-born competitors were held during 1923 to 1925 at Fallowfield (Manchester), Northampton and St Albans respectively. The only athletes to win the hat-trick of titles were Fred Gaby (120yh) and Reginald Goodwin (2M walk).

Athletes to have won AAA outdoor titles at each age grouping:
David Jenkins – Youths 220y and 440y 1968; Junior 100m and 400m 1969, Senior 400m 1971–6.
Brian Hooper – at PV, Youths 1969, Junior 1971, Senior 1973 and 1980. He also won AAA indoor titles in 1973, 1975–6, 1978–9 and 1981.
Sebastian Coe – Youth 1500m 1973; Junior 1500m 1975; Senior 800m 1981 as well as three indoor senior titles.
Steve Cram – Youth 1500m 1977, Junior 3000m 1979, Senior 1500m 1981.
Jenkins (400m 1980), Hooper (PV 1979) and Coe (800m 1979) also won UK titles.

Steve Ovett won at both youth and senior age groups but did not compete in the AAA Junior championships as he concentrated on senior competition.

The Harvey Memorial Cup is awarded annually to the man adjudged the best AAA champion of the year. It was presented by the family of the late Charles Harvey in 1907.
The most wins were three by Ron Clarke (3 miles 1965–7; in 1966 he shared the trophy with 440y champion Wendell Mottley).

The CN Jackson Memorial Cup is awarded annually to the athlete born in the UK who is adjudged the outstanding athlete of the year by the AAA Championships Committee. It was presented in memory of Clement Jackson in 1926.
The most wins were three by Steve Ovett 1977, 1978 (shared with Daley Thompson), 1980.

THE WAAA CHAMPIONSHIPS

The Women's AAA was formed in 1922 and in September of that year held championships at Waddon for two events, 120y hurdles and 220y. A full scale championship meeting was held the following year on 18 Aug 1923 at Bromley, on the Oxo Sports Ground. At these championships Mary Lines won four titles (100y, 440y, 120yh and LJ), still the record number of titles in one year.

Championships have been held annually except for the war years 1940–44, venues

Gladys Lunn wins her seventh WAAA title – at 800m in 1937. There was a record entry of more than 500, but few spectators. *(BBC Hulton)*

Joyce Smith ran the first sub-2½ hour marathon by a British woman in 1981, 22 years after she first won the national cross-country. *(M. Shearman)*

being: Waddon 1922; Bromley 1923; Woolwich 1924; Stamford Bridge 1925–6, 1928–32; Reading 1927; White City 1933, 1935–9, 1946, 1949–57, 1960–7; Herne Hill 1934; Tooting Bec 1945; Chiswick 1947–8; Motspur Park 1958–9; and Crystal Palace 1968–date.

The 1920s WAAA rule on kit read: 'Women shall wear loose tunics of optional length with elbow length sleeves. The knickers shall be dark and close-fitting and shall not be more than four inches from the ground when kneeling'.

The WAAA cross-country championships were first held in 1927 and road walking championships first held in 1933.

The WAAA indoor championships were held at Wembley from 1935 to 1939 and revived there from 1962 to 1964. Since 1965 they have been staged annually at Cosford.

The youngest ever WAAA champion and youngest ever British champion at any event is Sonia Lannaman, who was 14 years 312 days when she won the indoor 60m on 30 Jan 1971.

The youngest ever WAAA champion outdoors is Betty Lock at 60m in 1936 aged 15 years 72 days.

The oldest ever WAAA champion is Joyce Smith aged 42 years 281 days when she won the 1980 marathon. Joyce made her cross-country international debut in 1957 and her international track debut at 800m when placed third against Italy in 1960. After that year she had a 12-year wait before she again represented Britain on the track, during which time her daughter, Lisa, was born in 1968. In 1972 she made a superb return as she ran the 1500m in 4:12.8 for third against GDR and Netherlands from a previous best of 4:21.7. At the Olympic Games in Munich she twice improved the UK record: 4:11.27 and 4:09.37. Gradually longer distances were introduced for women, and Joyce moved into these new territories with alacrity. She five times set UK records for 3000m culminating in the first British sub nine minutes time, 8:55.53 in the heats(!) of the 1974 WAAA championships (she won the final in 9:07.15). At the European championships that year she won the 3000m bronze medal. Her second daughter Lia was born in 1976. In 1979 she made her marathon debut with a British best 2:41:37, a time she has subsequently improved five times to her 2:29:43 in the 1982 London marathon.

The most individual titles won outdoors is 14 by Suzanne Allday, with seven wins each at shot and discus. Allday also won indoor shot titles in 1962 and 1963 for a combined indoor and outdoor total of 16, but this is second to Mary Peters' 17.

Mary Peters first competed in the WAAA championships in 1956, when at the age of 17 she was second in the pentathlon. It was five years before she gained another placing, third 1961 for shot. Her complete list of titles are: **outdoors** Pen 1962–1, 1968, 1970, 1973; SP 1964, 1970; 100mh 1970; **indoors** SP 1964–6, 1970, 1972; 60mh 1970.

Nellie Halstead is second in the list of most outdoor titles and has the widest range of running events. In all she won 13 titles: 100y 1931; 220y/200m 1930–2, 1934; 440y/400m 1931–3, 1937; 800m 1935, 1938; cross-country 1935–6. She was also second at 1 mile in 1936. Uniquely she won the three sprint titles in one afternoon, running heats and finals on 11 Jul 1931.

The most titles at one event indoors and out are 11 by Ethel Raby at long jump (indoors and out 1935–9 and outdoors 1946), Dorothy Tyler (née Odam) at high jump (indoors 1937–9 as

Suzanne Allday, winner of a record number of WAAA championships, puts the shot in 1956, in which year husband Peter won the AAA hammer.
(Associated Press)

Lindsey Macdonald in the 4 × 400m relay in Moscow in 1980 when she became Britain's youngest ever Olympic medallist.   *(G. Herringshaw)*

well as eight outdoors) and Judy Farr, who added the 1½ mile walk indoors in 1966 to her ten outdoor walk titles. Farr won a record nine successive walk titles, and in 1971 seemed well on the way to a tenth, but she was disqualified while leading with a lap to go.

The most titles at each event
60m (1935–50): 4 Betty Lock 1936–9
100y/100m: 4 Eileen Hiscock 1930, 1933–5; Winifred Jordan 1937, 1945, 1947–8; Dorothy Hyman 1959–60, 1962–3
200m/220y: 6 Sylvia Cheeseman 1946–9, 1951–2
400m/440y: 6 Valerie Winn (née Ball) 1948–53
800m/880y: 5 Edith Trickey 1923–7; Gladys Lunn 1930–32, 1934, 1937; Joy Jordan 1958–62
1500m/1 mile: 5 Rita Ridley 1966–8, 1970–71
3000m: 2 Joyce Smith 1971, 1974; Mary Purcell (Ire) 1975–6
Marathon: 2 Joyce Smith 1979–80
Walk: 10 Judy Farr 1960, 1962–8 (at 1½M), 1969–70 (2500m)
80mh: 5 Elsie Green 1931–5
100mh: 2 four women
400mh: 2 Christine Warden 1976, 1979
High jump: 8 Dorothy Tyler 1936–9, 1948–9, 1952, 1956
Long jump: 6 Ethel Raby 1935–9, 1946
Shot: 7 Suzanne Allday 1954, 1956, 1958–62
Discus: 7 Suzanne Allday 1952–3, 1956, 1958–61
Javelin: 8 Susan Platt 1959–62, 1966–9
Pentathlon: 8 Mary Peters 1962–6, 1968, 1970, 1973

Rosemary Payne was the top placed British competitor at the discus for 11 successive years 1964–74. With strong foreign competition in many years, she was first in 1966–7, 1970, 1972–3, second 1964, 1969, 1974, third 1965, 1971, and fourth 1968. Her husband Howard achieved the same feat each year in the AAA championships from 1961 to 1974 with the exception of 1972.

The most placings in the first three at all outdoor events is 24 by Suzanne Allday, with 12 each at shot and discus between 1951 and 1964. Twelve years later she returned to athletics to accompany her daughter and reached UK top ten standards, with seventh and eighth places in the discus at the 1977 and 1978 WAAA championships and eighth at shot in 1977.
Judy Farr was placed in the first three 17

times in 16 years at the various WAAA track walks and Dorothy Tyler placed 14 times at HJ, over a record span of 22 years from 1935 (as 15-year-old Dorothy Odam) to her win in 1956. Second to her in 1956 was Mary Bignal, the first of her 17 places at six events, winning ten titles outdoors (five at LJ, two at Pen and one each at 80mh, 100mh and HJ), and indoor titles in 1966 at 60yh, HJ and LJ.

A unique walking/running double was achieved on 8 Jul 1950 when Joyce Heath won both the 1 mile run and 1600m walk.

Most indoor titles: Verona Elder 400m in 1972–3, 1975–7, 1979, and 800m 1978. She also won the outdoor 400m in 1976–7.

WAAA Intermediate Championships
These are for girls aged 15 or 16 on 1st September in year of competition, and were first held in 1949. Linsey Macdonald won a record four titles: 100m and 400m in 1979; 100m and 200m in 1980. Susan Mapstone won a record three titles in one year, 1972, when she won the 80m hurdles, long jump and pentathlon.

WAAA Junior Championships
These are for girls under 15 on 1st September in year of competition, and were first held in 1945. Ann Wilson won a record five titles: 70y hurdles and high jump in 1963; 80m hurdles, high jump and long jump in 1964.

Athletes to have won WAAA titles at each age grouping:
(J) = Junior, (I) = Intermediate, (S) = Senior
Sharon Colyear: (J) 200m 1969; (I) 200m 1970; (S) 200mh 1971, 100mh 1976 and 1978. Colyear also won the WAAA indoor 400m in 1974 and completed a list of all major national titles with UK 100mh wins in 1977 and 1978 and at long jump in 1977.
Susan Reeve (née Scott): all at long jump: (J) 1966; (I) 1967 (and at pentathlon); (S) 1976–7 and 1980. She also won WAAA indoor titles in 1969, 1976–8 and the UK title in 1978–9 to emulate Colyear.
Madeleine Weston (later Cobb): (J) 60m and 100m 1955; (I) 100m 1956; (S) 100m 1958. She also won the indoor 60m 1969, 1972.
Dorothy Hyman: (J) 100y 1956; (I) 100y 1957; (S) 100m/y 1960, 1962–3, 200m/220y 1960, 1962–3, 1969.
Maureen Tranter: (J) 150y 1962; (I) 200m 1963; (S) 200m indoors 1966. 'Mo' did not win any outdoor WAAA titles, but has a record

number of second places for a non-champion: four at 220y and one at 400m.
Marilyn Neufville: (J) 100y and 150y 1967; (I) 220y 1968; (S) 400m 1970. She also won the indoor 400m in 1970.
Ann Wilson: (J) five titles as above; (I) 80m hurdles and high jump 1965; (S) pentathlon 1972 and 1974. Also indoor long jump 1970, 60m hurdles 1971–2, high jump 1971–4.
Christina Boxer at 800m: (J) 1971; (I) 1972; (S) 1977–8. She also won the UK 800m in 1979–80.
Jane Colebrook won the junior 200m in 1972 and intermediate 800m 1973 and 400m 1974. Her senior best is second at 800m in 1980, but she won the UK senior 400m and 800m in 1978.

WOMEN'S ENGLISH NATIONAL CROSS-COUNTRY CHAMPIONSHIPS
These were first held at Luton in 1927, when they were contested by 108 women. A 'girls' race was added in 1966. From 1967 three age groups were catered for – senior, intermediate and junior, and from 1975 a fourth, for minor girls, was added.

The most wins are: six by Lilian Styles 1928–30, 1933–4, 1937; five by Rita Ridley 1969–72, 1974; four by Diane Leather 1953–6 and by Pam Davies 1965–8.
    The greatest winning margin is 1min 6sec by Roma Ashby in 1961.

The most top ten placings is 15 by Joyce Smith in 19 races between 1956 (7th) and 1982 (9th). She won in 1959, 1960 and 1973, and has been second four times (1966, 1967, 1970 and 1971) and third three times (1965, 1974 and 1978). Lilian Styles was in the first three each year from 1927 to 1938, with the exception of a fifth place in 1932.

The only winner at three age groups is Mary Stewart – junior 1970, intermediate 1971, 1972 and 1973, senior in 1978. Her only other race in the championships was in 1969 when she was 17th in the junior race. Her closest rival to this feat is Sandra Arthurton, whose complete record is: girls 6th in 1975; junior 3rd 1976, 1st 1977; intermediate 1st in 1978 and 1979; senior 5th 1980, 3rd 1981, 5th 1982.
    Helen Hill won the junior race three times, 1972–4, but did not compete thereafter.

The greatest number of finishers are: 1738 in 1980 (279 senior, 232 intermediate, 621 junior, 606 girls).

UK CHAMPIONSHIPS

These were first held at Cwmbran on 10–12 Jun 1977 as the first British championships closed to 'foreign' entries. The venue has moved each year, so that by 1981 when they were staged in Antrim, Northern Ireland, the championships had been held in each of the four home countries.

The most wins by an individual is four by Margaret Ritchie, women's discus 1977–80 and by David Ottley, javelin 1978–81. Sonia Lannaman has also won four titles, with 100m and 200m doubles in 1977 and 1978.

David Black is the only man to have competed in five finals at one event, at 10000m, winning in 1978, 1979 and 1981, fifth in 1977 and sixth in 1980.

WALKING CHAMPIONSHIPS – RWA

The Southern Counties Road Walking Association was formed by 16 clubs in September 1907 to hold walking championships on the road. The first, at 20 miles, was staged from Ruislip, Middlesex on 21 Mar 1908. The name was changed to the RWA (dropping Southern) in 1911.

In 1954 the AAA additionally entrusted the RWA with developing track walking, so the name was subtly changed to the Race Walking Association.

RWA Championships, with the date first held and the most titles won at each distance:

10 miles (1947) 6 Ken Matthews 1959–64
20km (1965) 6 Paul Nihill 1965–6, 1968–9, 1971–2
35km (1979), **20 miles** (1908–77), **30km** (1978): 6 Paul Nihill 1963–5, 1968–9, 1971
50km (1930) 8 Don Thompson 1956–62, 1966
100km (1979) one each

A 10 miles junior event was first staged in 1909 and a youths 3 miles was first held in 1961, but these eventually lapsed.

The most RWA titles won overall is 19 by Paul Nihill. In addition to the six at 20km and 20 miles shown above he won four at 10 miles (1965, 1968–9 and 1972) and three at 50km (1964, 1968, 1971). Uniquely he won all four RWA titles in 1968.

The oldest British champion at any event is Tebbs Lloyd Johnson, aged 49 years 70 days

Tebbs Lloyd Johnson finishing third in the 1948 Olympic 50km walk. At the age of 48 he is the oldest Olympic medallist ever. *(BBC Hulton)*

when he won the RWA 50km title in 1949. He had won his first RWA title, at 20 miles, 22 years earlier for the greatest span of any British champion. Johnson won Midlands championships over a 27 year span, 1922–49.

ENGLISH NATIONAL CROSS-COUNTRY CHAMPIONSHIP

The 'National' is the biggest cross-country championship in the world. Records for the number of competitors have been set almost annually, with peak numbers to date at Western Park, Leicester in 1980. Then there were 1710, of whom 1627 finished in the senior race; 602 of whom 532 finished in the junior and 734 with 628 finishing in the youth race.

The first race was in 1876, but all 32 runners got lost in Epping Forest, and the race was declared void. Thus the inaugural championships were in 1877 when 33 started and the individual winner was Percy Stenning of the winning team, Thames Hare and Hounds (formed in 1868), which had the first three to finish, a feat never subsequently achieved.

The teams with the most wins are: Birchfield Harriers 28 (1880, 1886–8, 1891–2, 1895, 1903, 1907, 1909, 1913, 1920–6, 1928–34, 1936–7, 1953); Salford Harriers 6 (1889–90, 1894, 1896–8); Tipton Harriers 6 (1969, 1972, 1978, 1980–2); Hallamshire Harriers 5 (1908, 1910–12, 1927); Gateshead Harriers 5 (1973, 1975–7, 1979).

Teams of nine runners, of whom six score, contest the race. **The greatest number of teams** finishing with six runners, is 173 in 1982.

The most individual wins have been: four Percy Stenning 1877–80; four Alfred Shrubb 1901–4.

The most placings in the first three have been seven for Ernest Harper (1st 1927, 1929; 2nd 1924–6, 1930; 3rd 1923); six for Bernie Ford, who has a remarkable record of always being placed in the top ten. From his senior debut in 1973 until 1981, he was placed successively 5-2-2-1-2-1-2-6-9. Frank Sando had a similar nine successive years, 1952–60 in the top ten, winning in 1957. Gerry North, the 1962 winner, had 13 successive years 1959–71 in which he was in the first 20 each year except for his 48th place in 1967.

The junior race was first staged in 1948. Four athletes have won twice: Walter Hesketh 1950–1; Mike Tagg 1966–7; Neil Coupland 1973–4; Nat Muir 1976–7.

The youth race was first staged in 1946. Three athletes have won twice: W. I. Williams 1950–1; Alan Cocking 1954–5; David Atkin 1964–5.

Athletes to have won at all three age groups Walter Hesketh had an almost perfect record in his only appearances from 1948 to 1952, winning: youth 1948, junior 1950–1 and senior 1952. He was third in the 1949 junior race. David Black won the youth 1971, junior 1972 and senior 1974. Narrow misses came from two men who won both youth and senior titles: Tony Simmons won the youth in 1967 and senior in 1975, but was third at junior in 1968 and 1969; Dave Bedford won the youth in 1968, then was second at junior in 1971 before winning the senior in 1971 and 1973. Mike Tagg was second in the 1965 youth race, won two junior titles (above) and the senior in 1969.

The biggest winning margin in the senior race is 1min 55sec by Julian Goater in 1981.

The closest senior race was in 1966 when Ron Hill beat Mike Turner by a 'chest'.

The increase in the number of runners in the senior race:
1877 **33**, 1878 **35**, 1879 **41**, 1880 **88**, 1881 **105**, 1882 **107**, 1895 **149**, 1902 **159**, 1906 **162**, 1907 **186**, 1908 **252**, 1914 **273**, 1923 **327**, 1927 **429**, 1949 **449**, 1950 **493**, 1955 **544**, 1957 **717**, 1961 **796**, 1963 **857**, 1965 **908**, 1966 **919**, 1968 **944**, 1969 **1046**, 1973 **1195 (1070 finishers, first over**

The 1925 'National' – from left: William Cotterell (first), Ernie Harper (winner 1927, 1929), Jack Webster (winner 1926, 1928).   *(BBC Hulton)*

1000), 1976 **1314**, 1977 **1458**, 1978 **1536**, 1979 **1672**, 1980 **1710**, 1982 **1743**.

Area Championships were first held as follows: Midland 1879, Northern 1883, Southern 1884. In 1970 Dave Bedford won the Southern senior race over nine miles by a margin of 55sec. Less than 20 minutes later he lined up for the junior race over six miles and proceeded to win that by 61sec from Jack Lane.

SCOTLAND
The Scottish AAA was formed on 26 Feb 1883, and in that year the first national championships were held at Powderhall, Edinburgh.

The Scottish Championships, now established at Meadowbank, Edinburgh, have always been held in that city or Glasgow, with the exception of Paisley 1885, Dundee 1892 and Grangemouth 1967–9 and 1979.

The most titles won have been 42 by Tom Nicolson between 1902–27, including 21 hammer (the most for any one event), 14 shot, 3 standing style hammer and 4 at 56lb weight. Nicolson was fourth in the Olympic hammer in 1908. In 1920 he missed the team boat to Antwerp, and eventually arrived after the qualifying round had been held. However, the other competitors insisted that he should be allowed to compete and he was placed sixth in the final. His brothers Hugh (one at shot) and Andrew (11 shot and five Scots hammer) also won Scottish titles.

The most wins at one event in recent years have been 13 successive high jump titles by Crawford Fairbrother 1957–69. Fairbrother also won AAA titles in 1959, 1961 and 1964.

Four track event titles were won in one day by Wyndham Halswelle on 23 Jun 1906 at Powderhall. His sequence was as follows: 100y in 10.4; 880y in 2:00.4; 220y in 23.2; 440y in 51.4. He served with the Highland Light Infantry in the Boer War in South Africa and only took up serious athletics in 1904 at the age of 22. He went on to win the Olympic 400m title in 1908 (qv) and his Scottish Native 440y record of 48.4 set that year lasted for 50 years.

Eric Liddell became the next British athlete to win the Olympic 400m title, and he won three successive trebles at the Scottish championships. In 1921, 1922 and 1923 he won the 100y, 220y and ran on the winning Edinburgh University 1 mile relay team. In 1924 and 1925 he won the 100y, 220y and 440y, and also in 1925, a fourth title, for the Edinburgh University 1 mile relay team.
   Liddell, British record holder for 100y at 9.7, went to the Olympic Games with a 440y best of 49.6, his winning time at the 1924 AAAs. It was therefore as an outsider that he won the title, improving to 48.2 in the semi-finals and 47.6, a British record, in the final. In 1925 Liddell returned to China, the land of his birth, as a missionary. He died in a Japanese internment camp in 1945.

The track treble of 100y/220y/440y was won in three successive years by Alfred Downer in 1893–5. 'Ming' Campbell achieved this treble in 1963 and 1964, but dropped out of the 440y at the last minute in 1965, when a win would have equalled Downer's effort.

The Scottish Cross-Country Union was formed in 1890, but the first Scottish cross-country championships had been held in 1886.

The Scottish women's championships were first staged in 1931. The most titles ever won are 18 by Alix Stevenson (née Jamieson) 1958–70, including seven long jump, six pentathlon, three at 80m hurdles, and two at 100y/m.

The largest attendances at athletics meetings in Scotland were those of the immediate post war years at the Rangers FC Sports in Glasgow with up to 70000 people. The 76th and last Rangers Sports were held in 1962.

WALES
The first Welsh championships were staged in 1893 at 100y and 1 mile, but it was not until 1951 that the championships were first held at Maindy Stadium, Cardiff, on a cinder track. Since 1975 they have been held at Cwmbran, with its all-weather surface track.

The most titles won are 20 by D. J. P. 'Dippy' Richards between 1923 and 1948. He started with four each at 1 mile and 4 miles in the 1920s and the rest were for walking from 1936.

The most wins at one event has been 10 by Laurie Hall with the hammer 1958–67.

Welsh Women's championships have been held annually since 1952.

The most women's titles at one event are 9 by Venissa Head at shot 1974–81. Head raised the Welsh record from 13.00m in 1974 to 17.84m at the 1981 Welsh championships, the latter her third British record of the year (as well as three UK indoor bests). She also won four discus titles, making a record total of 13 Welsh titles overall.

The most important meeting held in Wales was the 1958 Commonwealth Games in Cardiff. In commemoration Welsh Games have been held annually from 1959, first at Cardiff and now at Cwmbran.

Four Welshmen have won Commonwealth Games gold medals: Reg Thomas (running for England as Wales was not represented) 1 mile in 1930. Jim Alford (later the first Welsh national coach 1948–61) 1 mile in 1938; Lynn Davies long jump in 1966 and 1970; and Berwyn Price 110mh in 1978. Price and Davies are the Welsh athletes who have most often represented Britain internationally.

British International Matches
The first 'international' match was held at Lansdowne Road, Dublin between England and Ireland on 5 Jun 1876. A series of annual matches between Ireland and Scotland started on 20 Jul 1895 at Celtic Park, Glasgow and triangular matches between England, Ireland and Scotland were held between 1914 and 1938. The results of these series were: England 1st 8, 2nd 2; Scotland 1st 2, 2nd 3, 3rd 5; Ireland 2nd 5, 3rd 5.
   These inter-British Isles matches preceded the first British full international, against France

at Stade Colombes, Paris on 11 Sep 1921. The British team, called England as were all such teams prior to 1933 although athletes were drawn from the entire United Kingdom, won by 123 points to 118 in a very ill-tempered contest. The English team bus was stoned due to protests against action by the British Government over exchange rates which depressed the Franc.

The first British women's international match was held on 30 Oct 1921 when Britain beat France in an unofficial match in Paris in conjunction with an international soccer match. Two years later on 23 Sep 1923 the first official Great Britain–France match was held in Paris.

Crawford Fairbrother at the 1963 AAA championships when he was placed second.

BRITISH INTERNATIONAL MATCHES
(not including European Cup fixtures)

Summary of matches to 1 June 1982:		MEN				WOMEN	
Against		*First Score to GB*				*First Score to GB*	
		Outdoors	*Indoors*			*Outdoors*	*Indoors*
France	1921	23–10	1–3		1923	14–0	3–1
Germany	1929	1–5			1931	2–1	
Italy	1931	2–2	0–2		1952	2–1 (1T)	
Finland	1935	5–4	2–0		1972	2–0 (1T)	
Norway	1937	2–1			–		
Yugoslavia	1951	2–0			1976	1–0	
Greece	1951	4–0			1972	1–0	
Turkey	1951	1–0			–		
German Fed. Rep.	1953	2–11	3–6		1953	10–6	3–5
Sweden	1953	5–3			1973	5–0	
Hungary	1955	6–2			1954	8–2	
Czechoslovakia	1955	5–0			1954	5–0 (1T)	
USSR	1955	1–7			1955	2–6	
Poland	1957	1–13 (1T)			1957	8–7	
Commonwealth	1958	0–1			1958	0–1	
USA	1961	0–4	0–1		1961	3–0	0–1
Netherlands	1972	1–0			1963	8–0	2–0
Russian SFSR	1963	2–0			1963	1–1	
Switzerland	1968	2–0			1979	1–0	
Romania	–				1969	2–2	
GDR	1970	0–7	0–8		1970	0–7	0–7
Spain	1972	1–0	4–3		–		
Bulgaria	–				1973	1–1	
Belgium	1973	1–0	2–0		1975		1–0
Canada	1974	2–0	0–1		1974	2–0	0–1
Benelux	1974	1–0					

(T = ties. The first such tie was the men's match against Poland in 1964, 106 points each. Although Poland's men have a clear lead in the series, the matches have often been close, for in addition to the tie, Poland won by one point in 1961, two in 1974 and four in 1962. Britain's first win was by three points in 1976.)

The biggest margins of victory

To Great Britain: men 147–65 *v* Netherlands 1972; women 93–40 *v* Italy 1974 (greatest domination, although a higher points margin was the 182–95 win against Netherlands in a three-a-side match in 1976).

To opponents: men 29–73 *v* France 1945, 42½–93½ *v* Germany 1939, and in a three-a-side match 153–254 *v* USSR 1976; women 46–111 *v* GDR 1981.

Scheduled as the first GB v USSR match in Britain, the 1956 fixture was cancelled at the last minute as discus champion Nina Ponomaryeva was accused of shoplifting some hats from C & A Modes in Oxford Street. The USSR team withdrew and Mrs Ponomaryeva never appeared in court.

The oldest British international athlete is Harold Whitlock who was 48 years 218 days old when he came 11th in the 50km walk at the 1952 Olympic Games. He had won the event in 1936.

The oldest British woman athlete is Rosemary Payne who was 41 years 130 days old when she threw the discus against Finland in 1974.

The youngest British international athlete is Janis Walsh who was 14 years 324 days old when she ran at 60m and 4 × 200m relay against GDR indoors in 1975. Sonia Lannaman was just 16 days older when she made her senior international debut against GDR indoors in 1971, but she had run in a junior match against West Germany when she was 14 years 181 days in 1970.

The youngest British male international is Ross Hepburn, who was 15 years 316 days when he high jumped against USSR in 1977.

The most international appearances by a British man is 67 by Geoff Capes, all in the shot. He competed in three junior matches in 1967–8, before making his senior debut against Czechoslovakia on 6 Jul 1969. His first win came in his tenth match, which was against West Germany in 1971. In all he won 35 times, **the most individual event wins** by a British athlete. He won on his final appearance, against Sweden on 12 Sep 1980, but this was a very low key affair, for the paid attendance for the two days of the fixture at Meadowbank Stadium, Edinburgh was just 621, the lowest ever for a British international match. Capes' final defeat by a British athlete was at the hands of Jeff Teale in the 1970

AAA championships. He had 42 outdoor and 25 indoor GB internationals. At the European Indoor Championships he won twice (1974 and 1976), was second three times (1975, 1977 and 1979) and was third in 1978. He won the bronze medal at the 1974 European Championships, but was not allowed to compete in the 1978 finals in Prague for allegedly manhandling an official. At the Olympic Games he did not quite

Geoff Capes competes for GB v Finland in 1978. He won the shot with 20.68m, one of his record 35 event wins for Britain in 67 internationals. He ranked number one in Britain for ten years from 1971 to 1980. *(G. Herringshaw)*

do himself justice: he failed to qualify for the final in 1972 and was placed sixth in 1976 and fifth in 1980. Capes also represented England on six occasions including three Commonwealth Games – fourth in 1970 and first in 1974 and 1978.

The most appearances by a woman and the most wins including relays have been 67 by Verona Elder (née Bernard). Her individual wins include 17 at 400m, two at 800m and one at 200m. She has been Britain's most successful woman at the European Indoor Championships, winning the 400m in 1973 (world best 53.04), 1975 (52.68) and 1979 (51.80), and was placed second in 1977 and third in 1981.

The most outdoor international appearances is 61 by hammer thrower Howard Payne. He made his debut in 1960 at the age of 29 and his career closely parallelled that of his wife Rosemary, also a late starter, as she was aged 30 on her debut in 1963. Both made their final appearance against Finland in 1974.

The most international appearances for Great Britain

These include full international appearances for Great Britain in the Olympic Games, European Championships, European Cup and against other nations – indoors and outdoors, but do not include the Commonwealth Games or other appearances for England, Scotland, Wales or Northern Ireland.

Following each name their number of event wins is shown in brackets, first at individual events, and after the oblique on relay teams:

MEN
67 Geoff Capes (35) 1969–80
66 Mike Bull (10) 1965–77
61 Howard Payne (15) 1960–74
60 Brian Hooper (16) 1971–81
53 Crawford Fairbrother (4) 1957–69
53 Bill Tancred (6) 1964–76
50 Mike Winch (4) 1973–81
50 Alan Pascoe (24/6) 1967–78
48 Berwyn Price (13) 1971–81
46 David Travis (12) 1965–78
42 Alan Lerwill (10/1) 1967–76
41 Lynn Davies (26/1) 1962–72

WOMEN
67 Verona Elder (20/31) 1971–82
65 Brenda Bedford (12) 1961–78
51 Rosemary Payne (11) 1963–74
43 Mary Peters (6) 1961–73
43 Ann Wilson/Simmonds (9/1) 1966–78
41 Sonia Lannaman (25/16) 1971–80
41 Barbara Lawton (11) 1966–76
40 Tessa Sanderson (16) 1974–81
39 Mary Rand (30/9) 1957–67
39 Andrea Lynch (16/15) 1970–78

The best success rate for any of the above was by Mary Rand (née Bignal), an individual winner 30 times in 39 internationals. This total is comprised: 17 out of 30 long jump appearances, 5 out of 9 pentathlon, 4 at 80m hurdles, 3 at high jump and 1 at 100m hurdles. In all she competed in 79 events in these matches. On two occasions she contested four events: against West Germany in 1963 when she set British records at the pentathlon and 100m hurdles, shared a UK All-Comers record at the sprint relay and won the long jump; and against Poland in 1964, when she won the long jump, was second at 4 × 100mR, and third at 100m and 80m hurdles.

The most successive wins at one event is 16 (or 17 if the unofficial European Indoor Games are

Alan Pascoe (left) beats Berwyn Price at 110m hurdles for GB v West Germany in 1971.
(Press Association)

included) at long jump by Lynn Davies between 1963–7.

The most wins by a British man is 44 (25 individual, 19 relay) by David Jenkins in 36 internationals between 1967–81. He had 18 wins in 27 races at 400m, including 13 out of 15 in internationals against one or two other nations.

Progressive list of most GB internationals
MEN
11 Fred Gaby 1921–30
14 Reggie Thomas 1928–37
20 Robert Howland 1927–39
23 Don Finlay 1929–49
29 Peter Hildreth 1950–62
53 Crawford Fairbrother 1957–69
61 Howard Payne 1960–74
66 Mike Bull 1965–77
67 Geoff Capes 1969–80

WOMEN
19 Dorothy Tyler 1936–56
35 Suzanne Allday 1951–64
39 Mary Rand 1957–67
51 Rosemary Payne 1963–74
65 Brenda Bedford 1961–78
67 Verona Elder 1971–82

The most successful international season by a British athlete must be 1963 for Dorothy Hyman. In five internationals she won a sprint treble (100, 200 and relay) in every match except the final one of the season, when the British relay squad were disqualified against Hungary, though Hyman had the consolation of setting European records at both 100m (11.3) and 200m (23.2) in Budapest. In her 19 full internationals from 1957 to 1964 this Yorkshire girl achieved individual sprint doubles eight times as well as doing the same for England in the 1962 Commonwealth Games.

The record span for British international appearances is 20 years by Dorothy Tyler (1936–56) and Don Finlay (1929–49). Finlay first competed for Britain at long jump and was placed 6th against France in 1929. After that he had immense success at the high hurdles, winning 14 out of 16 individual races in dual internationals, as well as third and second places at the 1932 and 1936 Olympic Games and winning the 1938 European title. His two dual meeting losses were to Lord Burghley in 1931 and John Thornton in 1937, and in all he only lost nine races between 1933 and 1939. Finlay made an astonishing comeback after the war to win two internationals against France, and the 1949 AAA title. He also had, at the age of 40, a sensational win in Glasgow on 6 Aug 1949 over Richard Attlesey, who set a world record of 13.5 the following year. Sadly Finlay fell while leading in his heat at the 1948 Olympics. His final race in major events was for England at the 1950 Commonwealth Games, when he was placed fourth. He topped the annual British rankings for his event on a record 13 occasions, between 1933 and 1951.

Donald Finlay, whose 20 year span as an international is a British record. His 14.3 for 110mh was a British record 1938–61. *(H. W. Neale)*

The only perfect records at one event (minimum five races) in dual meet internationals have been:
McDonald Bailey 7/7 at 200m/220y from 1949–52. Bailey also won 7/9 at 100m/100y and from 1950 to 1952 won sprint trebles (including the relay) at six successive internationals.
Sydney Wooderson 6/6 at 1500m and 1 mile from 1935–45. Wooderson must take pride of place as **Britain's most successful international athlete**, for in addition to those six wins, he also won at 880y in his only international at that distance, in 1938, and the European titles at 1500m in 1938 and 5000m in 1946. His only international defeat was at the 1936 Olympic Games, when he was eliminated because of an ankle injury in a heat of the 1500m.
Ian McCafferty 5/5 at 5000m from 1966–72. He was also second in 1967 at 5000m in the European Cup and won his only international at 3000m.

JUNIOR INTERNATIONALS
The first full-scale British junior international match was held against France on 29 Jul 1967 at Portsmouth, and was contested by men under 20 at the end of that year.

The first British women's junior international was against West Germany on 26 Sep 1970 at Leicester. This was for those under 19 by the end of the year, although due to a misunderstanding the Germans included some girls of a year older.

The most seasons that an individual has been in the British junior team is four over five years for Sonia Lannaman, 1970–71 and 1973–4, and for Milton Palmer, 1974–5 and 1977–8. Lannaman made her junior debut at 14½ years and her senior international debut in 1971 at 15. Palmer started his senior high jump career in 1974, when he was 16 years 16 days old and Britain's youngest ever male international at the time.

Other British Meetings
The 'Coke' The Coca-Cola Bottlers International, organised by the International Athletes Club, was first held at Crystal Palace on 24 Aug 1968 when two world records were set: Ron Clarke 2 miles in 8:19.6 and the women's GB 4 × 200m relay team.

The Edinburgh Highland Games were first held

Barry Smith (left) and Brendan Foster (right)
dead-heated in the latter's last international race
at Gateshead over 5000m in 1978.   *(J. Burles)*

in 1947 before the first Edinburgh International
Festival. They are now held at Meadowbank,
where there was a peak attendance of 16000 in
1972.

The Gateshead Games were first held in 1975,
when they were sponsored by Rediffusion. They
have been sponsored by Phillips since 1977.

The Philips Night of Athletics at Crystal Palace
was first held in 1972.

The Talbot Games at Crystal Palace were first
held in 1980. They succeeded the Rotary
(Watches) Games.

The Inter-Counties Championships, organised
by the Counties Athletic Union (CAU), were
first held in 1925 at Stamford Bridge as a relays
meeting. Once established at the White City,
the venue now varies annually. **The most wins**
up to 1981 have been Surrey 25 Middlesex 23.

The British Games were first staged on 1 Aug
1923 at Stamford Bridge. They have usually
been held on bank holidays (both Whitsun and
August) and have often accommodated the
inter-counties championships or more recently
international meetings.

The Emsley Carr Mile has been held annually at
one major British meeting or another since
1953. Its perpetual challenge trophy is a book,
handsomely bound in red Morocco leather
identical to that used for the Queen's Coronation Bible in 1953. This book records the story
of mile running and its foreword opens with
these words:

'In the Coronation year of 1953, an outstanding ambition of world track athletes is to achieve
the four minute mile. In order to encourage
runners from home and overseas in this quest
the "News of the World" has instituted this
annual contest.'

The race is named in memory of Sir Emsley
Carr, Editor of the News of the World for more
than 50 years. The first Emsley Carr mile was
preceded by a motorised lap of honour by four
great milers: 79-year-old Joe Binks, whose
4:16.8 British record in 1902 was then the
second fastest ever; Paavo Nurmi, Sydney
Wooderson, and Gunder Hägg. The first race
was won by Gordon Pirie (GB) in 4:06.8 in an
amazing upset over Wes Santee (USA).

Four ex-1 mile record holders at the White City in
1953 (from left, after the driver) Wooderson,
Nurmi, Hagg and Binks.   *(H. W. Neale)*

The most Emsley Carr wins is four by Ken Wood
(GB) 1954–5, 1957 and 1961. The fastest time
is 3:53.4 by Kipchoge Keino (Ken) in 1966.

The first sub-four-minute Emsley Carr race was
in 1956 when Derek Ibbotson (GB) won in
3:59.4, and the most men to break this barrier is
eight in both 1976 and 1979, when the winners
were David Moorcroft (GB) 3:57.06 and Steve
Ovett (GB) 3:56.58 respectively.

LEAGUE ATHLETICS IN BRITAIN

Although league athletics had been tried before, it was as recently as 1967 that the current era of inter-club athletics in Britain was launched with the foundation of the Midland League for men's clubs. After a pilot league in 1968 the National League was formed in 1969, later changing its name to the British Athletics League (BAL), which now comprises five divisions of six clubs.

BAL records

The most successful club is Wolverhampton & Bilston, champions from 1975–81. Wolverhampton won all four matches in both 1975 (when they totalled a record 1112 points) and in 1981.

The highest points score by a club in a match was 302½ by Wolverhampton in Division 1 on 21 May 1977.

The highest individual points score in one match is 54 by Daley Thompson for Essex Beagles at

Gordon Pirie wins the first Emsley Carr mile at the White City in 1953 from the favourite, Wes Santee (USA) in 4:06.8. *(H. W. Neale)*

West London on 26 May 1979 when he scored at six events.

The highest individual points score in a season is 144 by Angus McKenzie for Shaftesbury Harriers in 1979.

The British Athletics Cup competition was launched in 1973 for men and in 1974 for women. The competitions are now staged for the Guardian Royal Exchange Gold and Jubilee Cups.

The most successful men's team has been Wolverhampton and Bilston, winners in 1973, 1976–7, 1979–80.

The most successful women's team has been Stretford, winners 1976–81.

Edinburgh Southern Harriers won both men's and women's cups in 1975.

The highest individual points score in a final is 34 by Sharon Colyear for Stretford in 1976. She was second at long jump and won 100m, 200m and 100m hurdles. The following year Colyear won 100m, 200m and long jump – the only individual trebles in the Cup Finals.

The highest male points score in a final is 28 by Angus McKenzie for Edinburgh Southern in 1976. McKenzie, uniquely, competed in all Cup Finals from 1973 to 1981, switching to Shaftesbury in 1978, and has in all amassed 120 individual points.

The most individual event wins have been eight by Margaret Ritchie, six at discus and two shot. Mike Bull won six pole vault victories.

The British Women's League started in 1975. Sale Harriers with three wins between 1976 and 1978 have been the most successful team.

OXFORD versus CAMBRIDGE

The great British Universities of Oxford and Cambridge played an exceptional role in the early growth of athletics.

The first University athletics meeting was staged by Exeter College, Oxford in 1850. The idea for the meeting was mooted on the evening of the College's steeplechase when it was suggested that a two mile run across country on foot rather than on horseback should be held and also flat races of 100y, 300y, 440y and 1 mile as well as

Oxford and Cambridge athletics in 1872. Throwing the hammer, 'a false start', and the pole vault.
(BBC Hulton)

140y over ten flights of hurdles. The steeplechase, run for stake money, was won by Halifax Wyatt, who had been 9–1 in the betting. Wyatt also demonstrated his all-round ability by winning the 100y. He also won a Cricket 'blue' in 1850 and 1851. Thereafter Exeter held their sports annually and were soon followed by other colleges.

Cambridge University first held their annual sports in 1857 and Oxford University sports followed in 1860. After the successful establishment of these fixtures the first Inter-Varsity contest was held on 5 Mar 1864 at Christ Church Ground, Oxford. Eight events were contested: 100y, 440y, 1 mile, steeplechase, 120y hurdles, 200y hurdles, high jump and long jump. The result was a tie, four events each.

The University match has been held every year since then, with the exception of the war years. Nowadays the demands of academic life and the rise in standards outside the Universities have relegated the fixture in importance, but for many years it was one of the most significant meetings in the British calendar despite an early season date. The 1864 and 1866 sports were held in Oxford and those of 1865 in Cambridge, but from 1867 the sports moved to London, where they stayed until 1977, when they once again reverted to alternating between Oxford and Cambridge.

From 1864 to 1937 scoring was by event. Points scoring was introduced in 1938. Oxford have won on 52 occasions to 48 for Cambridge with 7 ties to 1981.

A women's match was first held in 1975, and Cambridge have so far won 6–1.

The most individual wins have been nine by Adrian Metcalfe (O) – 100y 1962, 1964; 220y 1961–2, 1964; 440y 1961–4. Metcalfe set a world junior 400m record of 45.7 in 1961 when he was ranked first in the world, but despite an Olympic silver medal at 4×400m relay in 1964 injuries prevented him from fulfilling his potential. Since 1967 he has been the ITV athletics commentator. Another distinguished commentator, Harold Abrahams (C), held the previous record with eight wins: 100y 1920–3; 440y 1923; and long jump 1920, 1922–3.

The most wins in one year have been four by Robert Tisdall (C) in 1931 (440y, 120yh, LJ, SP) and Tom Blodgett (C) in 1963 (120yh, 220yh, PV, JT). The American Blodgett's records of 14.2 and 23.7 in the hurdles races held off Mike Hogan (O), who went on to win a second place at 440yh for the third time. Hogan won all three hurdles races in 1964 and 1965.

Doubles for three successive years were also won by Lord Burghley (C) 120yh and 220yh 1925–7 and Derek Johnson (O) 440y and 880y 1954–6, before winning the 1 mile in 1957.

Women's match: Most wins: 8 Gillian Smith (C) 1976–8, including a record four events in 1977, and by Kim Tuffnell (C) 1978–80.

The first Oxford v Cambridge cross-country race was held at Oxford on 2 Dec 1880. At Kingston Vale, 100 years later the race was won by Nick Brawn, who became the first to win for four successive years. The match score is 45 wins each.

The Achilles Club, based on Oxford and Cambridge blues was founded in 1920. In the 1920s and 1930s the club dominated British athletics. 23 Achilles members competed at the 1924 Olympic Games (18 for Great Britain, two for South Africa and one each for Canada, New Zealand and the USA) and at the 1928 Games (20 for Great Britain, and one each for Canada, New Zealand and South Africa).

LOUGHBOROUGH

Loughborough has been pre-eminent as the centre of athletics education in Britain. The AAA summer school, which was to play a vital role in the education of coaches, was first held there in August 1934 with the aim of improving field events standards. The School was initiated by Lt. Col. F. A. M. Webster with Evelyn Montague. In 1936 Webster was appointed the Director of the School of Athletics Games and Physical Education at Loughborough.

Harold Abrahams wins the long jump for the combined Oxford/Cambridge team against Harvard and Yale Universities at the newly opened Wembley Stadium in 1923. *(BBC Hulton)*

Loughborough went for a period of 22 years unbeaten by another college, until on 19 May 1971 in the second of their annual encounters, they lost 91–129 to Borough Road College. The previous year Borough Road, for whom Alan Pascoe and Alan Lerwill were the major stars – between them winning five events each year, had lost by just one point. The annual series of matches against the AAA started in 1959, to 1981 AAA have won 16 to Loughborough's 7.

SCHOOLS

The English Schools Athletics Association was formed in 1925. Their inter-county schools championships were first staged that year and have grown steadily to their current size and prestige. Until 1947 they were for boys and girls under 14 years old. In 1948 15–17 age groups were added and in 1951 17–19 age groups followed.

Before the last war the most important schools meeting was that organised annually for London AC. First held in 1890 the last meeting was staged in 1971.

In Scotland Inter-Scholastic Games were held in the 1870s and annual Scottish Schoolboys

A view from the grandstand of the London Athletic Club grounds at Stamford Bridge.
(By permission of the British Library)

championships for boys have been held since 1900; girls events were first included in the 1930s.

Famous British Stadia

THE WHITE CITY STADIUM, LONDON
Opened on 14 May 1908 by the Prince of Wales and designed for the 1908 Olympic Games it had seating for 90000 people, and cost nearly £50000. The first of more than 50 world records set on the track, was 3:59.8 for 1500m by Harold Wilson at the British Olympic trials on 29 May 1908. The AAA championships were held there on 4 Jul 1908 and nine days later King Edward VII was there to open the Games.

It was 24 years until the AAAs returned to the White City, which by then had been reduced in size and adapted for greyhound racing. In 1934 the British Empire Games and the Women's World Games were both staged on the track.

From 1932 to 1970 the White City was the home of British athletics. The biggest attendance was probably that estimated at 52000 on 6 August 1945, with thousands locked out of the ground, for the Bank Holiday match between the AAA, the Army, the RAF and the US Forces. The feature of the meeting was the mile clash won by Arne Andersson in 4:08.8 from Sydney Wooderson 4:09.2. There had also been a capacity crowd for the GB v Germany international in 1937, and in the immediate post-war years there were many 30000 plus attendances. There was a record two-day attendance of 71500 for the GB v USSR match in 1955. By the late 1960s, however, crowds had slumped so that its use was no longer an economical venture. Athletics moved to the Crystal Palace and the greyhounds were left to rule the White City.

LILLIE BRIDGE AND STAMFORD BRIDGE
The Lillie Bridge Athletic Ground in West London was opened in 1869, and burnt down by angry crowds on 19 Sep 1887. This was the culmination of a riot after two sprinters, Harry Hutchens and Harry Gent had failed to appear for a match over 120 yards for a prize of £200. Rival gangs each wanted their man to lose in order to succeed in a betting coup. Hutchens had dominated 'pro' sprinting for several years and Gent was reckoned to be his first serious rival.

Stamford Bridge, opened on 28 Apr 1877, was the major British athletics venue in the first thirty years of the 20th century. The record attendance was over 41000 for the USA v British Empire meeting in 1928.

CRYSTAL PALACE, LONDON
The 'old' Crystal Palace staged such first fixtures as those of the National Olympian Association in 1866 and the English Schools in 1925, but the modern track at the National Sports Centre was opened on 17 Jun 1964 with a match between London and New York, resulting in a 75–75 tie, sponsored by Guinness. Amongst the winners at this opening meeting was Al Oerter (DT 59.96m). He made his next visit to the track 15 years later when he was second to John Powell at the AAAs.

The official opening of the 'Tartan' track was on 19 May 1968, with Alan Pascoe winning four events.

The first 'full house' was on August Bank Holiday 1971 for the Great Britain v West Germany match, with a crowd of about 17000 and many more turned away. Recently the 'Coke' meeting has become an annual sell-out.

MEADOWBANK, EDINBURGH
The Meadowbank Sports Centre was opened on 2 May 1970. The first world record on the track was set on 13 Jun 1970 by the British 4 × 800m relay team of Rosemary Stirling, Sheila Carey, Pat Lowe and Lillian Board with 8:27.0. In July 1970 the Commonwealth Games were held at Meadowbank and a world record was set in the women's 400m by Marilyn Neufville (Jam) with 51.02. In 1973 Meadowbank hosted the European Cup Final, the only occasion that it has been held in Britain, and the Commonwealth Games are set to return in 1988.

Advertising

The IAAF rules are gradually being relaxed to allow 'amateur' athletes to appear in advertisements. Money has to be paid to governing bodies or clubs.

In 1960 the American pole vaulter Don Laz sued CBS and the Ford Motor Company for $840000 damages for 'invasion of privacy' as a film strip of him vaulting had been used in a commercial. The case was settled out of court for $35000. Two other top-class pole vaulters appeared in advertisements in 1970. Ron Morris, who like Laz had won an Olympic silver medal, appeared in the *Wall Street Journal* vaulting in suit, tie and hat, but John Pennel, still an active competitor, was suspended by the AAU for allowing his picture to be used in a cigarette advertisement without written permission.

In 1932 'Babe' Didrikson was barred from amateur competition by the AAU. She was charged with allowing her photograph and an interview with her to be used in an automobile advertisement.

Altitude

The highest ever venue for a major championships is over 3700m/12140ft for La Paz, where the 1981 South American Championships were staged.

The highest venue for an Olympic Games is Mexico City in 1968. Its altitude of 2240m/7349ft provides an atmosphere where the air is some 23% thinner than at sea level. This shortage of oxygen adversely affects the distance runners, and times at 5000m and 10000m are always considerably slower at high altitudes than at sea level. Explosive events, such as the sprints and horizontal jumps, on the other hand, are materially improved by high altitude. The cur-

rent men's world records for 100m, 200m, 400m, 4 × 400mR and long jump were all set at Mexico City.

Other notable high altitude athletics venues include: Bogota, Colombia 2610m, Addis Ababa, Ethiopia 2365m, South Lake Tahoe (Echo Summit), USA 2249m, Flagstaff, Arizona, USA 2105m, Johannesburg, South Africa 1733m, Nairobi, South Africa 1675m, Albuquerque, New Mexico, USA 1555m, Leninaken, USSR 1550m, Bloemfontein, South Africa 1492m, Provo, Utah, USA 1380m, Salt Lake City, Utah, USA 1372m, Pretoria, South Africa 1360m, El Paso, Texas, USA 1130m.

Notable venues at between 400m and 1000m include: Sao Paulo, Brazil 725m, Edmonton, Canada 690m, Madrid, Spain 650m, Sofia, Bulgaria 550m, Berne, Switzerland 548m, Munich, W. Germany 520m, Zurich, Switzerland 409m.

The highest track in the world is at Lhasa in Tibet at an altitude of about 4570m/15000ft.

Athletes at Other Sports

AMERICAN FOOTBALL
Numerous American athletes have excelled at American Football. Many college track stars are drafted annually by professional teams, having made their names for both speed and strength.

Those to have achieved the highest success at both sports are:
Bob Hayes was double Olympic sprint gold medallist in 1964. He turned pro in 1965 for the Dallas Cowboys and was selected as All-Pro pass receiver in 1966 and 1971.
Ollie Matson ran in the 1952 Olympics, when he was third at 400m and won a silver medal at 4 × 400m relay. After a brilliant college career for San Francisco, he turned pro and was an All-League selection at half back in 1952 and 1954–7.

O. J. Simpson (O.J. standing for Orenthal James) was on the University of Southern California's 4 × 110y relay team that set a world record in 1967. He had a best 100y time of 9.4sec. He holds the all-time Football records for the most touchdowns in a season, 23 in 1975; the most yards gained in a season, 2003 in 1975; and was four times the American Football Conference rushing leader, playing for the Buffalo Bills for most of his career.

Jim Thorpe won both the pentathlon and decathlon titles at the 1912 Olympic Games, although he had to forfeit these when it was revealed that he had received money for playing baseball (see p. 105). In 1950 Thorpe was voted the greatest Footballer of the half-century in an Associated Press poll. He had been college scoring leader while at Carlisle Indian School in 1912. Part Algonquin Indian, his Indian name was 'Wa-Tho-Huck', meaning Bright Path. He also played pro baseball in 1913–9.

Other All-Pro selections to have been notable athletes include:
Al Blozis (New York, Georgetown), AAU shot champion indoors and out 1940–2.
Cliff Branch (Oakland Raiders), best times of 10.0 for 100m, 20.4 for 220y and an indoor world best 5.9 for 60y in 1962.
Nolan Cromwell (Los Angeles Rams), 49.74 for 400m hurdles 1976.
Isaac Curtis (Cincinnati Bengals), second NCAA 100y in his first year of serious sprinting, 1970.
Russ Francis (New England Patriots), All-Pro 1978–80, set the still standing US high school javelin record of 79.18m/259ft 9in in 1971, when he had a meteoric rise to the top. He threw 56.40m/185ft in his first competition on 2 April. He improved to 67.64m/221ft 11in, then on 7 May set his first high school record of 77.14m/253ft 1in, thence to 77.70m/254ft 11in and finally that 79.18m on 12 June.
Mel Gray (St Louis Cardinals), best times of 9.2/9.1w – 100y and 20.4 – 220y in 1969–70.
James Lofton (Green Bay Packers), NCAA long jump champion in 1978, with bests of 8.23m/27ft for long jump, 20.5 for 200m and 46.2 for 400m.
Earl McCullouch (Detroit Lions), NFL Rookie of the Year in 1968. In 1967 he equalled the world record (13.2) and won the Pan-American title at 110m hurdles.
Mel Renfro (Dallas Cowboys), second NCAA 120y hurdles and ran on the first leg of the Oregon University 4 × 110y relay world record team in 1962.
Paul Warfield (Cleveland Browns and Miami Dolphins), 7.92m/26ft long jump in 1962, which ranked him fourth in the world.

Other star footballers with good athletics credentials
Terry Bradshaw (Pittsburgh Steelers quarterback), twice NFL most valuable player, set a high school javelin record of 74.64m/244ft 11in in 1966.

Isaac Curtis had a short but successful sprinting career (best 100y of 9.3) before turning to professional football. *(University of California)*

Jim Brown (Cleveland Browns), perhaps the greatest running back of all-time, was tenth in the 1954 AAU decathlon.
Glenn Davis (Los Angeles Rams), 100y in 9.7 and 220y in 20.9 in 1947 won the Heisman Memorial Trophy for the best college footballer in 1946. Other notable athletes to have won the Heisman have been O. J. Simpson in 1968 and Billy Cannon, who had bests of 9.5 for 100y and 16.57m/54ft 4½in for shot, in 1959.
Herschel Walker (University of Georgia) was runner-up for the Heisman Trophy in his first year of college football in 1981. An outstanding sprinter (10.10w for 100m in 1982) his future professional career is eagerly anticipated.
Harold Muller (California), All-American footballer at college, won the Olympic high jump silver medal in 1920.
Gale Sayers (Chicago) was voted best half back of the first 50 years of the NFL. He ranked third on the world junior long jump list in 1961 with 7.58m/24ft 10½in. He was a brother of Roger Sayers, one of only two men ever to beat Bob Hayes at 100y.

James Lofton, long jumping for Stanford University in 1978. He was runner-up in the 1982 World Superstars. *(Stanford University)*

Some star athletes have fared less well at pro football.
World record holders and Olympic champions who come into this category are: Frank Budd (Philadelphia, then Washington 1962), Henry Carr (New York Giants, then Detroit Lions 1965–7), who played as a defensive back but apparently couldn't learn the basic defensive tactic – running backwards!; Glenn Davis (Detroit Lions 1960–1); Jim Hines (Miami Dolphins 1969–70); Stone Johnson (Kansas City Chiefs), who died from injuries received in a pre-season practice game in 1963; Ray Norton (San Francisco 49ers 1960–1); Tommie Smith (Cincinnati Bengals 1969); Jerry Tarr (Denver Broncos 1962).

ARCHERY
Tapio Rautavaara (Fin), the 1948 Olympic javelin champion, won a team gold medal at the 1958 world archery championships. Also a well-known folk singer and actor, he died on 25 Sep 1979 after hitting his head on a concrete floor. He fell while posing for a photograph for a book depicting Finland's Olympic heroes.

BADMINTON
Ursula Smith won gold and bronze medals for England at Badminton at the 1966 Commonwealth Games. She had a best discus throw of 39.58m/129ft 10½in in 1964.

BASEBALL
Jackie Robinson of the Brooklyn Dodgers became the first black man to play major league baseball in 1947. In 1938 he headed the world long jump rankings with 7.78m/25ft 6½in. He won the 1940 NCAA title while at UCLA. His elder brother Mack was 2nd in the 1936 Olympic 200m.

Willie Davis starred for fifteen years with the Los Angeles Dodgers and the Montreal Expos. In 1958 at 18 he was ranked tenth in the world at long jump with 7.69m/25ft 3in.

Wilson Parma, who ran 100y in 9.6w in 1957, played on the 1963 US Pan-American baseball team.

Herb Washington, indoor world record holder for 60y at 5.8 in 1972 after tying the old mark of 5.9 many times, played in 1974–5 for Oakland as a stolen base expert.

BASKETBALL
Bill Russell ranked 11th in the world at high jump in 1956 with 2.06m/6ft 9¼in, just a quarter of an inch over his own height. His greatest glory that year, however, came as he was the star player on the US gold medal winning Olympic basketball team. He was five times (1958, 1961–3, 1965) voted most valuable player in the NBA (National Basketball Association) while playing for Boston Celtics, who won 11 NBA titles in 15 years from 1957. On his high jump style he commented 'I run a while and then take off'.

6ft 10in tall basketball star Bill Russell demonstrates his distinct high jumping style at Compton in 1956. *(Associated Press)*

Wilt Chamberlain, All-American basketballer while at Kansas University in 1957–8, before his magnificent pro career.   *(Kansas University)*

Wilt 'The Stilt' Chamberlain (2.16m/7ft 1in tall) holds the record for the most points in an NBA career, 31419 in 1960–73. He also holds the record for the most points in a game, 100 for Philadelphia Warriors v New York Knicks on 2 Mar 1962, and in that season set a total points record of 4029. He was NBA scoring leader for seven consecutive years from 1959/60 and was voted the most valuable player in 1960 and 1966–8. He too had some success as a high jumper with a best of 1.99m/6ft 6¼in in 1957, tying for first in the Drake Relays off a three-step run-up.

Other top high jumpers, **Walter 'Buddy' Davis**, Olympic champion of 1952 and **John Rambo**, Olympic third in 1964 were drafted by professional teams but were less successful.

At the other end of the scale the top Japanese sprinter, **Hideo Iijima** (10.1 for 100m in 1964), played professional basketball in Japan, but he was only 1.76m/5ft 9¼in tall!

Anne-Marie Colchen was captain of the French basketball team and played in more than 60 internationals. As a high jumper she won the 1946 European title at 1.60m and set a French record of 1.63m/5ft 4¼in in 1949.

BOBSLEIGH

The attributes of a top-class bobsledder, speed and power, are the same as those of the decathlete, so it is no surprise that many of the best bobsledders have been good athletes.

The most successful men at bobsleigh in recent years have been the GDR pair of Meinhard Nehmer and Bernard Germeshausen, each with three Olympic gold medals as well as many World and European titles. Nehmer had a javelin best of 81.50m in 1971, and Germeshausen, who took over as driver of the GDR four-man bob after Nehmer's retirement in 1980, had a decathlon best of 7534 in 1972. Also members of the Olympic gold medal winning GDR bobsleigh team were Hans-Jürgen Gerhardt (110mh – 14.05 in 1976) with whom Germeshausen used to train at Erfurt for the hurdles, and Bogdan Musiol (56.50m at hammer).

The GDR team was beaten in 1980 at the two-man bob by the Swiss pairing of Erich Schärer and Josef Benz. The former was a good athlete and the latter scored 6441 at the decathlon in 1973. 1976 Olympic bobsleigh medallists included the 110m hurdlers Raimund Bethge (GDR – 13.4 in 1973) and Manfred Schumann (Ger – 13.6 in 1972), both had won national titles at 110m hurdles. Edy Hubacher (Swi) won a bobsleigh gold medal at the 1972 Olympics. He had set Swiss records at shot (19.34m) and discus (56.78m) in 1970 and in all appeared in 51 internationals at athletics between 1962–76.

Willie Davenport competed for the USA at 110m hurdles four times at the Olympic Games from 1964 to 1976, winning in 1968 and was placed third in 1976. In 1980 he was a member of the US 4-man bob at the Winter Olympics which was placed 12th.

Colin Campbell ran for Great Britain at 400m in the 1968 Games, at 800m in 1972 and was in the 4-man bob at the 1976 Games (13th).

In recent years coach **Tom McNab** has recruited many British decathlon internationals to GB bobsleigh teams. John Howell and Nick Phipps competed in the 1980 Olympic Games, and Phipps was joined by Graeme 'Buster' Watson and Peter Brugnani in the 1981 world championship squad.

BOXING

Wladyslaw Komar, the 1972 Olympic shot champion, had been a member of the Polish national junior boxing team in 1956–9 and won 44 out of 56 bouts. Two world shot record holders had disastrous boxing careers, as both were knocked out in the first rounds of their one and only boxing matches – **Jack Torrance** and **Bill Nieder**, the latter just six months after he won the 1960 Olympic shot title.

Ken Norton (USA), a leading heavyweight contender in the 1970s threw the discus 49.50m/162ft 5in at high school in 1962, at the age of 16, and **Joe Bugner**, European, British and Commonwealth heavyweight champion had been a promising discus thrower. He had a 1kg best of 56.02m in 1965 when he was second in the English Schools intermediate age-group, having won the junior boys title in 1964. He turned professional at the age of 17 in 1967.

Ingemar Johansson, world heavyweight champion in 1959, ran the Stockholm marathon in 1981 in 4:40:10 at a weight of 110kg, and improved to 4:31:13 in New York.

CRICKET
Charles Burgess Fry was the epitome of the great all-rounder. At cricket he played in 26 Tests in England from 1895 to 1912, leading England to victory over Australia in 1912. At soccer he played for England in 1901 and earned a Cup Final medal with Southampton in 1902. He was also a fine rugby player and a brilliant scholar. He set a world long jump record of 7.17m/23ft 6½in on 4 Mar 1893 for Oxford University v London AC at Iffley Road.

The 1894 Oxford University athletics team. Amongst their inter-varsity winners were C. B. Fry (sitting centre), later England cricket captain, Sir George Robertson (sitting second from left), fourth 1896 Olympic discus and arts gold medallist, and W. J. Oakley (sitting extreme left), England soccer international.

The previous year he had added two inches to the British record with 23ft 5in. He was three times winner of the long jump in the 'varsity' match and tied for first at 100y in 1893. He edited 'Fry's Magazine', served on the League of Nations, and, having turned down the offer of the Kingdom of Albania, trained youngsters on the *Mercury* on the river Hamble.

An even more legendary cricketing figure, W. G. Grace was also a notable athlete in his younger days. He won the 440y hurdles (over 20 flights of hurdles) at the first National Olympian Association meeting at the Crystal Palace on 1 Aug 1866. He had scored the highest ever score in first-class cricket, 224 not out for England v Surrey at Kennington Oval on the two preceding days, before missing the final day of the match. He had considerable success at sprinting, hurdling and jumping between 1866 and 1870. His elder brother, E. M. was a top triple jumper.

Other Test cricketers to have been notable athletes: Charles Absolom – world amateur record 100y in 10.0 in 1868; Robert Barber – 60.12m at javelin in 1957; Peter Carlstein ranked 15th at 440y (49.2) at age 18 in South Africa in 1957. B.J.T. Bosanquet (pioneer of the 'googly' and father of newsreader Reginald) and the Hon Alfred Lyttleton both won 'blues' at the hammer.

Other early world record holders to have played first-class cricket:
Hon. Francis Pelham – 880y 2:02.5 in 1867; Lenox Tindall – 440y 48.5 in 1889; Alfred Lubbock PV 3.20m in 1868. John Le Fleming won the AAA 120y title in 1887, played cricket for Kent and was an England Rugby international, while Scottish Rugby internationals Augustus Asher and Kenneth Macleod also won athletics 'blues' and played first-class cricket. Asher was Scottish pole vault champion in 1885 and 1886.

Recently sportsmen have had to concentrate much more on their main sports rather than being free to indulge in many as did the Victorians, however one can still trace details of athletic prowess for many top names. In 1980 Vintcent van der Bijl did more than anyone to win the County Cricket Championship for Middlesex. Before he started his record breaking cricket career (most wickets in South Africa's Currie Cup competition) he was ranked ninth among South African junior shot putters and was third in the junior discus championships in 1967.

GOLF

Mildred Didrikson (later Mrs George Zaharias) was voted the greatest woman athlete of the first half of the 20th century in an Associated Press poll in 1950. Her track and field career was short, for after winning two gold and a silver medal at the 1932 Olympic Games she turned to golf. She had set world records at 80m hurdles (11.8 and 11.7sec in 1932), high jump (1.65m in 1932) and javelin (40.62m/133ft 3in as a 16-year-old in 1930). She was All-American at basketball for three years and set a world record for throwing the baseball 296ft/90.22m at Jersey City on 25 Jul 1931. She earned her nickname of 'Babe', after Babe Ruth, for her baseball prowess. At golf she was the top money winner in the USA each year from 1948 to 1951 and won the US Women's Open in 1948, 1950 and 1954, the latter by the record margin of 12 strokes. She won the US Women's Amateur Championship in 1946 and became the first American to win the Ladies' British Open Amateur Championship in 1947. To the dismay of all sports lovers she died of cancer on 27 Sep 1956 at the age of 42.

The Olympic 80m hurdles final in 1932, when 'Babe' Didrikson (right) beat team-mate Evelyn Hall, both running a world record of 11.7.

Robert Gardner, the first man to pole vault over 13ft in 1912, had won the US Amateur Golf Championship in 1909 at 19 years and 5 months, still the youngest ever champion. He won again in 1915 and was runner-up in 1916 and 1921 as he was for the British amateur in 1920. He was also US rackets doubles champion in 1926.

HANDBALL

Bent Larsen, who set a Danish javelin record of 78.32m/256ft 11in in 1975, had at that time played in 35 handball internationals for his country.

Alfred Sosgornik, third in the 1962 European shot, who set 15 Polish shot records, was a handball international before concentrating on athletics.

HOCKEY

Double internationals at hockey and athletics include, for England: Pru Carter (née French) – WAAA javelin champion 1972; for France: Anatole Vologe; for Ireland: Thelma Hopkins – world high jump record of 1.74m/5ft 8½in and an Olympic silver medal in 1956, Lorna McGarvey and Maeve Kyle; for Scotland: Alix Jamieson (later Stevenson) – fourth Commonwealth long jump and for New Zealand: Sue

Haden – second in the 1974 Commonwealth 800m. Also a hockey international was Janet Ruff, who set a world 440y record of 56.5 when she won the second of three successive WAAA titles in 1956.

ICE SKATING
Waclaw Kuchar won Polish titles at 800m, 110m hurdles, 400m hurdles, high jump and decathlon in the period 1920–3. He won six Polish speed skating titles, also played on national championship teams at ice hockey and soccer and was proficient in many other sports.

LAWN TENNIS
Two of the top women tennis players of recent years had strong athletics connections. Virginia Wade's brother Chris ran the marathon in 2:17:42 in 1969, in which year he was third at Kosice. Hana Mandlikova's father Vilem Mandlik competed in 32 internationals for Czechoslovakia as a sprinter. He won 11 national titles (four at 100m and seven at 200m) between 1956 and 1965, was fourth in the 1958 European 200m and set Czech records of 10.2 for 100m and 20.8 for 200m.

MOTOR RACING
Jean-Luc Salomon (Fra) was killed in a motor racing accident on 28 Jun 1970 just a week before he was due to make his formula one debut. He took up motor racing in 1968. As an athlete he set European Junior records at 1500m steeplechase in 1963 and was eighth in the European 5000m in 1966.

ROWING
Charles Lawes won the Diamond Sculls at Henley in 1863, and three years later won the first AAC mile title in 4:39.0. The leading light in the AAC was John Chambers, who won the 7 mile walk in 1863. Chambers coached Cambridge University to four successive boat race victories, just a part of his amazing endeavours in pioneering sporting competition. He also wrote the Queensberry Rules for boxing, rewrote the rules for billiards, was ground manager of Lillie Bridge and started championships in cycling and wrestling. He even accompanied Captain Webb on his first-ever cross-Channel swim and was editor of the magazine *Land and Water*. The strain of this work affected his health and he died just after his fortieth birthday in 1883.

RUGBY LEAGUE
Of the Rugby Union internationals on p. 232, the following went on to play Rugby League for their countries: George Smith (NZ), Mike Cleary (Aus), Keri Jones (GB). Another was **Keith Fielding**, a 7.29m long jumper at Loughborough, who went on to Superstars success (see p. 231). He made a conspicuous start at Rugby League, scoring a hat-trick of tries on his debut, Great Britain v France in 1974, having been signed by Salford in June 1973.
Berwyn Jones, British 100m co-record holder at 10.3 in 1963 when he was ranked fifth in the world, signed as a Rugby League professional for Wakefield Trinity in 1964 and missed the 1964 Olympics. He played three times for GB v France between 1964 and 1966 and toured Australia and New Zealand in 1966.
Emmanuel McDonald Bailey the great star of British sprinting in the immediate post-war era, signed as a professional for Leigh in 1953, but only played in one friendly match for them.
Arthur Rowe, who had improved the British shot record 15 times to a best of 19.56m/64ft 2in in 1961, and who had won both European and Commonwealth shot titles in 1958, signed professional forms for Oldham in 1962. He played only for their 'A' team, but enjoyed great success for many years on the Scottish Games circuit as a thrower, being proclaimed world caber-tossing champion in 1970.

The New Zealand Commonwealth sprint medallist Peter Henderson played for Huddersfield from 1950 to 1957 and Alf Meakin, who won sprint relay medals, Commonwealth gold for England and European bronze in 1962, later played for Blackpool.

RUGBY UNION
A great many athletes have achieved success at rugby and vice versa. Selecting as criteria the winning of an International cap at Rugby Union, and showing in brackets the country and span of their international rugby career, the list includes:
Olympic gold medallist: Eric Liddell (Sco 1922–3), 1st 400m and 3rd 200m 1924; UK 100y (9.7) and 400m (47.6) records. See p. 211.

World record: Hon. Marshall Brooks (Eng 1874) high jump 1.89m/6ft 2½in in 1876. H. E. Kayll (Eng 1879) pole vault 3.38m/11ft 1in 1877.

Olympic medallists
Georges André (Fra 1913–14), known as 'The Bison', competed at four Olympic Games from 1908 to 1924 at a wide variety of events, win-

Eric Liddell wins for the British Empire 4 × 440y team against the USA at Stamford Bridge in 1924. The US runner is Horatio Fitch.   *(BBC Hulton)*

ning medals at high jump (2nd equal 1908) and 4 × 400mR (3rd 1920). He set eight French records (at 110mh, 200mh, 400mh, HJ) and won 20 French championships.
Pierre Faillot (Fra 1911–13), 2nd 4 × 400mR 1912. He won nine French championships and set records at 200m and 400m.
Jack Gregory (Eng 1949), 2nd 4 × 100mR 1948, and 4th 1952. He was suspended by the Rugby Football Union for allegedly playing Rugby League.
Ken Jones (Wal 1947–57, 44 caps plus 3 for British Lions), 2nd 4 × 100mR 1948. In 1954 he won further medals: 3rd Commonwealth 220y and 2nd European 4 × 100mR.

Commonwealth medallists
Mike Cleary (Aus 1961), 3rd 100y 1962.
Peter Henderson (NZ 1949–50), 3rd 4 × 110yR 1950.
Cyril Holmes (Eng 1947–8), sprint treble in 1938, in which year he set UK records at 100y (9.7) and 220y (21.1).

Other internationals or national champions
Vinny Becker (Ire 1974), Irish 100m champion.
Fletcher Buchanan (Sco 1910–11), Scottish long jump champion 1910.
Denis Cussen (Ire 1921–7), 1928 Olympics and Irish 100y record holder (9.8).
Jeff Griffiths (Wal 1980), 1978 Commonwealth 400m and won 1976 AAA junior 400m.
John Hart (Sco 1951), Scottish 120yh champion 1947–52 (and 440yh 1947), President of the Scottish Rugby Union.
Rod Heeps (NZ 1962), NZ 100y champion 1961–3.

Bruce Hunter (NZ 1971), NZ 800m champion 1971, 1975.
Keri Jones (Wal 1967–8), 1966 Commonwealth (4th 4 × 110yR).
John Le Fleming (Eng 1887), AAA 120yh champion 1887.
Emile Lesieur (Fra 1906–12), French 100m and 400m champion 1906.
Christopher Mackintosh (Sco 1924), 6th Olympic long jump 1924. He was also a member of the British skiing team and the team that won the 1937 world bobsleigh title.
Phil McPherson (Sco 1922–32, 26 caps), Scottish long jump champion 1929.
William Peterkin (Sco 1881–5), Scottish 100y and 440y champion 1883.
Alain Porthault (Fra 1951–3), 1952 Olympics and French 100m champion 1949.
Franz Reichel (Fra 1893–1900), 1896 Olympics and French 110mh champion 1891. Won Olympic Rugby gold 1900.
Charles Reid (Sco 1881–8), Scottish champion at shot 1886–7 and hammer 1886.
Charles Reidy (Ire 1938), Irish hammer champion 1953.
Arthur Smith (Sco 1955–62, 33 caps and captain of 1962 British Lions team in South Africa), Scottish long jump champion 1953.
George Smith (NZ 1905–6), Australasian record holder at 120yh and 440yh and winner of nine NZ sprint championships.
Tony Steel (NZ 1966–9), NZ champion at 100y in 1966 and 220y 1965–6.
Alan Stewart (Sco 1913–14), Scottish 100y champion 1912, represented Australasia at the 1912 Olympics.
Robert Stronach (Sco 1901–5), Scottish champion at 120yh 1900–1, 1904–7, and long jump 1901.
W. R. Sutherland (Sco 1910–3), Scottish 220y champion 1913.
Ronnie Thomson (Sco 1960–4), 1958 Commonwealth (440y).
A. B. Timms (Sco 1886–1905), Scottish 120yh champion 1896–7.
Alec Valentine (Sco 1953), Scottish hammer champion 1960, 1961, 1963.
James Watson (Eng 1914), long jump for Scotland 1912.
William Welsh (Sco 1900–2), Scottish 100y, 220y and 440y champion 1900, also won 440y in 1899 and 1901.
David Whyte (Sco 1965–7), at long jump, AAA champion 1959 and Scottish champion 1959, 1962 and 1965, and Scottish triple jump 1965.
John J. Williams (Wal 1973–9, 30 caps plus 7 for British Lions), Welsh champion at 100m

1971, 200m 1968–9, 1971. Competed 1970 Commonwealth Games.

John Young (Eng 1958–61), AAA 100y champion 1956. Though selected for both the 1956 Olympic and 1958 Commonwealth Games, Young missed both through injury.

Other top rugby players with good athletics credentials include:

Edwin 'Slip' Carr mixed playing rugby for Australia with outstanding sprinting. He won 53 out of 54 races on a European tour in 1923 and was never beaten in Australia. His identically named son followed him as an Olympic athlete and Australian 400m record holder.

Gareth Edwards (Wal 1967–79, 53 caps plus 10 for British Lions), UK Junior 200yh record of 22.4 in 1966 in the heats of the *English* Schools championships, which he won for Millfield.

Joe Levula, the great Fijian rugby player, was second in the Australian 100y in 1954 and came, with two other Fijian double internationals, **Tomasi Nadole** (15.00 triple jump) and **Orisi Dawai** (9.8 100y) to play rugby league football in Britain in 1961.

Kenneth MacLeod (Sco 1905–7, making his debut at the age of 17), won 'varsity' 100y for Cambridge 1906–8. Scottish long jump champion 1906. He also played first-class cricket for Lancashire.

Jack Matthews (Wal 1947–51), Welsh junior 100y and youth 220y champion 1937.

Alan Stewart, Scottish 100y champion and rugby international. Note the sturdy hurdle that runners had to contend with.   *(BBC Hulton)*

Andy Ripley (Eng 1972–6), 24 caps the most by an England No. 8, best 400mh of 53.69.

Wavell Wakefield (Eng 1920–7) 31 caps which was a record until 1967, RAF 440yh champion in 1920.

Morris Kirksey and **'Dink' Templeton** of Stanford University were members of the gold medal winning US Olympic rugby squad in 1920. Kirksey won a sprint relay gold medal and a silver at 100m and Templeton, later a great coach at Stanford, was fourth at long jump.

SKIING (Nordic)

Martin Stokken as an athlete set 17 Norwegian records at 3km, 3km steeplechase, 5km and 10km. He won more than 20 national titles and was a consistently high placer in the major races from 1946 to 1952, though narrowly failing to gain a medal. His best was fourth in the 1948 Olympic 10km and fourth in the 1950 European 3km steeplechase. As a skier he represented Norway at the 1952 and 1956 Winter Olympics, winning a silver medal in the cross-country relay in 1952. His best placing at the world skiing championships was fourth at 50km in 1954.

Jussi Kurikkala won world Nordic skiing titles at 18km and relay in 1939 and went on to represent Finland in the marathon at the 1948 Olympic Games, finishing 13th.

Two Norwegian steeplechase champions won Olympic skiing gold medals: **Hallgeir Brenden**, steeplechase champion in 1953 and 1954 won the Olympic cross-country skiing at 18km in 1952 and 15km in 1956 and also won silver medals in 1952 and 1956; **Ole Ellefsaeter** was steeplechase champion in 1960–2 and won Olympic golds in 1968 for 50km and relay cross-country skiing.

SOCCER

Howard Baker of Corinthians and Chelsea won eight amateur caps and made one full international appearance for England at soccer as a goalkeeper. He set the inaugural English native high jump record of 1.95m/6ft 5in in 1921, a year after becoming the first British athlete to better Marshall Brooks' 44-year-old record of 1.89m/6ft 2½in. Baker's mark went unsurpassed for 25 years. He was sixth in the 1920 Olympic Games and won six AAA titles.

J. C. Clegg set a world record for 600y in 1873 and played for England against Scotland at soccer in 1872. As Sir James Clegg he was chairman of the Football Association in 1923. He is believed to have introduced the art of heading the ball into the modern game.

William Oakley, the AAA long jump champion of 1894, played 16 times for England at soccer and co-authored 'Association Football' for the Badminton Library.

Arthur Wharton, the AAA 100y champion of 1886 and 1887, was the first coloured player to appear in the Football League. During the 1890s he played for Preston North End, Rotherham Town and Sheffield United as a goalkeeper, thus presumably giving him little scope to exploit his speed.

Other England soccer internationals were **Reginald Macaulay**, AAC high jump champion 1879, and **Arnold Hills**, AAC 1 mile champion 1878.

James Crawford played for Scotland in 1932–3 at soccer and won Scottish titles at 100y in 1926, 1929 and 1930 and at 220y in 1928.

SUPERSTARS

The Superstars competitions have become a highly popular television phenomenon.

Bob Seagren, former world pole vault record holder, won the first Superstars competition at Rotunda West, Florida on 23 Apr 1973 for a first prize of $39700 and a bonus of $8500. In the USA Seagren was runner-up in 1973/4 and 1974/5 (when the winner was American Football and ex-track great O. J. Simpson), and he went on to win the first world title in 1977. That first world competition was heavily dominated by athletes with Kjell Isaksson, also a former world pole vault record holder, second, Peter Snell third, Frank Nusse, Dutch 400m hurdles and decathlon star sixth and Guy Drut ninth. Isaksson had been European Superstars champion in 1975 and 1976.

   In the UK **David Hemery** had the greatest success, winning the first Superstars in 1973, being placed second in 1974, and winning again in 1976. He was the leading UK sportsman in the 1975 European competition. In 1980 Keith Fielding (rugby see p. 231) won the UK title with John Sherwood second, but Sherwood went on to be placed second in the world competition to Brian Budd, the Canadian soccer player, who achieved his third successive world Superstars title. In 1981/2 the UK winner was pole vaulter Brian Hooper, with long jumper Alan Lerwill second and Keith Fielding third. Hooper went on to win the world Superstars

Brian Hooper won six AAA indoor titles, set 16 outdoor and 14 indoor UK bests at pole vault, but met greatest fame at Superstars. *(M. Shearman)*

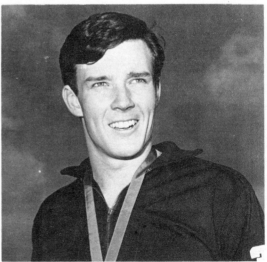

Bob Seagren, greatest Superstars money-winner with over $200,000, won the 1968 Olympic pole vault title.   *(University of Southern California)*

Above: Stan Vickers leads Ken Matthews in the AAA 2 miles walk at the White City in 1960. Both men broke George Larner's 56-year-old British record. Vickers was first in 13:02.4 and Matthews second in 13:09.6.

Above right: Al Oerter at Westwood, California in the UCLA Pepsi meeting in 1981, 25 years after he first struck Olympic gold.

Sebastian Coe (1), Willi Wülbeck (2) and Olaf Beyer (3), finish in the order of their numbers in the 1981 European Cup final.

Alan Wells (right) and Don Quarrie (left) in a heat of the Olympic 100m in 1980. Wells went on to win the gold medal but Quarrie went out in the semi-finals.

Mary Decker led from the start to set a world indoor 1500m record of 4:00.8 at the 1980 Millrose Games.

Above: Yuri Syedikh wins the hammer at the
1978 European Championships.

Right: Dave Bedford (274) and Emiel Puttemans
(61) in the heats of the Olympic 10000m in 1972.

Below: Donna Murray takes the baton from
Verona Elder.

title with former long jumper, James Lofton (see p. 226) second and Alan Lerwill, fifth. Renaldo Nehemiah, was sixth and he had twice won the USA Superstars. In 1981 his first prize was $43300 and Ed Moses was third. In 1976 the IAAF had ruled that amateur athletes could compete as Superstars was entertainment rather than athletics, but not in track events, and provided that the money went to their athletics governing bodies.

SWIMMING
Maureen Arnold (née Pitchfork) is the only double swimming/athletics international for Britain. A discus international in 1962, she had been placed sixth at 110y backstroke in the 1954 Commonwealth Games. Pam Piercy, fourth at 800m in the 1966 European Championships, had been a junior swimming international, while another top middle distance runner, Regina Kleinau, was a double international for the GDR.

TABLE TENNIS
The game was said to have been invented, as ping pong, by James Gibb, playing on his mahogany dining table with cigar-box tops as bats and champagne corks as balls. Gibb won three AAA 4 mile titles, 1875, 1877 and 1878, and set world records at 3, 6 and 10 miles.

WEIGHT-LIFTING
Weight-lifting as part of training has played a vital role for athletes in recent years. While there had been European advocates of its practice in the 1930s, notably Rudolf Harbig's coach, Woldemar Gerschler, it was not recommended in the USA until the late 1940s, when the major pioneer was Otis Chandler. Chandler, who became Publisher of the *Los Angeles Times* in 1960, ranked second in the world at shot in 1950 and 1951 and was successively placed fourth, third, and second at the NCAA for Stanford University 1948–50. His enthusiasm for weights was taken up by Parry O'Brien, who with his new technique revolutionised world shot putting standards and led the way to current training methods.

Judy Oakes, power-lifting success as well as six WAAA shot titles. *(M. Shearman)*

AAU weight-lifting titles were won by the above as follows: heavyweight Gubner 1966, Wilhelm 1975–6; super-heavyweight Patera 1969–72, Walker 1977, Feuerbach 1974. Bruce Wilhelm also represented the USA in the 1966 world graeco-roman wrestling championships.

Gubner was the first 16-year-old to put the shot more than 16m. The second was Gerd Bonk in 1968. Bonk was second in the 1969 GDR junior championships, but then concentrated on weight-lifting at which he won two Olympic and four world championship medals.

The greatest ever weight-lifter, with a total of 80 world records, is Vasiliy Alexeyev (USSR), and he tried his hand at shot putting in his younger days with a best of 15.20m.

World class athletes who have excelled as powerlifters include Jon Cole (USA), 65.90m discus in 1972, and George Frenn (USA), 70.88m hammer in 1970 and AAU champion 1970–1, who both set world powerlifting records. Bev Francis (Aus), 5th 1978 Commonwealth SP, set a world women's powerlifting record for the 165lb class in 1980 and for the 181lb class in 1981 when she won the world title. In those same championships the 165lb class was won by Judy Oakes (GB) – 3rd Com-

SEVERAL US SHOT PUTTERS HAVE EXCELLED AT BOTH SPORTS
(H = Heavyweight   SH = Super-Heavyweight)

Name	Best SP	SP competitions	Weight-lifting
Gary Gubner	19.80i	1st AAU 1962 1st NCAA 1963–4	World (H): 3rd 1962, 2nd 1965
Ken Patera	19.68	3rd NCAA 1967	Pan-Am 1st 1971; World: 2nd 1971; OG dnf 1972 (all SH)
Bruce Wilhelm	20.12		OG: (SH) 5th 1976
Sam Walker	20.50	3rd AAU 1973	OG: (SH) 10th 1976
Al Feuerbach	21.82	1st AAU 1973–5, 1978 OG: 5th 1972, 4th 1976	

monwealth SP 1978) from Pam Matthews (Aus
– JT) and at super-heavyweight Gael Mulhall
(Aus – Commonwealth SP record holder) was
second and Janis Kerr (GB – SP) was fourth.
Oakes and Francis swapped categories to win
world titles again in 1982.

Many of the top British male throwers have also
done well at lifting. Andy Kerr at super-heavy
was second in the 1974 Commonwealth Games
and at power-lifting was second in 1980 in
World Cup, European and World championships. He was the first British lifter to jerk
200kg/440¾lb and to dead lift 365kg/804½lb.
His shot/discus bests were 16.68m/51.46m.
Andy Drzwiecki was second at heavyweight in
the 1978 Commonwealth Games and tenth in
the 1980 Olympics. His shot/discus bests were
16.89m/53.24m. John Alderson, like Drzwiecki
a British junior shot international, with a best of
17.79m, was third at super-heavy in the 1975
world powerlifting championships. Paul Buxton
achieved a unique treble of AAA Junior championships, at the shot, discus and hammer in
1975 and in that year and in 1976 also won the
British junior weightlifting title. Tony Elvin,
shot international, set British powerlifting
records in 1969 and the top two British putters
Geoff Capes and Mike Winch also achieved
lifting successes.

THE WORLD'S STRONGEST MAN
This annual TV event was entered by Geoff
Capes in 1980 and 1981 when he was placed
third and second respectively to winner Bill
Kazmaier, the power lifter. Capes won the
British event in 1979 and 1981 and the 1980
winner was discus thrower Richard Slaney.
Bruce Wilhelm (USA) won the 'world' event
twice in the 1970s.

YACHTING
Ralph Craig won both 100m and 200m at the
1912 Olympic Games. 36 years later he was on
the US Yachting squad (11th Dragon class) and
carried the US flag at the opening ceremony for
the 1948 Olympic Games. This is the record
span between Olympic appearances.

Attendances
The biggest attendance for athletics have probably been for events staged with football
matches. There was a junior 1 mile held at the
half-time of the Scotland v England match, in
1962, with a crowd of 132000 at Hampden
Park, Glasgow. Then at Wembley the 100000

strong FA Cup Final crowds saw 3000m races in
1973 and 1974 won respectively by Emiel Puttemans (Bel) 8:10.6 and Brendan Foster, running in Newcastle United colours, 8:05.0.

Crowds of around 100000 were reported for the
1957 USA v Poland meeting in Warsaw, and for
the 1979 and 1980 China v Japan international
athletics matches in Peking.

Peak attendances at Olympic Games
1896 Athens – about 45000 in the stadium and
an estimated further 40000 watching from the
surrounding hills on 7 April.
1900 Paris – about 1000.
1904 St Louis – about 3000.
1908 White City, London – 90000.
1912 Stockholm – about 80000 on 14 July,
when the crowd was estimated at 30% above the
stadium's capacity!
1920 Antwerp – about 20000.
1924 Paris – about 40000.
1928 Amsterdam – about 40000.
1932 Los Angeles – 86443.
1936 Berlin – about 100000 every day.
1948 Wembley, London – 83000.
1952 Helsinki – 69106.
1956 Melbourne – 91119.
1960 Rome – about 75000.
1964 Tokyo – about 80000.
1968 Mexico City – about 80000.
1972 Munich – about 80000.
1976 Montreal – 71051.
1980 Moscow – about 80000.

**The largest attendance for an athletics meeting
in the USA** outside the Olympics was 81000 for
the USA v USSR at Stanford on 22 Jul 1962.
The largest for a national meeting is 62000 for
the Final Olympic Trials at Stanford on 2 Jul
1960, and the largest for a relays meeting 59661
at the Coliseum Relays, Los Angeles 21 May
1948.
The largest attendance for an indoor meeting in
the USA is 18310 for the Millrose Games in
Madison Square Garden, New York 8 Feb
1980.

Automatic timing
The first reported use of **electrical timing** was in
1892, in England and on 24 September at
Montreal, Canada when H. Jewett was timed at
21.95 for 220y. On 14 Nov 1902 Mimoru Fuji
was electrically timed, in Japan, at 10.24 for
100m, though the accuracy of this time must be
open to doubt.

Automatic timing was used in the USA in 1932 for the final Olympic try-outs at Stanford University with the use of the Kirby camera-clock, and this was also used at the Olympic Games in Los Angeles.

In Great Britain photo-finish cameras were in action at the 1948 Olympic Games at Wembley but only used in timing for place differentials, as hand times were used officially. Full photo-finish was installed at the White City in 1958.

The IAAF Congress in Rome in 1974 decided to inaugurate a separate list of sprint times recorded by fully automatic timing and since 1976 hand timing for sprints has not been permitted for world records.

It is conventionally accepted that hand times are 'faster' than automatic ones, and many statisticians use conversion factors of 0.24sec for 100m, 200m and 110mh and 0.14sec for 400m and 400mh to add to hand times in equating to automatic ones. The reason for such discrepancies is probably due to timekeepers anticipating a runner's finish, rather than allowing for the same delay as is caused by reaction to the flash of the starter's pistol. British timekeepers have so trained themselves that hand times in Britain equate very consistently with automatic times.

Awards

ATHLETES OF THE YEAR
WORLD

These are the winners of two of the leading polls: a) as published in the American magazine *Track and Field News* from the votes of international experts, and b) as published in the British magazine *Athletics Weekly* from readers' votes.

Women athletes of the year were selected for *Women's Track and Field World* from 1967 to 1975, before *Track and Field News* took over this feature.

Year	T&FN world male	AW world male
1959	Martin Lauer (Ger)	—
1960	Rafer Johnson (USA)	—
1961	Ralph Boston (USA)	Valeriy Brumel (USSR)
1962	Peter Snell (NZ)	Peter Snell (NZ)
1963	C. K. Yang (Taiwan)	John Pennel (USA)
1964	Peter Snell (NZ)	Peter Snell (NZ)
1965	Ron Clarke (Aus)	Ron Clarke (Aus)
1966	Jim Ryun (USA)	Jim Ryun (USA)
1967	Jim Ryun (USA)	Jim Ryun (USA)
1968	Bob Beamon (USA)	Al Oerter (USA)
1969	Bill Toomey (USA)	Bill Toomey (USA)
1970	Randy Matson (USA)	Ni Chih-Chin (Chi)
1971	Rod Milburn (USA)	Juha Vaatianen (Fin)
1972	Lasse Viren (Fin)	Lasse Viren (Fin)
1973	Ben Jipcho (Ken)	Ben Jipcho (Ken)
1974	Rick Wohlhuter (USA)	Ian Thompson (GB)
1975	John Walker (NZ)	John Walker (NZ)
1976	Alberto Juantorena (Cub)	Lasse Viren (Fin)
1977	Alberto Juantorena (Cub)	Alberto Juantorena (Cub)
1978	Henry Rono (Ken)	Henry Rono (Ken)
1979	Sebastian Coe (GB)	Sebastian Coe (GB)
1980	Edwin Moses (USA)	Miruts Yifter (Eth)
1981	Sebastian Coe (GB)	Sebastian Coe (GB)

Year	WTFW/T&FN world female	AW world female
1961	—	Tamara Press (USSR)
1962	—	Tamara Press (USSR)
1963	—	Shin Geum Dan (N. Korea)
1964	—	Mary Rand (GB)
1965	—	Irena Szewinska (Pol)
1966	—	Irena Szewinska (Pol)
1967	Liesel Westermann (Ger)	Liesel Westermann (Ger)
1968	Margitta Gummel (GDR)	Wyomia Tyus (USA)
1969	Chi Cheng (Taiwan)	Nicole Duclos (Fra)
1970	Chi Cheng (Taiwan)	Chi Cheng (Taiwan)
1971	Ilona Gusenbauer (Aut)	Renate Stecher (GDR)
1972	Heide Rosendahl (Ger)	Mary Peters (GB)
1973	Renate Stecher (GDR)	Renate Stecher (GDR)
1974	Irena Szewinska (Pol)	Irena Szewinska (Pol)
1975	Faina Melnik (USSR)	Irena Szewinska (Pol)
1976	Tatyana Kazankina (USSR)	Tatyana Kazankina (USSR)
1977	Rosemarie Ackermann (GDR)	Rosemarie Ackermann (GDR)
1978	Marita Koch (GDR)	Marita Koch (GDR)
1979	Marita Koch (GDR)	Evelyn Ashford (USA)
1980	Ilona Slupianek (GDR)	Tatyana Kazankina (USSR)
1981	Evelyn Ashford (USA)	Evelyn Ashford (USA)

BRITISH
As elected by a) British Athletics Writers (Wr) from 1963 and b) readers of *Athletics Weekly* (AW) from 1961:

Year	male
1961	(AW) Adrian Metcalfe
1962	(AW) Brian Kilby
1963	(both) Maurice Herriott
1964	(both) Lynn Davies
1965	(Wr) Maurice Herriott, (AW) Alan Simpson
1966	(both) Lynn Davies
1967	(both) Lynn Davies
1968	(both) David Hemery
1969	(both) Ian Stewart
1970	(Wr) Ian Stewart, (AW) Ron Hill
1971	(both) David Bedford
1972	(both) David Hemery
1973	(both) Brendan Foster
1974	(both) Ian Thompson
1975	(both) Alan Pascoe
1976	(both) Brendan Foster
1977	(both) Steve Ovett
1978	(Wr) Daley Thompson, (AW) Steve Ovett
1979	(both) Sebastian Coe
1980	(both) Steve Ovett
1981	(both) Sebastian Coe

Year	female
1961	(AW) Joy Jordan
1962	(AW) Dorothy Hyman
1963	(both) Dorothy Hyman
1964	(both) Mary Rand
1965	(both) Anne Smith
1966	(Wr) Pam Piercy, (AW) Anne Smith
1967	(both) Lillian Board
1968	(Wr) Sheila Sherwood, (AW) Sherwood and Lillian Board
1969	(both) Lillian Board
1970	(Wr) Rosemary Stirling, (AW) Sheila Sherwood
1971	(both) Barbara Inkpen
1972	(both) Mary Peters
1973	(Wr) Verona Bernard, (AW) Joan Allison
1974	(Wr) Joyce Smith, (AW) Andrea Lynch
1975	(both) Andrea Lynch
1976	(both) Sonia Lannaman
1977	(Wr) Tessa Sanderson, (AW) Sonia Lannaman
1978	(both) Tessa Sanderson
1979	(both) Christine Benning
1980	(Wr) Kathy Smallwood, (AW) Joyce Smith
1981	(both) Kathy Smallwood

BBC SPORTS PERSONALITY OF THE YEAR
The following athletes have been voted by BBC Television viewers to this coveted title since the first poll in 1954:

1954	Chris Chataway
1955	Gordon Pirie
1963	Dorothy Hyman
1964	Mary Rand
1968	David Hemery
1972	Mary Peters
1974	Brendan Foster
1978	Steve Ovett
1979	Sebastian Coe

SPORTS ILLUSTRATED SPORTSMAN OF THE YEAR
The great American magazine has awarded this title annually since 1954 to the sportsman or woman who 'symbolizes in character and performance the ideals of sportsmanship'. Track and field athletes to win have been:

1954	Roger Bannister
1956	Bobby-Joe Morrow
1958	Rafer Johnson
1966	Jim Ryun

SULLIVAN AWARD WINNERS
This award was instituted in the USA in 1930 in memory of James E. Sullivan, President of the AAU 1906–14, for 'the amateur athlete, who, by performance, example and good influence did the most to advance the cause of good sportsmanship during the year'. Track and field athletes to win have been:

1931	Bernie Berlinger
1932	Jim Bausch
1933	Glenn Cunningham
1934	Bill Bonthron
1936	Glenn Morris
1938	Don Lash
1940	Greg Rice
1941	Leslie MacMitchell
1942	Cornelius Warmerdam
1943	Gil Dodds
1948	Bob Mathias
1950	Fred Wilt
1951	Bob Richards
1952	Horace Ashenfelter
1954	Mal Whitfield
1955	Harrison Dillard
1957	Bobby-Joe Morrow
1958	Glenn Davis
1959	Parry O'Brien
1960	Rafer Johnson
1961	Wilma Rudolph
1962	Jim Beatty
1963	John Thomas
1966	Jim Ryun
1967	Randy Matson
1969	Bill Toomey
1972	Frank Shorter
1974	Rick Wohlhuter
1976	Bruce Jenner
1981	Carl Lewis

The Associated Press conducted a poll in the USA in 1950 to determine the greatest athletes of the first 50 years of this century at all sports. Track and field athletes in the list were: **Men:** 1. Jim Thorpe (also Football etc), 8. Jesse Owens, 12. Bob Mathias, 16. Glenn Cunningham, 17. Glenn Morris, 18. Cornelius Warmerdam. **Women:** 1. Mildred Didrikson (also golf), 3. Stella Walsh, 4. Fanny Blankers-Koen, 10. Helen Stephens. At track and field the leaders were: 1. Jesse Owens 201 votes, 2. Jim Thorpe

Jim Thorpe throws the discus 36.98m in the 1912
Olympic Games   *(BBC Hulton)*

74, 3. Paavo Nurmi 31, 4. Glenn Cunningham
30, 5. Cornelius Warmerdam 12, 6. Mildred
Didrikson 9, 7. Charley Paddock 8, 8. Gunder
Hägg and Bob Mathias 5, 10. Fanny Blankers-
Koen 3.

The Helms Athletic Foundation (founded in
1936) in 1960 selected the greatest teams in US
history as: **Club:** San Francisco Olympic Club in
1940, when they scored 159 points at the AAU,
including a world pole vault record from Cornelius Warmerdam and a sprint double from
Hal Davis; **College:** University of Southern
California 1936, when they scored a record
$103\frac{1}{3}$ points to win the NCAA Championships
under coach Dean Cromwell.

Boycotts

Sadly many major Games and Championships
in recent years have been the subject of
threatened or actual boycotts. The Olympic
Games, in particular, are such an important
focus of world attention that politics inevitably
play a part.

A chronology of some of the leading issues:
1956 The crises over the Suez Canal and in
Hungary during the year led to abstentions from
the Olympic Games in Melbourne. The Netherlands withdrew because 'events in Hungary had
spoiled the festive Olympic atmosphere'. Spain
withdrew for similar reasons and Egypt pulled
out, having unsuccessfully demanded that
nations 'guilty of cowardly aggression' against
her be expelled from the Games. Lebanon
withdrew in protest at Australian attitudes to
the Suez crisis, and the Republic of China
refused to compete after the admittance of
China (Taiwan).

1964 Mal Whitfield, double 800m gold medallist, suggested in 'Ebony Magazine' that black
athletes should boycott the Games as it was
'time for American Negro athletes to join the
civil rights fight'.

1967–8 There was much discussion on a possible
boycott by US black athletes. The issue was
raised by Harry Edwards (54.34m DT 1962),
Sociology Professor at San Jose State University
at the Black Youth Conference in November
1967 in Los Angeles, and the great black athletes Tommie Smith and Lee Evans were prominent in the discussions before the Games. In the
event there was no boycott but Tommie Smith,
and John Carlos made their point when they
appeared with black-socked feet and no shoes
(symbols of black poverty), on the victory ros-
trum after the 200m and gave a clenched fist
salute during the national anthem for black
power and unity. They were both expelled from
the Games village by the US Olympic Committee. There was later a token demonstration
by the 400m medallists Evans, Lee James and
Ron Freeman who wore black berets and raised
their fists when introduced, but they took off
their berets and kept their arms at their sides
during the anthem. Bob Beamon wore black
socks at the long jump victory ceremony and the
4×400m relay team also gave the clenched fist
salute after receiving their gold medals.

1968 There was a possibility of an Olympic
boycott by 39 nations, including 32 from Africa,
if South Africa were readmitted to the Olympic
Games. However at a special meeting in
Lausanne in April 1968 the IOC rescinded its
vote in favour of such readmittance.

1969 West Germany withdrew all but its relay
teams from the European Championships in
Athens in protest at the decision not to allow
Jürgen May to compete in the 1500m. It was
ruled that May, 5th in 1966 for GDR, had not
fulfilled the three-year residential qualification

needed before changing national affiliation. He had defected from the GDR, whose national federation had imposed a life ban on him for accepting money during the 1966 championships from a West German shoe company. This ban was reduced by the IAAF to two years and he was back in action in January 1969. He won that year's West German indoor 1500m title, but passed the opportunity of competing in the European Indoor Championships in Belgrade for 'reasons of personal safety'. Also in 1969, leftist Greek resistance groups threatened violence as part of their opposition to the regime of the Colonels. There was no such violence, but some Scandinavian athletes including Arne Kvalheim and Kenneth Lundmark did not compete because of their opposition to this regime.

1972 The IOC voted 31–36 to bar the entry of Rhodesia to the Olympic Games just a few days before the Opening Ceremony. Described by Avery Brundage as the IOC yielding to 'naked political blackmail' this followed threats by several African nations to withdraw if Rhodesia took part. Rhodesia had been invited in 1971, and Lee Evans threatened to lead black US athletes in boycotting the Games if the invitation stood. The Supreme Council for African Sport agreed to Rhodesia's participation only if it reverted to its legal title of Southern Rhodesia and used the British flag and anthem.

Several Arab nations withdrew in protest against Israeli policies towards Palestinians.

1976 Eighteen nations, including Iraq and Guyana as well as African ones withdrew from the Olympic Games in protest at New Zealand's planned Rugby tour to South Africa. The IOC took the view that as Rugby was not an Olympic sport it had no authority to sanction New Zealand.

1978 Nigeria and Uganda withdrew from the Commonwealth Games in protest against New Zealand's continuing Rugby links with South Africa.

1980 There was the greatest boycott in athletics history as about 50 nations (the number is difficult to determine as some of the so-called boycotters would not have competed in any case) did not compete in the Olympic Games in Moscow in protest against the Soviet invasion of Afghanistan. The boycotters included Arab nations and such major powers as the USA, West Germany and Japan. The American boycott, initiated by President Carter, meant that the USA missed the Games for the first time, and their lead prompted many other Western nations to follow suit. Despite considerable government pressure the British Olympic Committee decided to go to the Games, leaving it to individual sports and their athletes to decide their own courses of action. Although some sports did withdraw, the athletics team went and not one of the chosen team opted out. Despite the absence of many top names, such as the Americans, Germans and Kenyan runners, the Games went ahead at a very high level. Those who opposed the boycott could only note the irony as full USA v USSR sporting relations were resumed the following year including the visit of the US national team to Leningrad, while there had been no change in the Soviet situation re Afghanistan.

Careers

ASTRONAUTS
Two of America's pioneers in space were good class college athletes. **Major Edward White**, as a member of the Gemini IV crew, was the first American to walk in space on 3 Jun 1965. His 'walk' took 21 minutes over Hawaii to the US Atlantic coast. In 1952 he ran fourth in the NCAA championships at 400m hurdles and his best time for that event of 53.1 ranked him 25th equal in the world in 1952.

Colonel Edwin 'Buzz' Aldrin followed Neil Armstrong on to the surface of the Moon on 21 Jul 1969, and can be claimed as the first man to **run** on the Moon. 18 years before his journey on Apollo 11 he propelled himself upwards and achieved his best pole vault clearance of 4.16m/13ft 8in on 5 May 1951 at West Point, which rated him 37th equal in the world that year.

AUTHORS
Jeffrey Archer, author of the best-selling novels *Not A Penny More, Not A Penny Less; Shall We Tell The President?* and *Kane and Abel*, represented Great Britain against Sweden in 1966, and also won Canadian titles at 100y and 220y that year. His best marks at those events were 9.6 and 21.4, and he was also an Oxford Blue at gymnastics. He was Conservative MP for Louth from 1969 to 1974.

John Galsworthy, author of *The Forsythe Saga* was an outstanding schoolboy athlete, winning the Harrow School 880y in 1885 and the 880y and 1 mile in 1886.

John Cecil Masterman won the high jump for Oxford against Cambridge in 1912 and played for England at hockey and lawn tennis. He was a member of the XX Committee in World War II whose task it was to supervise the work of double agents. He wrote *The Double-Cross System – the War of 1939–45*, and several novels, including *The Case of the Four Friends* based on espionage.

Norris McWhirter, editor of the *Guinness Book of Records*, with his twin brother Ross (killed 1975) since 1955, was a Scottish international sprinter with best times of 100m – 10.7, 200m – 21.7. He also represented London v Gothenburg in 1951. Both Ross and Norris ran on the Achilles 4 × 110y team which won the AAA championship in 1948.

Jackson Scholz won fame as a writer of 'pulp' fiction. At the Olympic Games, he won the 200m in 1924 and was a member of the winning US sprint relay team in 1920, and was second at 100m in 1924.

Viscount Alverstone, Lord Chief Justice of England, was a double winner in the 1865 intervarsity athletics match.

Sir Leslie Stephen, editor of the *Dictionary of National Biography* and father of the novelist Virginia Woolf was a pioneer of athletics at Cambridge University. While a tutor he won the 1 and 2 miles in the University Games in 1860 and the 2 miles 1861.

Bram Stoker, the creator of *Count Dracula* was disqualified for 'lifting' after winning the 1868 Civil Service 5 mile walk championship in 40:05.

BEAUTY
The first Mr America, in 1939, was Bert Goodrich who, in 1927, had run 100y and 220y in 9.8 and 21.4 respectively.
The first Miss UK, in 1958, was Eileen Sheridan, later Mrs. Price. In 1981 she won three UK veterans titles in the 45–49 age group.

BIOLOGY
The biologist Julian Huxley was an Oxford high jump 'blue' in 1908 and 1909.

LEGAL MEN
Two Lord Chief Justices of England have been notable athletes: Viscount Alverstone (see p. 263) and Lord Goddard (1946–58), who as Rayner Goddard had run fourth at 100y for Oxford v Cambridge in 1898.

Lord Milligan, Lord Advocate and Solicitor-General for Scotland (1953) was a Scottish 1 mile international and a member of the Cambridge world record 4 × 880y relay team in 1920.

Thomas Curry QC, joint editor of *Palmer's Company Law* was AAA 2 mile steeplechase champion and an Olympic competitor in 1948.

John Creed Meredith, the 1896 AAC 440y champion, was a judge in the Supreme Court of Saorstat Eirann (Ire).

MEDICINE
Professor George Carstairs, former President of the World Federation for Mental Health, won the 1939 World Student Games 5000m, and was second in 1937.

MILITARY MEN
Air Vice Marshal Howard Ford competed in the 1928 Olympic decathlon, but completed only eight of the ten events. He also represented Great Britain five times at the pole vault, at which event he was the 1929 AAA champion

and had a personal best of 3.73m/12ft 3in in 1931, and the shot.

Field Marshal Earl Alexander of Tunis as a Captain in the Irish Guards in 1914, won the Irish 1 mile title in a time of 4:33.2 and represented Ireland in the triangular international against England and Scotland.

Colonel Arnold Nugent Strode Jackson is one of only 16 men to have received three bars to the D.S.O. (Distinguished Service Order). He achieved this rare gallantry distinction in the Great War of 1914–18. He was the youngest acting Brigadier-General in the British army. In 1912 he won the Olympic 1500m title in 3:56.8, having given little previous indication of such ability. He was the nephew of Clement Jackson.

Major General Robert Kotei, Ghana's Defence Chief, was shot in June 1979. His Ghanaian high jump record of 2.08m/6ft 10in set when he won the 1960 title, still stands. While in Britain as a Sandhurst cadet he won the 1958 Commonwealth high jump bronze medal.

POLICE
Sir Joseph Simpson was the first man to go through police ranks from constable to Commissioner of the Metropolitan Police. He won the 1930 World Student Games 400mh in a personal best of 54.2.

David Grigg of the Metropolitan Police, British discus international, was awarded the George Medal in 1940 for his bravery during the 'blitz'.

POLITICIANS
Great Britain
Baroness (Elaine) Burton, MP 1950–9, won a 'North of England' 100y in 13.0 at Old Trafford in 1919, one of the earliest women's races.

Lord (Frank) Byers, Liberal leader in the House of Lords since 1967 was an Oxford 'blue' and British Universities 440y hurdles champion in 1937. He was an MP in 1945–50.

Chris Chataway was Minister for Industrial Development 1972–4 following two years as Minister of Posts and Telecommunications. He was a Conservative MP in 1959–66 and 1969–74. On 25 Sep 1955 he became the first newscaster on Independent Television in Britain, a year after he had set world records at 3 miles and 5000m and had won the Commonwealth Games 3 miles title.

The Hon. H. R. Alexander (later Earl Alexander of Tunis) wins a mile in 1914, three weeks after placing second for Ireland. *(Mirrorpic)*

Terence Higgins was elected as Conservative MP for Worthing in 1964, having been President of the Cambridge Union Society in 1958 (46 years after Philip Noel-Baker had been President). He won a silver medal for England at 4 × 440y at the 1950 Commonwealth Games and was a member of Britain's 4 × 400m relay team placed fifth at the 1952 Olympics.

Sir Lees Knowles, AAC 880y champion 1878, was Conservative MP for Salford West 1886–1906, President of the Local Government Board 1887–92 and President of the Board of Trade 1895–1900.

Philip Noel-Baker won the Nobel Prize for Peace in 1959. He was a Labour MP in 1929–31, 1936–70; Secretary of State for Commonwealth Relations 1947–50, Minister of Fuel and Power 1950–1 and was created a Life Peer in 1977. In the Olympic Games at 1500m, he was sixth in 1912 and second in 1920.

Cecil Parkinson, an MP since 1970, was appointed Chairman of the Conservative party in 1981. He ranked 11th in Britain at 440y in 1954 with a time of 49.4.

United States of America

Jim Beatty, who set a world 2 miles record of 8:29.8 in 1962, and was the first man to run a sub-four minute mile indoors (3:58.9 in Los Angeles in 1962), served in the North Carolina state legislature, but failed in 1972 to win a seat in the House of Representatives.

Dave Bolen, fourth in the 1948 Olympic 400m, was appointed US Ambassador to Botswana, Lesotho and Swaziland in 1974.

Bob Mathias, double world record holder and Olympic decathlon champion, was elected a US Congressman in 1966. A Republican, he represented California's 18th District. In 1973 he introduced legislation to amend the US Olympic Charter, creating a 'Bill of Rights' for amateur athletes.

Ralph Metcalfe, world record holder and winner of four Olympic sprint medals 1932–6, was elected to the US House of Representatives in 1970 for the 1st District of Illinois.

Notable women athletes to be MPs include:
Chi Cheng, multiple world record holder, was elected a deputy in the Taiwan parliament in 1981.

Gunhild Hoffmeister, European 1500m champion of 1974, member of the GDR parliament.

SINGERS

Carl Kaufmann (Ger), 1960 Olympic 400m silver medallist, made his first recording with *Und Amor Lauft Mit (Love Runs Too)*.

Johnny Mathis has been a top singer and recording star for more than 25 years. His *Johnny's Greatest Hits* album was on the US charts for a record 490 weeks, from 1958 to 1968 and he had his first million-seller in 1956 with *Wonderful, Wonderful* which he recorded with the Ray Conniff Orchestra. However just a few years earlier he set a high jump record at San Francisco State College, being ranked equal 85th in the world at 1.97m/6ft 5½in, a performance set at Reno, Nevada on 7 May 1955.

Anne Pashley (later Mrs Irons) was an outstanding mezzo-soprano after her athletics career in which she won WAAA 100y titles in 1953 and 1954 and won sprint relay silver medals at the 1954 Commonwealth and 1956 Olympic Games and a bronze at 100m in the 1954 European Championships.

Jesse Owens (left) and Ralph Metcalfe (right). Metcalfe won their first four encounters, but then Owens won 4–1 in major races.
(Associated Press)

Paul Robeson was a promising high jumper (1.93m/6ft 4in) as well as an All-American footballer while at Rutgers University.

Clarence Treat was lead singer with the New Christy Minstrels, who had a golden disc in 1963 with *Green Green*. While at Occidental University in 1959 he had best times of 14.0 for 120y hurdles and 22.8 for 220y hurdles.

The first athlete to have a song named after him was **Dorando Pietri** after his experiences (see p. 92) at the 1908 Olympic Games. This was the first song composed by Israel Baline, later world famous as Irving Berlin.

STATESMEN

Mahamat Idriss was the first African high jumper to clear 7ft and he had a best of 2.17m/7ft 1½in in 1966. In 1963 at age 21 he became one of the youngest Ministers in the world, when he was appointed Minister of Youth and Sport in Chad.

Estes Kefauver, US Vice-Presidential candidate and senator, set a University of Tennessee discus record of 40.14m/131ft 8½in in 1924.

Dr Urho Kekkonen, President of Finland from 1956 to 1981 and Prime Minister 1950–3 and 1954–6, shared top ranking in his country in the high jump in 1924 when he won the Finnish title at 1.85m/6ft 0¾in, and had a triple jump best of 14.14m.

Paul Kruger, President of the Boer Republic of the Transvaal from 1883 to 1902, was reported to have set a world best long jump of 7.01m/23ft 0in in 1845.

Norman Manley, Prime Minister of Jamaica, set a national junior 100y record of 10.0sec in 1911.

Ratu Sir Kamisese Mara KBE has been Prime Minister of Fiji since 1970. He won his 'Blue' at Oxford for the shot in 1948 and 1949.

His Excellency Sir Arthur Porritt GCMG, GCVO, CBE, FRCS was one of the Queen's Surgeons and from 1967–72 was Governor-General of New Zealand. He was created a Life Peer in 1973. In 1924 he was third in the Olympic 100m, behind Harold Abrahams and Jackson Scholz (USA).

Habib Thiam became Prime Minister of Senegal in 1981. He had been French 200m champion in 1954 and 1957 and reached the semi-finals of the 1958 European 200m representing France, where he was studying.

George Washington, first President of the United States, is reputed to have long jumped about 6.78m/22ft 3in according to a reference by W. M. Thackeray in *The Virginians*.

TELEVISION
Top BBC television commentator **David Coleman** won a third place team medal at the 1952 English National cross-country championships. Running for Manchester A&CC he was 89th overall as his team-mate Walter Hesketh beat Gordon Pirie by almost a minute to win the race. Coleman also won the 1949 'Manchester Mile'.

TOYS
Alfred Gilbert, who tied for first place in the 1908 Olympic pole vault and was an innovator of the spiked pole, was President of A. C. Gilbert Co., a major toy firm which was particularly noted for magic sets and electronic games.

TRAVEL AGENT
Erna Low, founder of the Travel Agency to bear her name, was a javelin thrower, Austrian champion in 1930 and at the WAAA second in 1932 and third in 1933.

Coaches
The first AAA Chief Coach was the great Canadian all-rounder Walter Knox, appointed for three years in 1914. The First World War, however, cut short his stint. Knox had been due to coach the 1916 British Olympic team, but did coach the Canadian team in 1920. He set several Canadian records and won five Canadian titles (100y, PV, LJ, SP, HT) in one afternoon in 1907. He had travelled extensively as a professional athlete and was much involved in gambling, various 'interesting' deals and did not hesitate to use aliases to further his career.

The next man to be appointed Chief Coach was Geoff Dyson in 1947. A good all-rounder with a 120y hurdles best of 14.8, he joined the staff at Loughborough in 1938. Dyson was a highly successful coach and also introduced a new level of understanding of mechanical principles applied to athletics. However he had many disagreements with officialdom and resigned in 1961.

Walter Hesketh leads Gordon Pirie in the 1952 English National cross-country. *(H. W. Neale)*

A second coach, Tony Chapman, was appointed in 1947 and in 1948 three more: Denis Watts (North), Allan Malcolm (Midlands) and Jim Alford (Wales). Chapman moved to Scotland in 1949 and John Le Masurier took the Southern area. Since those early days there have been many significant improvements in coaching methods and a vastly expanded coaching service.

The current Director of Coaching in the UK is Frank Dick, who represented Great Britain in an indoor international at 400m in 1964, and had been AAA Junior 220y hurdles champion in 1960 and Scottish national coach since 1970.

In the 1940s and 1950s few, if any, coaches accompanied British teams overseas. In 1965 it was determined that one national coach could attend selection meetings, but only in an advisory capacity. Nowadays, of course, the coaches play a much wider role.

Canadian Walter Knox, the first AAA Chief Coach, with some of the trophies he gained in a globe-trotting career.

AAA National Coaches at a young athletes course at Motspur Park in 1957 (left to right) John Le Masurier, Lionel Pugh, Geoff Dyson, Jim Alford and Denis Watts. *(H. W. Neale)*

Crime

Pan Singh was an athlete turned bandit. With nine members of his bandit gang he was shot dead by police in a gun battle near Gwalior, India on 4 Oct 1981. After 22 years in the police force he had turned to crime, and the police said that 11 murders were against him. In 1960 he set Indian records at 3000m steeplechase (8:53.4) and 5000m (14:37.2).

Athletes to have been convicted of crimes include the Olympic 100m champion **Bob Hayes** (1964), sentenced to five years imprisonment in March 1979 at Dallas on charges of narcotics trading.

Drugs and Doping

The greatest problem in athletics today must be the use of doping substances. Greatest prominence has been given to the use of anabolic steroids to enhance muscle growth and aid the athlete's ability to take on heavier training schedules. No less serious is the use of stimulants such as amphetamines and cocaine. The practice of using drugs dates back to the sport's early days. For instance strychnine, in small doses a central nervous system stimulant, was used by the 1908 Olympic marathon champion Thomas Hicks. But there has been an alarming increase in drug usage and abusage since the 1950s. In the late 1960s and 1970s the sport's governing bodies introduced new rules barring specific drugs and setting up testing procedures.

The first athlete to be disqualified from a major competition was Eduard de Noorlander (Hol) after being placed sixth in the 1969 European decathlon. The first athlete to lose a medal was Vladimir Zhaloshik (USSR), disqualified after being placed third at the 20km walk at the 1974 European Championships.

In 1971 four West German athletes: Heinfried Birlenbach (SP), Erich Klamma (Dec), Reinhard Kuretzky (PV) and Hermann Latzel (LJ) were suspended for using illegal stimulants.

In 1972 dope testing was introduced at the Olympic Games and had earlier also been conducted at the US Olympic trials.

Technician Liz Johnson and testing equipment at the Drug Control Centre, Chelsea College, University of London.

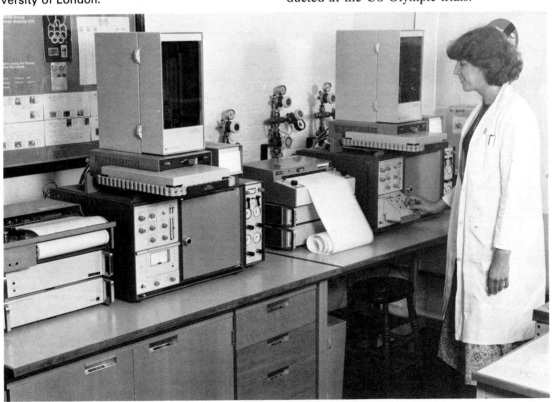

In 1974 British shot putter Jeff Teale was banned by the BAAB following newspaper statements that he had taken steroids.

From 1 Jan 1975 the IAAF introduced automatic disqualification for any athlete found to have used anabolic steroids. Since then the following have been banned for illegal use of drugs, most 'for life', only to have their bans reduced to 12 or (now) 18 months suspensions: (EC = European Cup)

1975 EC semi-final: Velko Velev (Bul) 1st DT; EC final: Valentina Cioltan 4th SP. Joan Wenzel (Can) was banned for life (lifted in 1976) after a third place in the Pan-American 800m (traces of ephedrine, from a cold capsule she had inadvertently taken, were the cause).

1976 Olympics: Danuta Rosani (Pol), who did not compete in the discus final after failing the test for steroids following the qualifying competition.

1977 EC semi-final: Vera Zapkaleno (USSR) 1st SP womens. EC final: Seppo Hovinen (Fin) 2nd JT, Asko Pesonen (Fin) 8th HJ, Markku Tuokko (Fin) 1st DT, Ilona Slupianek (USSR) 1st SP womens. Slupianek returned to win the European title just a year and 16 days later.

Knut Hjeltnes (Nor) and Walter Schmidt (Ger) were also banned as was Barry Williams (GB) after newspaper allegations of steroid use, but he was reinstated in 1978.

1978 European: Yevgeniy Mironov (USSR) 2nd SP, Vasiliy Yershov (USSR) 5th JT, Yekaterina Gordiyenko (USS) 5th Pen womens, Elena Stoyanova (Bul) 5th SP womens, Nadyezhda Tkachenko (USSR) 1st Pen womens. Tkachenko returned to win the 1980 Olympic title, and Stoyanova after a 22-month suspension, added 62cm to her personal best with 20.95m/68ft 8¾in for a second place at the 1980 Balkan Games, and was placed sixth at the Olympics.

W. German team champions: Hans-Joachim Krug 2nd SP, Hein-Direck Neu 1st DT. Two discus throwers, Dave Voorhees (USA) and Colin Sutherland (GB) were banned for refusing to take doping tests.

1979 EC semi-final: Ileana Silai (Rom) 2nd 1500m womens. Balkan Games: Natalia Marasescu (Rom) 2nd 1500m womens and 8th 3000m womens, Totka Petrova (Bul) 1st 800m womens and 1500m womens, Daniela Teneva (Bul) 1st 100mh womens, Sanda Vlad (Rom) 3rd LJ. The ban brought subsequent disqualification from later 'victories' for Marasescu, the World Student Games 1500m, and Petrova, the World Cup 1500m.

European Juniors: Yelena Kovalyeva (USSR) and Nadya Kudryavtseva (USSR) 4th and 6th DT (womens).

The five Balkan athletes were reinstated by a controversial IAAF vote (8–8 and decided by Adriaan Paulen's casting vote) from 1 Jul 1980 after less than a year.

1980 European Indoors: Ronald Desruelles (Bel) 1st LJ. World Champs: Rosa Colorado (Spa) 1st 'B' 400mh womens. She had had an injection, which contained steroids, to help heal a broken finger.

1981 European Indoors: Karoline Kafer (Aut) 4th 400m womens, Nonu Abashdze (USSR) 4th SP womens.

Pacific Conference Games: Gael Mulhall (Aus) 1st SP and DT womens; Ben Plucknett (USA) 1st DT. Plucknett later twice improved the world discus best, but his ban prevented ratification by the IAAF, although one was ratified by the TAC.

EC semi-final: Laszlo Szabo (Hun) 1st SP; Evelyn Ledl (Aut) 7th 400mh womens, for stimulants. Linda Haglund, the top Swedish sprinter, was also banned at the end of the year after a positive test at the Swedish championships. She claimed that her Finnish coach had given her drugs without her knowledge.

Rumours about 'blood-doping' of athletes, particularly in Finland have occasionally been heard. In 1981 Mikko Ala Leppilampi, 5th 1971 European and 10th 1972 Olympics at 3000m steeplechase, said that he had, prior to the 1972 Games, been blood-doped, wherein blood is taken from an athlete and added again later so as to increase the number of red blood cells. Lasse Viren was asked in 1976 whether he had been blood-doped. He made the celebrated reply that he 'drank only reindeer milk', and later denied the charges absolutely.

EQUIPMENT
Wind gauge. A report on wind assistance was prepared for the 1936 IAAF Congress. The German Federation claimed that the highest admissible following wind which did not affect a runner's time was 0.7m/s or if diagonal 1.0m/s. Despite this a rule was passed decreeing a maximum permitted following wind component

of 2.0m/s *4.47ft/sec* for straight races, long and triple jumps. At the time proposals to include wind speed conditions for 200 metres around a turn, pole vault, discus and javelin were not accepted, although later the 200m was added to the lists of events for which a wind gauge must be used for record times.

Starting blocks were perfected in 1927 by George Bresnahan and William Tuttle and were introduced into major championships in 1929, when George Simpson ran the first 9.4 for 100y at the NCAA Championships in Chicago. This time could not be ratified as blocks were not authorised by the IAAF until 1938.

The starter's red coat was pioneered by Teddy Vowles at the White City in 1934.

TRACKS

The introduction of 'all-weather' tracks has considerably altered the sport of athletics. Not only do the coloured tracks look attractive, but they have greatly reduced the effects of the weather, and as the name implies allow tracks to be used throughout the year in virtually any conditions and with much harder usage.

The first artificial surface track was probably that laid at Buffalo, New York State in 1950. This was a rubberised asphalt track put down by the US Rubber Reclaiming Co.

The first world record to be set on a rubberised asphalt track was Bob Hayes' 9.1 100 yards at St Louis in the 1963 AAU on Grasstex.

'Tartan' tracks were developed from 1963 from an idea of William McKnight, Chairman of the Minnesota Mining and Manufacturing Co. (3M), initially for pony trotting. The first 'Tartan' track for athletics was laid at Macalester College, St Paul, Minnesota. 3M quickly had considerable success with these tracks; the first to be used at a major games was at Winnipeg for the Pan-American Games in 1967, followed by the 1968 Olympics and the 1969 European Championships.

The first 'Tartan' laid in Britain was at Solihull, long and triple jump run-ups in 1967, and the first complete track (the first in Europe) was at Crystal Palace, the official opening being on 19 May 1968.

Such was 3M's success that their trade name of 'Tartan' came to be widely used for any form of artificial surface, but 3M were followed by many other companies, such as Chevron, Resis-

port and Rekortan, which was used for the 1972 Olympic Games at Munich.

The first all-weather surfaces in Britain were long jump runways at Eton Manor, East London made of Trinitrack, a bitumen/rubber mixture. A Trinitrack track was then laid at St Mary's College, Twickenham.

In 1980 the first ten-lane all-round synthetic track was laid, at Hughes Stadium, Sacramento, Cal. This was used for the 1981 TAC.

TWINS

Patrick and Pascal Barré ran together on the French 4 × 100m relay team. They won bronze medals at the 1980 Olympic Games, and were placed fourth in the 1978 European.

Christopher and Noel Chavasse, both eliminated in the heats of the 400m in 1908, are the only twins to have run for Britain at the Olympics. Christopher later became Bishop of Rochester and Captain Noel Chavasse was posthumously awarded a bar to the Victoria Cross on 14 Sep 1917, one of the only three men ever to have been so honoured.

Barbara and Wendy (later Hoyte) Clarke both represented Britain in three indoor internationals in 1979.

Haukur and Orn Clausen were both Icelandic record holders. At the 1950 European championships they were respectively fifth at 100m and second at decathlon.

Maurizio (1st) and **Giorgio Damilano** (11th) (Ita) contested the 1980 Olympic 20km walk.

Frank and Gerd Eisenberg both won GDR 5000m titles. Frank (best time 13:29.0) won in 1972 and Gerd (13:32.4) in 1967 and 1970. Frank was ninth in the 1972 Olympic 5000m and both ran at European Championships.

Jörg Freimuth was third in the 1980 Olympic high jump and his twin, **Uwe**, was third in the 1981 decathlon.

Robert and David Holt were consistently among Britain's top distance runners in the late 1960s and 1970s. Their best times were very similar: at 5000m/10000m/marathon – Bob 13:48.6/28:39.8/2:16.50, Dave 13:50.0/28:41.8/2:16.53.

Ross and Robert Hume ran their fastest mile (4:16.6) in tying for first place in the 1944 NCAA. A year later Ross was first and Robert second.

Christine (4th 1500m) and **Evelyn** (6th 800m) **McMeekin** both ran for Scotland at the 1978 Commonwealth Games. They alternated as Scottish 800m champions 1975–8. Their elder brother David was a British 800m international.

Shigeru and Takeshi Sou (Jap) have both run the marathon in less than 2:10. Shigeru ran his best of 2:09:05.6 when beating Takeshi to win at Beppu in 1978 and Takeshi's best 2:09:49 was when he was second at Fukuoka in 1980 with Shigeru fifth.

Malcolm and Melville Spence won gold medals at the 1962 Commonwealth Games on Jamaica's 4 × 440y relay team and at 440y they were placed fifth and sixth respectively. They also ran on the winning West Indian 4 × 400m team at the 1959 Pan-American Games; at 400m Malcolm was third in 1959 and Melville was second in 1963. They also competed at the 1956 Olympics.

Monique (6.03m LJ in 1970) and **Rita** (1.70m HJ in 1967) **Vanherck** set Belgian records. Their father Albert Vanherck was a pole vault international.

Jacques Vernier set French records at 5000m in 1948 and 1949 and his twin **Jean** set a record at 3000m in 1949. Both ran in the 1948 Olympics and 1950 European Championships.

Debbie and Diane Vetter with their sister Janis ran on the Blue Ribbon TC team that set a world 4 × 880y relay record of 8:46.4 at White Plains, New York on 28 Jun 1975.

Ann and Paula Yeoman both set British records: Ann (married to distance international Bernie Ford) at 3000m, and Paula (Mrs Fudge) at 3000m and a world record at 5000m. In the 1978 Commonwealth Games 3000m Paula was first and Ann third. They raced together for Britain three times, Paula beating Ann 2–1 and they also ran together for England in the 1979 World cross-country championships – Ann 9th, Paula 17th and in 1982 – Ann 13th, Paula 14th.

Two pairs of twins – Blaine and Wayne Rideout and Elmer and Delmer Brown set a world indoor medley relay best at the 1938 Millrose Games. The Rideouts ran their fastest miles (Blaine 4:10.1 and Wayne 4:10.4) at the 1940 Kansas Relays. Blaine won the 1939 AAU 1500m title.

Twins to have run for England at cross-country have been Graham and Grenville Tuck and Iris and Rita Lincoln. In ten races at the English national cross-country from 1969 to 1979 Grenville finished ahead of Graham 6–4, but Grenville has had a clear superiority on the track with eight GB internationals at 10000m. In the inaugural international women's cross-country race in 1967 Rita (later Ridley) was third and Iris (later Cook) tenth. Their 800m times were similar – Iris 2:05.8 and Rita 2:05.5, but Rita had much greater successes at longer distances achieving British records at 1500m and 3000m.

Notable American twins include: Ron (17.19m and 17.56m (w) triple jump) and Don (9.4 100y) Livers; David (10.2 100m) and Don (50.1 440y hurdles and 21.9 world record 220y hurdles) Styron; Herb (AAU indoor 1000y champion 1969) and George (800m international 1965) Germann.

BROTHERS AND SISTERS

The only sisters to have won Olympic titles and set world records are Tamara and Irina Press (USSR). Tamara won Olympic titles at shot in 1960 and at both shot and discus in 1964, and set six world records at each event. Irina won Olympic titles at 80m hurdles in 1960 and at the pentathlon in 1964 and set six world records at 80m hurdles and eight at the pentathlon.

Paula Fudge (4) leads her twin Ann Ford. They were first and second for GB v Finland in 1978.
(M. Shearman)

Brothers to have set world records at individual events

Thomas and Patrick Davin (Ire), both at high jump; Thomas 1.81m/5ft 11¼in in 1874 and Patrick 1.90m/6ft 2¾in in 1880 and also at long jump – 7.06m/23ft 2in in 1883. In 1881 Patrick won AAA titles at high jump and long jump while another brother, Maurice won the shot and the hammer. Between them the brothers won 30 Irish titles.

Timothy Ahearne and **Daniel Ahearn** (Ire) with 14.92m/48ft 11¼in in 1908 and 15.52m/50ft 11in in 1911 respectively at triple jump. The younger brother dropped the 'e' at the end of his name.

The three **Kolehmainen** brothers from Finland all set world bests: Viljami 'Willi' the eldest, ran the marathon on a track (!) in 2:29:39.2 in 1912 for a world professional best; Taavetti 'Tatu' for 20000m in 1913 and the youngest, Johannes 'Hannes' at 3000m and 5000m, as well as winning four Olympic gold medals.

Akilles and Matti Järvinen (Fin). Akilles set three decathlon records from 1928 to 1932 with a best on the 1964 tables of 7038 points, while Matti made ten improvements to the javelin record. Akilles won two Olympic silver medals and Matti a gold. They were the third and fourth sons of Werner Järvinen, winner of the Greek-style discus at the 1906 Olympics. Werner's two eldest sons were also good athletes: Yrjo (58.50m/191ft 11in javelin 1925) and Kalle (Finnish shot record of 15.92m/52ft 2¾in in 1932).

Brothers who have run together on world relay records

Gösta and Gunnar Fosselius 4 × 1500m IF Linnéa Stockholm 16:37.0 in 1925.
Alvin and Leslie Hables 4 × 440y Stanford University 3:12.6 in 1931.
Pentti and Martti Salovaara 4 × 1500m Finland 15:54.8 in 1939.
John and Dave Perry 4 × 880y Oklahoma State 7:18.4 in 1965.
Marvin and Curtis Mills 4 × 220y Texas A & M University 1:21.7 in 1970.

Other notable brothers/sisters

Brothers Platt and Ben Adams (USA) finished first and second in the 1912 Olympic standing high jump.
Horace Ashenfelter (USA) won the 1952 Olympic 3000m steeplechase title in a world record time of 8:45.4 and his brother **William** ran on the US team that ran a world record for 4 × 880y in 1952.

Godfrey and Audrey Brown won Olympic medals in 1936; Godfrey a gold at 4 × 400m relay and silver at 400m and his sister silver at 4 × 100m relay. Godfrey won gold (400m), silver and bronze (relays) at the 1938 European championships but Audrey missed out as the British 4 × 100m team finished third but were disqualified. Elder brother **Ralph** (later His Honour Judge Ralph Kilner Brown) was third in the 1934 Commonwealth 440y hurdles.

The four Howard sisters – Artra, Tina, Denean and Sherri set an American High School 4 × 440y relay record at 3:44.1 in 1979 for San Gorgonio HS of San Bernardino, California. At the 1980 Trials Sherri (1st) and Denean (3rd) at 400m became the first sisters ever to qualify for the US Olympic team. 15-year-old Denean was the youngest member of the squad. She went on to win the TAC 400m in 1981.

Patrick and Con Leahy won five Olympic medals: **Con** 1st HJ and 2nd TJ 1906, 2nd HJ 1908; **Patrick** 2nd HJ, 3rd LJ 1900. Con won four and Patrick two, AAA high jump titles and a third brother **Tim** gained AAA second places at high jump and pole vault.

Brother and sister **Carl and Carol Lewis** were both on the 1980 US Olympic team at long jump. Their mother, as Evelyn Lawlor, won the 1950 AAU 80m hurdles.

Sisters to have won WAAA titles: Hazel (1 mile 1951) and Sylvia (DT 1957) Needham; Edith (JT 1932) and Nellie (13 titles from 100y to cross-country 1930–8) Halstead. The Halsteads also both set British records: Edith 35.22m javelin throw in 1933 and Nellie at 200m, 220y and 440y, the latter a world record which lasted for 21½ years.

Bill and Peter Tancred both won AAA titles; Bill seven discus and two indoor shot and Peter two discus. At the Commonwealth Games at the discus Bill was third in 1970 and second 1974, and Peter was sixth in 1978. Another brother, Geoff, was an army hammer champion and father Adrian was a useful thrower.

Harold and Rex Whitlock both won RWA 50km walk titles and competed in that event at the Olympic Games; Harold was champion in 1936 and Rex was fourth in 1952.

Joe (1948) and **Bob** (1960) **Birrell** both ran for Britain at 110m hurdles at Olympic Games.

The most successful of all British families have been the **Stewarts**, brothers **Peter** and **Ian** and their sister **Mary**. All won European indoor titles – Ian 3000m 1969 and 1975, Peter 3000m 1971, Mary 1500m 1977. All set British records – Ian at 1500m, 2000m, 2 miles and 5000m;

Peter at 1 and 2 miles and Mary at 1 mile as well as a world indoor best (4:08.1) for 1500m. Ian (5000m 1970) and Mary (1500m 1978) won Commonwealth titles. Ian won the European 5000m in 1969 and the World cross-country title in 1975, thereby completing a unique double just a week after his European indoor win. All three also won AAA/WAAA titles. The brothers **Walter** and **Alfred George** between them won 16 national titles in Britain and America. Walter won two AAC and ten AAA championships and Alfred, ten years his junior, won one AAA and three AAU.

PARENTS AND CHILDREN
Olympic Champions and world record holders: Imre and Miklos Németh. Imre set a world hammer record each year from 1948 to 1950, and won the 1948 Olympic title as well as being placed third in 1952. He was later an Hungarian MP and manager of the Népstadion, Budapest. Son Miklos was fifth at the javelin in the 1966 European Games, but that remained his best major event placing for a decade. However in 1976 he came through in brilliant style to win the Olympic title with a world record 94.58m/310ft 4in on his first throw.

World record holders: Archie San Romani at 2000m (5:16.7 in 1937) and on the US 4×1 mile relay team in 1936. His son of the same name ran on the Oregon University 4×1 mile team that ran 16:09.0 in 1962. Their respective bests for 1 mile were 4:07.2 in 1937 and 3:57.6 in 1964.

British Olympic teams: Violet Webb (5th 80mh 1932 and 3rd 4×100mR and British record 11.7 for 80mh in semis 1936), was the mother of Janet Simpson (4th 400m 1968). Janet, European 4×400m relay gold medallist in 1969, married Philippe Clerc, the Swiss European 200m champion 1969. **Muriel Pletts** (4th 4×100mR 1948), was the mother of Sue Hearnshaw (9th LJ 1980). Sue was WAAA champion in 1979, bettering her mother's second at 100m in 1951.

US Olympic teams: Charles Moore, 110m hurdles 1924, and his son Charley first 400m hurdles 1952; Glenn Hardin, first 1936 and second 1932 at 400m hurdles, and his son Billy, semi-final 400m hurdles 1964 (both won AAU titles); Alice Arden, eighth equal high jump 1936, and her son Russ Hodge, ninth at decathlon 1964. Glenn Graham won the 1924 Olympic pole vault silver medal, losing to Lee

Barnes in a jump-off. His son Jim was third at pole vault in the 1956 Olympic Trials, gaining his place by the narrowest margin as four other men cleared the same height of 4.48m/14ft 8½in. Later in the year he injured his ankle and with superb sportsmanship gave up his coveted Olympic place to fourth placed Bob Gutowski, after the latter had shown his form with a 4.70m/15ft 5in jump. Yet on the day that he withdrew Graham vaulted 14ft 4in and could well have won an Olympic medal. As it was Gutowski was second to Bob Richards.

Other notable parents and children
The 1952 Olympic pole vault gold and silver medallists **Bob Richards** and **Don Laz** both had sons who vaulted higher than they had. Bob Richards senior had a best of 4.72m/15ft 6in in 1957, while his son Bob vaulted 5.33m/17ft 6in in 1973. Don Laz did 4.64m/15ft 3in in 1952 and son Doug 5.30m/17ft 4¾in in 1976.

Two pole vault world record holders also had vaulting fathers: Konstantin Volkov, 5.84m in 1981 and Olympic silver medallist, is the son of Yuriy who had a best of 5.16m/16ft 11in indoors in 1970. Philippe Houvion, 5.77m in 1980, is the son of Maurice, French national coach, who set seven national records and had a best of 5.10m/16ft 8¾in in 1968.

European medals were won by husband, wife and son: Karl-Friedrich Haas (Ger), second at 4×400m 1954 and 1958 and third at 400m 1958, Maria Sturm, third at pentathlon 1954, and their son Christian was second at 60m indoors in 1980.

Soviet discus throwers with notable sons: Aram Ter-Ovanesyan, top USSR man in 1933 at 42.59m, father of long jumper Igor (qv); Aadu Tarmak, USSR champion 1943–4, father of Yuriy, 1972 Olympic high jump champion; Sergey Lyakhov, father of Vladimir, both set USSR records, 50.74m in 1939 and 66.04m in 1976 respectively.

Yelizabeta Bagryantseva (USSR), second at 1952 Olympic discus; mother of Irina, first at 1980 Olympic 4×400m relay.

Irina Bochkaryeva, world 60m record of 7.2 in 1960 and European 100m champion 1954, daughter of Galina Turova, Soviet long jump champion 1934, 1943 and 1945, and Robert Lyulko, fastest Soviet 100m man in 1936 and 1938.

Jock Dalrymple set a British javelin record of 56.42m/185ft 1½in in 1929. His son, Malcolm emulated him with 64.25m/210ft 9½in in 1948, and Malcolm's son Philip had a hammer best of 50.42m in 1979.

Maria Dollinger set world records at 800m (2:16.8 in 1931) and on the German 4 × 100m relay team in a heat of the 1936 Olympic Games but they dropped the baton in the final. Her daughter Brunhilde Hendrix won an Olympic 4 × 100m relay silver medal in 1960.

Helmut Dombrowski, German youth 100m champion 1939 and a 7.18m long jumper, father of Lutz, 1980 Olympic long jump champion.

Yuriy Dyachkov (USSR), sixth 1962 European decathlon, son of Nina Dumbadze, women's discus world record holder, and Vladimir Dyachkov, coach of Valeriy Brumel and with a best pole vault of 4.20m in 1939.

Jack Higginson set an English triple jump record of 14.25m/46ft 9in in 1926 and his son Jack improved this to 14.43m/47ft 4in in 1938.

Andrea Matay, European Indoor high jump champion 1979, daughter of Ilona Vekony, 1948 Hungarian high jump champion. With a best of 1.98m/6ft 6in, Andrea outjumped her mother by 50cm!

Yuriy Nikulin (USSR), fourth 1964 Olympic hammer, father of Igor, European Junior champion 1979 and at 19 in 1980 much the youngest man to throw over 80m.

Heinz Rosendahl, German discus champion 1951 and 1953, father of Heide, long jump world record holder and Olympic champion.

Ernst Schmidt, winner of ten GDR titles (shot, discus and decathlon between 1950–4), father of Wolfgang, world discus record holder.

Gerhard Stöck (Ger) won the 1936 Olympic javelin title; his daughter Jutta won a European 4 × 100m relay silver medal for Germany in 1966 and 1969.

Grandparents and grandchildren
Jim Espir, 1500m international and AAA junior 3000m champion 1977, is the grandson of Ellis Smouha, third Olympic 4 × 100m relay 1928, and the nephew of Brian Smouha, second

Peter Allday talks to his wife Suzanne through the wire fence of the Olympic women's village at Melbourne in 1956.　*(GOPA)*

World Student Games 200m 1961. Ellis had perhaps the ultimate address – Smouha City, Egypt.

Tom Lockton, winner of the 1938 AAA decathlon, was the grandson of Charles Lockton, winner of the first AAA long jump title in 1880.

MARRIED COUPLES
Married couples to have won Olympic titles
Harold and Olga (née Fikotová) Connolly, Harold Osborn and Ethel Catherwood (HJ 1928), Bill and Mary (then Rand) Toomey, Emil Zatopek and Dana Zatopková (Cze). See Olympic section for further details.

Although crossing into the world of gymnastics it is also worth mentioning that double Olympic medallist Valeriy Borzov married Lyudmila Turischeva, winner of four Olympic gold medals.

Married couples to have set world records
Erwin (59.00m hammer 1938) and Dora (née Voigt, 4 × 200m relay 1938) Blask; Harold (2.03m/6ft 8¼in high jump and 6668 decathlon 1924) and Ethel (née Catherwood, 1.60m/5ft 3in 1928) Osborn, Emil Zatopek (see p. 173–4) and Dana Zatopková (see p. 15).

Married couples to have set British records

Peter (HT) and Suzanne (SP, DT) Allday; Robbie (400m) and Ann (400m, 800m) Brightwell; John (3000m S/C) and Sylvia (200m) Disley; Geoffrey (PV, Dec) and Pam (80mh) Elliott; Derek (1M, 3M) and Madeline (3 × 800mR) Ibbotson; Alan (110mh, 200mh) and Della (100m) Pascoe; Howard (HT) and Rosemary (DT) Payne; Gordon (2000m–10000m) and Shirley (200m, 400m) Pirie.

John (400mh) and Sheila (LJ) Sherwood won gold medals at the 1970 Commonwealth Games and won medals (3rd/2nd respectively) at the 1968 Olympic Games.

The Connolly, Payne and Allday couples, in each case a hammer thrower married to a discus thrower, all had twins!

Harold Connolly and his two wives have the record for the **most Olympic appearances by married couples**. Harold threw the hammer for the USA at four Games (1956–68). His first wife Olga (from whom he was divorced in 1975) went one better by throwing the discus at these four Games and the 1972 Games and his second wife, Pat (formerly Daniels, Winslow and Bank) competed at the three Games from 1960 to 1968 for a Connolly total of 12.

Bill Toomey married Mary Rand a week after his 8417 world record decathlon. This was Bill's seventh score of over 8000 points in 1969 and 13th in all out of 33 ever to that date. Supposedly his final competition he actually competed in one more decathlon in each of the next three years. In 1972 they had car licence plates of BIL2ME and MAR2ME respectively.

Films

Notable athletes who have appeared in films

The 1960 Olympic pole vault champion, **Don Bragg**, had the ambition of playing Tarzan. In 1956 his kit bag was labelled *Tarzan* and *15-9 or bust.* He made the latter with his 1960 world record 4.80m/15ft 9¼in but didn't quite make the former. He began filming *Tarzan and the Jewels of Opar* in 1964, but the project was abandoned.

Herman Brix, 1928 Olympic shot put gold medallist and world record holder with 16.07m/52ft 8½in in 1932. As Bruce Bennett he made his name as Tarzan in *The New Adventures of Tarzan (1935)* before moving on to many dramatic roles.

Herman Brix (above) puts the shot for the USA v British Empire after winning the 1928 Olympic silver medal *(BBC Hulton).* (Left) As Bruce Bennett he is Tarzan swinging through the trees in 1935.
(National Film Archive/ Stills Library)

Dean Smith, the 1952 AAU 100m champion, became a great film stuntman. He also ran 100y in 9.9 at the age of 38. *(University of Texas)*

Roscoe Lee Browne, ranked second in the world at 800m in 1951, was in *Topaz (1969)* and many other films.

Ricky Bruch, world discus record holder, played an Italian priest in *Charleston (1974)*.

Giuseppe Gentile, triple jump world record holder and 1968 Olympic bronze medallist, played Jason to the Medea of Maria Callas in *Medea (1970)*.

Roosevelt Grier, with a best shot putt of 17.16m/56ft 3½in in 1955, appeared in the television smash hit, *Roots*. Grier and Rafer Johnson were among Robert Kennedy's bodyguards when he was shot dead in Los Angeles on 5 Jun 1968.

Glenn Morris, 1936 Olympic decathlon champion, after first making a short film, *Decathlon Champion*, also played Tarzan in *Tarzan's Revenge (1938)* and the same year made *Hold That Coed*.

Several other Olympic decathlon champions have appeared in films: **Bruce Jenner** appeared in *Can't Stop the Music (1980)* and the decathlon bronze medallist in 1948 and 1952, **Floyd Simmons** was in *South Pacific (1958)*.
Rafer Johnson made many movies from his first *The Fiercest Heart (1961)* and his arch-rival **C. K. Yang** played a prisoner in *The Crooked Man (1969)* amongst other parts.
Bob Mathias played himself in *The Bob Mathias Story (1954)* and also appeared with Jayne Mansfield in a spoof of the 1896 Games, *It Happened in Athens (1961)*.

Jim Thorpe acted as an extra in many Westerns in the 1930s and 1940s and was the subject of a film biography, *Man of Bronze (1951)*, called *Jim Thorpe–All-American* in the USA, starring Burt Lancaster.
Dennis Weaver is the most successful ex-decathlete film star. As Billy Weaver he was sixth with 6588 points in the 1948 US Olympic trials. Starting with *The Raider (1952)* he became famous for his television roles in *Gunsmoke, McCloud* and *Stone*.

Norman Pritchard, Indian Olympic silver medallist in 1900, featured in many Hollywood silent films.

Bob Seagren, 1968 Olympic pole vault champion and world record holder, has appeared in numerous television roles including one in *Soap*.

Adhemar Ferreira da Silva, double Olympic triple jump winner and world record holder, had a major part in *Black Orpheus (Orfeu Negro) (1958)*.

Dean Smith, fourth at 100m and a relay gold medallist at the 1952 Olympic Games, has for many years been a film stuntman and has appeared in hundreds of films and television programmes, including *Stagecoach*, *True Grit* and *Rio Lobo*. He was noted for his fast starting, and it is said that in his home state of Texas starters instructions were: 'Get to your marks', 'Get set', 'Go Dean' and then they fired the gun.

One of the first black actors to be given serious 'heroic' roles was 'Woody' Strode, whose first film was *The Lion Hunters (1951)*. He was fourth in the 1938 NCAA discus, with a best of 49.32m/161ft 10in.

Oliver Reed, British film star, was seventh at the 1965 English Schools cross-country championships (juniors).

FILMS ON ATHLETICS
One of the earliest films to have included athletics sequences was *College (1927)* in which Buster Keaton endeavours various activities in order to impress a girl. Lee Barnes, 1924 Olympic pole vault champion, was Keaton's only stand-in ever as he is shown vaulting up and through a first-floor window to rescue the heroine.

In the 1938 film *A Yank at Oxford* starring Robert Taylor, the latter, wearing cap and gown, is shown winning a 440y race despite starting late. His stand-in was Harold Smallwood, second in 46.4sec in the 1936 NCAA 400m.

Filming for *The Games* incorporated the 1969 Southern area cross-country championships. Michael Crawford, playing Harry Hayes, was shown beating the actual winner, British Olympian Tim Johnston but Crawford had not run the full 9 mile course!

Of purely sporting films the most celebrated have been the official films of the 1936 and 1964 Olympic Games. Leni Riefenstahl's *Olympische Spiele 1936* is a magnificent and beautifully photographed epic dedicated to physical health. Kon Ichikawa's 1964 Olympic film is rather less of a documentary coverage, leaving that to the television cameras, but concentrating on the competitors' struggles against their adversaries and their own nerves and doubts.

Charlie Chan at the Olympics (*1937*) included footage of the 1936 Games. There is a pole vaulting competition, but the purported American vaulter is in fact Shuhei Nishida of Japan, the silver medallist.

The Oscar winning British film *Chariots of Fire* (*1981*) was a moving and highly successful depiction of how Harold Abrahams and Eric Liddell won their gold medals at the 1924 Olympic Games. The realistic performances of the actors were largely due to the training of Tom McNab, former Scottish triple jump champion and British national coach, and also a keen historian.

Chariots of Fire won the Oscar as best film of the year. Above is the film depiction of Eric Liddell (Ian Charleston) chaired in triumph with Harold Abrahams (Ben Cross) on extreme right. Top right the real Abrahams wins his gold medal. *(Roland Grant Archive)*

Fund Raising

The greatest ever fund raising by running was the 24 million dollars brought in by the 'Marathon of Hope' run across Canada by the one-legged Terry Fox. The money was donated to cancer research. Terry Fox, who had lost his right leg through cancer in 1977, started his run in St John's, Newfoundland in April 1980, hoping to raise 100000 dollars. The discovery of cancer in his lungs forced him to end his run at Thunder Bay, Ontario in September when, having stumbled about 25 miles a day, he had covered 3339 miles/5373km. He died of cancer on 29 Jun 1981, a national hero. Canadian Prime Minister Pierre Trudeau said that 'Candians mourned the passing of a young man whose courage and awesome determination inspired this country as no one else has ever done'.

Indoor Athletics

The first indoor athletics meeting ever held was at the Ashburnham Hall in London on 7 Nov 1863. A programme of four running events (100y, 220y, 440y and 880y) and a triple jump was organised by the West London Rowing Club. Four years earlier *Bell's Life* reported that W. Priestley would jump 500 hurdles, 10 yards apart in under 40 minutes for a bet of £22 at the Lambeth Baths in London, but this was presumably not a true meeting.

The first indoor meeting in the USA was organised by the New York Athletic Club in a building at 3rd Avenue and 63rd Street, later known as the Empire City Skating Rink, on 11 Nov 1868, a Wednesday evening. From then indoor athletics rapidly became established in the USA, which was the first nation to hold indoor championships. (See p. 143.)

Indoor athletics was much slower to become important in Europe although meetings were held in various countries, notably in Germany.

The first European nation to hold national indoor championships was England at Wembley from 1935–9 although these were not revived after the War until 1962. The original track at Wembley was a 12½ laps to the mile flat floor circuit. A banked board track was first installed in 1937. From 1965 RAF Cosford has been the home of British indoor athletics. The first indoor meeting at Cosford was held on a 160y flat floor track on 9 Nov 1955. A larger, 250y circumference, track was marked out on con-

Terry Fox, whose Marathon of Hope on one leg aroused deep admiration throughout Canada.
(Photo-Canada Wide)

crete from 1961. From 1965 a banked board track was used. This was re-surfaced in 1972 (with Uni-Turf) and in 1980 (Mondo surface).

The biggest board track in the world was that installed in the Houston Astrodome in 1968. Its six-lane banked boards measured 352y/322m in circumference. There was plenty of room for it in the Astrodome, with a clear span of 642ft/196m, and 208ft/63m to the highest point of the dome. Many remarkable times have been set on this oversized track.

The fieldhouse of Washington State University at Pullman is large enough to stage indoor discus, hammer and javelin competitions.

During the Second World War several indoor meetings in the USA were held outdoors, as the armouries in which they were traditionally staged were closed to track meetings.

It took **11 months** to determine the winner of the 1950 Wanamaker Mile held at the Millrose Games on 28th January. Both Fred Wilt and Don Gehrmann were timed in 4:09.3 and the judges were deadlocked before the Chief Judge, Asa Bushnell, voted for Gehrmann. this decision was reversed by the Metropolitan AAU a fortnight later and an appeal by Bushnell failed, but the National AAU convention on 8 Dec 1950 declared for Gehrmann. Two years later at the NYAC Games, Gehrmann again beat Wilt, but only after an hour-long examination of the photo-finish.

Largest fields

The greatest number of runners in any race is about 80000 in the 6½ mile/10.5km 'Round the Bays' race in Auckland, New Zealand on 28 Mar 1982.

Europe's greatest mass-participation race is the 22km 'Stramilano' in Milan, Italy, with about 50000 participants each year since 1979. It was first staged in 1972 with 1500 runners.

The greatest number of runners in an all-women's race was about 7300 in the Bonne Bell national 10km at Boston, Mass., USA on 12 Oct 1981. The winner was Jan Merrill in 32:04.

27000 boys and girls took part in relay races in East Berlin, GDR in 1980. Seven to eight year olds ran 20 × 50m, nine to sixteen year olds ran 20 × 200m.

The largest cross-country fields have been in Sweden's 'Lidingoloppet', with the main race at 30km. There were a record 10085 runners in 1981, of whom 9650 finished.

The greatest number of runners in a track race is 355 at 10000m at Trondheim, Norway on 5 Oct 1973. The winner Knut Bórö weaved his way to a time of 29:47.0.

The Cross du Figaro cross-country races have been held annually in Paris since 1961. In 1979 there were 35849 runners divided into several races.

Longevity

Duncan MacLean set a world best for his age, 92, of 21.7 for 100m in 1977. This was 73 years after his career best 100y of 9.9 in South Africa in 1904. He trained regularly at Crystal Palace in the early 1970s.

Duncan Maclean, whose career began in the 1890s, with Chi Cheng before her WAAA 100m win in 1969 at Crystal Palace.   *(All-Sport)*

Joe Deakin ran his first race 1887 at the age of eight and ran in the Surrey AC winter handicap up to his 90th birthday. He was Irish champion at 1 and 4 miles in 1901 and won a gold medal for the 3 miles team event at the 1908 Olympic Games, winning the race in 14:39.6 he was also sixth at 1500m.

Wilhelm Häfner was still jogging at the age of 94 in 1974, reckoning to run 5000m in 38–42 minutes. He had won six South German titles in 1900–5.

Names
Perhaps the ultimate commentator's nightmare came in the heats of the 100m at the 1972 Olympic Games. Vassilios Papageorgopoulos (Gre) was first and Jean-Louis Ravelomanantsoa of Madagascar second. The winning time 10.24 seconds being about the time taken to get out the names. It was perhaps fortunate that Benedict Majedkodunmi and Sunil Gunawardene were in the next race!

The 1978 Commonwealth shot bronze medallist, Bishop Dolegiewicz (Can) got his first name because school authorities so interpreted the heavy accents of his parents, who had emigrated from Poland to Canada after the World War II. His real name – Zbigniew.

Officials
Primo Nebiolo was appointed **President of the IAAF** in 1981. His three predecessors were notable athletes:
1912–46 J. Sigfrid Edstrom (Swe) – best times for 100m of 11.0 and 150m of 16.4 in 1891.
1946–72 Lord Burghley (from 1956 the Marquess of Exeter) – Olympic 400m hurdles champion in 1928 and fourth in 1932 when he won a silver medal for 4 × 400m relay. He won eight AAA titles (3 at 120yh, 5 at 440yh) and set many British records. Following 12 years as MP for Peterborough he was created KCMG in 1943 and was Governor of Bermuda 1943–5. Lord Burghley became the first man to run round the Great Court of Trinity College, Cambridge (370y/338m) in a dinner jacket while the clock was striking twelve (it took 44.9sec). He is also reputed to have run round the upper promenade deck of the Queen Mary in full evening dress immediately after dinner, taking 58sec for about 400y. 'The Hurdler' public house at Stamford near his ancestral home has a sign depicting him in running vest and shorts.

1972–81 Adriaan Paulen (Hol) – set Dutch records at 400m (48.2) and 400m hurdles (57.4) in 1924 and at 800m (1:55.1) in 1923. He also set a world 500m record of 63.8 in 1924, in which year he was an Olympic semi-finalist at 400m and 800m. In 1920 he was placed eighth in the Olympic 800m. He went to Rice University in the late 1920s and served in the US Army in World War II.

John Holt (GB) was appointed **Secretary-General of the IAAF** in 1972. He had been second in the 1959 World Student Games 800m, and had a best ever of 1:49.2.

Two of the eight **Presidents of the IOC** have been good athletes. Sigfrid Edstrom (above) was in office 1946–52 and was succeeded by Avery Brundage. Brundage had earlier been President of both the AAU and the US Olympic Committee (from 1929). His long career as a forthright defender of amateurism was preceded by athletic achievements including AAU all-around titles in 1914, 1916 and 1918. In the 1912 Olympic Games he was fifth at the pentathlon, but failed to finish the decathlon.

Other IOC members to have been notable athletes include: Charles Sherrill (USA) (IOC 1922–36) – AAU 100y champion 1887 and a pioneer of the crouch start in the USA (Bobby McDonald had earlier used a crouch start from 1884 in Australia). Sherrill was later US Ambassador to Turkey.
Karl Ritter von Halt (Ger) (1929–64) – 8th 1912 Olympic Dec.
Marquess of Exeter (GB) (1933–81) – see opposite.
Lord Porritt (NZ) (1934–67) – 3rd 1924 Olympic 100m.
Bo Ekelund (Swe) (1948–65) – 3rd 1920 Olympic high jump.
Ivar Vind (Den) (1959–77) – 1st 1947 World Student Games high jump, Danish champion and record holder.
Sylvio de Magalhaes Padilha (Bra) (1964–) – 5th 1936 Olympic 400mh, and winner of five South American titles.
James Worrell (Can) (1967–) – 2nd 1934 Commonwealth 120yh.
Maj. Gen. Niels Holst Sorensen (Den) (1977–) – 8th 1948 Olympic 800m, 1st 400m and 2nd 800m 1946 European.
Kevan Gosper (Aus) (1977–) – 2nd Olympic 4 × 400mR 1956; 1st 1954 Commonwealth 440y.

The first two women members of the IOC were admitted in 1981. One of them was Pirjo Häggman (Fin), who won World Student titles at 200m and 400m in 1975 and competed in three Olympic Games, with a best placing of fourth at 400m in 1976.

Ollan Cassell was appointed **administrator of the AAU** in 1966 and later their first director of track and field athletics. On the formation of The Athletics Congress (TAC) of the AAU in 1979 he was appointed its secretary. At the University of Houston he had been known as 'The Chief' due to his practice of painting his nose with a white streak of zinc oxide to protect it from the sun. He won AAU titles at 220y in 1957 and 440y in 1965 and won a gold medal on the world record-setting US Olympic 4 × 400m team in 1964.

Presidents of the Amateur Athletic Association
1880–90 The Earl of Jersey – second at 1 mile and fourth at 2 miles in the 1865 Inter-Varsity Sports.
1891–1915 Viscount Alverstone. As Richard Webster he won both 1 and 2 miles at the 1865

match (above), having been second in the steeplechase in the inaugural Oxford v Cambridge match in 1864, when as Secretary he had penned Cambridge's challenge. He became Attorney General and later Lord Chief Justice of England (1900–13). Amongst his famous cases was the trial of Dr Crippen in 1910.
1916–30 Sir Montague Shearman – AAC 100y champion 1876, and inaugural AAA 440y champion in 1880. He was secretary of the AAA 1880–3 and was also an Oxford rugby 'blue' and international lacrosse player. He wrote the classic *Athletics and Football* in the Badminton Library (1887). In 1914 he became a judge in the King's Bench division.
1930–6 Lord Desborough – as William Grenfall he was an Oxford 'blue' at rowing and athletics (second at 3 miles in 1876). Chairman of the British Olympic Association at the time of the 1908 Games, he was uniquely President of five national sports associations: fencing, cricket, lawn tennis, wrestling and athletics.
1936–76 Marquess of Exeter – see p. 262.
1976–8 Harold Abrahams – 1924 Olympic 100m champion and British record holder with bests of: 100y – 9.6w; 100m – 10.5; 220y straight – 21.6, LJ – 7.38m/24ft 2½in. He retired from athletics due to a broken leg while long jumping in 1925 and devoted a lifetime of ser-

Douglas Lowe retains his AAA 440y title in 1928. He won the 440y/880y double in both 1927 and 1928.

vice to the sport as team captain, broadcaster, journalist and official, serving on the AAA's general committee from 1926. He was Hon Treasurer of the BAAB 1946–69 and its chairman 1969–75.

Harold's elder brothers Adolphe and Sidney were both knighted, the former for services to medicine and the latter for legal work, which included being Chief Justice of Uganda, Tanganyika and Ceylon. Sidney won the 1913 AAA long jump title and competed in the 1906 and 1912 Olympics (5th and 11th at long jump).

1978– Squire Yarrow – 1946 AAA marathon champion. At European championships he was second in 1938 and seventh in 1946, with a best time of 2:37:50.

BAAB Secretaries have included:
1932–8 Douglas Lowe – 1924 and 1928 Olympic 800m champion, world record holder at 600y (1:10.4); hon. secretary of the AAA 1931–8. He was Recorder of the Crown Court 1972–5.
1965–77 Arthur Gold high jump international in 1937 with a best ever of 1.90m/6ft 2⅞in and coach to many top British jumpers.
1977–8 Robert Stinson – Cambridge 'blue' at 220y hurdles, best 25.4 in 1954.
1978–81 David Shaw, the first full-time general secretary – Steeplechase international, winning against France in 1958, with a best time of 8:57.0 while in the RAF.

Pacemaking

Pacemaking, while prevalent in many major races in which records have been set, has been officially deprecated. National records to have been refused ratification due to pacemaking include a 4:02.0 1 mile by Roger Bannister (GB) in 1953 and a 3:39.0 1500m by Francesco Arese (Ita) in 1968.

People

In 1962 **Gerry Carr**, former British discus record holder, ran in a weightman's sprint relay for UCLA v Stanford. Running the first leg he got so excited he squeezed the baton so hard that it broke.

Ed Morland was known as the 'Human Mortar' while serving in Vietnam for his deadly accuracy in throwing grenades. Perhaps unsurprisingly he was a fine javelin thrower, with a best of 79.26m/260ft in 1971 at Kansas State University.

Larry Doubley, 1977 NCAA long jump champion and fourth in the 1980 US Olympic long jump trials, had a wind-aided best of 8.26m/27ft 1¼in, but achieved permanent fame with a world record for jumping over cars. Because of his brashness he was known as 'Baby Ali'.

Kip Keino was renowned for wearing an orange cap. When asked why he did not wear it indoors, he said it was because 'the light doesn't affect my eyes the way the sun does outdoors'.

Boyd Gittins failed to qualify for the 400m hurdles final in the US Olympic semi trials because he was hit in the eye before the first hurdle by pigeon's droppings which knocked out his contact lens and blinded him. However he won a run-off for an extra qualifying place for the Final Olympic Trials, when he came second and thus qualified for the Olympics. Further misfortune came with an injury causing him to miss the Games.

Two deaf mutes have won European Championships medals. Vyacheslav Skomorokhov (USSR) won the 400m hurdles in 1969 and Gerhard Sperling (GDR) was second at the 20km walk in 1971.

Bill Alley (javelin best 83.48m/273ft 10½in in 1960) threw a 3lb hand grenade a record 298ft/90.84m.

The US Army track arena at West Point was named Shea Stadium in honour of Lt. Dick Shea, ICAA indoor 2 miles champion 1951–2, who was awarded the Congressional Medal of Honour posthumously for valour in Korea.

The record for running up the Empire State Building in New York – 1575 steps to the 86th floor was set by Pete Squires in 1981 at 10min 59sec.

Statues of famous athletes include those of Paavo Nurmi outside the Olympic Stadium in Helsinki, and Don Quarrie in Kingston. The first woman to be so commemorated was Fanny Blankers-Koen.

Christchurch, New Zealand has streets named after Halberg, Landy, Lovelock and Snell, all world record holders.

Larry Doubley, at 2.03m/6ft 8in the tallest ever 27ft long jumper, who won the NCAA title in 1977. *(University of Southern California)*

Professionals

The first professional athletes may be said to be those who competed at the ancient Olympic Games, for though they only competed for glory and prizes of branches of wild olive, they certainly subsequently cashed in on their fame. In the more modern era footmen were employed by the aristocracy from the 17th century to run messages. Rivalry was stimulated by wagers and the practice developed of specially trained footmen. Meanwhile prize money was contested at rural sports and during the 19th century at the growing Scottish Highland Games and Border fairs.

In the early part of the 19th century pedestrianism was in vogue with feats of endurance being attempted for bets. A celebrated example was that of Robert Barclay Allardice's 1000 miles in 1000 successive hours. Known as Captain Barclay, he was watched by thousands of spectators as for 42 successive days and nights he walked a mile each hour on Newmarket Heath from 1 June to 12 July 1809.

Barclay must have been tough to have achieved this and even more so to have survived his training regimen, which included purging by drastic medicines, sweating by walking under a

Robert Barclay Allardice (Captain Barclay) whose walk of 1000 miles in 1000 hours made him the most celebrated of the pedestrians.

weight of clothes and by lying between feather beds. His diet was lean meat, beef or mutton, no vegetables or milk, but butter and cheese were allowed, and to drink, strong ale.

In 1877 William Gale walked 1½ miles each hour, for 1500 miles in 1000 successive hours.

In the middle of the 19th century the most notable professional running was in matches between leading athletes and in the 'go-as-you-please' events known as wobbles. Meanwhile, particularly in the universities amateur athletics was developed and rules of competition formulated. Gradually amateur athletics took over in importance in England, although the Scottish Games, still professional, flourished for many years. Betting scandals and distaste by the increasingly puritannical Victorians at the more unsavoury elements of mobs following the professionals contributed to the demise of this side of the sport, but many so-called amateurs profited from their sport.

The first great amateur athlete to turn professional was Walter George in 1885 for his series of matches against William Cummings, highlighted by his mile in 4:12¾ the following year. In April 1887 William Snook, former world record holder for 2 miles, was suspended by the AAA for allegedly deliberately losing the national cross-country championship. The biggest shock of all came in 1896 when six prominent athletes were suspended by the AAA for having received appearance money. The six included world record holders – Charles Bradley and Alf Downer, each of whom had run 9.8 for 100y; George Crossland, records at 20 miles and 2 hours; Fred Bacon 4:17.0 for the mile; Harry Watkins, who later set a professional 1 hour record of 18878m (11 miles 1286y) in 1899 and the sixth man was Yorkshire mile champion Alexander Blair, the only one to be reinstated later. These men were joined in professional ranks, and gained a major boost by the addition of Edgar Bredin, the 440y world record holder, and the USA middle distance champions Thomas Conneff and Charles Kilpatrick and high jumper Michael Sweeney who were among the many who turned pro.

In 1905 Arthur Duffey was banned by the AAU, after he had admitted receiving money since 1898. He had run extensively in Britain and Australia as well as in the USA, had won AAU and AAA sprint titles and was the first man to run 100y in 9.6. All his records were expunged from the lists by the AAU.

Following the 1908 Olympic marathon there was a **professional marathon craze** in the USA. The main contestants were the Olympic champion John Hayes, the race's hero Dorando Pietri, Alfred Shrubb and the Canadian Indian Tom Longboat. Dorando won the first of these races against Hayes running 260 laps indoors at Madison Square Garden. Dorando then ran four more marathons in two months, losing the first two to Longboat, then winning two. Longboat beat Shrubb in the latter's first race at the distance and all met in the first Marathon Derby on a five-lap-per-mile course at the New York Polo grounds on 3 Apr 1909, but the winner was a 40–1 outsider Henri St. Yves, for the first prize of $10000, with Dorando second and Hayes third.

Since those days, however, **professional athletics in Britain** has been totally overshadowed by the amateurs, except perhaps in Scotland, where the most famous event is the annual Powderhall handicap sprint. This was first held in Edinburgh in 1870 over 130y (118.9m). The distance was reduced to 120y in 1958.

Alf Shrubb (left) and Tom Longboat (right) in January 1912 at the start of one of their professional matches. *(BBC Hulton)*

The most important professional athletics for most of this century has been in Australia. The most famous event is the Stawell Gift, first run in 1877 for a prize of £24. Like the 'Powderhall' it is run over 130y and is a handicap race. The first man to win from the scratch mark was Jean-Louis Ravelomanantsoa of Madagascar in 1973 for a prize of 4585 Australian dollars. The main feature of the Australian professional scene has been sprinting, from the great rivalry between the 'Blue Streak' Jack Donaldson, who ran such times as 9⅜sec for 100y, 11.25 for 120y, 12.0 for 130y and 21.0 for 220y, and Arthur Postle (6sec for 60y and 9.5 for 100y) in 1910–15, to the present day.

Among the top sprinters who have gone to Australia to race for money have been Olympic champions or world record breakers like Reg Walker (1912), Eddie Tolan (1935), Barney Ewell (1950), Lloyd La Beach (1951), Mel Patton and Herb McKenley (1954). Henry Carr and Jim Hines (1969). Many raced in gimmicky ways such as against horses in handicap races. Hines for instance won a 220y race by 30y having given the horse an extra 110y to run. Jesse Owens also used to race against horses after his amateur days were over. He said that the trick was 'to get the biggest gun, fire it close to the horse's head, and you've gone 50 yards by the time the jockey gets the horse going'.

Other famous athletes who have been suspended for infringing amateur rules: 1912 Jim Thorpe; 1932 Jules Ladoumègue and Paavo Nurmi; 1945 Gunder Hägg and Arne Andersson; 1946 Henry Kälarne, like Hägg and Andersson suspended from all amateur competition (six other Swedish runners were suspended for 1–2 years); 1956 Wes Santee; 1961 Dan Waern; 1976 Guy Drut (reinstated 1980).

Lee Calhoun was suspended by the AAU for a year after he had been married on the 'Bride and Groom' television show in August 1957. His bride won $2500 of gifts on the show and a $6000 swimming pool, although the Calhouns gave the latter to a boys club at Durham, NC. However Calhoun returned in January 1959, and won the AAU 120y hurdles title that year before winning a second Olympic title in 1960.

ITA CIRCUIT
The first major professional athletics promotions of the modern era were those of the International Track Association (ITA), the formation of which was announced at Munich in 1972.

The first ITA meeting was a warm-up one indoors at Pocatello, Idaho on 3 Mar 1973. A ground record crowd of 10480 saw three world indoor bests recorded: 100m Warren Edmonson 10.2; 600m Lee Evans 1:16.7 and high jump John Radetich 2.25m/7ft 4¾in. Each winner received $500 and there was a $500 bonus for record breakers.

The first official ITA meeting was at the Los Angeles Sports Arena on 24 Mar 1973, with attendance of 12280.

The first outdoor ITA meeting was at Tokyo on 6–7 Apr 1974. The runners included Bob Hayes, ten years after his Olympic triumphs in the same stadium. The first outdoor meeting in the USA was at El Paso on 27 Apr 1974.

The ITA folded in 1976. Principal reasons for its failure to become established permanently were poor attendances and the ITA's inability to continue to recruit new star names, probably because many were better off as 'amateurs'.

Leading ITA money winners
1973 $10375 Brian Oldfield. However, Lee Evans, fourth on the official list with $7900 won an extra $6000 from Post Cereals for the Grand Prix at his event.
1974 $16700 Ben Jipcho (including $6000 from Post Cereals).
1975 $27500 Ben Jipcho.

The boom in road running in the USA led to the early stages of development of professional races in the 1980s.

The first professional road race to be held in the USA for more than 50 years was run at Atlantic City, NJ on 21 Sep 1980 over the marathon distance and sponsored by clothing manufacturers, Jordache. Winners Ron Nabers (2:31:10) and Katie McDonald (3:04:51) each won $15000 for mediocre performances. However Nabers improved sharply to win a further $12500 when he ran 2:18:49 to win the second pro race at Pasadena, when the women's winner Cindy Dalrymple (2:42:54) also won the same amount.

A series of six professional road races was organised by the newly formed Association of Road Racing Athletes (ARRA) in 1981. The first race was a 15km race, the Cascade Run-Off at Portland, Oregon on 28 June. As a result TAC first banned the four leading foreign runners – the first three women, all New Zealanders: Ann Audain ($10000), Allison Roe ($4000) and Lorraine Moller ($2000) and third placed man Domingo Tibaduiza of Colombia from TAC sanctioned meetings. They followed this by banning the leading eight American money winners, including men's winner Greg Meyer. However no action was taken against other runners, including Bill Rodgers, who did not take prize money. The irony of the situation was emphasised by the fact that Rodgers admits to earning well over $250000 in 1980 from running and related activities. Allison Roe, however, paid her cheque into a trust fund administered by her national federation and was reinstated, in time to run in the New York Marathon in which she set a world best. Despite the TAC's actions many leading runners continued to run openly for money. The second ARRA race, the Nike Marathon had $20000 first prizes for Benji Durden (2:12:12) and Lorraine Moller (2:31:19).

The biggest prize is $25000 won by the winners of the 1981 Jordache Los Angeles marathon, Tom Fleming (2:13:15) and Cindy Dalrymple (2:39:33). However, in real terms, the greatest earnings were those of the Six Day runners in Victorian times. In 1878 promoters set up a series of world championship races for the Astley Belt. Charles Rowell won $20398 (then £4191) from his first Astley Belt race and $19500 plus $6500 entrance money (total £5343) from the fifth race.

'Kate the Great' Schmidt in the 1977 World Cup. She won seven AAU titles and Olympic bronze medals. *(All-Sport/Tony Duffy)*

Rod Milburn high hurdles in 1981. He returned to the top after six years as a pro. *(J. Burles)*

ITA meetings were held in Britain in 1975: On 18 June at Meadowbank, Edinburgh and on 20 Jun at Crystal Palace, London.
ITA records, better than the world amateur records, were set by Brian Oldfield at the shot, culminating in his massive 75ft put on 10 May 1975 (see p. 60).

After the ITA folded several of the leading participants petitioned the AAU and the IAAF for re-instatement as amateurs. Eventually they were re-instated for domestic meetings at the end of 1979. On 5 Jan 1980 Rod Milburn ran his first race as an amateur since 1973, and he was followed by other ex-pros such as John Smith, Brian Oldfield, Henry Hines and Lance Babb.

The ex-ITA men were, however, at first prevented from competing at the 1980 US Olympic Trials. Milburn missed his event, but after pole vaulter Steve Smith had taken the matter to court, both he and Oldfield took part.

On 29 Jun 1978 the AAU suspended four athletes for receiving **prize money from a Superstars contest** the previous January. Dwight Stones ($33400), Jane Frederick ($17600), Kate Schmidt ($3900) and Francie Larrieu ($3100) were also suspended by the IAAF. The three women were re-instated at the end of the year and Stones followed a year later after he had paid over the money to the governing bodies.

The least well paid professionals were the transcontinental runners of the late 1920s (see p. 46). The 1929 winners were never paid their money, and Johnny Salo and Sam Richman won the grand sum of $5 each for winning a six day relay race at the Ascot Speedway, Los Angeles on 13–18 Jul 1929. They covered 749 miles 696y (1206km) – just 0.66 cents per mile!

Sex Tests

The first woman to be disqualified from a meeting for failing the 'sex test' was Ewa Klobukowska (Pol) at the European Cup Final in Kiev in 1967. Sex testing had been introduced the previous year at the Commonwealth Games and European Championships. At the latter Klobukowska was allowed to compete, winning two gold and a silver medal to add to the gold (relay) and bronze (100m) medals she had won at the 1964 Olympics, despite reportedly failing the visual inspection.

In the relay she had run, taking over in fourth place 8m down on the final leg, what was widely regarded at the time as the greatest ever piece of sprinting in a woman's race, to take Poland to victory.

Ewa Klobukowska wins for Poland v GB at 100m in 1965, two years before being the first to fail a sex test. No. 4 is Liz Gill.   *(Photo-Reportage)*

The basis for the test is a chromosome check, a normal woman having XX chromosomes. Klobukowska was one of those unfortunate people who are apparently borderline cases, and she had had two operations to make her female, but these were not enough and she failed at Wuppertal at the European Cup semi-final as well as at the final when she was ruled out of competition. The IAAF withdrew recognition of her world 100m record set on 9 Jul 1965. Before the tests were introduced several of the top women athletes had been 'doubted' by athletics followers. In this category came such top names as the Soviets Tamara and Irina Press, Tatyana Shchelkanova and Maria Itkina, all of whom dropped out of competition when the tests were introduced, and from an earlier generation Aleksandra Chudina and Stella Walsh.

Before the war two 'world records' had been set by people posing as women who were later confirmed as men: Zdena Koubkova (Cze) at 800m (see p. 71) and Dora Ratjen (Ger) at high jump (see European Championships). Herman Ratjen, for so he really was, said that he had lived the life of a girl for three years. Stefania Pekarova (Cze), third at shot in the 1934 World Games was also later found to be a man.

Two French European relay silver medallists of 1946 also later lived as men; Claire (later Pierre) Bresolles, who also was third at 100m, and Léa (later Leon) Caurla. Fortunately the advent of sex testing has enabled distinctions to be drawn and so ended the use of those unfortunate to be living in a kind of twilight zone between the sexes. Even so the suspected use of male sex hormones remains a major problem in women's athletics.

Sprinters

Patrick Morrison was dropped from the Stanford University team as a freshman on 7 May 1966 for refusing to have his hair cut. A highly promising British sprinter, who had made his international debut in 1965, he had won a sprint double in 9.6sec (100y) and 21.0 (220y) the previous week, but apart from the AAA championships later that year never ran seriously again. He did however complete his university education.

Delano Meriwether (USA) did not start his sprinting career until he was aged 27 in 1970. Within a few months he ran a 9.4 100y and

Above: Jesse Owens, quadruple Olympic gold medallist in 1936, at home with his trophies.

Left: Filbert Bayi (613) leads Mike Boit (inside) and John Walker (in the all-black strip) on his way to a world record and the Commonwealth Games 1500m title in 1974. Number 123 is Graeme Crouch.

A selection of stamps depicting athletics; hundreds are issued for each Olympic Games.

indeed ran 9.6 in his first ever race. A research scientist whose studies and work had not permitted serious sports he had a sensational season in 1971 at an age when most sprinters would have retired. In his first major indoor race he ran 6.0 for 60y, just a tenth of a second off the world best. Outdoors he won the AAU 100y title in a wind assisted 9.0, the fastest time ever run, ahead of a fine line up. Following Meriwether were Jim Green, Don Quarrie, Charlie Greene and Ivory Crockett, and Eddie Hart was last (8th) in 9.2! The auto times went 9.22 – 9.23 – 9.24 for the first three and 9.41 for Hart. Meriwether was a colourful addition to the track scene for apart from his sprinting talent he ran in yellow swimming trunks and braces. After 1971 he ran only intermittently, but recorded classy 10.2 times for 100m in 1974 and 1978.

Stamps and coins

The first postage stamps concerned with sport were those issued by Greece on 6 Apr 1896 to commemorate the first Olympic Games. There were eight different designs in a series of 12 stamps, depicting subjects from the ancient Games, including a discus thrower and the stadium. They were designed and printed in France. Greece also issued a set of 14 stamps for the 1906 Games. The next sporting stamps were issued by Belgium for the 1920 Olympic Games and since then every host country, and nowadays many others, have issued stamps.

The first identifiable athlete to be featured on a stamp must be Hercules, depicted on two of the 1906 issue. The first athletes of international repute to appear on stamps bearing their names were those on a set of eight issued by the Dominican Republic in 1957. The series of athletes, each shown with their national flag was: 1 cent Fanny Blankers-Koen, 2 cent Jesse Owens, 3 cent Kee Chung Sohn, 5 cent Lord Burghley, 7 cent Bob Mathias, 11 cents Paavo Nurmi, 16 cents Ugo Frigerio, 17 cents Mildred Didrikson. The last was also one of the first two sports personalities to be featured on a US postage stamp, in 1981.

The first coins to honour sports were those issued in 1951–2 for the Helsinki Olympic Games.

In 1968 Sharjah featured 1936 Olympic champions, but the stamp captioned Jesse Owens was not of Owens!

Tragedies

Several top athletes have met with tragic deaths, some while at the early stages of their careers.

Notable athletes killed in car crashes include:
Bob Gutowski at the age of 25 on 2 Aug 1960. He won the 1956 Olympic silver medal and set a world record in 1957 at pole vault.
Ove Jonsson (Swe) on 29 Sep 1962 aged 21, just thirteen days after winning the European 200m title.
Jorma Valkama (Fin), aged 34, on 11 Dec 1962. He won the bronze medal in the 1956 Olympic long jump.
Ugandan marathon runner **John Mwanika** was killed by a car at about the 22 mile point in the 1970 East African Championships.
Steve Prefontaine (USA) on 30 May 1975 aged 24. Prefontaine, who at 5000m had won the 1971 Pan-American title and was placed fourth in the 1972 Olympics, held US records at each distance from 2000m to 10000m and was undoubtedly the most popular American track and field athlete with a growing industry in 'Go Pre' sloganed T-shirts. Following a win at 5000m in 13:23:8 in his home town of Eugene, Oregon, he was killed as his sports car apparently went out of control as he was returning from having dropped off Frank Shorter at Kenny Moore's house following a post-meeting party.
Ivo van Damme (Bel) on 29 Dec 1976, aged 22. He had demonstrated his enormous potential with Olympic silver medals at both 800m and 1500m in 1976 following his fourth place behind Steve Ovett in the 1973 European Junior Championships and his second in the 1975 European Indoor Championships. In his great year of 1976 he improved dramatically,

Steve Prefontaine won a record four successive NCAA 3 mile/5000m titles 1930–3. He was killed in a car crash in 1975. *(University of Oregon)*

with best times of 1:43.86 for 800m and 3:36.26 for 1500m as well as a European record 2:15.5 for 1000m. His fatal accident on autoroute A7, near Orange, Belgium happened as he was on his way home to see a recording of his performance in the European Superstars Final on television.

Bronislaw Malinowski (Pol) on 26 Sep 1981 near his home town of Grudziak, aged 30. From his win in the European Junior 2000m steeplechase in 1970 to his Olympic 3000m steeplechase victory in 1980, Malinowski compiled a magnificent record, mostly at the steeplechase at which he was also European champion in 1974 and 1978 and had a best of 8:09.11 for second place at the 1976 Olympics. His range of ability was shown by his 1 mile best of 3:55.40 and his fourth placing at the 1974 European 10000m.

Malcolm Ford, who won 15 AAU titles and set a world long jump record of 7.08m/23ft 3in in 1886, shot and killed his brother Paul in New York on 8 May 1902 and then committed suicide. He was a dollar millionaire and a Brooklyn lawyer.

Amongst those **killed in a terrible air disaster** in France on 3 Mar 1974 was **John Cooper** (GB), aged 33, winner of Olympic silver medals at 400m hurdles and 4 × 400m relay in Tokyo in 1964. He was Marketing Manager of the Adidas Footwear Division and was on his way home after watching the England v France Rugby International in Paris.

Sol Butler (USA), the 1920 AAU long jump champion, died from gunshot wounds at the age of 59 in 1954 after 'bouncing' a bar customer.

Ron Copeland, the 1966 NCAA 120y hurdles champion, collapsed and died 22 May 1975 after a challenge 60y race with one of the athletes at Mt San Antonio College where he was assistant coach.

French hammer thrower **Michel Decker** was shot dead on leaving a young lady's apartment on 6 Jul 1981 the day after he had been placed third for France in an international against Germany.

Dick Howard (USA), bronze medallist at 400m hurdles in 1960 and AAU and NCAA champion in 1959, died of an overdose of heroin in a Hollywood motel on 9 Nov 1967 at the age of 32. His team-mate in 1960, **Cliff Cushman**, who

had won the silver medal was killed in action in Vietnam in 1966 aged 28, while another American athlete to die in that war was **Ron Zinn** on 6 Jul 1965 at the age of 26. Zinn was sixth in the 1964 Olympic 20km walk.

Stanley Johnson (USA), AAU hammer champion in 1942, died after shooting himself with a shotgun on 13 Nov 1960.

Nathan Ndege Lagat (Ken) who was world ranked in the 3000m steeplechase in 1975 at 8:23.98, shot himself in July 1979 in his army barracks in Nairobi.

The Lamar Tech mile relay team of 1968 was killed when their private plane crashed a mile from Beaumont, Texas airport after the pilot suffered a heart attack.

Boughera El Ouafi the French Algerian, who won the first ever Olympic gold medal by an African, at the marathon in 1924, was killed in a family quarrel in 1959.

Cliff Schnedar (USA) died on 4 Apr 1980 following a pole vault training session five days earlier at San Diego, when he hit his head on concrete. His best vault was 5.36m/17ft 7in in 1979.

Yuriy Styepanov (USSR), former world high jump record holder, committed suicide in 1965 after a year in hospital suffering from psychiatric disorders.

Charlie Tidwell (USA) apparently committed suicide with his wife in Denver on 29 Aug 1969. Tidwell was NCAA champion at 100m in 1959 and 1960 and 200m champion in 1960, but pulled a muscle in the US Olympic trials 100m causing him to miss the Games, for which he would have been one of the favourites.

Kokichi Tsubaraya (Jap) was third in the 1964 Olympic marathon, having been overtaken on the final lap by Basil Heatley (GB). On 9 Jan 1968 as a 2nd Lieutenant at the national military PT school, he committed suicide. A year earlier his right achilles tendon was injured and he left a note saying 'I can't run any more'.

Stella Walsh (USA), who as Stanislawa Walasiewicz of Poland won the 1932 Olympic 100m, set many world sprint records and won a record 41 AAU titles, was found shot dead in a discount store car park in Cleveland, Ohio on 4

Dec 1980 (see pp. 136 and 189). A post mortem report revealed that Stella Walsh had male sex organs and no female sex organs.

Serious accidents have finished the careers of several great athletes.

Abebe Bikila (Eth), the first man to win two Olympic marathon gold medals suffered a broken neck and spinal cord injury in a traffic accident in Ethiopia in 1969. He was brought to Stoke Mandeville Hospital in England. He died on 25 Oct 1973 at the age of 42 of a cerebral haemorrhage. An estimated 60–70000 people, including Emperor Haile Selassie, attended his funeral.

Valeriy Brumel (USSR), world high jump record holder and Olympic champion suffered multiple fractures in his right leg in a motorcycle accident on 7 Oct 1965. He had five hours of surgery and there were fears that his leg might have to be amputated due to gangrene. His leg was in a cast for nearly three years but, trying to exercise too soon, the leg broke again. However following more operations his perseverance paid off and although unable to approach the form that had made him the greatest ever high jumper, he succeeded in clearing 2.06m/6ft 9in on 7 Jun 1969.

Brian Sternberg (USA) at the age of 19 set world pole vault records in 1963 at 5.00m on 27 April, 5.05m on 25 May and 5.08m/16ft 8in on

Brian Sternberg (left), paralysed in a trampoline accident in 1963 at the age of 20, after an unbeaten outdoor season.
(University of Washington)

7 June. On 15 June he won the NCAA title and, on his 20th birthday on 21 June the AAU title, but his tremendous undefeated season and indeed his career was finished by a terrible accident on 2 Jul 1963 on a trampoline which left him paralysed from the neck down having fallen on the back of his neck attempting a double back somersault with twist. He met his disaster with indomitable courage and two years later had recovered partial use of his arms.

Veterans (men of 40 and over, women of 35 and over)

The first major veterans championships were the US Masters in 1968, although in Britain the Veterans AC had been formed in London in 1931.

The World Masters Championships have been held biennially since 1975 when they were staged at Etobicoke Stadium, Toronto. Winners in that first year included such past greats as Thane Baker, Albie Thomas, Stig Pettersson, Roy Fowler and Howard Payne in the 1A category (40–44), while 1948 Olympic pole vault siver medallist Boo Morcom won the 2A (50–54) long jump. In 1976 Morcom set a world age 55 best for the pole vault of 4.12m/13ft 6¼in, this was a quarter of an inch higher than when he had won the 1945 AAU title! In 1975 there was just one event, the 400m, for women, but the programme has now expanded to include a full range of events.

In 1977 two former Olympic champions won 1A titles: Gaston Roelants, five distance events, and Al Oerter the discus, in which his 60.36m/198ft 0in was well ahead of the 57.78m of Ludvik Danek, the man who succeeded him as Olympic champion in 1978.

Win streaks

The greatest ever sequence of successive wins is 140 by woman high jumper Iolanda Balas from her fifth place at the 1956 Olympic Games on 1 Dec 1956 to 11 Jun 1967 when she lost with 1.68m to Dagmar Melzer (GDR) 1.71.

The greatest win streak by a man is 116 by Parry O'Brien at the shot from 7 Jul 1952, a week after he had been placed second to Darrow Hooper in the US Olympic tryouts, to 15 Jun 1956. Seven days later his long run ended when Ken Bantum beat him by two inches at the AAU. The man O'Brien succeeded as the world's number one shot putter, Jim Fuchs, had the previous win streak best – 88 until O'Brien beat him at the 1951 AAU.

Athletes to have gone through their careers undefeated include: Helen Stephens, the 6ft American sprinter, unbeaten at any track event. She won the Olympic 100m title in 1936 but had a fairly short career.

Athletes unbeaten at specific events this century include:
Paavo Nurmi at any distance more than 5000m; Hal Davis in 25 races at 200m or 220y 1940–3; Charlie Moore in 23 races at 400m/440y hurdles 1949–52; Henry Carr in 8 races at 400m or 440y 1961–4: Eric Liddell in 14 races at 400m or 440y 1922–5; Robert Tisdall in 6 races at 400m (or 440y) hurdles 1930–2.

Athletes who have won all their decathlons include:
Jim Thorpe, his only one when he won the 1912 Olympics, a perfect career indeed at the event for he also smashed the world record, although he lost the title when he was declared a professional.
Glenn Morris, all three decathlons, all in 1936, including the Olympic title.
Bob Mathias, all 11 decathlons 1948–56, including the 1948 and 1952 Olympic titles.

Helen Stephens (right) wins the Olympic 100m at Berlin in 1936. The farm-girl from Missouri was never beaten at sprints.   *(BBC Hulton)*

Jim Fuchs set four world shot records, with a best of 17.95m/58ft 10in in 1950, and was unbeaten from 1949 to 1951.   *(Yale University)*

The most famous win streaks include:
Harrison Dillard, nicknamed 'Bones' won 82 consecutive sprints and hurdles races at various distances indoors and out from 31 May 1947 to 26 Jun 1948. Then Bill Porter beat him at 110m hurdles the AAU in Milwaukee and the next week came one of the most amazing results in athletics history as he hit three hurdles and failed to finish the 110m hurdles at the US Olympic tryouts. He had qualified, nonetheless for the Games with a third at 100m, and went on to win the Olympic title at his second string event. Four years later he qualified safely and went on to win the Olympic 110m hurdles title. He ran on the winning sprint relay team at both Games. In his collegiate career for Baldwin-Wallace College he won 201 out of 207 sprint and hurdles finals. Indoors he won 37 consecutive hurdles races from 1949 to 1954 when Jack Davis beat him in a disputed decision at the AAU.
Dillard's **indoor win streak record** was broken in 1963 by **Hayes Jones**, who went on to win 55 consecutive high hurdles as well as three low hurdles races indoors from 30 Jan 1960 to 27 Feb 1964. His loss to Les Calhoun in March 1959 was the last of his indoor hurdling career. He won five consecutive AAU titles, and set world hurdles records at 50y, 60y and 70y. His very last race was his fastest, a world record 6.8 for 60yh at Baltimore.
Chi Cheng won all her 83 competitions in 1970 (see p. 144).
Edwin Moses was, at the time of writing, still composing the greatest record of the current era, with 78 consecutive wins at 400m/440y hurdles to the end of 1981 (see p. 50).

Ron Delany, Olympic 1500m champion, was supreme indoors. Here he wins the 1956 Wanamaker Mile at the Millrose Games. *(United Press)*

Other great win streaks by men include:
George Brown – 41 long jump competitions 1950–2.
Ricky Bruch – 54 discus competitions 1972–3. Bruch's habit was to wear a black bowler hat and a garish kimono, and emit a 'Tarzan' yell on entering the arena. It seemed to work.
Ludvik Danek, the Czech discus thrower won 45 competitions from 28 Jul 1963 to 15 Oct 1964 (second at Olympic Games). Then he had seven wins before a loss to Jay Silvester on 4 Jun 1965, then a series of 40 wins. Then second to Al Oerter on 28 May 1966 before 26 more wins.
Ron Delany was undefeated in his indoor career 1956–9 in 40 races, including 34 at 1 mile.
Craig Dixon – 59 hurdles races 1949–50.
Herb Elliott – 44 at 1500m/1 mile 1954–60. His only loss at a mile came as a 14-year-old, and he won the 1958 Commonwealth and 1960 Olympic titles, setting two world records at 1500m (3:36.0 and 3:35.6) and one at the mile (3:54.5).

Manfred Germar – 70 sprints 1956–58.
Rudolf Harbig – 55 at all events from Aug 1938 to 28 Sep 1940.
Glenn Hardin was unbeaten at 400m/440y hurdles from his Olympic second place in 1932 to his retirement in 1936.
Bob Hayes – 49 finals at 100y or 100m from second at the 1962 NAIA (1 Jun) to his last race, the Olympic gold medal in 1964.
Michel Jazy – undefeated at middle distances for 26 months to 26 Oct 1963, including all 49 races in 1962.
Romuald Klim – 42 hammer competitions 1965–8.
Janis Lusis – 41 javelin wins 1967–70. Lusis had undefeated seasons in 1962 (15), 1963 (19), 1966 (20), 1968 (20), 1969 (13).
Randy Matson – 47 shot competitions from second at the 1964 Olympics to 12 Jan 1967.
Imre Nemeth – 73 hammer competitions 1946–50.
Paul Nihill won 51 consecutive walking races from 17 Oct 1968 to 20 Jun 1970. That first date was his retirement in the Olympic 50km walk in Mexico City. Apart from that his sequence was

for 86 races back to 9 Dec 1967. In Britain he won 96 consecutive races at this time. In his career 1960–77 Nihill won 355 races.
Steve Ovett – 45 at 1500m/1 mile (see p. 30).
Greg Rice – 65 distance races from 17 May 1940 until Gunder Hägg beat him by 60m in the 1943 AAU 5000m. During this period he set world indoor bests at 2 miles (8:51.0) and 3 miles (13:51.0).
Bob Richards – 50 pole vault competitions 1950–2. Also unbeaten outdoors 1953–5.
Gaston Roelants – 45 wins in 3000m steeplechase finals from 5 Aug 1961 to his third place at the European championships on 3 Sep 1966. He also won two heats, but was second in another at the Olympic Games in 1964, before winning the final.
Ernie Shelton – 46 high jump competitions 1953–5.
Adhemar Ferreira da Silva – 60 triple jump competitions 1950–6.
Jiri Skobla – 68 shot competitions 1952–5.
John Woodruff was unbeaten at 800m/880y from his loss to Charles Beetham at the 1936 AAU until the end of his career, in 1940.
Emil Zatopek – 69 races 1949–51; 48 races at 5000m 1948–52; 38 races at 10000 from 1948–54 (see p. 173).

Notable win streaks by women include:
Nadyezhda Chizhova – 57 shot competitions 1969–73.
Gisela Mauermayer – 65 discus competitions 1935–42.
Faina Melnik – 52 discus competitions 1973–6.
Renate Stecher – at 100m and 200m won 90 successive races outdoors from Aug 1970 to Jun 1974, though she was beaten at 60m indoors during this period.
Irena Szewinska won the first 34 finals at 400m that she ran from 1974 until her first loss against Marita Koch at the 1978 European Championships. In 1974 she also won all 23 of her races at 100m and 19 out of 20 at 200m, but then her only defeat was in a heat.

With the intensity of competition worldwide nowadays it is increasingly difficult for athletes to go through a season undefeated. Among the most impressive records in recent years have been:
Udo Beyer – seasonal records at shot from 1977: 1977 – 14/15; 1978 – 17/18; 1979 – 16/16; 1980 – 11/12; 1981 – 8/8. His longest win streak was 34 from second to Yevgeniy Mironov on 24 Jun 1978 until his surprise third place at the 1980 Olympics.

Paul Nihill won 355 races in his career including 19 RWA and six AAA titles and the 1969 European 20km walk. *(E. D. Lacey)*

Ruth Fuchs – unbeaten at javelin in 1972, 1973 and until 4 Jul 1974 for 30 successive wins. From 1970 to 1980 inclusive her career record was 113 wins in 129 competitions.

Alberto Juantorena was unbeaten at 400m in 1973, 1974, 1976 and 1978, and at 800m in 1976 and 1977 (winning at least 24 successive races).

Rod Milburn won all his 28 races at the high hurdles in 1971. In 1972 he was placed only third at the US Olympic trials, hitting the 7th and 10th hurdles, after winning 27 consecutive finals. He went on to win the Olympic gold and record a further win streak of 31 until he lost as a pro on 4 Apr 1975.

Viktor Saneyev – unbeaten at triple jump in 1969 and in 27 successive competitions from his second place at the 1973 World Student Games to 29 May 1977. From 1968 to 1977 Saneyev won 96 out of 110 competitions, a ten year record hard to better.

Cornelius Warmerdam (see p. 55) lost only once at pole vault at his peak, to Willard Schaefer in 1941.

Mal Whitfield lost only three of 69 races at 800m or 880y from June 1948 to the end of the 1954 season. During that period he won every major championship he contested. In 1953 he set world indoor bests at 500y (56.6) 500m (62.9) and 600y (1:09.5) and world records at 880y (1:48.6) and 1000m in 2:20.8, which he followed an hour later with a 45.9 400m, the best time in the world that year, just a tenth of a second outside the world record. At all distances he won 49 of his 51 races in 1953, losing once to Herb McKenley at 400m and once in his debut at 1500m.

Miruts Yifter at 10000m was unbeaten from 1972 until 1981.

World Rankings

The best performance in the world at one event has most often been achieved by John Flanagan who topped the hammer lists 13 times 1895–1901, 1904–6, and 1908–10; and by Nina Dumbadze 12 times at women's discus 1937, 1939, 1943–4, 1946–52 and 1954. At all events Aleksandra Chudina achieved this 18 times between 1945 and 1955 – 8 Pen, 4 HJ, 3 JT, 2 400m, 1 LJ.

'Track and Field News' have published annual top ten merit rankings for men's events since 1947, chiefly compiled by Roberto Quercetani and Donald Potts. Leading performers have included:

The most years at No. 1 at one event: 9 Viktor Saneyev TJ 1968–76; 9 Janis Lusis JT 1962–3, 1965–9, 1971–2; 8 Bob Richards PV 1949–56; 8 Ralph Boston LJ 1960–7; 7 Emil Zatopek 10km 1948–54; 7 Parry O'Brien SP 1952–6, 1958–9.

The most years at No. 1 at all events: 13 Emil Zatopek 10km – 7 (see above), 5km – 5 (1947, 1949–50, 1952–3), Mar – 1 (1952); 10 Bob Richards PV – 8 (see above), Dec – 2 (1951, 1954).

The most years ranked: 18 Janusz Sidlo JT 1953–70; 16 Gyula Zsivotzky HT 1957–72; 16 Parry O'Brien SP 1951–64, 1966 (DT 1952–7, 1959, 1961–2, 1965). 15 Jay Silvester DT 1958, 1960–5, 1967–73, 1976.

The highest points scorer (10 for 1st to 1 for 10th):
At one event 139 Janusz Sidlo (JT). At all events 182 Parry O'Brien (126 SP, 56 DT); 170 Emil Zatopek (79 10km, 76 5km, 15 Mar).

Ranked No. 1 at three different events: Zatopek 5km, 10km, Mar (above); Kip Keino 1500m 1968, 1970; 5000m 1966; 3000m S/C 1972; Henry Rono 5km, 10km and 3000m S/C 1978; Ben Jipcho 1500m and 3000m S/C 1973, 5000m 1974.

Annual top ten merit rankings for women have been compiled by Jan Popper since 1956.
The most years at No. 1 at one event: 9 Iolanda Balas HJ 1958–66; 8 Ruth Fuchs JT 1972–9; 7 Irena Szewinska (Pol) 200m 1965–8, 1974, 1976–7; 7 Tamara Press SP 1959–60, 1962–6; 7 Irina Press Pen 1959–62, 1964–6; 7 Faina Melnik DT 1971–7.

The most years at No. 1 at all events: 16 Irena Szewinska 200m – 7 (above), 400m – 4 (1974–7), LJ – 3 (1966–7, 69), 100m – 2 (1967, 1974). Szewinska is the only athlete to be ranked at No. 1 at four events. 10 Tamara Press SP – 7 (above), DT – 3 (1961–2, 1964); 10 Irina Press Pen – 7 (above), 80mh – 3 (1960–1, 1965).

The most years ranked: 14 Irena Szewinska 1964–9, 1971–9.

The highest points scorer (10 for 1st to 1 for 10th):
At one event 131 Irina Szewinska 200m 1964–9, 1971–9. At all events 343 Irena Szewinska (200m 131, 100m 83, LJ 61, 400m 55, 400mh 8, Pen 5); 182 Tamara Press (SP 92, DT 90).

INDEX Athletes, Coaches and Officials

Dates of birth where known are shown in the format, day, month and year. Thus 27 Feb 19 = 27th February 1919. Alternative formats are year of birth and death, e.g. (1734–93) or where year of birth only is known e.g. (b.1938). To save space some Christian names have been omitted, these will normally be found in the text. Page nos. in italics denote illustrations.

MEN

WOMEN See also cross-reference list at the end of index of athletes maiden or married names.

Women's Cross Reference Index

The name in capitals is that by which the woman is indexed in the main index. This list is in alphabetical order of athletes' alternative names to that by which they are indexed. These names are included in the left-hand column if a maiden name or in the right-hand column if a married name.

Subject Index